The JORDAN RULES

SAM SMITH

SIMON & SCHUSTER

New York · London · Toronto · Sydney · Tokyo · Singapore

SIMON & SCHUSTER
Simon & Schuster Building
Rockefeller Center
1230 Avenue of the Americas
New York, New York 10020

SIMON & SCHUSTER and colophon are registered trademarks
of Simon & Schuster Inc.
Designed by Irving Perkins Associates
Manufactured in the United States of America

5   7   9   10   8   6

Library of Congress Cataloging in Publication Data
Smith, Sam, date.
The Jordan rules / Sam Smith.
p.   cm.
1. Chicago Bulls (Basketball team)   2. Jordan, Michael, date.
I. Title.
GV885.52.C45S65   1992
796.323′64′0977311—dc20   91-32973
CIP

ISBN: 0-671-74491-7

To Kathleen and Connor, Bet and Lee, and Ernie

The JORDAN RULES

JUNE 1991

EVERYWHERE PHIL JACKSON looked he saw red.

The city of Chicago, celebrating the Bulls' first-ever National Basketball Association title, was wearing the Bulls' red like an expensive suit. It was a city more used to disappointment and failure from its teams, finally able to puff out its chest and do a little strutting. And on this night, as the Bulls players gathered at the Four Seasons Hotel downtown for the last team party in what seemed like a month of celebrations since winning the title, Jackson could see from the crimson coloring around his players' eyes that they had joined the city in its reveling. But he could also see that their eyes still twinkled from the night they had shone brightest.

He could see his young stars, Horace Grant and Scottie Pippen, who had flashed across the NBA this season like comets, growing brighter and stronger, helping lead the way to a four-games-to-one victory in the Finals over the Lakers. They had joined with the baby-faced kid, B. J. Armstrong, in a dance line at the team's postgame party, and were swaying to the music and singing as the band played into the early morning hours.

Jackson could see his backup center, Will Perdue, in many ways a symbol of his team, long maligned but lately cheered. The Bulls had been the team of Michael Jordan, a one-man show whose sup-

9

porting cast strived but usually failed to overcome its limitations.
Few had more limitations than Perdue, but he had become a competent player, a nice piece of the puzzle, and he was now celebrated
by the hometown fans, perhaps as much for his ability to survive
the once-angry mob as for his contributions. Perdue had survived
as a test track that daily wore the tire marks of veteran center Bill
Cartwright. So he sat this night with Cartwright and pounded playfully on Cartwright's head and shoulders, yelling, "This is for the
elbows to my head, and this is for the elbows to my nose, and this
is for the elbows to my side. . . ." And the two banged and hugged
and laughed and looked like two of the biggest teddy bears anyone
had ever seen.

And then there was Cliff Levingston, a spare part for most of the
season who had proved his worth down the stretch in the playoffs.
And Stacey King, the bouncy kid who'd taken his lumps in a dis-
appointing season for him, and Armstrong, and Dennis Hopson,
who also had been more wallflower than dancer for long stretches
at a time. All had been discouraged by the intricacies of the offense,
known to the players as "the triangle," adapted from the teachings
of assistant coach Tex Winter. But now they were serenading the
grandfatherly coach in a rap version of the championship shuffle.

"Oh, we believe in the triangle, Tex, we believe, yeah, we believe
in that triangle. It's the show for those in the know. Goin' to the
triangle and goin' to win a title."

Jackson could feel his thin lips curling into a smile. He admired
the quirky Winter, and he had stuck with him, even when his star,
Jordan, said he didn't care for that particular system because what
had Winter won with it anyway? And Jackson stayed with it even
when the players grumbled early in the season and Winter came to
him and said he should drop the system because the players had to
believe in it for it to work. He would make them believe, Jackson
insisted. And now they were singing.

There was Jerry Krause, the Bulls' general manager, joyous perhaps less from the win than from the fact that the players were
treating him like one of the guys. A humorless man who lived for
his job, Krause was the object of the anger some of the players felt
toward the Bulls over money. Overweight and sensitive about it,
Krause had been the kind of kid who'd had trouble making friends.

But here were the guys, his guys, yelling out to him just as if he were one of them.

"Getting laid tonight, Jerry?" came the shouts. Manly stuff, guy talk. "Gettin' any, Jerry?" said one player as Krause's devoted wife, Thelma, stood by.

"You know it," Krause said happily.

"Pax, Pax," Perdue chimed in, "What was it? About $100,000 per shot? Like a cash register. $1.1, 1.2, 1.3. . . ."

Owner Jerry Reinsdorf, nearby, could only laugh. John Paxson, the veteran with the all-American-boy looks, one of the lowest-paid starters in the league, had made five straight baskets down the stretch in the final game. Every time the Lakers had threatened, there was Paxson to take the big shot. And now his contract was up. "What were those shots worth, Pax?" bubbled Perdue. "Just going for the new deal?"

And then there was Jordan. Jackson knew that was a smile that wouldn't wipe off. The crying was done; it had come, unexpectedly and touchingly, in the locker room right after the game, in a huge release. He was the star who couldn't win, they had said all these years, and now not only had his team won, but he had too in the biggest way, the way he'd always dreamed it would be: He was the Most Valuable Player of the series, chosen unanimously. One of the eleven electors had all but refused the ballot, saying, "Who else could it be?" And Jordan had done it against his archrival Magic Johnson, who had been held up by basketball purists as the exemplar of all that Jordan wasn't: a great passer, a great teammate, a winner. Well, they couldn't say that anymore.

First they prayed. After rushing into the locker room, the Bulls gathered in a circle for the Lord's Prayer, and then popped champagne bottles while looking for beer to slug down. Jordan collapsed into his seat for the TV cameras, but it was all too much. His head fell into the lap of his wife, Juanita, and he sobbed. His dad, James, who had never stopped telling him that he'd get to this moment, massaged his neck. But Jordan couldn't stop. His body trembled and he tried to wipe away the tears of joy, of relief, of promise fulfilled at last. His stomach ached and his breath was short. He'd never felt better. Better than in college when he was a freshman and his North Carolina team won the NCAA title. That one was too easy. This one was a struggle, against odds and doubters for seven seasons, and now it was over. He sucked down champagne like a baby sucking on a bottle. He cried and he wouldn't sleep. He was feeling pure, unrestrained joy.

The morning after that final victory, Jordan clutched the championship trophy like a long-lost friend. He wouldn't put it down, and everyone saw him walk off the plane with it. He slept with it all the way back to Chicago and he wouldn't let it get farther than five feet away from him on the team bus. It was the symbol of the struggle and it had to stay close, just in case anyone still questioned him.

Jackson saw all of this as they assembled before him this night. They had flown back to Chicago, where they were met at the airport by a few hundred fans, and the players went right up to the fence so they could touch one another, to form the kind of bond they enjoyed in the raucous Chicago Stadium. And they had gone to Grant Park in the city's heart to give their hearts to the city. They had formed a short motorcade and the fans reached out just to touch them as if they were holy men, and Paxson waved and the hands were grabbing, clutching all over until his wife drew their two sons in close together because the hands were everywhere. And then they had gone up on stage and hundreds of thousands cheered and rained gratitude down on their every word.

And they hadn't come down yet, nor slept much, buoyed as they were by the affection and exuberance, until they were standing there before Jackson for the last time after this magic carpet ride of a basketball season. This would be the last team party, for the players and staff and management only, before they would head their separate ways for the summer. Jackson had asked his players to get together once more as a group, twelve men of various faiths and faculties. They had endured much this season. They had lived together since last October, sharing sweat and glory, sometimes as compatible as a roomful of alley cats, as distant as former lovers. But they had grown with one another, accepting each other's faults and sharing in each other's successes. None had ever come this far before, and from the lonesome kid, Scott Williams, to the proud loner, Cartwright, their eyes reflected their relief and glee. Jackson didn't want it ever to end for them.

"You should know that many championship teams don't come

back," Jackson started out, the buzz of excitement quieting down for a while. "This is a business. I'd like to have all of you back, but it doesn't always happen. But this is something special you have shared and which you'll never forget. This will be yours forever and it will always be a bond that will keep you together. I want to thank you all personally for this season. Now, get back to the party."

Who could have imagined, only one year earlier, that there'd be this party, this joy, this togetherness on this night?

I

SPRING 1990

MICHAEL JORDAN SURVEYED his crew and got that sinking feeling.

It was just before 11:00 A.M. on May 24, 1990, two days after the Bulls had fallen behind the Detroit Pistons two games to none in the Eastern Conference finals. The city of Chicago was awash in spring—all two hours of it, as the old-time residents like to say— but Jordan wasn't feeling very sunny. He didn't even feel like playing golf, which friends would say meant he was near death.

The Bulls had gathered for practice at the Deerfield Multiplex, a tony health club about thirty-five miles north of Chicago, to try to get themselves back into the series. Jordan's back hurt, as did his hip, shoulder, wrist, and thigh, thanks to a two-on-one body slam in Game 1 courtesy of Dennis Rodman and John Salley. But his back didn't hurt nearly as much as his pride or his competitiveness, for the Bulls were being soundly whipped by the Pistons, and Jordan was growing desperately angry and frustrated.

"I looked over and saw Horace [Grant] and Scottie [Pippen] screwing around, joking and messing up," Jordan told an acquaintance later. "They've got the talent, but they don't take it seriously. And the rookies were together, as usual. They've got no idea what it's all about. The white guys [John Paxson and Ed Nealy], they work hard, but they don't have the talent. And the rest of them?

14

Who knows what to expect? They're not good for much of anything."

It was a burden Michael Jordan felt he had to bear. The weight of the entire team was on his tired shoulders.

The Pistons had taken the first two games by 86–77 and 102–93, and Detroit's defense had put the Bulls' fast break in neutral: The Bulls had failed to shoot better than 41 percent in either game. Jordan himself had averaged only 27 points, stubbornly going 17 for 43. No team defended Jordan better than the Pistons, yet he refused to admit that they gave him a hard time, so he played into their hands by attacking the basket right where their collapsing defensive schemes were expecting him. The coaches would look on in exasperation as Jordan drove toward the basket—"the citadel," assistant coach John Bach liked to call it—like a lone infantryman attacking a fortified bunker. Too often there was no escape.

Although Detroit's so-called Jordan rules of defense were effective, the Bulls coaches also believed the Pistons had succeeded in pulling a great psychological scam on the referees. It had been a two-part plan. The first step was a series of selectively edited tapes, sent to the league a few years earlier, which purported to show bad fouls being called on defenders despite little contact with Jordan. The Pistons said they weren't even being allowed to defense him. "Ever since then, the foul calls started decreasing," Jordan noted, "and not only those against Detroit."

Step two was the public campaign. The Pistons advertised their "Jordan rules" as some secret defense that only they could deploy to stop Jordan. These secrets were merely a series of funneling defenses that channeled Jordan toward the crowded middle, but Detroit players and coaches talked about them as if they had been devised by the Pentagon. "You hear about them often enough— and the referees hear it, too—and you start to think they have something different," said Bach. "It has an effect and suddenly people think they aren't fouling Michael even when they are."

It only added to Jordan's frustration with Detroit.

At halftime of Game 2, with the Bulls trailing 53–38, Jordan walked into the quiet locker room, kicked over a chair, and yelled, "We're playing like a bunch of pussies!" Afterward, he refused to speak to reporters, boarded the bus, and sat in stony silence all the way home. He continued his silence—other than a few sharp postgame statements—for the next week. He would not comment on his teammates. "I'll let them stand up and take responsibility for themselves," he told a friend.

Jordan had really believed that the Bulls could defeat Detroit this time. Of course, there was no evidence to suggest it could happen, since the Pistons had knocked the Bulls out of the playoffs the previous two seasons and had taken fourteen of the last seventeen regular-season games between them. But hadn't there been similar odds in 1989 when the Bulls had faced Cleveland in the playoffs? The Cavaliers had won fifty-seven games that season to the Bulls' forty-seven, and they were 6–0 against the Bulls, even winning the last game of the regular season despite resting their starters while the Bulls played theirs. The Bulls' chances were as bleak as Chicago in February.

Jordan promised that the Bulls would win the Cleveland series anyway.

Playing point guard, Jordan averaged 39.8 points, 8.2 assists, and 5.8 rebounds in the five games. And with time expiring in Game 5, he hit a hanging jumper to give the Bulls a 1-point victory. The moment became known in Chicago sports history as "the shot," ranking with Jordan's other "shot" in the 1982 NCAA tournament, a twenty-foot jumper that gave North Carolina a last-second victory over Georgetown. It also sent the Cavaliers plummeting; over the next two seasons, they would not defeat the Bulls once.

The playoffs had become Jordan's stage. He was Bob Hope and Michael Jackson, Mick Jagger and Frank Sinatra. His play transcended the game. It was a sweet melody received with a grand ovation. Others jumped as high and almost everyone slammed the ball, but Jordan did it with a style and a smile and a flash and a wink, and he did it best in the postseason.

"There's always been the feeling on this team," Bach had said after that Cavaliers series, "that if we got to the Finals, Michael would figure out some way to win it. He's the greatest competitor I've ever seen and then he goes to still another level in the big games."

It was true: Jordan's playoff performances had been Shakespearean sonnets, beautiful and timeless. And like Shakespeare, he was the best even though everyone said so. In just his second season in the league, after missing sixty-four games with a broken foot, Jordan demanded to return to the court despite warnings by doctors that he might exacerbate the injury to his foot. The Bulls, and even Jordan's advisers, said he should sit out the rest of the season. Jordan angrily accused the team of not wanting to make the playoffs so it could get a better draft pick. He was reluctantly allowed to return with only fifteen games remaining in the regular schedule. The Bulls made the playoffs, and in Game 2 against the Boston Celtics (who would go on to win the NBA title) Jordan scored 63 points. Larry Bird put it this way: "It must be God disguised as Michael Jordan."

In the 1988 playoffs against the Cavaliers, Jordan opened the series with 50- and 55-point games, the first time anyone had ever scored back-to-back 50s in the playoffs, to lead the team to victory and establish an all-time five-game-playoff-series scoring record of 45.2 points per game. Jordan had become perhaps the greatest scorer in the game's history. He would never equal Wilt Chamberlain's 100-point game or his hundred-plus 50-point games, but by the end of the 1990–91 season, Jordan had become the all-time NBA scoring average leader in the regular season, the playoffs, and the All-Star game. And he'd won his fifth straight scoring title, putting him behind only Chamberlain's seven.

And now, facing the Pistons in 1990, he was coming off a series against the 76ers in the second round of the playoffs that was un-believable even by his own amazing standards. The Bulls won in five games as Jordan averaged 43 points, 7.4 assists, and 6.6 re-bounds. He shot nearly 55 percent in 42.5 minutes per game. He drove and he dunked. He posted up and buried jumpers. He blocked shots and defended everyone from Charles Barkley to Johnny Dawkins.

"I never played four consecutive games like I did against Philly," he said of the first four, in which he led the team in scoring in thirteen of sixteen quarters.

And then the Bulls, storming and snorting, headed for Detroit to take on the Pistons. The two teams hailed from hard-edged, blue-collar towns, Chicago with its broad shoulders and meat-packing history, Detroit with its recession-prone auto industry. For some reason, though, Detroit's sports teams seemed to have a perpetual edge over Chicago's. In 1984 the Cubs finally won a piece of a baseball title, but it was the Detroit Tigers who won the World Series, just as they had in 1945, the year of the Cubs' last World

Series appearance. Many times Gordie Howe's Detroit Red Wings had come into the Stadium and ruined the dreams of Bobby Hill's Black Hawks. And now there were the Pistons. Detroit had made a habit of beating Chicago. It was a habit Michael Jordan was determined to break.

But no matter how hard he tried against the Pistons, he couldn't beat these guys. In earlier seasons, Jordan had some of his biggest scoring games against the Pistons: a 61-point mosaic in an overtime win in March 1987, an Easter Sunday mural on national TV in 1988 in which he'd scored 59 points. And Jordan *was* an artist, the ninety-four-by-fifty-foot basketball court being the canvas for his originals, signed with a flashing smile, a hanging tongue, and a powerful, twisting slam. Pistons coach Chuck Daly, a man who appreciated the arts, was not particularly enamored of Jordan's work, and after that 1988 game the Pistons instituted "the Jordan rules" and the campaign to allow what the Bulls believed was legalized assault on Michael Jordan.

The Pistons had two of the league's best man-to-man defenders, Joe Dumars and Dennis Rodman, to carry out those assignments. Jordan grudgingly respected Dumars, with whom he'd become somewhat friendly at the 1990 All-Star game; Dumars was quiet and resolute, a gentlemanly professional. But Jordan didn't care much for Rodman's play. "He's a flopper," Jordan would say disdainfully. "He just falls down and tries to get the calls. That's not good defense." Rodman once "flopped" so effectively back in the 1988–89 season that Jordan drew six fouls in the fourth quarter to foul out in the last minute of a close loss to the Pistons.

But Jordan's frustration against the Pistons was much larger than his dislike for Rodman, his team's lack of success against Detroit, or even his failure to score effectively since that Easter Sunday game. Detroit simply beat up Jordan, battering him through picks and screens whenever he tried to move. For Jordan, it was like trying to navigate a minefield of bullies. First he'd take a forearm shiver from Dumars when he tried to get past, then perhaps a bump from Bill Laimbeer and a bang from Rodman or Isiah Thomas. The Bulls were so concerned about some of these tactics a few years ago that they focused a camera on Laimbeer throughout the playoffs to see what he was doing and found that he was grabbing players at their pressure points to deaden their arms. They complained to the league, but got no action. And while Thomas is not generally considered a good defender because he doesn't like to play a helping game, whenever the Bulls play Detroit he is quick to double-team Jordan. He knows Jordan despises him and he doesn't care much for Jordan being the hero in Chicago, Isiah's hometown.

Jordan's resentment toward the angelic-looking Thomas is deep. Much of it stems from an alleged freeze-out of Jordan in the 1985 All-Star game, when Thomas and several other players apparently conspired to keep Jordan from getting the ball—and their paths have continued to cross along with their swords. During the 1989–90 season, Magic Johnson suggested a one-on-one match between himself and Jordan. Jordan wasn't too interested, but Johnson was looking at a big pay-per-view payoff and had already worked out a deal with a cable TV company. When word surfaced, though, the NBA voiced its disapproval, and Thomas, head of the Players' Association, said it was not in the best interests of the players to have such unsanctioned off-season games. Suddenly Jordan was very interested. He said he always thought the Players' Association "was supposed to be for the players." And anyway, Jordan said, Thomas was just jealous. "He wasn't asked," snarled Jordan. "And do you want to know why? It's because if he were in it no one would be interested enough to watch."

But the Pistons get their shots back at Jordan. They love to taunt Jordan during games about his selfish play, his baldness (that's a specialty of John Salley), and how he enjoys being a loser. Salley, a bad stand-up comic who has earned a stage because he is seven feet tall and looks like Arsenio Hall, is a particularly bitter antagonist.

"There's not one guy who sets the tone on our team," Salley liked to tell reporters during the 1990 playoffs. "That's what makes us a team. If one guy did everything, we wouldn't be a team. We'd be the Chicago Bulls."

And this, too, from Salley: "We don't care who scores the points as long as we win. It would be hard for Michael Jordan to play on this team because he's got to score all the points. I don't think he'd fit in here."

Jordan burned over comments like that, but he seemed helpless to pay back the Pistons. Jordan was perhaps the league's best when angered, dunking over seven-footers after they'd blocked his shot,

scoring wildly against boastful rookies, and surging to great heights
when opponents scored on him regularly or tried to show him up.
But Jordan couldn't make it happen against the Pistons, and his
teammates were unable to ease the burden he felt.

In Game 1, John Paxson and Craig Hodges missed all 8 of their
field-goal attempts and Scottie Pippen was thwarted by Rodman. "I
seem to spend too much time worrying about how he's going to play
me," Pippen would say later. Among Detroit starters, only Joe
Dumars would score in double figures, with 27 points, but it would
be enough.

In Game 2, Jordan limped on his injured hip and leg, and the
Bulls fell. Pippen and Horace Grant scored 17 each, but it was hardly
enough to make up for the ailing Jordan, who scored only 20. Dumars scored 31.

And so Jordan left the game without speaking to anyone, leaving
the media scrambling for reasons and Jordan's teammates searching
for answers. It was not a happy group that headed back to Chicago
for Game 3. Jordan believed his team had let him down when he
was hurt. The team believed he'd let them down by failing to face
the media after such a crucial loss. Sure, several noted, he was there
long into the night after he scored 50 points, but where was he when
he scored only 20? And his man, Dumars, had burned him in two
straight games, and had clearly been the difference in Detroit's
taking a 2–0 lead. The players agreed: We hear it from him when
we don't play well, but when *he* doesn't play well it's still our fault?

Center Dave Corzine, a former Bull, had once explained it well:
"It's hard playing on a team with Michael Jordan because you're
always the reason the team lost." It certainly couldn't be Jordan's
fault, everyone usually agreed; he was the best, wasn't he? There
was not much anyone on the team could say publicly.

But Jordan would be ready for Game 3 back in the Stadium. He
was angry and chastened, a little contrite perhaps, but also demanding payment for assorted sins.

•

PHIL JACKSON DID the talking for the next few days following Tuesday's Game 2. Jordan, usually playful during practice, wasn't saying
much. After practice Wednesday, with the media waiting and watch-

ing, most of the players skipped out the back door directly to the parking lot, which is what they always did when they wanted to avoid the press. But after complaints from the media, Jackson told Jordan he would have to go out the front door on Thursday—to run the gauntlet, as the coaches liked to say, although the demands on Jordan from the local media (and the national media, too, for that matter) were never threatening. Jordan carefully cultivated his image, maintaining an air of affability while the media fed a Jordan-crazed public a series of well-crafted clichés. It was a formula that played in Peoria, with sponsors like Wheaties, McDonald's, Chevrolet and Nike lining up to quadruple his $3-million-a-year basketball salary in outside income. He was annually selected to the national basketball writers' all-interview team, and local TV reporters liked to put their arms around him during interviews. "But I don't have to talk to anybody?" Jordan said.

"No, you don't have to talk to anybody," Jackson agreed.

So following Thursday's practice Jordan did as he was told, exiting through the front door but ignoring the waiting media. Even his teammates wondered what was going on. "Did the General have anything to say?" Craig Hodges wondered when he came out afterward. Hodges liked to call Jordan "the General," explaining that Jordan gave the commands, ordering players around and out of his way, determining whether the play called by the coaches should be run, and jawing with officials. It was up to his teammates to carry his orders out, which they rarely seemed to do to his satisfaction these days.

"What'd he say?" asked John Paxson when he left the floor of the glass-enclosed Multiplex gym.

"Did he say anything to you guys?" a reporter asked.

"No," Paxson said. "He talked generally, like calling plays or positions, but he didn't say anything else."

"Did he say what was bothering him?" asked another reporter.

"No, he didn't say much of anything," Paxson repeated.

But Jackson had. He read Jordan's actions as a demand for his teammates to step up and be held accountable for their poor play. He agreed with the sentiment, but didn't want to see it in the papers. (Actually, Jackson rarely read the sports pages, but his family and his assistants had summarized the reports of Jordan's fit and the team's sense of betrayal.) He told the team that what happened in their locker room was their business and no one else's. He talked of character and "owning up," and said that if a little adversity could destroy the team, they weren't the team they believed themselves to be. It was a desperate time, Jackson said, a time to be angry and emotional. It was a time to be held accountable. It was up to them.

As for tactics, the team had to stop its headlong charges into Detroit's interior defense. The Pistons played a zone, simple and effective, Jackson noted. And the Bulls had to get good shots and take them rather than crash in where they had no room to maneuver. They had to retreat better on defense, and they had to rebound.

In Game 3, they did. And it was a series again.

"Tonight," Jackson offered after the victory, "we showed that it wasn't the rules against Jordan, but that Jordan rules."

Jordan scored 16 points in the first half, but the Bulls trailed 51–43 after a typically withering Detroit second quarter in which the Bulls were outscored 32–19. Jordan fumed in the locker room and made a decision. "If we're going down," he thought to himself, "we're going down my way."

By the time the third quarter was over, a roaring cascade of cheers was tumbling down on the Bulls from the overcrowded Chicago Stadium. The result was no longer in doubt, as the third quarter turned into a Jordanfest. Jordan drove and tipped in his own miss to open the quarter, and blew a pass inside to Pippen for a lay-up for the second Bulls basket of the quarter. He hit a ten-footer for the third. He sliced inside for the fifth, and later added a driving basket for a three-point play and a pair of free throws to close the quarter as the Bulls outscored Detroit 17–6 in the last three and a half minutes to gain control of the game. The fourth quarter saw Detroit push back, but Jordan pushed harder. He scored 18 more points and found himself smashed to the floor by Rodman. He got up, drove again, and was fouled. Then he hit a three-point field goal with time running out on the twenty-four-second clock. The Stadium was shaking in pandemonium.

Jordan had scored 31 points in the second half to finish with 47 points and 10 rebounds. Pippen had added 29 and 11 rebounds while Grant had climbed on the boards for another 11 rebounds, 6 of them offensive. The Bulls had gotten another big assist from Ed Nealy, who had played 22 minutes and scored 8 points. He was slow and couldn't jump much, but Jackson labeled him "his favorite player, the smartest player on the team."

Jordan was curt afterward. He didn't smile or joke, as he usually does in postgame sessions. He went to the podium and said he wouldn't talk about the locker-room incident in Game 2. He said he never criticized his teammates. He said he only spoke as "we," not "they."

"He said that?" Grant exclaimed later when told about Jordan's comments. "Really, no, he really said that?"

Cartwright, sitting next to Grant, shook his head. "Crazy," he said with a wry smile.

Jordan said he would not talk to the media again until after the next game.

The Bulls would do again in Game 4 what they couldn't do in Detroit. They shot well and scrambled the game. The Bulls' play was to get the game above 100 points, so they trapped Thomas and Dumars into 12 turnovers and Jordan was brilliant in scoring 42 more in a 108–101 win. Bill Laimbeer was 1 of 7 and now just 1 of 13 in the two games in Chicago after shooting 8 for 10 in Detroit.

The Pistons were now 24–5 in the playoffs over the past two seasons, with the Bulls having defeated them four times. The Pistons had lost two straight in the playoffs for the first time in two years. But the Bulls hadn't defeated Detroit in the Palace of Auburn Hills yet.

After Game 5, the Bulls still hadn't. It was a classic Pistons win over the Bulls. Dumars scored 20, holding Jordan to 7 of 19 and 22 points. The Pistons outrebounded the Bulls 45–36, the Pistons' bench outscored Chicago's 35–13, and the Bulls hit just a third of their shots. And it was rough: Thomas slammed Pippen to the floor midway through the third quarter. The Bulls trailed 72–64 to open the fourth quarter, but after scoring a basket, Jordan signaled that he wanted to come out for a rest. He was out for two minutes, and in that time Detroit outscored the Bulls 11–2 and the Bulls never got close again. The Bulls had begun to ignore Laimbeer, and he scored 16 points while Pippen labored through a 5-for-20 game. Grant was brilliant off the boards, with 8 offensive rebounds, compared with 9 for the entire Detroit team. Mostly, though, Detroit was tougher and more aggressive.

In a play that summed up the problems Chicago faced in Detroit, with 10.4 seconds to go in the first quarter Jordan took the ball after a Pistons turnover and tossed up a shot from midcourt. The ball swished through to give the Bulls a 25–25 tie. Vinnie Johnson then missed a drive to end the quarter.

As Jordan went to the bench, he explained to Jackson, "I thought [the clock] said one point four seconds."

Trainer Mark Pfeil pulled Jordan aside. "We'll go over numbers later," Pfeil joked.

The only number that mattered for the Bulls now was one. One loss and their summer began. One win and they would get a chance to start over.

Pistons players talked about being mentally tough, saying that now the games would go to whoever wanted them most, whoever played the hardest, whoever was a champion.

In Game 6, the Bulls looked like the champions. The Bulls bolted from a narrow 57–54 lead midway through the third quarter with a 23–9 run to close the quarter and close out Detroit; the final margin was 18. The Bulls grabbed loose balls as if they had Velcro on their fingers. Craig Hodges and Jordan ignited the crowd with long three-pointers. Even Will Perdue was banging around after Bill Cartwright picked up his fourth foul. Everybody was talking about the chance of a lifetime after the game. John Paxson, sidelined with a sprained ankle, said he'd tape his ankle and try to play. Hodges said the sixth didn't mean anything without the seventh. There was a lot of talk about a one-game season and about how the momentum was now theirs.

Jordan still wasn't granting mass interviews by his locker after the game. Since Game 3, he'd chosen to come out, sit on a podium next to Jackson, answer a few questions from the dozens of assembled reporters, and then leave. Jordan would then go to his locker, dress, and be ignored as if he had an infectious disease. Reporters made a wide arc to avoid even getting close to him as they squeezed into the cramped locker room in the old Chicago Stadium.

As Jordan slipped on a sheer, brown floral shirt, his father, James, leaned over. "Son," he said, "we're there. Now's our chance and we're gonna do it."

"Right, Dad," Jordan agreed.

•

MICHAEL JORDAN RETURNED to his team. The dam of silence was swept away by a flood of hope. Jordan was joking on the team bus as it traveled to the Palace, and in the locker room, as if nothing had happened the last two weeks. He made fun of Pippen's shoes and Grant's after-shave lotion. It smelled like a lawn, Jordan said, one just fertilized. They asked Jordan where he'd left his comb. The scene seemed to relax everyone, and it was a calm, outwardly confident Bulls team that readied for the game. This was all Jordan had asked for, a chance. This was a chance to get to the Finals. Let the better team win. Throw it all out there and go on or go home. It was the farthest one of his teams ever had gone.

But the Bulls would go no farther. As Jordan feared, even suspected, his teammates disappeared. Paxson tried, but couldn't go. His ankle was too sore and swollen, and he would need surgery in a week. Hodges, rusty from months of virtual inactivity, couldn't sustain his effort for two games and shot 3 for 13, 2 for 12 on three-pointers. His big, toothy smile was gone and he'd soon be contemplating his feet.

It wasn't much of a game. The Pistons hit 9 straight shots in the second quarter while the Bulls went 2 of 12. The score was 48–33 at halftime and the game was over. The score was 61–39 in the third quarter, and even though the Bulls closed the gap to 10 after three quarters, they never had a chance.

Scottie Pippen was 1 of 10 for 2 points. Stricken by a migraine headache, he was blinking his eyes madly before the game and putting an ice pack on his head during time-outs. He played forty-two minutes, but could barely distinguish his teammates from the Pistons. He broke down and drowned himself in tears in the locker room afterward. Grant was ferocious on the boards, pulling down more offensive rebounds than the entire Detroit team and grabbing a game-high 14 overall, but he shot 3 of 17. Cartwright had worn down and would need knee surgery, and Hodges also would go under the knife. The rookies were deadly—B. J. Armstrong flew out of control in front of the Detroit crowd and was 1 of 8. The Pistons' bench outscored the Bulls' 33–21, as Mark Aguirre had 15 points and 10 rebounds and John Salley had 14 points. Thomas was brilliant in orchestrating the Pistons' break with 21 points and 11 assists. "They may have the best player, but we have the better team," noted Laimbeer, the mockery in his voice scratching at Chicagoans like fingernails on a chalkboard.

Jordan was left to consider the 93–74 loss. He agreed Detroit was better. The Bulls had to get better. He wasn't the general manager, but if he were . . . It was obvious the team needed veterans. But he wasn't just slapping at the rookies. Where was Pippen? This was the second straight year he'd vanished in the last game against the Pistons; he'd received a concussion in the first minute of the final conference playoff game in 1989. Were he and his buddy, Grant, serious enough? Paxson had broken down and the other guys hadn't done much. Jordan had scored 31 points, 21 more than anyone else, but he'd also attempted 27 shots. And many were wondering how the Bulls were ever going to win if he was to continue to shoot at that pace.

As for Jordan, he believed he *had* to continue at that pace. Otherwise, who would?

Just before he stepped from the postgame podium and onto the golf courses of America, Jordan offered one final thought: "We have to do some things. We need to make some changes."

2

SUMMER 1990

JERRY REINSDORF SAT back, surrounded by his fellow National Basketball Association owners, at one of their regular meetings, enjoying another wonderful day in the summer of 1990.

He was going to lose a player he would have liked to keep for his Bulls, but little setbacks like that didn't bother Reinsdorf much; he was having too much fun being Jerry Reinsdorf.

Being Jerry Reinsdorf didn't look like it would be worth much when he was growing up. He was just another face in the crowd at Brooklyn's Erasmus High School, which has a reputation for producing special students. Among its graduates are actor Eli Wallach, singer Barbra Streisand, writer Bernard Malamud, playwright Betty Comden, and chess champion Bobby Fischer. And Reinsdorf, the son of lower-middle class parents, his father a sewing machine repairman, vividly remembers his high school graduation day. He was in a class of nearly 1,000 students and the school had given out literally hundreds of awards, for everything from proficiency in English and math to excellence in hall monitoring. Reinsdorf's name hadn't been called. He remembers walking home a long time in silence with his mother, Marion, who finally said, "Couldn't you at least have gotten one?"

He had been just another sports-crazed kid growing up in Brook-

lyn, but he went on to amass a fortune in real estate after moving
to Chicago, eventually selling his business, Balcor, to American
Express for $53 million. By then he had fulfilled his lifelong dream
of running a baseball team by leading a group that bought the Chicago White Sox. But the White Sox were a financial drain, so much
so that Reinsdorf sought to buy an interest in the Chicago Bulls so
he could remain in sports if he lost the team. Basketball had never
thrived in Chicago, where the Stags disbanded in 1950 and then the
Packers/Zephyrs moved in 1963 to become the Baltimore (now
Washington) Bullets. The Bulls came along in 1966, but were averaging just over sixty-three hundred fans per game in 1984 when
Reinsdorf began negotiations. George Steinbrenner, then the New
York Yankees' principal owner, was a Bulls part-owner then and,
by chance, mentioned to Reinsdorf that he was embarrassed by the
team and wanted to get out. Reinsdorf said he wanted in, but didn't
say why. A deal was quickly put together; Reinsdorf would acquire
more than half the team's stock for about $9 million. He then
watched as NBA revenues soared, aided in no small part by one
player, Michael Jordan, who was just joining the Bulls when Reinsdorf bought in. Chicago Stadium was now a complete and constant
sellout, and, all in all, Reinsdorf was feeling pretty good.

Ed Nealy, the player the Bulls were about to lose, was a thirty-
year-old barrel-chested forward from Kansas who had joined the
team for a second go-round before the opening of the 1989–90 season. He was one of those players the newspapers liked to call "much
traveled." Coaches called him "smart." Both were euphemisms for
Nealy's pokiness, his inability to jump very well, and the fact that
he was rarely in demand. But he'd had a steadying influence on the
Bulls, even a motivating one, for his teammates could look at Nealy
and see what hard work could do for a player. Here was a guy with
so little talent, yet he was still around after seven years in the NBA.
It was tempting to look at him and think, "If he can play seven
years, I ought to be able to play until I'm forty," but it wasn't as
easy as that, as most would eventually learn. Nealy didn't cruise the
clubs at night and he was always the first one to practice or to work
out in the weight room. He never complained when he didn't play
and he rarely shot when he did. Playing time and shots: Even more
than money, they are the pro basketball player's measures of self-

worth. Nealy didn't make an issue of either, so he was a favorite of both management and his teammates. And the Chicago fans took to Nealy because he personified their city—hardworking and blue collar (even though tickets had become so expensive that only the whitest of collars could afford them, assuming they could even find a ticket to buy).

Yes, he worked hard. He set screens, boxed out, took on the strongest inside player. He did the basketball dirty work, even if his limited talent didn't allow him to do it often enough. Still, he had had a 9-rebound, 9-point game in the playoffs against Philadelphia as the Bulls won without Scottie Pippen, who was home after the death of his father. Nealy took several rebounds away from Charles Barkley in the fourth quarter and was chosen player of the game by the CBS broadcasters.

He'd come to Chicago that season unwanted. The Bulls had traded him to Phoenix the previous season for Craig Hodges, but even Suns coach Cotton Fitzsimmons, who had originally drafted Nealy as the 166th pick in 1982 for Kansas City, had no use for him. Fitzsimmons promised to find Nealy a spot in the NBA, and the Bulls agreed to take him back as a twelfth man. He played in little more than half the regular-season games, earning about $250,000, so the Bulls were stunned when he rejected their two-year offer of $400,000 per year; Nealy said he could get almost $700,000 per year for three years. Bulls coach Phil Jackson argued that the team should keep Nealy, but he understood it was impossible at that cost.

Reinsdorf was laughing about the Nealy offer and shaking his head when he turned to Phoenix president Jerry Colangelo. "Somebody's going to give Ed Nealy seven hundred thousand dollars," Reinsdorf said. "Jerry, who'd do something that stupid?"

Colangelo mumbled something about not knowing. The next day, Phoenix announced it had signed Ed Nealy for three seasons.

Losing Nealy posed a problem for the Bulls. They were a young team, and Michael Jordan didn't think young teams won titles. Jordan made that clear following their seventh-game loss to the Pistons in the 1990 playoffs. Rookie guard B. J. Armstrong shot 10 for 38 and averaged 4.4 points in fifteen minutes per game in the series, and rookie forward Stacey King went 9 for 28 and averaged 5 points in his fifteen minutes per game. Jordan had reserved much of his anger for King, screaming at him to rebound and "hit somebody" several times. "Management knows where we can improve," said Jordan. "And I don't think they'll be looking at the draft."

Jordan respected Nealy, even if he doubted his overall athletic talent, for Nealy was the basketball version of rolling up your sleeves, spitting on your hands, and going to work. Jordan would always go to Nealy's side of the court when they were playing together, no matter where Jordan was supposed to be in that particular set. "He's the only one who'll set a good pick," Jordan said. "He's a tough guy."

That kind of respect is hard to earn from Jordan, who can be as cold and demanding as a landlord on the last day of the month. Just ask Brad Sellers, whom Jordan regularly derided for his soft play and eventually helped evict from the team. In 1987, the Bulls drafted Sellers, a seven-footer from Ohio State who was projected as a small forward. The obvious pick appeared to be Duke guard Johnny Dawkins, but the Bulls decided they needed a small forward since they were getting rid of Orlando Woolridge and had already arranged a deal to get point guard Steve Colter from Portland. And the Bulls were, to some extent, drafting Sellers to accommodate Jordan: "They liked Sellers because you couldn't leave with your three [small forward] to double on Michael because Brad could hit the jumper," Jackson explained.

But Jordan believed that Dawkins would be the choice, and he had told Dawkins so in pickup games they'd played in North Carolina before the draft. So when the Bulls skipped Dawkins for Sellers, Jordan felt both betrayed and embarrassed. He felt the team made him look like a fool, and he took it out on Colter, a quiet kid from New Mexico, and later on Sellers, likewise sensitive and uncertain about how to respond to a superstar. Jordan's famous tongue became a whip for these plowhorse players, as he saw them. Sellers would eventually break under the strain of Jordan's attacks, the constant derision during practice, and the physical attacks when Jordan had him in his sights coming downcourt in practice, and Sellers's game would plummet to such depths that he was out of the NBA by the 1990–91 season.

Jordan can be demanding on the court, and it's always been his habit to wave off the point guard to get the ball. That's one reason Paxson had been the most successful point guard to play with Jordan;

Paxson isn't a creator. Unlike most point guards, who need the ball to make plays and set up teammates, Paxson feeds off creative players like Jordan and Pippen. He's more comfortable passing the ball upcourt and then spotting up for a jump shot. Not so Colter— or most point guards, for that matter. But Jordan kept running Colter off the ball, demanding the ball in every crucial situation, and criticizing him whenever he'd made a mistake.

It wasn't always Jordan's fault, since his coaches, Kevin Loughery, Stan Albeck, and Doug Collins, all permitted Jordan to stay back to pick up the ball in the backcourt and then run the offense. Jackson tried to change that and Jordan balked much of the 1989–90 season, but Jackson would continue to work on him for the 1990–91 season. He knew what a great weapon Jordan would be for the Bulls if he would just take off downcourt, because the defense would have to follow him and leave the court clearer for the ball handler to advance the ball.

Colter wasn't strong enough to stand up to Jordan; few Bulls ever have been. It's one reason some people felt the Bulls should have pursued Danny Ainge after the 1989–90 season, when the feisty point guard was being made available by Sacramento. The Bulls were looking for a scorer for their second team, but they also needed someone to stand up to Jordan when he routinely ordered his team-mates out of the way late in the game. "He'll tell Michael to fuck off when he starts screaming for the ball," said assistant coach John Bach at the time. "And sometimes we need that."

Another Bull who appeared to be wilting under Jordan's heat was Will Perdue. "You've got to get Michael's respect to do well on the Bulls," said John Paxson. "Will had trouble."

"I never really understood," admitted Perdue. "I'll always set a screen for him when I'm in there and I know no one else but Ed [Nealy] would. I know Bill [Cartwright] would never do it. But I know Michael hated me and Bill."

Perdue came out of Vanderbilt, known perhaps more for his size-22 shoes than his game. Although he was Southeastern Conference Player of the Year in 1988, he had yet to find a role in the pros. He was slow afoot, although he had a good passing touch and could score. But he often shrank back from contact, which doomed him almost immediately as a pro center. The lane in pro basketball is an area Bach appropriately describes as "an alligator wrestling pond." All sorts of holding, pushing, grabbing, and clawing is allowed among men who are seven feet tall and weigh more than 250 pounds. The center has to establish his position and then fight to keep it. Perdue often backed away from combat. The daily beatings he took in practice from Bill Cartwright, whose flying elbows had already given Perdue a cauliflower left ear, made him instinctively wary. To many on the team, it didn't even look as if he enjoyed basketball. He appeared to be a big kid who was told he had to play basketball, so he did. That almost was the case, although Perdue had come to appreciate the game for what it could do for him, having been a so-so football player growing up in Florida, where football is king. Finally, he took up basketball at age thirteen.

"I thought, 'Hey, I can do this. This might get me something,' " Perdue recalls about his introduction to the game. And maybe that was enough for him. He refused to go to the pro summer league after his unsuccessful first season, souring some among the Bulls on his work habits. He'd been described as looking like a character from the painting *American Gothic* and he seemed to have about as much movement. Some of his teammates called him "Shytown."

Jordan's dislike for Perdue was palpable. He called him "Will Vanderbilt." "He doesn't deserve to be named after a Big Ten school," Jordan would explain. Jordan rarely talked to the big center, whom general manager Jerry Krause had projected as the team's pivot player of the 1990s. By Perdue's second season, it was clear that Krause had overstated Perdue's potential. "If Bill Cartwright plays until he's fifty, Will Perdue will still be his backup," Bach once told Krause. Krause would grow angry at such observations, but Perdue never did much to change anyone's feelings.

It didn't help that Perdue was backup to one of the most respected players on the Bulls (if not by Jordan), Bill Cartwright.

"Bill's always the one we look to when things aren't going right on the floor or if there's a problem in the locker room," said guard B. J. Armstrong. "That's just the way it is."

It was Cartwright who organized players to buy some gag gifts for the coaches at a team party around Christmastime, one that Jordan didn't attend. It was the first time in twenty years in the NBA, Bach remarked, that he'd seen players buy anything for the coaches.

Cartwright admired Jordan's talent and saw him as one of the great individual players ever, an artist and a genius of the hardwood, a man who could spin the straw of effort into the gold of brilliance. Cartwright said he respected that, even if he didn't always care for Jordan's habits. Jordan usually worked hard in practice, but sometimes so effectively that Bulls' practices became disorganized because no one could stop or guard him. It was one reflection of the eternal Bulls problem: Jordan so focused on what he could do that he lost sight of the team's goal in practicing. Journeyman Charles Davis stayed on the team much of one season because he gave Jordan trouble in practice, thus enabling the coaches to conduct some reasonably competitive scrimmages.

But the trouble between Jordan and Cartwright ran deeper than most observers realized. Much of it stemmed from the Bulls' acquisition of Cartwright in a trade for Charles Oakley, Jordan's last good friend on the team. Cartwright wasn't a great rebounder or shot blocker, but he was still a smart, effective center, and in the 1991 playoffs Jordan finally offered him some grudging credit. Adlai Stevenson, talking about journalists, had once said that they do not live by words alone, although sometimes they have to eat them. Jordan would chow down heavily on his words about Cartwright, but he wouldn't sit at the table alone. "You guys," Jordan told reporters when asked whether he regretted the negative remarks he'd made about the trade for Cartwright, "didn't know either."

·

ONE PLAYER JORDAN did want on his team was Walter Davis, the high-scoring sixth man for Denver. Davis had been something of an idol for Jordan, who hadn't been very highly sought after in high school. The five-foot-ten-inch Jordan hadn't made the varsity at Laney High School in Wilmington, North Carolina, as a sophomore. He started to gain some recognition after his junior year at the meat-market summer camps where college coaches do their scouting. Jordan was interested in UCLA, but he didn't hear from the school. He thought about North Carolina State because of David Thompson, who was to kids then what Jordan is now: a high-flying basketball magician who could excite the crowd with his daring moves. But Jordan eventually decided on the University of North Carolina, whose symbol was Davis. Where Thompson represented the flam-

boyance of State, Davis's professionalism and cool demeanor reflected the integrity of UNC. Jordan spoke of Davis often when he
first arrived in Chicago, although he stopped dropping his name
after Davis's flings with cocaine. But one thing Jordan learned at
North Carolina was loyalty. Coach Dean Smith always told his players to stand up for their own, and Jordan was always trying to get
the Bulls to trade for someone from his alma mater.

Davis had kicked his habit and was staying out of trouble, which
was vital to Jordan, for when he arrived in Chicago he found himself
surrounded by very talented but very confused players. "I've always
said, the best talent I ever played with was my first year with the
Bulls," Jordan noted. "But I call them 'the Looney Tunes.' Physically, they were the best. Mentally, they weren't even close." One
of the reasons for this was made clear to Jordan when, as a rookie,
he popped into a teammate's room and saw loads of white stuff that
definitely wasn't baby powder. Two of his teammates, Quintin
Dailey and Orlando Woolridge, would eventually go into drug rehabilitation, and others like Steve Johnson, Jawann Oldham, Sidney
Green, and Ennis Whatley would fade into lesser roles. Actually,
the dismantling of that team when Reinsdorf took over became
general manager Krause's greatest achievement. He liked to call it
"addition by subtraction" combined with the search for "OKPs"
(our kind of people).

In the short run, Krause's strategy worked brilliantly. He traded
Oldham to the Knicks for a first-round draft pick, which he later
exchanged with Seattle for the pick that allowed him to select Scottie
Pippen in the 1987 draft. That draft was, perhaps, Krause's greatest
achievement in sports and the foundation for the Bulls' championship of 1991. Krause also traded Woolridge to the Nets for a first-
round pick that he used to select Stacey King, who remained an
uncut stone even as the Bulls pushed toward their title.

The title was Krause's goal, although few thought him capable of
getting there. He really was just a scout, they'd say. He was a pretty
good one, though. He'd grown up in Chicago and attended Bradley
University in Peoria, where he liked to hang out with the athletes.
He wasn't much of one himself, being roundish with narrow, distant
brown eyes, so he became the manager for the basketball and baseball teams, charting plays and running errands. That willingness to
do just about anything would mark Krause's climb up the ladder of

sports management. He started hanging around with the baseball scouts who drove to the numerous semipro games around central Illinois in those days, and he eventually hooked on as a small-time scout. That led to a contract with Bob "Slick" Leonard, then playing with the old Chicago Packers. Leonard would become player-coach when the team moved to Baltimore, and he took the twenty-three-year-old Krause along as a sort of PR man and gofer. Krause scouted some for the Bullets; there are differences of opinion about whether he discovered Earl "the Pearl" Monroe, as he says he did. Krause eventually left to run a minor-league team in Oregon and then joined the Bulls in the late sixties. He was an exceptionally hard worker, almost single-minded in his pursuits and truly a believer in the notion that chance favors the prepared mind. His genius, if it would come, would be from the 99-percent-perspiration part. But his personal habits, like dressing in gravy-stained clothes and striving hard for a sense of humor, kept him from being accepted by the people he worked with. Krause would tell long stories of how various legends of the game had praised him for his work habits. He did work hard, but he could never understand that modesty is the only sure bait when you angle for praise. Krause also had an annoying habit of repeating his opinions. He'd scout a player and offer something like, "This kid can really get the ball. I mean, this kid can really get the ball. I mean really, this kid . . ." He drove Dick Motta nuts when Motta coached the Bulls, and that antipathy hurt the Bulls in 1990 when Motta was trying to trade Danny Ainge from Sacramento. Krause had some successes, like tabbing Cliff Ray in the third round of the NBA draft in 1971; Ray later ran into Krause and said, "Hey, aren't you the guy who was following me around campus?" Krause, one of the first in basketball to recognize the need to search for skeletons in players' closets, had been sneaking behind trees on the University of Oklahoma campus to watch whom Ray met with. But Krause had also touted Kennedy McIntosh as a first-round pick in 1971 and Jimmy Collins over Nate Archibald in 1970, and Motta lost faith in him. Krause moved on to Phoenix to scout for a while, returning to the Bulls as player personnel director only after Motta left.

Jordan didn't know anything about Krause when he joined the Bulls, but their relationship would sour quickly. Jordan was the one who nicknamed the GM "Crumbs" ("He always had doughnut crumbs on his lapel," says Jordan), and by the 1990–91 season he was convinced that Krause was incapable of acquiring the kind of veteran talent Jordan felt was needed.

Jordan, who has been known to lead the team in mooing like a cow when Krause would appear in the locker room (others would hum the theme from "Green Acres"), lobbied extensively during the 1988–89 season for a trade that would bring New Jersey's Buck Williams to the Bulls. Jordan didn't particularly care for Horace Grant, Krause's other pick in the 1987 draft, never believing Grant would develop into a responsible player, and lobbied hard for Williams, who was represented by Jordan's agent, David Falk. But the Nets were still angry over the Woolridge deal; Woolridge had gone into drug rehabilitation and then left the team as a free agent after two seasons, so they weren't making it easy on the Bulls. Also, Krause has a deep reluctance to trade first-round picks, so Williams eventually went to Portland, and made it to the Finals before Jordan did, in 1990, when his team was beaten by Detroit in five games.

Jordan never cared for the Oakley–Cartwright trade—he never understood why a team would trade for a veteran like Cartwright and then the very next season go into the draft for three first-round picks (Chicago's own, the No. 6 pick from the Woolridge deal, and a No. 18 pick obtained in the Brad Sellers trade)—and he began to wonder more and more whether the Bulls were serious about winning or whether they merely wanted to keep the Stadium filled. He often believed they were content just to compete while he was at his peak, knowing that would be enough to draw the crowds, while they focused their efforts on building the winning team they'd need to keep attendance up in the years when his abilities would lessen or after he retired. Jordan understood, too, that a great effort was being made to shift some of the spotlight away from him and onto some of his teammates. "I know they're into this de-Michaelization," he said during their 1989–90 season. "So I've just got to get mine now."

Jordan had grown more and more resentful during the summer about his salary, even though it was easily the highest on the team. He knew that the Bulls, especially Krause, privately resented him because everyone credited the team's success to him rather than to good management and planning. Initially, the new organization focused its marketing on Jordan, selling Jordan as the Bulls. The campaign was a huge success. But now the marketing and basketball people, Jordan felt, were beginning to view him with jealousy. Jordan had heard about Krause bragging that he'd have two titles by now if the Bulls had Akeem Olajuwon instead of Jordan. And the marketing people had come to believe that their promotions, fancy light shows, and other gimmicks in the Stadium were as much responsible for a three-year run of sellouts as Jordan. So Jordan wasn't surprised when he saw a photo of Scottie Pippen on the team's pocket schedule for the 1989–90 season, the first time a player other than Jordan had been featured alone on a team publication during his time with the team. And now Jordan could see the plan for Yugoslavian superstar Toni Kukoc, whom the Bulls had drafted in hopes that he could be convinced to come to America. Already, he'd heard that the marketing staff was concentrating on endorsement opportunities for Kukoc; the Bulls had told Kukoc that even though they were offering him $1 million less than a team in Europe, he'd easily make that up in endorsement money. Jordan had become less and less cooperative with the team about promotions in recent years, so they decided to let him worry about himself; Kukoc would be "their" player.

Jordan's reservations about Kukoc weren't limited to marketing strategies. He would tell friends he didn't expect Kukoc to be a star in the NBA anyway. "Wait until he gets an elbow in the face from Laimbeer. He won't be going to the basket again. I know he looks good, but that's against college players. He has no idea what the NBA is all about." And while the Bulls continued to pursue Kukoc, even Reinsdorf wondered what would occur when another player, one the Bulls would market as a future star, joined Jordan. "Does he want to share the spotlight?" Reinsdorf asked. "I wonder."

One answer to that question was offered when Jordan refused Krause's requests to telephone Kukoc and urge him to come to America. "I don't speak no Yugoslavian," Jordan told Krause with a mocking smile.

•

THE BIGGEST FREE-AGENT catch available over the summer was Sam Perkins, the Dallas forward from North Carolina. He seemed a perfect match for the Bulls. Jordan loved North Carolina players

and Perkins, at 6-9 and 235 pounds, averaged about 15 points, could
rebound some and was a good defensive player at both forward
positions and even at center. But he'd already turned down $3 mil-
lion from the Mavericks. Jordan had told the Bulls he doubted
Perkins would leave Dallas because North Carolina players were
drilled to be loyal. But the Bulls had other concerns. They were
paying Jordan less than $3 million, and while they felt they could
get away with Jordan being paid less than several other players
around the league, they knew it would be intolerable for him to be
the second-highest player on his own team.

"Falk [Jordan's agent] was getting ready to start knocking on the
door," acknowledged coach Phil Jackson.

Falk had pulled off what seemed like the deal of a generation
when word leaked early in 1988 that Jordan would sign an eight-
year, $25 million contract with the Bulls. It dwarfed other deals for
superstars, but so did Jordan's popularity. Indiana general manager
Donnie Walsh said, "We should all be chipping in to pay him. He
does so much for the league." Teams sold thousands of extra tickets
whenever Jordan was in town, not to mention what he did for attendance in Chicago. The year before Jordan came, the Bulls' average attendance was 6,365. That grew to 11,887 in Jordan's first
season, and to 17,794 by 1988. At the Bulls' average 1990 ticket
price of about $25, it's easy to estimate Jordan's value to the Bulls
at $5 million per year. And that's just in admissions.

When NBC outbid CBS for the NBA's TV rights starting in the
1990–91 season, it was a bonanza for the players. Under the players'
basic agreement, players and owners had agreed to split league
revenues, and the players' salaries were capped at a total of 53
percent of these revenues. With the new TV deal, revenues boomed
and the amount of money available to players under the salary cap
jumped way beyond any earlier expectations. By the start of the
1990–91 season, Jordan was only the seventh-highest-paid player in
the league (moving up to third highest for the 1991–92 season). And
Reinsdorf had Jordan locked up for six more seasons in what now
looked like a brilliant deal for the other side.

Reinsdorf knew Jordan wanted more money as others around
him, like Cleveland's John (Hot Rod) Williams, signed huge contracts thanks to the expanded salary cap. Everywhere Jordan went
were the signs that he was underpaid even at $3 million per year.

Leafing through a preseason basketball publication, Jordan came across a picture of Williams and his children. Williams had on a Nike shirt and the kids were wearing Air Jordan sneakers. "He's making five million dollars," Jordan would later note, "but he's got to pay me for the sneakers."

While Reinsdorf was opposed to renegotiating earlier contracts, he recognized that Jordan was different—in fact, the eight-year deal had been a renegotiation of the seven-year, $6.3 million contract Jordan had signed when he first came into the league. Reinsdorf told Jordan after the 1989–90 season that he'd do something for him, even if Reinsdorf felt no personal urgency. There was talk about real estate partnerships and other equity deals, perhaps paying Jordan in cash up front for the season to give him quicker use of the money. Reinsdorf recognized what he had in Jordan; he'd often say Jordan was the Babe Ruth of basketball, that in generations to come people would talk about having seen him the way Reinsdorf's grandfather talked about having seen Ruth.

But Reinsdorf felt he had an ace in the hole against Jordan: "He's too worried about his image to complain about only making three million dollars," Reinsdorf said.

If Jordan was a product of the American consumer society, with endorsement contracts from many of the most wholesome companies, he was also a prisoner of the image he'd created. He'd become the most visible spokesman for these products because of his unsullied image. He was handsome, with a quick, ingratiating smile. His name was never linked to scandal or even questionable habits, even though his first son was born out of wedlock.

Fear of public criticism controlled many of Jordan's actions. When teammates once suggested he come out publicly against then-coach Doug Collins, who was splitting the team in two with his incessant criticism of certain players, Jordan refused. "I'm not getting into one of those things like Magic did," he said, recalling the damage to Magic Johnson's image and endorsement potential when he orchestrated the firing of Lakers coach Paul Westhead. Westhead was fired eleven games into the 1981–82 season (after guiding the team to the NBA title in the 1979–80 season) when the team rebelled against his playing style and Johnson spoke up. Jordan agreed with his teammates about Collins, but he was unwilling to be that kind of lightning rod.

But image aside, Jordan simply was not going to stand for making less than Sam Perkins. And the full weight of the public's support would be on Jordan's side, the Bulls well knew. The team had to think about Scottie Pippen as well; Pippen had made the All-Star team in 1990, but was earning only $765,000 in 1990–91 under his first contract. So the Bulls backed away from Perkins, which didn't concern Jordan too much, for he was sure Walter Davis would accept the Bulls' offer.

.

THE BULLS HAD identified two principal weaknesses after the 1990 playoff loss to Detroit. They needed more frontcourt strength, preferably a tough guy. They had had a chance to get Rick Mahorn from Minnesota the summer before when Detroit lost him in the expansion pool, but they were concerned about his back. With Krause reluctant to give up the first-round draft choices Minnesota wanted, a deal wasn't made, even though Jackson had interceded with Timberwolves GM Billy McKinney, who had left the Bulls and was not on speaking terms with Krause.

The Bulls also needed a scorer off the bench to counter Detroit's strength. The Bulls' starting five usually played well against Detroit's starters, but Chicago couldn't compete with Detroit backups like Vinnie Johnson, Mark Aguirre, and John Salley. Davis was a big-time scorer, a former All-Star, and a player whom the coaches felt answered that need.

Meanwhile, the Bulls also wanted to add a big guard. All their guards other than Jordan were 6-2 or under—that's why they rejected the overtures of Detroit free agent Vinnie Johnson—and a big guard playing alongside Jordan would give Detroit matchup problems the way Milwaukee did with Jay Humphries, Alvin Robertson, and Ricky Pierce. The Bucks were clearly inferior to the Pistons, but always did better against them than the Bulls did. There was ample sentiment for acquiring Ainge, the former Boston Celtics star who'd been shipped off to Sacramento and was now being offered around as the Kings tried to rebuild under Dick Motta. It was not going to be easy for the Bulls, given the relationship between Motta and Krause. But few teams really liked dealing with Krause,

who had developed a reputation around the league as a bargainer
who often demanded something for nothing.

That was never clearer than before the 1990 draft when Krause
tried to get Atlanta's first second-round pick, No. 36 in the draft.
The Hawks weren't anxious to add rookies to their team, so they
were willing to deal the pick. "What will you give me?' asked Hawks
president Stan Kasten.

"Nothing," replied Krause.

"Then why should I give you the pick?" responded Kasten.

"Because you can get the same guy with your second pick [No.
41], and then you won't have to pay him as much," explained
Krause. The Hawks were not impressed by the logic.

The search for that big guard ended with the acquisition of Dennis
Hopson of New Jersey. Hopson was the third player selected in the
1987 draft, two places ahead of Pippen. But he had been a bust
with the lowly Nets, shooting poorly and eventually getting into
several disputes with Bill Fitch when the former coach of the Cavaliers, Celtics, and Rockets took over the Nets in 1989. Fitch had
coached Phil Jackson when Jackson was at the University of North
Dakota, and he assured Jackson that Hopson had talent that might
develop in the right atmosphere. The feeling in New Jersey was that
there was too much pressure on Hopson to produce with a bad team
and that he could help a good one. But Jordan had his doubts.

"When you play a guy, you know," said Jordan. "You can see it
in his eyes. He's scared. He's got no heart." Later, Jordan would
regret not speaking up against Hopson. "Especially when I heard
he needed knee surgery (the summer before joining the Bulls),"
said Jordan. "Nobody told me that. If I had spoken up, he wouldn't
have been here."

But when the Bulls began talking to Hopson, the season had
ended and Jordan was just anxious to get a big guard and get to the
golf course. So when the Bulls couldn't fit Hopson in under their
salary cap because the new TV money wouldn't increase the salary
cap until August 1, Jordan agreed to defer $450,000 of his $2.95
million 1990–91 salary. There was one condition: The Bulls had to
try to sign Davis. Done, said Krause.

Jordan had been talking to Davis regularly. He would become a
free agent and select his team if he desired. But Reinsdorf refuses

to make a player an offer and allow him to shop around; his practice is to tell a player to get his best offer—"Find out what your market is"—and then come in to talk. Reinsdorf told Jordan to bring Davis in and they'd make a deal. But Jordan couldn't deliver. Davis's wife had concerns about Chicago; the family was comfortable in Denver and the kids liked their schools. "She says there's too many gangsters in Chicago and she's not moving there," Davis told Jordan.

Jordan was stunned. "Was she watching too many TV shows?" he wondered.

The deal Davis signed with Denver paid him less than the $1.3 million a year for two years that Chicago was willing to pay. Davis had wanted to continue to play for Denver coach Doug Moe, and Jordan knew that was important because Moe had played at North Carolina and the loyalties remained strong. But when Moe was fired and replaced by Paul Westhead, Davis found himself unhappily trying to figure out how to keep his thirty-five-year-old legs going in Westhead's idiosyncratic running system. Davis would later tell Jordan how much he regretted his decision.

"I'm just glad it was Michael who tried to get him," Reinsdorf said. He knew the kind of fallout there'd be if Jordan saw this one as another opportunity screwed up by Krause.

·

IN NORTHWEST INDIANA, near a small town called La Porte, Craig Hodges had purchased a farm. Hodges was a city kid, having grown up in the projects in Chicago Heights, a suburban ghetto community about forty miles south of Chicago. Hodges was raised in what he called an extended family. "I called my grandma and grandpa 'Mom' and 'Dad,' and I had lots of uncles and aunts around who were like brothers and sisters." All lived within a few blocks of one another. The young Hodges says he was a gym rat at four, even though he didn't know it, because his grandfather ran the local park. And although Hodges became a good basketball player, he was not highly recruited. He eventually won a scholarship at Long Beach State University from coach Tex Winter, who had been at Northwestern and had heard of Hodges. Hodges was 6-2 and an excellent shooter who would find a place in the NBA as a specialist, mostly coming in to hit the three-point shot. But he also was a player teams liked

to have around, upbeat and full of encouragement for younger players, active in the community and always the first to accommodate
the team when it needed speakers at high schools. He'd even started
his own youth organization to help teenagers with their problems;
it got little publicity, which wasn't unusual for any venture that didn't
involve Michael Jordan. "My idea was to stay on course and get an
education," said Hodges, who had majored in Afro-American history in college with the full intention of becoming a history teacher.
"I felt I had to use basketball instead of letting it use me."

Unlike most of his teammates and colleagues around the NBA,
Hodges looked at basketball as a transitional phase in life, which
was why he had begun working with black entrepreneurs in hopes
of landing contracts, some for NBA merchandise. "Change in our
community must come through economics," said Hodges, who had
strong beliefs about black development. "We need businesses to
give us jobs." He was viewed with alarm by some players for his
association with radical black militant groups and his devotion to
the Muslim religion and the Koran, which he often quoted to his
teammates. But Hodges realized it was a white world he worked
in, even if most of the workers were black, and he kept his views
shielded from management and the general public.

Hodges had tried to interest Jordan in going into the shoe business
for himself when his first Nike contract expired after the 1987–88
season. "Just think of the jobs and contracts you can provide for
your people," Hodges told Jordan. But Jordan wasn't interested,
and he always wondered later whether Hodges had anything to do
with the Operation PUSH boycott of Nike products, which proved
embarrassing to Jordan in the summer of 1990. Here he was, the
hero of every black ghetto kid at a time when perhaps the most
prominent black citizens' organization in the nation—at least in the
Midwest—was accusing Nike of profiting from the black community
and giving little back.

And it was Hodges who was among the strongest backers of an
additional pension program for the players that went into effect late
in the summer of 1990. The plan was to provide money for players
in the years after they retired until their pension plan went into
effect at age forty-five. It sounded good, but it also meant that each
team would have about $1.5 million less under the salary cap to sign
players now. The concept upset the players' agents, who earned 4

percent commission on contracts and clearly preferred a bigger cap; with more money under the cap, the teams presumably could renegotiate some deals, like Jordan's. One of the leaders of the opposition was Jordan's agent, David Falk, who had enlisted Jordan's support. Publicly, it should have been an embarrassing position for Jordan to take, seeking a raise at the expense of players who were less fortunate. But the issues became muddied by charges and countercharges and never became clear publicly. Late in the summer, Hodges got a message to call Falk. "You know, Michael is against this proposal," Falk told Hodges, the Bulls' player representative, who would cast the team's vote at the upcoming union meeting. "He'd really like to see it rejected." Hodges heard the underlying warning—go against Michael and you risk your position on the team—but he believed the issue was more important than his own security. "If Michael's got a problem, tell him to call me," Hodges told Falk. Jordan never did, and Hodges joined in a near-unanimous vote in support of the proposal. As Hodges walked out of the meeting, smiling broadly if a little nervously, he went up to a friend and joked, "You know he's going to have me traded now."

And, frankly, Hodges wouldn't have minded, even if it meant leaving home again. It seemed as if he'd had his chance and never would again. Late in the 1988–89 season, Hodges's first with the Bulls, Doug Collins had inserted Hodges into the starting lineup and shifted Jordan to point guard, a move that helped the Bulls sweep a four-game Western Conference road trip for the first time in their history. Jordan then played perhaps the best series of games in his career, recording seven straight triple doubles—at least 10 points, rebounds, and assists—as the Bulls won ten of eleven games. One of those wins was over Golden State, and Hodges recalls Don Nelson, the Warriors coach, generally regarded as the best strategist in the NBA, telling him, "Well, they finally figured it out there. I would have been playing him at point guard from the day he showed up as a rookie."

Putting Jordan in the middle of the floor as point guard instead of to the side as a shooting guard made it more difficult to double-team him effectively. But Jordan was assured by Collins the move was only temporary, and after the season he told the team he preferred to return to his shooting guard role. Why? The official reasons were that he would get too tired playing point guard and that he'd have trouble defending against the smaller, quicker point guards and that, too, would wear him out. But the fact was that Jordan continued to have grave doubts about his teammates' ability to score, saying, "How am I supposed to be the principal ball deliverer and the main scorer?" Phil Jackson would later reject his assistants' suggestion to move Jordan to point guard, arguing that Jordan's passing was not consistently good enough and that giving Jordan the ball even more would reduce the chances of dividing up the scoring load, one of Jackson's main goals.

Hodges, meanwhile, suffered an ankle injury in that game against Golden State in March 1988 after averaging 18 points, almost double his career average, and shooting 22 for 31 from three-point range in his previous six games. He would miss the rest of the regular season, be hampered in the playoffs, and never truly regain his health the next season. With Hodges still hobbling at the start of training camp in 1989, John Paxson moved in as starting point guard, and Hodges went on to have the poorest season of his career.

The team never truly believed there was anything wrong with Hodges. Their reports merely noted some soft-tissue buildup and said that Hodges would be able to play through it. The Bulls were also angry because Hodges had been a free agent after the 1988–89 season and, fearing they might lose him to Portland (which was prepared to make an offer), they gave him a four-year, $2.6 million contract, and now he couldn't play effectively. Hodges kept saying something was wrong, but he wasn't getting much response from the team, which had a reputation for such things (such as downplaying the extent of Scottie Pippen's back problems in 1987–88 until after the season, when it was finally determined he needed disc surgery).

With the Davis negotiations dead, the team called Hodges and told him to see the team doctor so they could determine once and for all what his status was. It was mid-July and Hodges was preparing to go to a golf school for a week and then on a cruise with his family, but the Bulls wanted to try to package Hodges for the shooter or rebounder they were seeking.

The doctor determined that Hodges needed surgery on his ankle. And another chance to add a player went away.

•

THE FREE-AGENT LIST was not deep and the Bulls had already turned down Adrian Dantley, whose style of play, Jackson felt, wouldn't fit with the passing, motion, and fast-break concepts he sought. David Falk, Dantley's agent, was relentless and would call Reinsdorf or Krause all year after Bulls losses to suggest that the Bulls wouldn't have lost if they had Dantley. Purvis Short of New Jersey was a scorer who could fit in, and assistant John Bach had coached him when Bach was head coach at Golden State, but it was determined that Short had played too many minutes over the years to do that job now. Same with Charlotte's Robert Reid, whom the Bulls had considered the previous season but rejected.

That's when the Bulls began to talk about Cliff Levingston of Atlanta. Levingston wasn't a scorer—he was known in Atlanta as "House" for putting up so many bricks when he shot—but he was active and could play small forward to back up Scottie Pippen. The Bulls had let Charles Davis go in order to have enough money available—along with Jordan's contribution—to trade for Hopson. And while Krause talked about Hopson as a possible backup to Pippen, the coaches felt Hopson would have enough difficulty trying to fit in as a backup shooting guard.

Levingston, who liked to go by the nickname of "Good News" because of his friendly demeanor, was not a favorite of Reinsdorf's. "I watched all those Atlanta games and I don't ever remember seeing him," Reinsdorf told Jackson. But Reinsdorf left personnel decisions in basketball principally to Krause and Jackson. Krause didn't care much for Levingston either, and wanted to go after an old personal favorite, Joe Wolf, who was a restricted free agent. But Jackson was lobbying hard for Levingston. He believed Levingston, though only about 6-7, would help on defense and rebounding and fit well into the open-court style of basketball Jackson felt the Bulls had to play. Krause was resisting, saying Hopson would do as a backup small forward. Jackson believed otherwise, and he was now getting additional pressure from the assistant coaches. They all knew the Bulls simply didn't have the players to contend for a title without some additions. They couldn't go into a new season with just Hopson, if only because it would demoralize Jordan. But Jackson was hesitant to get into a fight with Krause. He'd seen Krause and Collins battle desperately over trade possibilities, with Collins going over Krause's head to Reinsdorf and even trying to get Krause fired. This proved fatal in the long run to Collins, for Reinsdorf hadn't wanted Collins as coach in the first place, and only agreed to hire him after a desperate appeal from Krause. And a year later here was this brash kid trying to get his sponsor fired.

Perhaps the dispute that had made the strongest impression on Jackson was the Collins–Krause battle over Ricky Pierce. The talented scorer for the Bucks was a holdout in 1987, demanding renegotiation of his contract. The Bucks made him available, but after dealing with the likes of Dailey, Woolridge, and Oldham, Krause wanted no part of another public holdout who might also be a clubhouse lawyer. He refused to trade Brad Sellers to the Bucks and Collins was livid, ranting and accusing Krause of trying to cost him his job. It was a common habit of Collins's, blaming either Krause or the players for team failures.

"I'd seen this organization almost come apart over Ricky Pierce," Jackson told his assistants at a meeting. "I'm not going to let that happen here over Levingston."

But finally Jackson, in his softer way, made Krause see the obvious: The Bulls needed help. "Jerry," he told Krause, "you're going to blow this one." Krause didn't blow it, but the Levingston negotiations provide a revealing look at life on the edge at the NBA.

Unbeknownst to the Bulls, Levingston was in serious financial trouble and needed to put $200,000 in the bank by the last day of September or face action by his creditors. He had been earning about $425,000 per year, which would seem to be enough to live on, especially when your room is paid for on the road and you get $55 meal money per day during road trips. Despite their garish wealth—the average NBA salary approached $1 million by the 1990–91 season—players often are remarkably stingy. They get so used to having their way paid as highly recruited high school and college stars that they often don't think about paying their own way, especially when it comes to tipping. Some coaches, like Al Attles when he was with Golden State, used to go into restaurants his teams frequented on the road and leave $50 in tips to be divided among the waitresses because he knew that invariably the players would not tip.

Nonetheless, players often find themselves in financial problems, especially when trying to keep up with their teammates, as Levingston had tried to do with the Hawks' Dominique Wilkins, who owned almost a dozen automobiles and liked to travel home from games by limousine, a habit Levingston then acquired. That was okay on Wilkins's multimillion-dollar salary, but it was something else at Levingston's level of pay. Levingston was frustrated in Atlanta; Dominique wasn't ever going to share the scoring spotlight. He was there to rebound and pick up loose balls; there'd be none of the glamour scoring for him. In fact, point guard Glenn "Doc" Rivers once told him that coach Mike Fratello had instructed him never to pass the ball to Levingston on the fast break. And it only got worse when the Hawks picked up Moses Malone and Reggie Theus.

So Levingston decided to test the free-agent market. Levingston was the team's player representative, and union officials had told him it would be good for free agency if more players would try that route. Levingston figured the Hawks were about to start making moves anyway, and he might be traded, so this way maybe he could pick his team. Detroit had some interest, as did Indiana. Denver would later take notice, as would New York. But Levingston decided he wanted to come to Chicago.

Krause called Levingston's agent, Roger Kirschenbaum, and said the Bulls were interested, but had some other issues to handle first, including the matter of Davis. Levingston was looking for a four-year deal worth about $5.6 million. And why not? The Hawks had offered $4 million for four years and Levingston, Kirschenbaum felt, could be the missing veteran the Bulls needed. And after the Davis deal fell through, even Jordan said he'd like to have Levingston. He'd called Reinsdorf to tell him so, and Levingston and Kirschenbaum assumed that would assure a deal. That was their first mistake.

The Bulls didn't want the risk of a long-term contract with a thirty-year-old player, which was fine with Levingston.

"We're talking one point three, one point four [million dollars for one year]," Kirschenbaum told Krause.

"That's no problem," Krause said. "Money shouldn't be a problem."

Kirschenbaum and Levingston's second mistake was misreading Reinsdorf's business sense. Although Reinsdorf loved sports, he lived for business. Earlier in his career, he was a lawyer at a Chicago firm representing several local doctors. "They all kept getting screwed in these real estate deals," related Reinsdorf. "I'd look at them and tell them these were shit deals, but it didn't do any good, they'd go into them anyway. Finally, one of these guys said, 'If you're so smart, why don't you put something together?' " So he did. And it led to the start of his real estate empire and Balcor. For all his interest in what happened between the first- and third-base lines, or between the sidelines and the endlines, he never wavered in his commitment to the bottom line.

Levingston pretty much assumed he was coming to Chicago when Krause never questioned Kirschenbaum's demand. In fact, Krause told Levingston not to bother with those other teams, that the Bulls would work out something, so Levingston didn't worry when Detroit signed Tree Rollins, leaving itself little room to add Levingston also. And then the Players' Association voted for its prepension plan, effectively knocking out teams like Indiana, which needed the larger cap to sign Levingston as a free agent. Levingston still wasn't concerned, even when Atlanta was forced to relinquish his rights to sign first-round draft pick Rumeal Robinson. So Atlanta, which would have been permitted to exceed the salary cap to re-sign Levingston because he was Atlanta's own free agent, was now out of the running until at least two months into the season under NBA rules.

Still, Levingston was certain he was headed for Chicago. But he hadn't bargained on two things. One was the Bulls' fears about Scottie Pippen's salary. He desperately sought a new deal, especially when, in August, his close friend Horace Grant was awarded a new contract extension that would pay him $6 million over three seasons. But Grant was coming into the final year of a four-year deal, while Pippen still had three years remaining on his six-year deal. The Bulls had some leverage, but they knew Pippen wouldn't react well to being paid less than his backup, which Levingston would be.

Of even greater importance to the team, though, was the Yugoslav Kukoc, who wouldn't even be with the Bulls in 1990–91. Krause had never scouted in Europe before, but the Lakers' success with Vlade Divac made him think twice. Jackson had urged Krause to take a look at Divac in the 1989 draft, but Krause, like a lot of NBA general managers, doubted Europeans could play effectively in the

NBA. He'd realized his error, and went to Europe in the spring of 1990 to see Kukoc, advertised as the best player there. And he came back with an obsession.

The word was that Kukoc, just twenty-two, didn't want to play in the NBA yet, but the Bulls went after him anyway, betting he would want to play with Jordan, his American equal. "Great players want to play against the best, and Kukoc is going to be a great player," Krause said, and immediately began planning to sign him. That meant they would have to keep almost $2 million available under the 1990–91 salary cap, in case Kukoc was suddenly ready to sign.

The NBA's rule for such a deal required that the first-year offer to Kukoc would have to go under the salary cap as soon as the deal was made. That meant as early as December 28, 1990, the first day the Bulls were allowed to make an offer. The Bulls tried to get Kukoc to visit Chicago before then, hoping that the crazed basketball atmosphere in the Chicago Stadium would help sway his decision. They sent him a Bulls jersey with his number, and made contacts in the Yugoslavian community in Chicago, and arranged with an interpreter to join the staff as "assistant trainer" and sit on the bench in games.

Because the Bulls needed to keep so much money free under the cap, it's doubtful that they ever considered paying Levingston as much as $1.3 million. And while the negotiations dragged, Levingston's other options were vanishing. By late August, Levingston was sure he'd made a mistake; he should have taken the Atlanta offer, the security, and forgotten about it. Now it was beginning to look like one year in Europe and another bout with free agency in 1991.

"From the start, there hadn't been a question about money," said Levingston. "It was always Krause saying, 'You don't need to talk to those guys,' or 'We'll take care of you, don't worry.' I was dealing straight and he said he'd be straight. So I cut my options instead of letting them barter. Businesswise, it wasn't a very smart thing to do. But it did help me one way. I learned who my friends are and I learned who not to trust."

And now Jordan was getting in on it. He would become close with Levingston, as close as he'd been with anyone since Rod Higgins and Charles Oakley had left the team, although the players would come to regard Levingston with some cynicism. "So how many times Cliff kiss Michael's ass today?" somebody would invariably say as the season wore on. But Levingston saw immediately who mattered with the Bulls and he decided he wasn't going to be stupid again. Jordan had told him not to take less than $1 million. But Reinsdorf had other ideas.

Levingston came in for one last negotiating session in September. A week before, he'd come to Chicago with Kirschenbaum, who didn't have any other basketball clients and wasn't used to sports negotiations; he considered himself a close friend of Levingston's and constantly told the Bulls it was important to have such a good guy on the team. This made Reinsdorf laugh. "This guy's much too personally involved in this thing," he thought. "He's not negotiating for a client, he's trying to help out a friend." And that was no way to do business. Business was business. This guy just wasn't going to understand.

The Bulls offered Levingston $750,000. That was less than Pippen made, so Reinsdorf figured that would hold Pippen off for a while. And that left the Bulls about $1.8 million under the salary cap to pursue Kukoc. Kirschenbaum was shocked. "What am I going to tell Cliff? What's he going to say to me?" Kirschenbaum pleaded.

"If you can get a better deal, go ahead," Reinsdorf said.

Everyone in the room knew Levingston couldn't, at least in the NBA. He had no other options. New York could not sign him without first making a deal to free cap space, Denver had decided to make an offer to Wolf, and that September 30 creditors' deadline was approaching. "Screw them," Levingston decided. He was going to Europe and he called Krause to tell him so.

The Bulls figured Levingston would fold—he'd told Jordan he didn't want to go to Europe—so Krause was surprised to get the call. He huddled with Reinsdorf and a deal was made. It would be a two-year deal worth about $2.15 million, but with only the first year guaranteed. They'd pay Levingston $750,000 for the 1990–91 season and guarantee to buy out the remaining year of his contract for $400,000 if they didn't want him after the season. That meant if the Bulls didn't pick up Levingston's option, which they didn't plan to, he'd be paid about $1.1 million for his one year in Chicago. If they did, he'd get his $2.15 million. They agreed to send $200,000 right away to Levingston's bank.

•

Training camp opened the first Friday in October. Jordan was the star, of course, back from the golf course and wearing a diamond stud in his ear. Cartwright took one look at the earring and said that if it were his team, the stud would be gone. He was presumably referring to the diamond. A press release was distributed announcing that Levingston had signed for two seasons. Terms were not disclosed, but reports were out. A radio reporter asked Levingston how he felt about turning down $4 million in Atlanta to sign for less than $1 million with the Bulls. "Good News" Levingston wasn't smiling.

The Bulls crew for 1990–91 had been assembled and its air show was about ready to take off. There was plenty of turbulence ahead.

3

OCTOBER 1990

PHIL JACKSON WAS wondering just how he was going to win with Michael Jordan on his team.

The Bulls hadn't been able to—at least they hadn't won the big prize, the NBA title. They had become the most successful team in franchise history, winning fifty-five games in the 1989–90 season and going to the conference finals for the second straight season, a feat achieved only once before, when Dick Motta coached a highly competitive Bulls team in the early 1970s. And much—if not all—of the Bulls' recent success could be attributed to Jordan.

"I can't stand losing and I hate people who accept losing, although I had to learn to deal with it better when I came to the Bulls," Jordan once said. "But I made a vow that every year I played for the Bulls we'd make the playoffs."

For six years now, the Bulls had tried it Jordan's way, and while they hadn't exactly failed, they hadn't truly succeeded. The Pistons stood in the way, and they figured to again in 1991, while other teams, particularly those in the Western Conference, were getting better.

Jackson couldn't think of any teams that had ever won the NBA title with the league's leading scorer. It had happened only once—

the Milwaukee Bucks in 1971 with Kareem Abdul-Jabbar—since the NBA adopted the shot clock for the 1954–55 season. Jackson thought about his former Knicks teammates Walt Frazier, Earl Monroe, and Willis Reed, any of whom could have scored 25 or 30 points per game if he wanted to. But by sharing the ball and getting everyone involved, the Knicks became a five-man threat, refusing to let defenses cheat or double-team because they always looked for and found the open man. Jordan's style of play made it too easy for the defense.

"I knew it would be a hot issue and I would be on the hot seat. I was nervous, sure," Jackson conceded later, "but the Bulls had been through the era where Michael would average thirty-six or thirty-seven and still came up short against the top-echelon teams. Michael having to score so much and everyone else scoring only eight or ten hurt our chances in the long run, I believed. I felt the team had exhausted that. We'd gotten rid of half a dozen point guards to find someone to play with him, and we had to keep moving people around to accommodate him."

That would have to stop, Jackson decided. It was time for Jordan to start accommodating others, and the coach didn't believe that doing so would limit Jordan's greatness. He still intended to use Jordan as a weapon, especially at the end of the game. He was not, as Jordan would suggest later, trying to make him just another player. "Even if you put [Jascha] Heifetz in the orchestra, he's still going to be the featured player," Jackson said. "Michael still will be the featured player in our system."

Jackson did not reach this conclusion overnight; he is not a spontaneous man. He is deeply contemplative and tends to internalize. While Jackson rarely discusses his team problems at home, where the frenzy of his four children are a welcome escape, his wife, June, would occasionally turn over in bed at 5:00 A.M. and see Phil lying on his back, his eyes closed and his glasses on.

"Phil, you're awake," she'd say. "Why don't you get up?"

"I'm thinking," was Jackson's reply.

"So take your glasses off."

"I think better with them on."

And even better with a fly reel in his hand, the snow-covered peaks of Galcier National Park over his shoulder, and his lure bobbing in Flathead Lake. Jackson used his playoff share from the 1973

Knicks title win to buy about nine acres just west of the Continental Divide in Montana, where he built a home to return to each summer, a peaceful retreat near his childhood home. He didn't get there until late in the summer of 1990, as Krause dragged him off to the Goodwill Games in Seattle to watch Toni Kukoc and then to watch the Bulls' summer-league team, but finally Jackson went home. He didn't hike the bumping foothills quite as much as he used to or attack the great billowing waves of mountains at the Continental Divide for his solitude. His hip and back injury from his playing days no longer allowed it. But he loved the country nonetheless. It was the real Montana described best by Ivan Doig in books such as *This House of Sky* and *English Creek*. Jackson could lose himself for days in the thick, lumbering forests and craggy mountain ranges, or wander the arteries of limpid creeks with a fishing rod. It gave him time, again, to enjoy the land and consider his team's options for the 1990–91 season. The Bulls still weren't the team they should be. Perhaps the media were right when they called the Bulls "Michael and the Jordanaires." Jackson and the rest of the Bulls resented the implication, but there was some truth to it, he knew, and Jordan didn't seem to mind much. That had to stop if the Bulls were to become a team.

The principal change would come from the use of "the system," although Jordan, and later Pippen, would spend as much time outside of it as in. But it would be there for the players who needed to feel a structure and for Jordan, who needed to learn to work within a team concept. In the clear air and open sky of Jackson's Montana retreat, anything seemed possible.

•

SEVERAL WEEKS BEFORE training camp was to open, Jackson called Jordan, trying him again and again, but he was still out on America's back nine. Jackson had much to discuss with his star: the upcoming season, the system, and his strong feeling that maybe Jordan shouldn't win the scoring title this season.

The system that Jackson chose to implement was one he had started with the previous season. It had been refined by assistant Tex Winter and explained in a book Winter wrote some thirty years ago called *The Triple-Post Offense*. It relied upon quick passing and very few play calls, so the idea was uncomplicated. Players moved the ball quickly while they moved to certain spots on the floor. Since they weren't running plays, but instead using tendencies, the defense couldn't anticipate their movement, and the tendencies depended on where the defense moved. That's what made the system difficult for some players, and Jackson had introduced it in bits and pieces his first season as coach. But its strength was that when the defense tried to double-team—and any player could move into the post at any time—the quick passing allowed for open shots. The downside, as some (including Jordan) saw it, was that in theory it allowed as many shots for John Paxson and Bill Cartwright as it did for Michael Jordan.

Jordan had spit out the words "equal-opportunity offense" a lot during Jackson's first season, although it hardly worked out that way, and Jackson never planned it to. You don't take the best scorer in the game and reduce him to just another player among five. Jordan would still have ample opportunity to go one-on-one, for Jackson would bastardize the system to open the floor up and provide Jordan those opportunities even as other players moved within the system's constraints. The system was a form of motion offense in which players formed triangles on different parts of the floor, exchanging positon in the post as the defense rotated. Of course, Jackson used pro-style screen roll and post-up plays, but the triangles would always be there for the players to fall back upon. The offense had helped Winter's smaller Kansas State teams stand up to Wilt Chamberlain's great Kansas team in the 1950s, but some wondered whether it was merely a college system, outdated for the bigger pro players of the day.

The important thing, Jackson felt, was that the Bulls have some system. "Cream always rises to the top," he noted. "Michael is always going to find a way to score, but if he could play within a system then he might also find ways to score more easily."

And, more importantly, so would others.

"I frankly didn't like the game they played here," Jackson said about his impressions when he arrived. "I didn't want to set up a conflict between Michael and the organization, but I always knew there was something better that could come from what he did. So much of the game here had been 'Throw him the ball and then clear out and he's going to go one-on-five and everyone's going to stand there and watch and everyone's going to come running at him and maybe he makes some outstanding move and pops through or he crashes to the floor and burns.' But how many times does this guy have to go down before he's putting himself in more jeopardy and taking unnecessary risks?

"We don't want to see this guy burn himself out in forty-minute games just trying to keep it close when there are other guys who can step up and help us. Because if you play a system, eventually he and his teammates are going to learn certain routes and they'll be able to find him at critical situations and they'll be in position to contribute.

"This system utilizes passing and shooting skills, what we consider clean basketball, where you're passing the ball within two seconds so that when you're shooting you don't have the pressure of defense on you quite as much. The basic idea, though, was we'd moved as far as we could with what we were doing. We were not going to beat Detroit with this one-on-one dribble-penetration game, which they're so good at defensing."

Jordan finally putted out the first week of October and gave Jackson a call. He would come into camp more serious this year than in the past. The failures were beginning to haunt him, although he doubted anything would change. To some extent, he believed he was reaching—or had reached—the apex of his majesty. "Yeah," he said as camp was about to begin, "people may have seen my best, although it's not that much due to me. Defenses are not going to let me get to the basket like I used to. Everyone's going to make me take the outside shot. When Detroit started knocking me on my ass, everyone started playing me that way, so I'm not allowed the creativity in the halfcourt game as much. But I feel like this is the most serious I've ever been at this time of year because [a championship] is something I want to achieve so badly. Before, I was more or less relaxed and enjoyed this time of year, this kids'-game time. But now it's like a business for me.

"I want to prove the critics wrong. We may not ever get a chance to win a world championship, and we may not ever get a chance like this again. This is the strongest team I've ever played on here, assuming we don't have any injuries. So I want to see some serious moves from management, which I really haven't seen that much of yet, and I want to see more serious attitudes from my teammates

this year when it comes to the playoffs. In the past, it's been more
or less a joking thing, sort of a 'Well, we're here, so let's have a
good time.' Not this year. It's time for us to get serious because
that's the only way we'll win.''

Jordan and Jackson would finally have their conversation when
Jordan stopped by the coach's office in the Multiplex. He was
wearing a diamond stud in his ear, but the sparkle in his smile soon
faded.

"Look, M.J.," Jackson said, "we're going to stick with the system
this season.''

Jordan wasn't thrilled.

"I know I can recognize what to do," Jordan said, "but I'm not
sure they can.''

Jordan often thought his teammates about as reliable as a newspaper street-corner sales box when all you had was twenty-five cents
in your pocket.

"This is what you've got to remember," Jackson said: "Maybe
these guys are not as talented as you'd like them to be, but this is
as good as they're going to be. And this is as good as we can get
under the present situation. But if we run a system, everyone is
going to have an opportunity to perform. They can't do the spectacular one-on-one things that you can do, but they can have some
level of success and perform on some level, even in critical situations.''

Jackson talked about his Knicks teams from the early 1970s
again, and about how many weapons they had at the ends of
games.

"Teams just don't win with one man doing all the scoring," Jackson said, "because when you need to you can shut down one individual, and Detroit has done that to us.''

"But that's when they're supposed to score," said Jordan.

It didn't work that way, Jackson said. Jordan's teammates had
to be worked into a system so they were prepared for those opportunities. They just couldn't shoot in times of desperation, with
a few seconds left on the shot clock. When they were open, they
had to get the ball, not afterward. The Bulls had good shooters;
Paxson, Grant, and Cartwright had all been 50 percent shooters
in their careers, and Pippen was on the cusp of some form of greatness. This was a team going into its third year together. It was time

to take advantage of the group, for what was a team, Jackson said, but a collection of individuals with a common goal? The best thing for the Bulls, Jackson said, was for everyone to move the ball around so the threats might come from anywhere on the court.

"We need to score as a group, and score consistently as a group, to win," Jackson said.

It might not be a bad idea, Jackson added, if Jordan didn't win the scoring title this season. It wasn't necessary. And Jackson said he was going to curtail Jordan's playing time, perhaps down to thirty-six or thirty-seven minutes per game, probably fewer than Pippen and maybe even Grant.

The last was met with silence. The talk was over.

"Well," Jackson thought to himself, "at least now he's been warned. He knows, and we're going to stick with this. We'll see what he does."

•

JACKSON, LIKE HIS predecessors, admired Jordan's skills, although he refused to compare him with players of previous eras. He would only say that Jordan was among the best in the game in his own era. Jackson was not a man of hyperbole.

He had once thought he was going to be a man of the Lord, telling coach Red Holzman when he first arrived in New York after being drafted by the Knicks in 1967 that he intended to become a minister. Jackson's father was a Pentecostal minister and his mother was an evangelist. They embraced the then mystical and charismatic Pentecostal wave sweeping some of the upper Midwest. Jackson remembers attending services where the congregation would speak in tongues, and his mother always preparing him for the apocalypse. Their house was without TV or any conveniences, and Jackson's family did not believe in conventional medicine.

The Jacksons did believe in competition. He vividly remembers playing games with the family on Saturday nights at the dining-room table. He would become a great athlete, excelling in baseball and then basketball in Montana, where he was raised, and then in college basketball for Bill Fitch at North Dakota. He would score, but he became celebrated for his defensive play, his long arms always flailing about. They were so long, in fact, that Fitch would do a little

trick to impress pro scouts: He'd have Jackson sit in the middle of
the backseat of a conventional automobile and open both front doors
without getting up. Jackson had an odd gait, which was later aggravated by hip fusion surgery that gave him an awkward look compared with the smoother, more graceful athletes who mostly
populated the game. At Knicks practices, the players would usually
be watching out for Jackson, who played hard, though seemingly
out of control. This is perhaps one reason that Jackson has remained
the Bulls' biggest supporter of Bill Cartwright.

Jackson rarely watches entertainment shows on television and
rarely reads the sports pages; you're more likely to find him watching
the debate over a civil-rights bill, as he did in his Stadium office
only minutes before the start of the first game of the NBA Finals,
or sitting with a *New York Times* crossword, one of his favorite
pastimes on the road. He has a playful wit—he once explained after
a low-scoring game in Atlanta the night after President George Bush
had spoken there that Bush's defense buildup had caused so many
missed baskets—and he can be absentminded and evasive.

He enjoyed a fairly successful eleven-year career in the NBA,
mostly with the Knicks, though he's remembered as much for his
actions off the court in the turbulent 1960s and early 1970s as for
anything on the court. He grew a beard and became a vegetarian;
he went to Earth Day and antiwar rallies; he wrote a book entitled
Maverick in which he talked about his drug use and his teammates'
karma; he experimented with mysticism and spiritualism and was a
veritable storehouse for the era's "isms." He believes that because
of his reputation he was blackballed from coaching jobs for years.
He coached five years in the CBA and attained great success, winning a title in Albany in 1984 and Coach-of-the-year honors in 1985.
But he couldn't attract much interest from the NBA.

Jerry Krause tried to bring him to Chicago as assistant coach in
1985–86 when Stan Albeck was coach, but Jackson came to his
interview with a beard that made it look as if he was eating a muskrat
and wearing a big Ecuadoran straw hat of which he was very proud;
it had a big bird feather looping out of the brim, and Jackson tried
to tell Albeck a story about the tropical bird from which it was
taken. Jackson's long, bony face was nearly black from the sun of
Puerto Rico, where he was then coaching, and his hair was still
longish.

"Er, no, I don't think so," Albeck would tell Krause.

Jackson was about ready to give up. He'd been coaching in the CBA for four years by then and he was wondering if he'd ever get a shot at the NBA. Maybe it was time to join the establishment and get a real job.

"Most of them had long given it up," Jackson said of his sixties radical friends. "They all explored until they found out you're not going to make money and you're going to be an outcast, so they fell in line and joined the establishment. But I never had to. I always had this basketball life of not having to pay the piper.

"I'd done some TV and coaching after my playing career was over [in 1980] and I had this business in Montana [Second Wind Sport and Fitness, an athletic club] and I came back to basketball on my own terms [in 1983 with the Albany Patroons of the CBA]. I was living in Woodstock, and that's not only a great place for a person to enjoy freedom, but it's an open, mind-expanding place where they're doing mental work and creative physical and artistic things, although I realized I wasn't coming out of the CBA unscathed. I knew I would have to conform somewhere."

He decided to quit basketball after the summer of 1987. He knew the world of basketball could exist comfortably without him, for Jackson had been taught about being humble all his life. The reminder was always there on his father's desk, a cardboard figure with small feet and a big balloon for a head. The message Jackson constantly received was not to have too big a head, for then one couldn't fill one's shoes.

"I had a talk with my wife and I decided I had to put myself in God's hands and quit," Jackson recalled. "I'd given it three or four years, but it was time to get on with my life. I had kids growing up who were going to college and I also had to be a provider, so I had to look at another line of work." Jackson decided either to pursue a law degree or to go back to school in counseling psychology, which had been his college major.

Then, in October 1987, Bulls assistant coach Gene Littles was hired by the expansion Charlotte Hornets as director of player personnel. With the season about to begin, the Bulls' list of available assistants was small, since most were already under contract for the season.

At this time, a friend of Jackson's was looking for him and had

called the Bulls because he knew Jackson had interviewed with them
once. The call rang a bell with Krause, who called Jackson about
the job after head coach Doug Collins agreed to take on the one-
time flower child.

"That's how lucky and happenstance life is," said Jackson. "I
recognized this was my last opportunity, so I had to stick my head
down and put on my zoot suit and shave down to a mustache and
be ready to step back into the establishment. It was something I
knew I could do. I was a fraternity guy [Sigma Alpha Epsilon] and
a college campus leader [he was listed in the 1967 *Who's Who of
American College Students*] and I knew how to behave establishment
if I had to. I knew all the rules. I was a good minister's son and had
lived in suits when I was a kid. It was no problem to step back in.
It was time to conform. I didn't have to stay an outcast forever."

●

WHEN JACKSON WAS a player, he admired the Bulls for their defensive strength. But just as the current team relied on one or two
players on offense, so had the Bulls teams of Jackson's era: The
team was built around their great forwards, Bob Love and Chet
Walker. Jackson believed basketball could be nothing but a team
game, and when he came to New York in 1967, he told Holzman
he thought the Knicks were selfish and poorly coached under Holzman's predecessor, Dick McGuire. But Holzman's emphasis on team
play would eventually catch on and lead the Knicks to two titles.

It would also catch the attention of Jerry Reinsdorf, a Brooklyn
boy who, when he purchased the Bulls, said he would watch then-
coach Kevin Loughery's style before deciding whether to make a
coaching change.

"Kevin Loughery has to be able to convince me that he can coach
a basketball team like Red Holzman," Reinsdorf said at the time.
"The New York Knicks of the Red Holzman era epitomized the
way basketball should be played. Total unselfish basketball. That's
going to be Chicago Bulls basketball."

Loughery thought Reinsdorf was a meddling buffoon, and kept
running plays for Jordan. He was fired at the end of the 1984–85
season, not only for his headstrong insistence on using Jordan, but

for allegedly losing a game on purpose to get a better playoff seeding; the home crowd—on Fan Appreciation Day, no less— taunted the Bulls with shouts of "Tulane, Tulane" as the team left the floor, a reference to the Tulane University team accused of shaving points.

Jordan didn't think much of Reinsdorf's theories either. All he knew was that when he came to the Bulls, Loughery was largely responsible for making him a superstar. Jordan insists his first season and his first coach made all the difference.

Jordan was rookie of the year in 1984–85, averaging 28.2 points per game, but more importantly, he was being shaped into the dominant individual player in the game by Loughery. Loughery immediately turned the offense over to Jordan. "I feel like I was able to relate better with him than any coach I've ever had," said Jordan. "He was a player's coach. He liked my game and wanted me to be the leader. I didn't want to do that, didn't feel I should with veteran guys around, Dave Corzine, Caldwell Jones, and Steve Johnson. I just wanted to get along."

But Loughery, emphasizing a one-on-one style for Jordan that mirrored his own play in the NBA, put Jordan in a position to demonstrate his skills and gain confidence.

"The truth was, I didn't know how good I'd become or what I could do against pros," said Jordan. Jordan never really thought much about the NBA other than as another place to play, and never really cared for the game, even after several years in the league. He said he rarely watched games, thought they were boring, and doubted he'd ever come to an NBA game after his retirement. But Jordan said that Loughery's decision to allow him to test his individual skills proved to him that he could be a great player. "And that's the most important thing in this league, confidence," said Jordan.

When Loughery was fired in 1985, Stan Albeck was brought in. But the bushy-haired coach would have a hard time getting along with Jerry Krause. Krause didn't care for Albeck's coaching techniques, although Albeck was generally regarded as highly knowledgeable about the game. Albeck routinely threw Krause out of team meetings; he deeply resented what he perceived as Krause's meddling, and in succeeding years, when he went to coach at

Krause's old school, Bradley, Albeck compiled embarrassing stories about Krause, which he'd feed to Jordan, who would pass them on to the rest of the team.

When Jordan broke his foot in the third game of the 1985–86 season and insisted on rejoining the Bulls earlier than the team wanted him to, Albeck got caught in the cross fire between Jordan and Krause. Management wanted Jordan on the bench, since he had already missed more than fifty games and could hardly help the team; Jordan accused Krause of not wanting to win so the team could get a better draft pick. A deal was finally made that allowed Jordan to play a limited number of minutes per game. When Albeck left Jordan in a game for an extra three minutes once because the Bulls were within striking distance of a win, Krause told Albeck that if it happened again he'd be fired. A few games later, with Krause's words ringing in his ears, Albeck pulled Jordan with thirty seconds left in the game and the Bulls down by 1. Jordan seethed. After the Bulls dropped three straight to Boston in the playoffs— despite a record 63-point game from Jordan—Albeck was fired.

Jordan had never heard of Jackson when Jackson came to the Bulls, and he didn't know anything about the Knicks of the seventies, but he did have an astute eye for the game and he believed that era had ended. "The players today can do things they couldn't do twenty years ago," Jordan said. "The game isn't played any more like Tex Winter taught it or even P.J. [Jackson]. Those concepts don't work against bigger, faster players who jump higher. You don't need that with players who can create."

Jackson thought otherwise. Just a few weeks after joining the Bulls as an assistant coach under Doug Collins in 1987, he was sitting in a coaches' meeting, explaining that his Knicks teams had played so well together because of their philosophy of teamwork.

"We had a rule of thumb in New York" Jackson said: "A star makes the players around him better. That was our belief. That was the measure of what a star was, Frazier or Reed picking up for you, covering you defensively, allowing you to play harder because they could intimidate an opponent, Walt with his quick hands and ability to make a pass to you, and the same with Dave DeBusschere."

Collins listened for a few seconds. He didn't disagree with Jackson, but he knew Jordan wouldn't see it quite that way. To anyone who would listen, Collins would complain of his inability to get the

Bulls into a running game. "Do you know who's the biggest obstacle to us running?" Collins would ask. Then he'd offer a thin, weak smile and shake his head. "Michael Jordan, that's who. He won't let go of the ball."

But Collins had no power to do anything about it by then—Jordan had little or no respect left for his coach. During a preseason scrimmage before the start of Collins's second season with the Bulls, Jordan angrily left practice accusing Collins of intentionally misstating the score in a practice game so that Jordan's team would lose. Collins quickly tried to smooth over the argument, and the next day at practice even kissed Jordan in front of the media to show they were friends again. But Collins had already made his fatal error.

Jordan knew he had behaved badly, even childishly, but despite his seeming sophistication in dealings with media and public, Jordan was often like a child searching for discipline, pushing matters as far as he could until someone came forward to punish him. Jackson was quick to catch on, and would use Jordan's need for a father figure to his own advantage; he would not tolerate Jordan's childish fits. But when Collins caved in so quickly to Jordan's admittedly puerile tantrum, Jordan realized two things: He could do what he pleased without threat of punishment, and he could no longer respect his coach.

The power struggle between Jordan and Collins was never more evident than in the 1990 playoffs against Detroit. In the fifth game of the conference finals, Jordan attempted just 8 shots; the Bulls lost, and were eliminated at home in the next game. Questions flew at Jordan and Collins after the game, only to be met by the standard response about double-teaming tactics. But Collins and Jordan knew otherwise. The coach had told Jordan he was shooting too much; he had taken 31 percent of the team's shots in the first four games. Collins felt more players had to be involved in the offense for the team to be effective. Jordan, who usually took such suggestions as criticism, took only 8 shots just to make a point.

It was all about pride. Despite his fame and acclaim, Jordan still sometimes reacted like the high school sophomore who failed to make the varsity basketball team; he still remembers not wanting to cheer for that team even though his close friends were playing. "I guess I wanted them to lose to prove that they had made a mistake by leaving me off the team," Jordan recalls, and years later he still felt the same way. Even as a young pro, Jordan conceded once, "I thought of myself first, the team second. I always wanted my teams to be successful. But I wanted to be the main cause."

That pride had driven him to his extraordinary accomplishments. Jordan takes being guarded by only one man as a personal insult. He torched Cleveland for 69 points in the 1989–90 season when the Cavaliers insisted on single-teaming him throughout the game. A reporter asked during the 1990–91 season who defensed him the best. "No one, really," he said. "Everyone uses two or three players to guard me."

But which player is the toughest? the questioner persisted.

"I don't really ever see one guy," Jordan said again, "but I'd guess you'd have to say [Joe] Dumars, but one guy really never plays me."

Jordan even got into a brief public debate with the Cavaliers after that 69-point game when several Cleveland players said it was no big trick to score a lot of points if you're taking 37 shots a game, as Jordan did.

"I wouldn't be shooting so many times," Jordan shot back, "if I weren't open."

Tales of his competitiveness are legendary around the Bulls. When former teammate Rod Higgins beat him in Ping-Pong when both were rookies in 1984, he went out and bought a Ping-Pong table and became the best player on the team. He took up golf in college and was playing to a reported 6 handicap by 1990. He'd play games of cards with the ferocity of Mike Tyson going for a knockout. He hated to lose and took it personally.

One unforgettable demonstration of his competitive drive was in 1988 against the Utah Jazz. Jordan stole a pass and got out ahead of the field to dunk over guard Bobby Hansen to a thundering roar. Even on the road Jordan's dunks are cheered, especially in Western Conference cities where the Bulls make just one visit a year. Utah owner Larry Miller was sitting at center court in the first row and yelled to Jordan as he passed by, "Why don't you pick on someone your own size?"

A few sequences later, Jordan again made a steal, but this time was closing in on a basket guarded by 7-4 center Mark Eaton, Jordan sped up just a bit and appeared to grab hold of Eaton's shirt, boosting himself up and dunking over the powerful center.

Running back to his defensive end, Jordan turned to Miller and yelled, "He big enough for you?"

And so when Phil Jackson explained to Collins his theory about superstars and team play and sharing the ball, Collins just stared and said, "Why don't you go out and tell Michael that?"

"Okay," Jackson said earnestly, "I will."

So Jackson confronted Jordan, who still knew Jackson only as an odd-looking man who moved as if he had left the hanger in his suit, and told him about the Knicks and Frazier and what stars should do and how they had to help their teammates.

Jackson remembers Jordan saying "Thanks" politely and walking away. Jordan remembers rolling his eyes afterward and thinking Jackson was nuts. "It's a hell of a lot easier to make Earl Monroe look good than it is Brad Sellers," he thought.

But now, in 1990, Jackson was in charge. Jordan was dubious, but he liked Jackson and had come to respect his knowledge of the game and the way he handled the team. "He's the coach," Jordan would say after meeting with Jackson. "I'll follow his scheme, but I don't plan to change my style of play. I'm sure everything will be fine if we win, but if we start losing, I'm shooting."

Hardly a vote of confidence. "I know what I would do if I were coach," he added a few weeks into the season. "I'd determine our strengths and weaknesses and utilize them. And it's pretty clear what our strength is."

.

THE FIRST WEEK of October the players started drifting back to the Multiplex, the suburban health club where the team practiced. Jordan said he was getting in shape on the golf course, as always: "I'm walking instead of using an electric cart." But Jordan had also been to Europe on a promotional trip for Nike, and now he was talking about playing there after his Bulls contract ended in 1996, perhaps for a team he'd co-own with Nike. Jordan was mobbed everywhere he went in Europe, and his agent assured him he could earn perhaps $10 million per year there. Then he could buy his own golf course.

The Bulls had finally assembled the team that would begin the 1990–91 season. Charles Davis and Ed Nealy were gone, as was Jeff Sanders (a 1990 first-round draft choice who was a flop); the Bulls gave him to Miami with the condition that if the lowly Heat kept him, they would have to pay his salary. He would last a week. The Bulls wanted to keep free-agent forward Scott Williams from North Carolina, in part because Jackson thought he was a better athlete than Sanders, with the ability to be a backup at both the forward and center positions; Sanders, whom the players had dubbed "Sleepy" and whose languid ways had made him an object of almost constant ridicule, hadn't even been an adequate backup power forward. Also, Jordan had wanted a North Carolina player on the team, and when Walter Davis wouldn't come, the Bulls agreed to take Williams, whom Krause had scouted extensively before the draft and homed in on as soon as the draft was over.

So the twelve spots were filled: Jordan, Pippen, Grant, Cartwright, and Paxson, the starting five, plus holdover reserves Armstrong, King, Perdue, Hodges, and new additions, Hopson, Levingston, and Williams.

Grant had worked out almost all summer and looked strong, having put on about twenty pounds of upper-body muscle. Cartwright and Paxson, after minor surgeries, were starting to work out again, as was Hopson. Levingston was back in town, finally ready to sign a contract. And King and Armstrong, rookies in 1989–90, were thinking that they might even become starters this season.

Scottie Pippen was thinking he'd just let the Bulls see how they would do without him.

He had left Hamburg, Arkansas, about ten miles from the Louisiana border, and was heading for Memphis in his $80,000 black Mercedes, to the office of his agent and friend, Jimmy Sexton. He had been staying with his mother, Ethel; though Pippen took quickly to the fast NBA life, with new cars and clothes and plenty of nightlife, he most enjoyed returning to Hamburg for the summer. His father, Preston, who had been disabled by a major stroke and confined to a wheelchair after working for years in the local paper mills, had died the previous spring during the playoffs. For Pippen, the youngest of twelve children, who had been babied by his parents and brothers and sisters, home was a place of sweet memories.

"We were poor," Pippen recalls, "but I always had enough. I'd do baby-sitting for my sisters or wash dishes or run errands. It seemed like there was always something for me to do."

Pippen's rise to the NBA is perhaps the most remarkable success story among the Bulls. Sure, Jordan didn't even make his high school varsity as a sophomore, and John Paxson would have to stay back a grade to make his high school team; Craig Hodges couldn't get a college scholarship in his own city, and Grant was still thinking about becoming a marine when he was in college. "Players from places like Sparta, Georgia, don't get to play in the NBA," Grant figured at the time.

But neither do poor kids from Hamburg, Arkansas, especially those whose collegiate goal is to be the manager of the football team. "I just liked hanging around with the guys," Pippen explained, not at all offended at picking up the dirty uniforms. "I really preferred that, because then I could hang out, but I wouldn't get hurt playing. I had the best job of anyone.

"You always idolize professional sports guys when you're small. But I just liked football a lot when I was young, and I still do. I didn't have the size to play the game, but I wanted to be around it as much as I could. I can't say I had any ambition to be a pro basketball player."

College wasn't a high priority in the Pippen family; only one of Pippen's eleven brothers and sisters had gone. But the family urged Scottie to go; everyone wanted the best for the youngest. Money was scarce, and he wasn't exactly being offered scholarships. Pippen had finally made the varsity basketball team as a senior, although in Hamburg that wasn't a major achievement. His coach, Donald Wayne, recommended Pippen as a possible walk-on candidate, to Don Dyer, the basketball coach at the University of Central Arkansas in Conway, just north of Little Rock. Wayne felt Pippen had potential, but he had accomplished so little that no scholarship offers were forthcoming, so Dyer helped Pippen obtain financial aid.

"I was glad about that," said Pippen, "but I wasn't really thinking about playing basketball. I was going to college to be the manager of the football team."

In high school, Pippen played point guard, which would prove vital to his development; like Julius Erving, he learned the game as a small man who then grew, and in college he would eventually play all five positons. Pippen was a barely six-foot-one-inch, 150-pound guard in high school, so when he grew about four inches after his freshman year in college, he became an offensive force. He was that rarest of players, one who could take down the rebound at one end of the court, dribble the length of the court, and then finish strong at the other end with a slam dunk. Only a few NBA players can consistently do it.

But those thoughts had hardly entered his mind when he prepared to attend the University of Central Arkansas. Pippen had never traveled much, and life was changing fast. He had grown into a terrific athlete almost overnight. He had the coordination and talent, but was small, so he started lifting weights and working on his conditioning. He improved his diet and grew those four inches after his freshman year, when he played in twenty games but averaged just 4 shots per game, 4.3 points, and 2.9 rebounds. When he came back to school as a sophomore, he was not just better, but better than everyone else.

"I was really a nobody my freshman year," recalls Pippen, who would grow to a muscular 6-7 and 220 pounds by the 1990–91 season. He remained wispy-looking, his long, flat nose and angular Native Indian features providing the look of an intense warrior. "But then as a sophomore, I was better than any player on the team by far, including the juniors and seniors. I had been playing all the time that summer, so I never lost my coordination as I grew."

When he was a sophomore, his averages suddenly increased to 18.5 points and 9.2 rebounds on 56 percent shooting, most of that from dunking. Although Pippen would become a proficient three-point shooter in college, his weakness even as an NBA All-Star was his shot. Perhaps because he was so explosive to the basket and dangerous when close by, scouting reports recommended giving Pippen the outside shot. But unlike Jordan, who turned himself into the best shooting guard in the NBA after coming out of college as a suspect shooter, Pippen had a shooting style, with a floppy elbow and loose wrist, that would limit development. Still, he had enough talent to dominate his conference, where he became an NAIA all-American as a junior, when he averaged 19.8 points and 9.2 rebounds, and then again as senior, when he averaged 23.6 points and 10 rebounds.

The NBA pretty much assumes that if you're a good player, good enough to play professional basketball, somebody has discovered you by the end of your high school career and you've gone to a major college. Central Arkansas didn't fit that category, and NBA scouts always looked with suspicion at players with great statistics against inferior competition. There wasn't much interest in Pippen. Not that he expected much; he had become something of a local celebrity in college and was pretty happy with that. But Marty Blake, the director of collegiate scouting for the NBA, checked up on Pippen and sent out a report suggesting he had potential to be a good player. The Bulls listened.

Krause sent his top assistant, Billy McKinney, to check Pippen out, and McKinney discovered in Pippen the characteristics Krause loved in players: long arms, big hands, quickness, and jumping ability. But McKinney, who would later take a brief stint as general manager of the expansion Minnesota Timberwolves, said he couldn't tell how good Pippen was because the competition was so bad. Maybe he was a second-round pick. Krause thought he might have a diamond in the rough and figured he'd fool everyone, but Pippen's stock began to soar after impressive performances against some of the nation's best players in postseason all-star games, which are attended by executives from every NBA team. Krause would eventually grow desperate in his bid to snare Pippen and would ask his agent, Jimmy Sexton, to take Pippen to Hawaii for a few weeks before the draft—the Bulls would pay all his expenses—which could make other teams think Pippen irresponsible so they wouldn't draft him. "Thanks, Jerry, but we'll stay here," Sexton told him.

A player's value rises and falls dramatically in those all-star games, and a classic Krause tale would emerge from one such gathering: In 1988, Krause had his eye on Dan Majerle, a rugged kid from small Central Michigan University, who would eventually make the Olympic team and become a first-round draft choice of the Phoenix Suns. Krause went to Majerle before the first of those games and asked him to pretend he was injured.

"Then we could get you with our third-round pick," said Krause.

Majerle looked at Krause as if he were nuts.

"I think I might make a little more money if I were a first-round pick, Mr. Krause," Majerle said.

Krause had not tried the same tactic with Pippen, though the proposed trip to Hawaii was close. The Bulls had the eighth and tenth picks in that draft, but Krause knew Pippen would not last until No. 8 because Sacramento, which had pick No. 6, was ready to grab him. So when Georgetown's Reggie Williams was picked fourth by the Los Angeles Clippers, Krause worked a deal with

Seattle, which had the fifth pick and had wanted Williams. The deal was an exchange of draft choices (Seattle got Chicago's No. 8, plus its second-round pick in 1988 or '89 and the option to exchange first-round picks in 1989). Krause had Pippen, and the Executive of the Year award, as he also came up with Grant a few picks later.

Pippen had some money coming his way for the first time in his life, although not the ability to shake his insecurity about what he had become. He was the fifth pick in the draft, behind big-time stars like David Robinson, Armon Gilliam, Williams, and Dennis Hopson. After him came all-Americans from major universities like North Carolina's Kenny Smith and UCLA's Reggie Miller.

So Pippen wanted, almost demanded a long-term deal from the Bulls, six years for $5.1 million. The Bulls were agreeable, for Krause was ecstatic about Pippen. He viewed him not only as a potential All-Star but as a personal discovery, a case of outsmarting his peers, as every general manager yearns to do (but few with Krause's intensity). And he would be right, so much so that when the Bulls later went shopping for talent, the only players they considered untradable were Jordan and Pippen.

But coming out of Hamburg, Pippen wasn't even sure he could play in the NBA. His representative, Sexton, remembers Pippen asking how much he could get from his contract if he were released after his rookie season.

"He wanted security," recalls Sexton. "That's what he was most concerned with."

Although he was a rural version of a street kid, wild, somewhat irresponsible and subject to running with people of questionable character, Pippen was intensely conservative with money. His father's illness, which had put him out of work when Pippen was in junior high, and crippling illnesses to two brothers left Pippen obsessed with providing for the future. He never, never wanted to be without money now that he had some. When he signed a deal, he talked about an annuity before he talked about a new car, Sexton said.

"I just had my mind set on one thing after going through college," Pippen said. "I wanted to get money to help my family. I felt this was a chance for me to give my mom some of the things I wanted her to have."

So Pippen began sending home a regular allowance, bought his mother a new car, and built the family a sprawling ranch-style home to accommodate his father's wheelchair needs. In later years, Pippen would always return there. "It's real comfortable, the most comfortable house for me," he says. "I could just sit there and know we're all enjoying it and that made me feel good."

But now, as his teammates were in Chicago preparing to begin the 1990–91 season, Pippen wasn't feeling so good. He'd just left that big house in Hamburg and was driving east through Mist and Thebes on U.S. 82. He was heading into Mississippi toward Memphis, Tennessee, where he would meet with Sexton. It was the first of October, just a few days before the opening of camp, and Pippen had made a decision: "I just thought I'd sit out a few days and see what they said. Maybe I'd even sit out all of training camp."

Pippen was outraged at the bigger salaries being paid to teammates like Stacey King, who Pippen thought was lazy and lacking spirit. He'd heard rumors all summer about Levingston, about the Bulls being willing to pay him more than $1 million per year, and he wondered: How good is this guy? Could he play my position and replace me? Is that why they wanted him?

Pippen was to earn $765,000 in 1990–91 with two unguaranteed option years to come at the club's discretion at $1.1 million and $1.25 million. When he had signed in 1987, those were considered lucrative figures, but the impact of the NBC TV deal had thrown all previous deals out of whack. Reggie Miller was about to sign a five-year, $16 million deal with Indiana, and Reggie Lewis, picked even farther down in that 1987 draft by Boston, was about to sign a $3-million-a-year deal. And Pippen's next two years were still unguaranteed. Pippen bought a multimillion-dollar insurance policy, but he remained frightened that it could all vanish quickly.

He'd had that fear since his rookie season, when he averaged 8 points per game in about twenty minutes on the floor. From midseason on, Pippen had experienced pain in his back and legs, but team physicians couldn't agree on the problem. Trainer Mark Pfeil told Pippen he only needed to stretch, and the general feeling was that Pippen was a malingerer. Pippen knew otherwise, and also knew that if something wasn't done, his career was over. Sometimes he'd have to stop two or three times during his forty-minute drive to the Stadium to walk or stretch because he couldn't sit in the car anymore. He'd never realized how far away his feet were before; he could never seem to reach them. He could dunk a basketball more easily than he could put on his socks. But the team insisted nothing was seriously wrong. Pfeil, who'd had a long career in Chicago listening to the whining of lazy athletes, became the team's enforcer, telling Pippen he was weak and lazy. It was something Pippen would not quickly forget.

Eventually, the team would recognize that Pippen needed disk surgery, which he had after his rookie season. And he admits that as he lay in bed, he wondered if he'd ever play again. "I was scared," he recalls. "I thought that was the end."

But Pippen had a full recovery and moved into the starting lineup by late December of the following season. And now he was an All-Star, yet teammates like King and Hopson and Cartwright were all making more than he was. And the Bulls could hold him to three more seasons without the kind of raise he deserved. Pippen had worked out most of the summer back in Chicago and was quicker, jumping better, even shooting better. He felt lithe and strong—and underpaid.

As he rolled north, he came up with a plan. He was going to get a room in Memphis and hide out for a few days so the Bulls couldn't find him. He'd enjoy knowing that Krause was squirming before the local media, unable to find him. His anger, as it is for most of the Bulls during contract negotiations, was directed at Krause.

Krause had gone to Pippen when Pippen started mumbling about wanting a new deal after the 1989–90 season, and said it was team policy not to renegotiate when a player has three years left on his contract. Pippen cursed out Krause and later told Sexton he wouldn't talk to him anymore. Krause had had the same effect on John Paxson earlier in the summer, when Ed Nealy signed with Phoenix for almost $700,000 per year. Krause knew Paxson and Nealy had become close friends, so he told Paxson not to expect that kind of money when his contract ran out. Paxson didn't want to make a scene, but he asked his lawyer to call Reinsdorf and request that Krause no longer talk with him—about anything.

And Krause had so angered Horace Grant during talks late in the 1989–90 season that Grant demanded to be traded on the eve of the playoffs. Krause had said Grant was unworthy of a big contract, unlike A. C. Green, whom Sexton, also Grant's agent, had brought up for comparative purposes. When Sexton told Grant what Krause had said, the sensitive Grant could think of nothing but trying to hurt Krause in return.

But Reinsdorf was shrewd. He knew Krause annoyed players and their agents. He'd offer ridiculously low contracts just to make them fume. Krause initially told Grant he'd never get more than $800,000 per year; he eventually added $6 million over three years to his contract. Krause would compare a player unfavorably with others around the league and tell him the Bulls fully intended to enforce his contract. There was no bargaining with Krause.

So Reinsdorf would enter the negotiations. He was smooth and smart. He'd assure the agent and his player things could work out, that the Bulls thought highly of him, and immediately increase any "last" offer Krause had made. He was comforting and he'd order Krause to keep quiet, often right in front of the agent. It was a tactic Reinsdorf would use again and again, even as agents came to realize what was going on.

"I was told that's the way it worked with the Bulls," said rookie agent Roger Kirschenbaum, who represented Levingston. "But Krause makes it so hard and gets you so mad you seem to forget."

Then Reinsdorf would move in with a seemingly generous offer and a deal would quickly be agreed upon. It would be the price Reinsdorf was going to give them in the first place, but they'd be so glad to be dealing with someone so reasonable that they'd take it.

But Pippen had had it with Krause. There would be no talking with him, not even with Reinsdorf, this time. "Why bother?" he told Sexton. Sexton urged Pippen to go to camp, that he had to be there to get a deal done, that Reinsdorf wouldn't deal any other way.

Pippen was stubborn. "Let them see how many games they'll win without me," he said.

Sexton, though, persuaded Pippen to call Reinsdorf and at least tell him he wasn't coming.

Reinsdorf was stunned. Pippen had to come to camp, he insisted. He was under contract. He'd be taken care of, but he had to be there. It was an obligation. This was a contract, for God's sake. You live up to contracts. That's the way it was.

Pippen said it was a bad contract and he had no intention of honoring it. He said he'd think about it, and hung up.

"The thing was," said Pippen, "I really wanted to go to camp. I'd worked out all off-season and I wanted to show what I could do, not sit around."

Sexton persuaded Pippen that it was important to him to make the All-Star team again, that many had thought his previous appearance a fluke, especially after the migraine incident in the play-offs. Also, Nike had offered Pippen a shoe deal, and Sexton said a holdout might embarrass Nike and hurt Pippen's endorsement opportunities.

Finally, Pippen changed his mind. "I'm going to camp," he told Sexton. "But they better do something quick."

•

THE PRIME ROLE of the exhibition season for the Bulls is to make money, which they do exceptionally well thanks to Jordan. And while Jordan hardly needed the playing time, Jackson often felt compelled to play him.

"I know the people are here to see him and that we're not only playing basketball, we're in the entertainment business," said Jackson. "They want Jordan."

To what extent was often beyond belief. In Vancouver, kids hung from the team bus like spiders trying to get a view of Jordan. In Seattle they threw firecrackers around the bus. Exhibition games are usually played in cities without NBA teams, so the security is often poor; the NBA cities and regular team hotels have learned how to deal with the Jordan phenomenon, but this year the Bulls went to Nashville and Iowa City, Vancouver and Chapel Hill, and capacity crowds watched the team everywhere, as opposed to the few thousand who attend most exhibition games.

The Bulls played well, frighteningly so at times, running up 30- and 35-point leads in some games. "We've been solid, really overwhelming at times," admitted Jackson, "although we won't be that overpowering all season. The key for us will be to run the system and force everyone into recognition of that system, which will take time." Yet Jackson would welcome a gradual ascent. He experimented repeatedly with different combinations, something that would continue throughout the season. He'd play the reserves as a unit, then try them with Jordan or Pippen or both; he'd squeeze the offense so that Jordan ended up in corners it was almost impossible to score from, and then Jackson would ask Jordan to do so. He'd challenge Grant with verbal attacks and encourage Pippen with soft praise. "This is a ball club that has to be extended all the time," Jackson would tell the coaches. "We have to give them things to extend them and put them in negative situations so they learn to recover, not only in practice but in games. They're going to have to figure out situations as a group all season and find something to hang their hat on."

Jordan remained a phenomenon of epic proportions. The Bulls attracted more than twenty-five thousand to the Kingdome in Seattle, and just as many in the new Sun Coast Dome in Saint Petersburg, where Reinsdorf had almost moved the White Sox. At the last minute a new stadium deal convinced him to stay in Chicago, but he appreciated Saint Petersburg's interest and asked how he could repay the favor. Bring the Bulls to our new dome, he was told. So the Bulls were scheduled for the first basketball game in the new arena on October 18, facing Seattle, and it was the top story in all the local newspapers. Like most big stars, Jordan performs when the stage lights go up. No matter how he might feel or how routine the games seem, he always seems energized by the crowd and the demands placed on him. He knows the fans are rooting for the big breakaway dunk or the slashing baseline jam or the reverse hanging lay-up.

He also knows this style of play goes against Jackson's best instincts about how the game should be played.

"I almost wish sometimes that we could put in a play where Michael can dribble around like Marques Haynes and everyone would clear out and we could do a Globetrotter backdoor and jam the ball at the end of the twenty-four-second clock," mused Jackson once. "Then we'd give them that one play where they could see him dribble and pass and slam. Maybe if we just asked the other team they'd lay down for one play and it would be all over and out of the way and we could get on with playing the game."

But Jordan wasn't thinking that way in Saint Petersburg after an unusual 0-for-7 shooting half when his jumpers were bounding off the rim and his lay-ups were sliding away.

The fans were growing restless. Jackson felt an obligation to leave Jordan on the court, playing him thirty-five minutes in a meaningless exhibition game, and Jordan felt an obligation to score. The first five times the Bulls had the ball in the second half he dribbled around, drove, and shot. His teammates stood around watching helplessly, hopelessly. They had seen it before and they knew they would not be seeing the ball much. The Bulls ended up losing the game down the stretch when Sedale Threatt hit several jumpers in a row.

Bill Cartwright had attempted 3 shots to Jordan's 18, even though Seattle had Olden Polynice and Michael Cage, both natural forwards, playing center.

"I've got one fear," said Cartwright later. "It's that I'm going to play all this time in the league and come so close and never get a ring. I only want to win. He's got so much talent and can do so much for this team, but I keep thinking he's going to keep us all from it unless he changes."

4

NOVEMBER 1990

11/2 v. Philadelphia; 11/3 at Washington; 11/6 v. Boston; 11/7 at Minnesota; 11/9 at Boston; 11/10 v. Charlotte; 11/13 at Utah; 11/15 at Golden State; 11/17 at Seattle; 11/18 at Portland; 11/21 at Phoenix; 11/23 at L.A. Clippers; 11/24 at Denver; 11/28 v. Washington; 11/30 v. Indiana

IT DIDNT TAKE long for the Bulls to discover they weren't as good as they thought they'd be.

Before the opening game against Philadelphia, Jordan sent a diamond ear stud over to Charles Barkley with Barkley's number 34, on it, just like the number 23 Jordan was now wearing in his ear. Rick Mahorn had told Jordan that Barkley had seen a picture of Jordan with his ear stud during training camp and liked it, so Jordan picked one up for Barkley. "Maybe it will keep him from hitting me," Jordan joked.

Actually, the two had become good friends. After the 1989–90 season, Jordan played in a celebrity golf tournament in Philadelphia with Barkley caddying for him. "Charles is a nice guy, a fun guy to be with; he makes me laugh," Jordan would explain about how Oliver Twist and the Artful Dodger had come together, how the league's Goody Two-Shoes and Peck's Bad Boy could coexist. "We're friends," added Barkley, "because most of the guys in this league are jerks and you wouldn't want to spend any time with them."

As the season went on, the two would engage in a personal race for the league scoring title, and one would often call the other to taunt him about how many points behind he was. In December, Jordan would take over the scoring lead for the first time all season, after a slow start; he'd been playing by Jackson's rules. But Perdue remembers Jordan sitting in the locker room before a game, saying that Barkley needed to score 45 that night to pass him. "No way he'll do that," Jordan said. But sure enough, Barkley did, and Jordan would go for a season-high 42 in this next game to keep pace.

Jordan, like most players in the league, studied his statistics, for that was, in the end, how players were paid. Play as a team, they were told; but in negotiating sessions, statistics were always held up as the barometer of value. It was hard to find an NBA player who did not know his current statistics, and those of most of the players in the league. During the 1988–89 season, when Collins switched Jordan to point guard, he started picking up triple doubles, and it became something of a contest to see how many he could get and whether he could pass Magic Johnson, who usually led the league in that category. For several games, Jordan would check with the official scorer during the game to see how many more rebounds or assists he needed for another triple double; it only stopped when the league got word and ordered the scorer to refrain from giving out the information during the game. But Jordan has always kept his point totals in his head as he's played: Late in the 1989–90 season, during a time-out in a close game, the overhead scoreboard in Chicago Stadium listed Jordan's point total as 38. "Go tell them it's got to be thirty-nine," Jordan told trainer Mark Pfeil. "I know I shot an odd number of free throws, so it's got to be an odd number."

Jordan liked Barkley's brashness and respected his ability, which some said made him the most unstoppable player in the game, although their personalities were different. Jordan could be razor-sharp of tongue with an implicit, cutting message, like when he saw struggling rookie Stacey King walking into the locker room carrying a box: "I hope there's a jump shot in there," Jordan cracked. Or when then-reserve Charles Davis was sorting through tickets for friends and family when the team was playing a game in Atlanta: "They don't need a ticket to watch you sitting on the bench. They can go to your house for that."

Barkley, who doesn't own an unexpressed thought, rarely worries about whether outsiders hear his taunts. Everything about him is on public display, as in the 1990 playoffs, when he signaled with his thumb for coach Jim Lynam to yank Mike Gminski during a game. He's annually the most fined player in the league, once saying he'd considered donating his annual total to the homeless, "but then they'd have better homes than I do." In the 1989–90 season, he and New York's Mark Jackson were fined for saying they had bet on which of them would make the winning shot in a close Knicks–76ers game. Barkley would be called in by the commissioner for a slap on the wrist and lecture, only to say, when asked if he were going to be fined, "Wanna bet?"

Barkley angered women's groups for saying, after a loss, that it was the kind of game after which you go home and beat your wife. "Screw the women's groups," he said when asked if he'd actually like to see that in print. He slammed New York: "It's my kind of town . . . because I've got a gun." He said of Larry Bird, "As long as he's around, I'll only be the second-worst defensive player in basketball." He talks throughout games to anyone who'll listen, and he once told lead referee Tommy Nunez to make a call because "you know Moe and Larry won't."

"Charles says what's on his mind," says Jordan. "I like him because it's like I'm the good brother and he's the bad brother. He says a lot of good things the good brother wants to say, but doesn't. And I like that. I know I'm always laughing when we're together."

But Barkley's play is no joke, and despite his developing friendship with Jordan, Barkley said he was going to show all the preseason prognosticators that the Eastern Conference race wasn't just between Detroit and Chicago. In the season opener in Chicago, he went out and outscored Jordan 37–34 and added 10 rebounds as the 76ers won rather easily, 124–116, after building a 19-point halftime lead.

The Bulls went into Washington the next night to play a Bullets team they'd defeated easily in the preseason. With Chicago trailing by 1, Jordan had a last-second shot attempt blocked, and the Bulls were now 0–2.

The Bulls had come to expect last-second heroics from Jordan. After all, who could forget that stunning fifth and final game of the 1989 opening-round playoff series in Cleveland? With Jordan promising a victory and Collins fearing for his job, there were half a dozen lead changes in the fourth quarter when Cleveland ran a brilliant screen play from Larry Nance to Craig Ehlo and scored to take a 1-point lead with three seconds left.

Collins called time-out, gathered everyone in a tight circle, and began to draw a play for Dave Corzine. "Everyone started to look around," recalled backup forward Jack Haley, who would call the moment the most thrilling of his life. "Doug could see everyone sort of frowning, and he started to explain that they wouldn't be expecting Corzine to get the ball. Michael just slammed his fist down on the clipboard and said, 'Give me the fuckin' ball.'

"Doug looked at him, drew up the play Jordan wanted, and he hit that amazing hanging jumper to win the game. Now that's what I call taking charge," said Haley, who would later go to the Nets.

Taking charge: It was what Jordan was there for. But Jackson had been drilling his team—including Jordan—about moving the ball and hitting the open man. And on the final, decisive play in the Washington game, no one was near Craig Hodges in his favorite spot in the corner, yet four Bullets jumped at Jordan and blocked his shot. It happens, but some began to wonder when it happened again the next game: Boston squeezed out a 110–108 victory in Chicago when Jordan missed an eighteen-foot jumper with about twenty seconds left, and then Brian Shaw, whom Jordan was supposed to be guarding, rebounded a missed Robert Parish jumper over Jordan and put the ball in at the buzzer to win the game.

A week before at the Bulls' kickoff luncheon, player after player had talked about winning a title; management was saying this was the year; national publications were picking the Bulls as one of four or five teams with the best chance to win a championship.

The Bulls were 0–3.

After this start, Jordan told reporters he'd talked it over and decided to become more assertive on offense. And just whom had he talked that over with? "I talked it over with myself," Jordan explained.

The Bulls ended the first nine days of the season 3–3, but two of those wins were over expansion teams—Minnesota and Charlotte—

and some were worrried. But not Jackson. He's a patient man, well suited for coaching the modern athlete. From his experience in the game he can relate to players, particularly big men, which is rare for a coach. Many eventually fail because they lose the respect of the bigger players, who doubt that a smaller man who never played the game can understand what they do. It's one reason Golden State's Don Nelson remains so successful. But Jackson is successful for another reason: He refuses to blame his players for the team's failures, which is something that eventually doomed Collins. "It would be either that *he* won or *we* lost," recalls Will Perdue. "It was always 'The coaching staff did all they could.' It was 'you guys' who let down when we lost, and then when we won it was 'What a great job of preparation the coaches did and how hard they worked watching those films.' "

Collins had been a great player, a three-time All-Star with the Philadelphia 76ers, because of his hustle, enthusiasm, and impassioned, almost insane desire. His own personal demons drove him to be a standout while also keeping him on a highly emotional edge. But that same intensity eventually took him down as a coach.

When Stan Albeck was fired in 1986, Krause felt that Collins, then an analyst for televised NBA games, would relate better to the current generation of players because he had been one so recently.

"You mean the TV guy?" said Reinsdorf incredulously. "As our coach?"

But Krause was adamant, and he was right—at first. Collins was enthusiastic and let Jordan loose to average 37 points per game. But as time passed and the Bulls failed to join the NBA's elite, Collins became desperately controlling, calling every play and privately blaming Jordan for his inability to get the team to play a fast-breaking transition offense.

And in 1988 when the team traded for Cartwright and drafted center Will Perdue from Vanderbilt and Krause proclaimed the team set at center for the 1990s, Collins found himself under great pressure to develop a low-post game at a time when he didn't know how, never having studied the position or played it. In the 1988 exhibition season, by which time the team was fully expected to win—they had crashed the fifty-win barrier, they had Jordan, and they now had the center everyone always said the team lacked—Collins was near a breakdown, strung tighter than piano wire. He was breaking

out in a rash that the players noticed whenever he was nervous, he
wasn't sleeping or eating much, and his permed Little Orphan Annie
hair sat on top of an ever-shrinking face that was a mask of rage
one day, tears the next.

Once at a charity exhibition, Jordan sat with players from around
the league, swapping stories, when the subject turned to coaches.
Everyone had something to add, from Dominique Wilkins telling
about Mike Fratello's demonic rages to Isiah Thomas telling about
his willful exchanges with Chuck Daly. So everyone had a good
laugh, but there was silence after Jordan said. "You may think
you've got problems with your coaches, but, well, mine cries every
day."

Finally, Krause and Collins became bitter enemies, with Krause
compiling indiscretions by Collins, and Collins calling Reinsdorf and
demanding Krause be sent home from a road trip or remain out of
the locker room. Collins's mania had become too draining on everyone around. He had to go.

Jackson was never predictable, though in a different way than
Collins; he still mystified his players, although they liked and respected him. He was a guy who could wear his hat sideways during
practice, but then confront them in the harshest terms about their
play. To some, Jackson was a master of psychology, using a variety
of ploys to produce results. "I think it's important to do anything
you can to make them play hard," he'd say.

"Phil's always playing with your head," said Craig Hodges.

In his first season, Jackson started giving books to players at the
start of the team's annual two-week November road trip. This season
he would give the novel *Glitz* to high-priced, fast-talking Stacey
King, *Tar Baby* to rookie Scott Williams, and *The Great Santini* to
Will Perdue. Michael Jordan received *Song of Solomon* and the
aging Bill Cartwright got *Things Fall Apart*. Jackson considers himself a guide for these young men as well as a coach, and given the
long duration of the NBA year, he tries to break up the routine.
That's why the team took a bus trip from Seattle to Portland, instead
of flying, because Jackson thought they'd enjoy the scenery. Instead,
they all slept. He'd occasionally administer psychological tests during bus and plane trips, although most of the players would invariably scribble aimlessly while listening to their headphones. Jackson
sometimes wondered if he could reach a generation that didn't un-

derstand how Thoreau could live by a pond but not own water skis or snorkeling equipment. The players often considered Jackson too didactic.

"I have to spend a lot of time thinking about people," says Jackson. "I remember my dad thinking in terms of the congregation, and it was the pastor's responsibility to remember everyone, sort of like a shepherd with his flock, and I believe that about a team. You can't think of them as just players for a coach, but you have to think of them as a group and relate to them that way, even without words. Sometimes just a wink or a pat on the shoulder will do it.

"Basketball is a very fragile thing because as coaches we can do everything and prepare everybody and have everyone physically ready and still if there's not the group reflex and reaction at the right moment, if you don't have that oneness of the group, it starts to be five starters on the floor. That bond, that unity, is a very fragile thing. It's really almost something holy, which is where the word *whole* comes from in a sense. So you've always got to try to do things to break down the routine."

But Jackson wasn't a goofy innocent. He could make backs straighten and stiffen with his messages.

Like his game films. After the Bulls had fallen behind two games to none in the 1990 playoffs against Detroit, Jackson decided he'd edit the game film himself for the next day's meeting. First there was Joe Dumars slashing by Jordan for a basket. Then came a snippet from the movie *The Wizard of Oz,* with the Tin Man talking about not having a heart. The players laughed loudly. Then Bill Laimbeer was drifting off a screen for an easy lay-up past Scottie Pippen, followed by the Scarecrow pining for a brain. More laughing, but not as much, and finally Isiah Thomas drove down the lane untouched past John Paxson, Bill Cartwright, and Horace Grant, and the Cowardly Lion was wishing for courage. There were still some giggles.

"He's telling us we've got no heart, no courage, and no brains," snapped Paxson to a suddenly deathly quiet room.

"One of my functions, as I see it, is to try to enlarge their lives in an intellectual–athletic combination," says Jackson. "This is a human behavioral laboratory, but not like white rats and lab research. You know, ideas lead to buildings and bridges. I like to think about these people and visualize their being better players through schemes, and how to encourage and motivate them through bringing them to look at film and game critiques. If you spend time wishing you had other players and scheming to get rid of them or not being loyal, either you end up hating them or they end up hating you, and that cannot be productive.

"I love the action of the game, the stimulation of a competitive event and being thrust into a situation where a person has to survive by making inituitive decisions, sort of riding on the edge like a surfer," says Jackson. "To make the right decisions at the right time and respond to competitive pressures and needs is a tremendous feeling. I always looked at basketball as a temporary thing, but that macho man-to-man aspect and the group interaction almost makes it a form of a higher plane. It takes you out of the mundane space of life, and sometimes I wish that we could play in a gym without any people and try to play the perfect game where you don't make any mistakes and maybe if there's a mistake it's of omission, not commission, and everything is done at the right moment, at the right time, and each decision is the right one and everyone can ride that decision-making wave."

•

As THE TEAM headed out west for a seven-game trip, Reinsdorf was questioning everyone's decisions. He had been sure that with the team's off-season pickups, the Bulls had a chance to win a title this year, yet they were playing miserably. So he called Jackson on the road to ask what was wrong.

"My teams always are slow-starting teams," Jackson explained to Reinsdorf. "Even in the CBA. I like to put guys out there and let them find their roles, let them find out how they'll react in times of stress, leave them on the floor sometimes to see what they'll do in situations. I like them to be able to find their space out there."

Jackson had told the players as much in meetings. He suggested he might even experiment with them, in a sense, leaving them out on the floor and in jeopardy in tough situations. He might not throw them a lifeline time-out to see how they could get through. It would build the kind of bond he sought. His assistant coaches weren't so sure. Bach, at times, thought Jackson a little strange, and Winter had his doubts, too.

Despite his assurances, even Jackson was getting a little concerned; not only was the team feeling the weight of great expectations, but there were outside factors as well. Both Paxson and Cartwright would be free agents after the season, and the Bulls had seen fit to offer neither a secure deal. They'd offered Cartwright a one-year extension at $1.5 million, his 1990–91 salary, which he'd rejected. Two years before, when the Bulls had acquired Cartwright, the coaches had agreed he'd be good for two solid seasons, and then perhaps one more, before, as Bach likes to put it, "he'd be an elephant looking for a graveyard." But Cartwright had surprised them all. The surgery on both knees in the off-season had gone well, and he was moving better than at any time in the past two seasons. And Perdue looked as if he would never be able to provide more than a few backup minutes.

As for Paxson, the Bulls didn't plan to ask him back. It was agreed that now that he was thirty his skills would soon start slipping, and Krause wanted Armstrong to be the starter by the end of the 1990–91 season. Also, the team needed the money that they might have given Paxson to pay Kukoc. And should they get Kukoc, Paxson would easily be expendable. Reinsdorf had given Paxson a $200,000 bonus the previous season, recognizing that at $320,000 he was vastly underpaid for a starting point guard. He liked Paxson and was willing to go for a new deal, but his basketball people, especially Krause, insisted against it. Reinsdorf would let them decide. And then there was Pippen, searching for a new contract and upset at being the sixth-highest-paid player on the team.

The biggest issue, though, remained Jackson's attempt to weave Jordan into a coordinated, egalitarian team game and still win. He needed the team to win a game that Jordan didn't dominate.

•

THE BULLS OPENED the trip in Salt Lake City against a backdrop of natural splendor and spiritual reminders, the Mormon church and the spectacular Wasatch range dominating the area. Winter always was on the doorstep here, and the craggy mountains showed a carpet of snow. The two-week November trip, the longest of the season, often began here and branded on the team a reminder that it was just the beginning of a long, dreary season. But the Bulls would be getting a break. The Jazz had been to Japan for a two-game opening set with the Phoenix Suns that had left coach Jerry Sloan feeling as if they were on their fiftieth game of the season instead of the fifth. His team was slumping badly already and he'd thrown the owner out of the locker room in a fit of rage not long after the team's return. He lamented to the Bulls coaches before the game that he was certain to be fired soon. Sloan no longer delighted in defeating the Bulls as he once did, having been fired by them during the 1981–82 season after a reasonably successful run as coach. He was, perhaps, the franchise's biggest star before Jordan, and the only player ever to have his number retired. His ferocious approach to the game had made him a success as a player, but it seemed to doom him as a coach: He had once thrown a chair at one of his players, Larry Kenon, for being too lethargic on the court. He'd hooked on as an assistant with the Jazz and eventually became head coach when Frank Layden stepped down. His teams had great success against the Bulls with their halfcourt power game behind Karl Malone.

It was an excruciating game. Both were good shooting teams—Utah had led the league the previous season at 50.5 percent to the Bulls' 49.8 percent—but neither team would shoot even 40 percent on this night as the game slowed and became a wrestling match. Utah was one of the toughest teams in the league, as befitted Sloan's rugged image. Early in the game, Horace Grant, who'd started wearing prescription goggles in the preseason to correct a vision problem, tossed the goggles away; Karl Malone kept pushing them off and then going up for a rebound while Grant fumbled helplessly to get them back on straight. "If he killed someone on the court I wonder whether they'd call a foul," Grant moaned afterward.

But it was a happy locker room after Jordan hit a long fallaway jumper at the buzzer to give the Bulls an 84–82 win, once again bailing the Bulls out on a night when the team was faltering. Pippen and Grant combined to shoot 5 for 25, but Paxson was solid as usual, if not spectacular, and had come through with a late jumper that had tied the score and set up Jordan's heroics. Jazz owner Larry Miller also remembered a game a year earlier in which Paxson had scored 27, although the Jazz scored 7 points in the last 40 seconds to win by 1.

"You shot the ball well," said Miller, who was bouncing around the Bulls' locker room to the surprise of the players.

"You know, I'm a free agent," Paxson responded quickly.

The exchange left Paxson in a gregarious mood, and later in the hotel lounge he was explaining how he was going to change his uniform number.

"I'm getting number ninety-nine," he cried. "Then maybe I won't get called for so many fouls because the refs won't be able to figure out how to flash nine-nine."

Paxson laughed, but his reputation with the referees was no laughing matter to him. He is slower than many of the guards he faces, so he often gets beaten and ends up fouling. His reputation for being a slow player who doesn't jump well had created an attitude among many referees that if there is contact, it was initiated by Paxson. And it doesn't help that Paxson has been considered a marginal player throughout most of his career.

Because there is so much improper contact in the NBA, referees tend to make their calls on the fouls that have some impact on the game. But as in every other aspect of the NBA, a star system exists. Players like Jordan are called for violations less often than players like Paxson, who are called for fouls less often than rookies. Understandably, Paxson resents being considered just a step up from rookies.

During one game, referee Hue Hollins tooted his whistle and Jordan, thinking it was on him, spun around. "Don't worry," Hollins said, "I'm not going to make the call on you, Michael." Whereupon he turned around and shouted: "Five [Paxson], hold."

"You get tired of all this star stuff," says Paxson. "I know I can play pretty good defense, and then if I'm a step to the side it's a call. I know I ought to keep my mouth shut, but when you're out there those things bother you." And more often than not, Paxson complicates the situation by loudly pleading his case.

"He's got a reputation for challenging the referees," notes Jackson, "and they don't like it. So he probably needs to take the calls and live with it."

But were Paxson to do that, he likely wouldn't survive in the NBA. In fact, had he ever done that in his life, he wouldn't even be in the NBA.

Even John Paxson doesn't really know where his toughness comes from. But it's there, a hard shell that allows him to bounce off the floor and play with injuries that would put other players out for a

week. His stubbornness has defined his career; it made him an NBA
player. Paxson's father, Jim senior, played in the NBA for a few
seasons back in the 1950s; he was 6-6, pretty big in those days, and
did reasonably well, averaging almost 10 points per game for the
Cincinnati Royals, the fourth-best scorer on the team behind Clyde
Lovellette, Jack Twyman, and Maurice Stokes, all three All-Stars.

But playing in the NBA didn't mean much money or fame then.
Al Bianchi, then playing for Syracuse, remembers trips to Fort
Wayne in which the train didn't go through downtown, so they'd
have to get off thirty miles north of the city. Someone would arrange
for teenagers to pick them up in four or five cars, and the team
would ride into town with the kids and reward them with a few
bucks and some tickets. There were eight teams in the league and
nobody counted on the future.

And so when Jim junior was born, Jim senior had decisions to
make. He didn't know then that his oldest son would go on to break
his basketball records at the University of Dayton and become a
star NBA player at Portland, the first player in team history to score
more than 10,000 points, before finishing his career with the Boston
Celtics. At the time, his wife was having medical problems and he
didn't want to be on the road, so he quit after two seasons and
became an insurance agent.

While many NBA players grew up with just one parent and others
struggled mightily, Paxson lived a simple middle-class suburban life
in Ohio: neat house with a fence around it, kids, church, and a
basketball hoop. The players often refer to Paxson as "the nine-to-
five pro" because of his businesslike life-style. While many of the
players go to nightclubs, even when the team's at home, Paxson can
more often be found wheeling his son around a mall. On the road,
if he can't find some old friend from Notre Dame, he delights in
room service and a TV movie. Even his groupies are wholesome:
When Paxson is trailing along in Jordan's wake, it's the eleven- and
twelve-year-olds who are usually screaming for his autograph. "At
least someone notices," he says.

His thin, fine brown hair flops down Prince Valiant style and his
blue eyes are soft and inviting. He shaved his mustache a few years
back, and now his upper lip forms a slight snarl when he smiles.
But he is all-American all the way, from his reliable backyard jumper
to his high school sweetheart of a wife, whom he used to take on

hayrides, to two sons for whom the word *moppets* was practically invented.

Growing up, John was the runt of the family, three years younger and smaller than his brother Jim. Because his birthday fell just before his school's enrollment, he was always one of the youngest and smallest kids in class, so he didn't make the teams. But his parents decided to let him repeat the eighth grade. He went to a small military school in Rolling Prairie, Indiana, and when he returned to the Dayton school system he found himself playing against kids his size. He became a top player at Archbishop Alter High School in Kettering, Ohio. "I never would have become a pro player if I hadn't done that," he insists.

Paxson played his college ball at Notre Dame, where he averaged 17.7 points per game as a senior and made some second-unit all-America teams (he was a first-team academic all-American) and was chosen in the first round of the NBA draft by the San Antonio Spurs. But he never got much of a chance to play; George Gervin and Johnny Moore were already there, and John Lucas and Alvin Robertson were brought in during his first two seasons. The Bulls picked him up as a free agent before the start of the 1985–86 season, but he would remain haunted by the team's own doubts about his abilities.

First he would back up Kyle Macy, and then Steve Colter, before finishing the 1986–87 season as a starter with an 11.3 scoring average, his career best. But then the Bulls brought in Sedale Threatt and he started, then Rory Sparrow and he started, then Sam Vincent and he started, then Craig Hodges and *he* started. But when the 1989–90 season opened, Paxson was starting, and he would continue to do so throughout the season. By the start of the 1990–91 season, the team was privately talking about starting B. J. Armstrong, but they stuck with Paxson. Hodges was now down to fifth guard, and all the others were long gone.

"It is satisfying to know," Paxson was saying early in the 1990–91 season, "that after all these years and all these guards I'm still starting."

Paxson is a realist; he knows that you can have a long career in the NBA by accepting your limitations and finding a role. More important, he learned better than anyone else that the only way to remain a starting point guard with the Bulls is to satisfy Jordan. The

Bulls always say that to play the point opposite Jordan you have to be a great shooter; since Jordan always draws double or triple coverage, the tandem guard has to be able to hit the jumper. Paxson can do that. But so could Threatt, Macy, Vincent, Hodges, and Armstrong, and yet Jordan regularly said he most preferred playing with Paxson. The difference was that Paxson was the one who most deferred to Jordan on the court. Many wondered whether Jordan would be able to play with a great, penetrating point guard like Kevin Johnson, whom Krause always said he was trying to obtain. But Johnson needs the ball to be effective; Jordan demands to have the ball in his hands, and his corrosive glare has worn down those who have tried to ignore him. And Paxson knows that. His first pass upcourt is usually to Jordan, and then he drops off into a spot-up shooting position, ready if called upon.

Paxson's son, Ryan, once said to his father after watching a game on TV, "Daddy, you don't shoot the ball too many times."

"Get used to it, son," Paxson answered.

But if Paxson learned how to deal with the Bulls on the court, he never did off the court, particularly during the 1989–90 and 1990–91 seasons, when he remained among the lowest-paid starting guards in the league. "I guess my big problem was I was always too realistic and dwelled on what I couldn't do rather than how important I was," said Paxson. "Other guys would say how they couldn't be replaced. I knew I could. But so could they." Paxson had settled for a three-year deal ending in 1991 that paid him about $330,000 per year. He negotiated it without an agent, but the Bulls proved a little too shrewd for him. They held out a carrot, saying that after he retired they'd make him a TV announcer, a possibility that seemed more and more remote as the 1990–91 season went on. And Paxson had already decided he'd like to return and work at Notre Dame in some capacity.

So Paxson finally hired Jordan's agent, Falk. And Paxson began to see conspiracies abounding. After informing the Bulls that he'd hired an agent, and not just any agent but the nettlesome Falk, whom Krause detested, Paxson noticed his playing time shrinking and began to wonder whether the change had been ordered by management. Bulls players always wondered if the front office was controlling their playing time. Sam Vincent felt it was when he negotiated a major incentive based on minutes played and suddenly found himself being lifted repeatedly in the fourth quarter. And Paxson remembers Charles Davis telling him during the 1989–90 season that when Davis asked Jackson why he wasn't playing, Jackson said he was ordered not to play him.

Paxson was now certain he wouldn't be offered a new contract by the Bulls. Moreover, Paxson suspected that his next contract would be his last, and he needed to start putting up some numbers. He began coming to every game determined to shoot every time he got the ball to build up his statistics. Pippen, who had given him the idea, was planning to do the same since he was about to begin negotiations on a new deal.

But Paxson couldn't bring himself to follow through on the plan. "I say I'm going to do it, I'm going to shoot, and then when I get out there I just can't if it's not the right situation for me," Paxson lamented one day. "I'll never change." He was, in a way, too good a basketball player for his own good.

•

PHIL JACKSON'S PROBLEM, meanwhile, was with the player who was too good for his team's good. Jordan showed no signs of changing his game, and for the team's sake Jackson was hoping that a game Jordan couldn't dominate would come soon. Fortunately, a game against the Golden State Warriors, in Oakland, was coming up on the schedule.

It was in Oakland that Jordan broke his foot in 1985, and for seasons to come he despised and feared the Oakland Coliseum. The following year Jordan admitted he was afraid to play there and shot 11 of 30. The next year he would record a season-low 16 points there. It's the arena in which he's averaged by far his fewest points since he's been in the NBA.

Jordan has tried to overcome the Oakland jinx, and in the 1989–90 season he felt he succeeded, leading the Bulls to an easy win with 29 points and 14 rebounds. This night, though, would not start out well for Jordan. Upon arriving at the arena, he'd heard the word that was sweeping both locker rooms: Lakers star James Worthy, a North Carolina teammate of Jordan's and one of the more respected gentlemen around the league, had been arrested for soliciting prostitutes. Worthy had contacted an escort service and requested sex of two women who turned out to be undercover police officers, it was alleged; they arrested him when they came to his hotel room in Houston before that night's game.

Jordan was stunned and kept asking reporters whether it was true. "What are they going to say back home?" was Jordan's principal concern. Several players began to offer weak jokes about the situation. "You'd think he'd have been tired of being double-teamed by now," said one, while another offered, "This gives new meaning to the concept of the pregame meal."

The life of any professional athlete is filled with temptation, which is one reason Horace Grant likes to bring his wife, Donna, on road trips, although the Bulls would order Grant not to. There's an old joke around the NBA:

Question: What's the hardest thing about going on the road?
Answer: Not smiling when you kiss your wife good-bye at the door.

All of this reminded one of the Bulls coaches of an incident that occurred a few years ago involving a professional baseball player who was with his wife in the delivery room for the birth of their child. When the baby was delivered, everyone was shocked: The baby was black; the player and his wife were white. She had been having an affair with one of his teammates. Shortly thereafter, the teammate was traded; the team said it had an excess of players at the teammate's position and was making room for a promising minor leaguer.

Jordan felt badly for Worthy and his family, for he knew Worthy's life would never be the same.

"It's the biggest fear you have," said Jordan. "I know it's my greatest fear. I've spent a life building something positive, and I know any mistake I make could damage that for the rest of my life. People look to their role models to be almost flawless and I guess I'm the closest thing to being viewed positively, very little being flawed in my life. It's hard to live up to something like that, really harder than basketball. It's really the biggest job I have."

But that night, Jordan's job was just to play basketball. Golden State would take a 7-point lead after three quarters and hold on to win by 10, although the Bulls pulled within 6 midway through the final quarter. The ball was moving around, but not always to Jordan, and by the time he got back into the game in the fourth quarter he was cold and angry. He protested a foul call, and when Chris Mullin missed both free throws he told referee Jack Madden, "See, cheaters lose." The referees had become accustomed to Jordan's kidding and usually dismissed it with a smile, but this season he seemed testier. Was it the offense? The drive to finally win? Or, as Jackson and Jordan would suggest later in the season, lack of protection for the Bulls star from the referees? Jordan then missed his only 2 shots of the quarter and the Bulls fell to 4–4 on the season. Game line for Jordan: 14 points on a season-low 12 shots, as every starter had at least 10 shots, a rarity in Jordan's seven seasons with the team.

Jordan was furious after the game. He kicked a chair when he came into the locker room, and in his comments to the media he came just short of losing his temper: "He's the coach. I have to abide by his decisions. He chose to play me that way, so that's the way I'll play. I guess they figured in my first six years we didn't have the success they wanted, so they figure the success will come from everyone being involved." Jordan was, by now, seeming to count the letters in each word, as they came out slow and measured. His voice was almost quivering.

"But then I see Mullin on me," he went on, "and I'm licking my chops, and I still didn't see the ball. But I have to accept his explanations."

Jackson had seen immediately how angry Jordan was and went to him after the game to ask him to "say the right thing" when the media were allowed in after ten minutes. It was a tense scene. Krause usually went into the locker room a minute or two after the players went in. This time, Jackson kicked him out. He wanted to talk to Jordan alone.

Warriors coach Don Nelson walked by long after the game and smirked to Jordan, "I hope they keep playing you that way."

Jordan went out to a local club with his old friend Rod Higgins, now with the Warriors, and bashed the new system long into the night.

"I just hate it," he said, "and now in the newspapers tomorrow they're going to be saying I didn't perform, that they shut me down. I hate when I have to read that in the papers the next day, that I couldn't do something. It wasn't my fault."

Jordan's anger simmered as the team moved on to Seattle the

next day. And at practice late in the afternoon, his mood hadn't changed any. He was still burning.

"He just passed the ball, even at times when he was supposed to shoot," Grant would say afterward, somewhat delighted because he was beginning to think that he might get some shots in the next game. The Bulls' offense, like most around the NBA, denied shots to the power forward, whose job it was to rebound. But Grant felt he could become an active part of the offense. He'd worked hard on a post-up move in the summer and had an accurate jump shot, but usually didn't get more than 7 or 8 shots in a game, most off offensive rebounds. He liked the new offense. But it was clear Jordan didn't. "Michael wouldn't say a word to anyone. He just passed the ball and took maybe one or two shots and that was it for two hours," said Grant.

•

THE BULLS HAD played Seattle three times during the exhibition season, winning two. In the one loss, brash SuperSonics rookie guard Gary Payton had played well, and told *USA Today*'s Peter Vecsey that he could defend anyone, including Jordan. Later that night the two met by chance at a Seattle nightclub and Payton began to taunt Jordan: "I've got my millions and I'm buying my Ferraris and Testarossas, too."

"No problem," said Jordan. "I get them for free."

Jordan liked his little comeback, but he wasn't through. A challenge always invigorates Jordan, and if it's on the basketball court, all the better. Before the Bulls were about to go out and play Seattle that night, Jordan reached into his bag and pulled out that *USA Today* story with Payton's quotes from the preseason. B. J. Armstrong watched. He's a thoughtful kid and he enjoys studying others, particularly Jordan. "You watch what the best do and then you learn from it," says Armstrong. But Armstrong wondered to himself as he watched Jordan, "This guy's the best there is. Why is he so worried about what a rookie says?"

Just before Jordan walked out of the locker room he promised, "I'm going to show that little sucker."

The first time Payton had the ball, Jordan stole it, drove for a lay-up, and was fouled. The next time Payton had the ball, Jordan stole it again and drove all the way down court and slammed for a 6–0 Bulls lead. The third time Payton had the ball, Jordan destroyed his dribble; Scottie Pippen came in to steal the ball and hit Bill Cartwright for a lay-up, and Seattle coach K. C. Jones took the rookie out of the game. It would be an easy Bulls win, 116–95, as Jordan had 33 points and 7 steals before the end of the third quarter. It was the kind of game he loved, when nobody who ever played the game was better than he was, the kind of game that would carry him for a few days. He was headed for a 50-point game, at least the high 40s, with easily a few more fan-pleasing cradle dunks, but Jackson took him out early. And as Jordan sat on the bench during the fourth quarter after having played just 27 minutes, less than every starter but Paxson, he finally came to a realization, something he'd considered but never really believed. He turned to Armstrong on the bench: "He's not going to let me win the scoring title." The reality was finally sinking in.

The Bulls moved on to Portland, where the perpetually gloomy November skies wouldn't begin to clear over the city, and then would start to follow the Bulls. They were unable to pierce either the curtain of rain draped over the city or the storming Trail Blazers. The Bulls would absorb a 125–112 drubbing that would open some old wounds. Portland had become the team the Bulls should have been, acquiring Buck Williams and Danny Ainge, whom Jordan had tried to persuade management to chase. But they hadn't, and the Blazers had been to the Finals; no one seemed to care anymore that Portland had passed on Jordan in the 1984 draft. Now the Blazers were walloping the Bulls.

And Horace Grant was ready to wallop Stacey King. Grant was feeling pressure from King, although not because of his playing ability—the second-year power forward had come to training camp grotesquely overweight at almost 280 pounds. But King had been talking among friends about how he should be starting, and Grant believed it was management's plan to replace him in the starting lineup anyway. Earlier, Grant had been taken out of a game with the starters but not put back in, and when Grant asked why, Jackson said, "I want to run the fat kid's butt into shape." But Grant remained unconvinced that was the only reason.

King, meanwhile, also doubted team management. Despite coming to camp thirty pounds overweight and apparently having done little to improve his game after an indifferent rookie season, King felt he deserved to be starting. He was 7 for 19 so far on the West Coast trip, and would go 1 for 5 against Portland.

Grant had heard the rumors about King. His twin, Harvey, had told him when the Bulls drafted King that he wouldn't play hard and was lazy. And he had been right. Rookies often come in over-weight, as Miami's Glen Rice and San Antonio's Sean Elliott did in their rookie years, but a year of pounding and disappointment usually persuades them to get into shape by their second seasons. But not King. Yet King was blaming his problems on a lack of playing time, and had told Armstrong he was going to quit the Bulls after the 1990–91 season to play in Europe. Once again, King wasn't paying attention: He didn't know that he could not break his NBA contract to play in Europe.

Grant's friend Pippen had taken to snarling openly at King, letting loose some of Grant's irritation and some of his own. "How can that piece of shit be making more money than me?" he'd ask.

Like Grant, Paxson believed his time as a starter was coming to an end. His off-season ankle surgery didn't appear to have worked well and he was worried. He still had pain and soreness in the ankle and he wasn't moving well. Great contract I'll be able to command, he thought.

Cartwright, too, was frustrated. "We just don't seem to have any purpose," he said. He had come to a decision: He was going to leave Chicago after the season unless the Bulls' offer substantially topped that of any other team. He would be an unrestricted free agent, meaning he could sign with any team, and he always liked the idea of finishing his career in California. His wife had talked at times of returning there and his family and closest friends were there. He thought about Golden State and playing for Don Nelson, whom he admired and who had tried to get him to turn pro after his junior season when Nelson had a top choice in Milwaukee and promised to take him.

Cartwright had grown tired of Jordan's approach to the game. He was getting fewer shot opportunities than almost any of the starting centers in the league, despite the fact that Jackson constantly urged players during the games to "get the ball inside." He liked Jackson's offensive concept, but couldn't stand the way Jordan ig-nored it. So he thought perhaps the right opportunity might come along in the off-season and he'd get a chance at a title somewhere else. He thought the Bulls had the talent to make a run, but wasn't sure the tension between Jordan and his teammates regarding the offense would allow it.

Jordan rarely stopped griping about the offense. "If I had come up under Phil," Jordan said to friends, "I'd never have become the player I did. He'd have had me all screwed up and doubting what I could do with that system like these other rookies. And what's Tex Winter ever won, anyway?"

Jerry Krause almost couldn't speak when he heard what Jordan had said. Krause viewed Winter as something of a holy man and often promoted him for the Basketball Hall of Fame. Months later, when the Bulls would win the NBA title, Krause would run directly to Winter and yell, "You did it. You did it."

Winter was a student of the game's legendary scholars, Sam Barry at USC and Purdue's Piggy Lambert. This was before the NBA even existed, when college basketball was king of the sport, the era of two-hand set shooters and patterned play. Winter earned great success at Kansas State in the 1950s and national Coach of the Year honors, but did little on the pro level except for a brief stint as head coach of the San Diego/Houston Rockets. Krause had become something of a disciple of Winter's, treating him as a great basketball guru, and to many around the Bulls it seemed as if Winter had a Svengalilike hold over Krause. The kindly, grandfatherly Winter had befriended Krause some years before and would spend time with him whenever he was in town, lecturing him on the game and his precepts. Krause had sworn a lifetime oath: "Tex Winter will never be unemployed as long as I'm running a team." Winter was Krause's first hire when he replaced Rod Thorn as Bulls general manager in March 1985.

He is a character, but an endearing one, and a favorite of Jackson's; the head coach chides him for his idiosyncrasies as one does an eccentric but lovable uncle. He behaves as if he's still a poor Texas kid, often rushing into the media room before games to eat and shoveling in the food as if someone were about to take it away. He can also be found scouring around an arena for an abandoned newspaper. A friend remembers when Winter was coaching the Houston Rockets in the early 1970s, just after the team moved from San Diego. The Rockets were trying to persuade Jimmy Walker, the tough, streetwise New York playground great, that Houston was a great place to play. "Jimmy, you're gonna love it here," said Winter. "They've got the best cafeterias in the world."

Jordan's game clashed head-on with Winter's. It was Jordan's Testarossa, which could only seat one or two, against Winter's lumbering station wagon, which would accommodate everyone. Jordan liked to hold the ball, survey the defense, and make his move as defenders edged nearer to him. No one had ever seen anyone split defenses the way he did, twisting his way through two or three players and then popping up and *Boom!* slamming the ball through the basket. But he didn't always make room for his teammates, and Jackson was trying hard to change that, although he wasn't getting much help from the players; they were resigned to the fact that Jordan would never change.

A few days before their November 21 game in Phoenix, the players had moved lethargically through the drills, seemingly bored with the offense, which required movement based on who had the ball and where it was.

Suddenly, Winter slammed a ball against the wall and shouted, "It's not the offense; it's you guys. You're not working hard or playing hard. You're not trying to get it to work."

The players just sort of shrugged. They knew that their going with the system wouldn't matter much if Jordan didn't.

And he wasn't. He scored 34 points but attempted a whopping 32 shots as the Bulls lost at the buzzer on Thanksgiving Eve in Phoenix. Everyone saw turkeys, and not on the dinner table.

•

BEING A MEMBER of the Chicago Bulls meant many things: fame, usually; fortune, mostly; and never having to carve a Thanksgiving turkey. The NBA schedule is one of the most virulent in sports with its back-to-back games in different cities, its stretches of four games in five nights in four different places. Thoreau once mused that it wasn't worth going around the world to count the cats in Zanzibar. Traveling the United States to try the room service wasn't much better, yet that was the biggest part of an NBA player's life. In many ways, it was a dull routine. Other than the travel, which had improved dramatically with the charter flights, days on the road went like this: practice from 11:00 A.M. to 1:00 P.M., lunch, and then a nap—most NBA players had long worked naps into their routines as a means of being close to their best for their serious work, which came from 7:30 P.M. to 9:30 P.M. Many lifted weights in the afternoon to stay in condition, and the Bulls usually had one of their strength coaches, Al Vermeil or Erik Helland, on their road trips.

The Bulls were in Phoenix almost three full days before playing that Thanksgiving Eve game. That rare situation was because the Stadium was always leased to the circus the last part of November, so the NBA sent the Bulls on a long Western Conference road trip at that time. It's why the players were never home for Thanksgiving. For a few years, the team met for a meal together, but that custom was discontinued in 1988; the players preferred not to eat together anymore. Grateful Pilgrims they were not. The Bulls had become a disparate group. Jordan rarely socialized with any of the players, although it was hard for him to go out in any case because of his celebrity. He liked to have friends in for long card games or to sneak out to a golf course. In some cities, like Oakland, where he had friends like Higgins, he could try out a nightclub they'd know. Jordan just didn't socialize much with his teammates, and he even skipped mandatory events like the team's preseason promotional bowling night or the Christmas party, preferring to pay a fine instead. Grant and Pippen were close, but Grant had become a TV junkie and liked to stay in his room these days. When many of the players went out to celebrate later in the season after the win over the Pistons in the playoffs, Grant went home to watch the game again with his father-in-law. He always went straight to his room after games to watch the half-hour national sportscast, and he might have dinner with Pippen. Paxson was a loner, though he had friends from his NBA days and Notre Dame connections in many cities. Cartwright, too, was a loner. He enjoyed movies and would go out to one when he'd exhausted those in his room. He also had to bathe his knees in ice, which he did several hours each day. In Phoenix, he went to a movie each night and then a quiet dinner. Hodges often would try to find a mosque to visit and he, too, went to the movies, but he and Cartwright, though friendly, could rarely agree on films to see and usually went separately. Armstrong and Hopson had become friendly and started to spend time together, and occasionally might join King. Williams tended to stay by himself and walk the malls;

it was a favorite pastime of many of the players, and the team always tried to arrange for hotels within walking distance of shopping. Perdue and Helland had become close and they'd often take off somewhere for dinner after a workout, while Levingston, who liked the company of groups of people, drifted in and out of Jordan's circle, having developed contacts throughout the league.

Those few days in Phoenix were warm, so several of the players hung around the pool, which is a favorite location for Jackson and the coaches. They'd usually meet in the mornings, then run practice, watch films afterward, and then break up for dinner and perhaps a movie. It was a relaxing if unexciting few days, unusual only for the length of time the team went without playing a game. It wasn't what one might consider a holiday with first-class travel, but it wasn't with kids, either.

The only thing that could have improved things was a win; the Bulls lost to the Suns by 109–107 when Kevin Johnson scooted around like a water bug and hit a running shot at the buzzer. Jackson still thought it was a good game for the team, a close loss against a championship-quality team on the road. But Krause was apoplectic afterward outside the team locker room, complaining about an illegal-defense call. He was flapping his arms like a drowning man and convulsing with anger. He was raging at reporters to question the referees about the call and demanding that the assistant coach get league operations director Rod Thorn on the phone.

"Jerry," said Suns president Jerry Colangelo, "relax, you're going to have a heart attack."

Colangelo wasn't joking, as Krause's face had turned completely red.

"Hey, you didn't have a game stolen from you like we just had," Krause screamed at him. "Out of my way."

It would be the third time already this season that Krause had called the league to complain about an official's call.

Expectations were taking a heavy toll.

•

JACKSON TRIED TO lighten the mood as the Bulls flew into Los Angeles to play the Clippers. "If we don't win a road game," he warned, "Mr. Reinsdorf is going to take away our plane." While his tone may have been light, he could not have hit upon a more important improvement in the Bulls' life on the road than the team's charter aircraft.

Jackson himself had called the plane "our flying limousine." It was specially equipped with captain's chairs for lounging and sleeper compartments. It made for more rested players, especially on quick trips in which they would have had to catch the first flight out of town to get to a game the next night.

The presence of the plane was one of the more puzzling contradictions of a Bulls management that seemed so determined to nickel-and-dime players in other ways. While management was doubling or tripling travel costs to ensure the players' comfort, it was direct-depositing some paychecks a week or more after payday. On matters of money owed, like retroactive per diem money, the Bulls were one of the slowest teams in the league to make payments. These practices irritated the players, and there seemed to be little reason for them.

There would be more than a game going on in Los Angeles. There were rumors flying that the Clippers were going to make a deal for Isiah Thomas. The rumors turned out to be false, but one thing was true: The Clippers' owner, Don Sterling, desperately sought a headline star to compete with the crosstown Lakers' Magic Johnson. One he'd tried to acquire was wearing Bulls jersey number 23.

Sterling had called Reinsdorf during the 1987–88 season. The Bulls were about to be eliminated by the Pistons four games to one after losing nine of ten playoff games the previous three seasons with Jordan. It was already a popular theory that the Bulls would never win a title because Jordan's style of one-on-one play eliminated the other players as contributors. But the fans loved it, and to Reinsdorf, that meant money. Reinsdorf believed he could never trade Jordan: As unpopular as he already was because of his threats to move the White Sox out of Chicago, he knew such a trade would force him right out of town. Still, there was the looming prospect of moving the White Sox to Florida, so maybe he'd have to move anyway. Collins had always told him the Bulls couldn't win with Jordan, and Reinsdorf had always told friends he knew only two things about basketball: "You win with defense and team play." He could have one, he knew, but perhaps not the other as long as Jordan dominated the scoring.

Sterling offered any combination of five players or draft choices. The Clippers didn't have many players the Bulls desired, but they had two of the first six picks in the upcoming draft, and Krause loved 7-4 Rik Smits, a top prospect that year. And with another high pick, the Bulls could select Kansas State guard Mitch Richmond, whom Jordan later would compare favorably with himself. That would give the Bulls Smits and Oakley, Scottie Pippen and Horace Grant, and still allow them to select a point guard, perhaps De Paul's Rod Strickland, or trade for a point guard now that they had depth and draft choices. Krause had always wanted Kevin Johnson, and he thought he might get Johnson (then with Cleveland) for Oakley or Grant, leaving the Bulls a starting five of Johnson, Richmond, Pippen, Grant or Oakley, and Smits.

The Bulls thought about it long and hard; they were almost sure the deal could get them to a title faster than staying with Jordan. But in the end, Reinsdorf held firm: Michael Jordan was untradable. Period.

The Bulls beat the Clippers easily with perhaps their best effort of the season. Paxson hit for 26 and Pippen scored a triple double. Six players were in double figures, including Jordan with 14 points on 12 shots. Jackson was feeling pretty good. Perhaps it was finally working. Perhaps Jordan was going to go along. Several players said it was the best game the team had played in years.

But the next night, before the Bulls played the Denver Nuggets in the final game of the trip, Jackson noted something unusual. Jordan was on the floor long before the game, shooting. Jordan *never* engaged in pregame shooting drills. He liked to relax before the game, sorting out tickets for friends, chatting with out-of-town reporters. But since the other players were required to shoot before games, the Bulls offered a flimsy excuse, saying that the crowds around Jordan would be too disruptive. That didn't fool the other players, for they knew fans weren't even allowed in the arena during pregame shooting drills. And it wasn't long before Pippen, whom assistant coach Winter called "the imitator," had taken to skipping pregame shooting drills too.

But because he didn't shoot before the games, Jordan never felt comfortable shooting when games opened, so he usually surveyed the defense, examining where the double-team was coming from and how the overall defense was reacting, and passed the ball at the start, which is what Jackson wanted anyhow.

As he watched Jordan warming up on the court, Jackson thought about the predictions that Jordan would perhaps score 100 points against the Nuggets' new style, which employed little defense and was creating talk of 200-point games. Jordan knew Jackson would never allow it to happen; Jackson was almost insulted by the thought. "That's not basketball," he'd say.

Jordan had 18 by halftime on the way to 38 points, and the Bulls won, 151–145.

But when the team returned home, Jackson noticed that Jordan had continued his pregame shooting routine. Suddenly he was taking shots early in the game as never before, scoring 15 in the first quarter of an easy win over the Bullets, then 20 in the first quarter in another easy win over the Pacers to end November. Jordan would score 13 in the first quarter the next night in Cleveland, then 15 and 16 in the first quarter the next week in games against the Knicks and Trail Blazers. Jordan was averaging more points in the first quarter than anyone else on the team was averaging the entire game. Jackson thought he'd come up with the rules the team needed to go all the way; Jordan was rewriting the rules.

His rebellion was becoming clear to his teammates and coaches. Jordan realized he wasn't going to get as many minutes as before, and in the current offense he was not going to get as many opportunities. He was desperately unhappy, and completely at odds with the rest of the team. Several players felt Jordan cared only about winning the scoring title, while Jordan believed he was uniquely responsible for the team's success: If he didn't do it, who would? It remained the Bulls' classic chicken-and-egg problem.

"I can't go out and win games at the end if I'm not in the flow," Jordan had told assistant coach Bach in explaining his opening offensive assaults. "I can't just take twelve shots a game and then hit the winning shot."

Bach, usually a loyal soldier to Jackson, had somehow come between the coach and the player, encouraging Jordan to be aggressive with his shots early in games, which was contrary to Jackson's game plan. This was fine with Jordan, who called Bach his personal coach. "When I'm having trouble, I go to coach Bach and ask him if he has any suggestions," Jordan once said.

Jordan, meanwhile, told reporters it was a new team strategy to come out more aggressively, although he did belie his motives in accompanying statements.

"I always could count on playing forty minutes before, but I can't anymore," he explained. "So in the past I could start out slow and then come on strong, but now I'm not out there as much. I found my minutes and opportunities going down, so I decided I needed to get more production out of the minutes I was playing."

Jackson had long studied philosophy and he knew you get the chicken by hatching the egg, not smashing it. So when he was asked about Jordan's theory, Jackson offered a narrow smile. "I find as I get older I become more patient," he said.

5

DECEMBER 1990

12/1 at Cleveland; 12/4 v. Phoenix; 12/7 v. New York; 12/8 v. Portland; 12/11 at Milwaukee; 12/14 v. L.A. Clippers; 12/15 v. Cleveland; 12/18 v. Miami; 12/19 at Detroit; 12/21 v. L.A. Lakers; 12/22 v. Indiana; 12/25 v. Detroit; 12/27 v. Golden State; 12/29 v. Seattle

THE BULLS WERE heading into the calmest part of their schedule. December would bring only three road games out of fourteen, and the first one was against the Cavaliers, who were about to learn that night that their star guard, Mark Price, would be out for the season. The Cavaliers were forced to start guards John Morton, the worst shooter in the league the previous season, and Gerald Paddio, a free agent from the CBA who had failed with several teams.

The game was a quick rout, with the Bulls bolting away by 17 in the first quarter and leading by 30 before the third period was half over. Fewer and fewer NBA games were being decided in the last two minutes since expansion hit; the dilution of talent had weakened many teams and created so many have-nots that a team with talent, like the Bulls, would have an easy time many nights.

Jordan was enjoying himself on the ride home after the game, joking about the Cavaliers, against whom he'd enjoyed so much success. Stretching out a stat sheet, Jordan, with 32 points in thirty minutes, had some lighthearted instruction for the younger players: "That's the kind of game where you get your points and get out of there," he told Armstrong.

Horace Grant shook his head.

He and Jordan had become antagonists a few years back when he became the first Bulls player ever to challenge Jordan, although not publicly. It was on a plane ride home from a playoff loss against Detroit, and tensions were high. Jordan had scored 18 points and wasn't too happy about it, and he had taken a beating. Grant, the Bulls' power forward, had just 1 rebound, and had supplied little protection for Jordan. Jordan enjoyed taunting Grant, whom he felt was not very bright, but Grant, who could be as sensitive as an open wound, finally tired of the kidding.

"Screw you, M.J.," Grant shot back. "All you care about is your points and everyone knows it. You don't care about anything but yourself."

"You're an idiot," Jordan screamed at Grant. "You've screwed up every play we ever ran. You're too stupid to even remember the plays. We ought to get rid of you."

The rest of the players sat stunned as the verbal assaults continued back and forth, Jordan being derisive and Grant warily fending off the arrows, until the two were finally separated. And after the season, Jordan tried to get management to trade Grant for Buck Williams.

But Grant had bigger concerns than Jordan as the season headed into its second month. In the rout against Cleveland he played just twenty minutes, far fewer than any of the other starters, and he was taking it as an ominous sign. His playing time, PT in the players' vernacular, was diminishing, and he saw the team trying to move King in as a starter to justify the high pick in the draft. Jackson had outlined an expanded role for Grant when he became head coach because of Grant's speed; he's the fastest runner on the team, and Jackson envisioned getting Grant open downcourt ahead of the opposing power forward for easy baskets. But Grant was also the Bulls' best rebounder, so he had to stay back to rebound. Meanwhile, he was invariably assigned to guard the best offensive forward, making it difficult for him to break quickly downcourt. And even when he could, it really didn't matter, given Jordan's demands for the ball and his feelings about Grant.

"I have a dream," Grant would sing one day later in the season on the team bus after a few players had gone to the Martin Luther King, Jr., Center in Atlanta. "I'm going to get the ball."

But it didn't stop him from trying. Grant had become perhaps the hardest-working player on the team, spending every day in the off-season working out with strength coach Al Vermeil, brother of former Philadelphia Eagles coach Dick Vermeil. Grant could now lift weights with the strength of a football defensive lineman. When Grant came to the Bulls as the tenth pick in the 1987 draft, he was known in coaches' talk as a three and a half: He had the height of a big forward (a four), but without the power and strength to play the position, and he wasn't deft enough offensively to handle the scoring at the small-forward position (a three). But eventually Grant would build up to nearly 230 muscular pounds from less than 210, his rookie weight.

The adjustment to the NBA had been hard for Grant. He was from a rural Georgia town and had been raised by a single parent. When he was young, his ambition was to be a marine. "I'd watch the commercials on TV about how they wanted a few good men and I was fascinated by the nice suits and the swords and everything," Grant recalled. He was not a good student, but he started to develop as a basketball player, earning himself and twin brother, Harvey, scholarships at Clemson. "We were a package deal," Horace remembered. But Horace always was a little ahead of Harvey, and when Harvey didn't make the varsity team as a freshman he started missing class and eventually transferred to Oklahoma, where he was a teammate of Stacey King's.

Harvey would eventually come to add to Horace's frustration, although unintentionally. Every year they played together, Horace was dominant—in high school, in college, and even in the NBA during Harvey's first two seasons with the Washington Bullets. Horace always averaged more points and was the bigger star. And the joke between the twins was that Horace flaunted it. "He's nine seconds older," Harvey once explained, "so he thinks he can boss me around." But with the lack of talent in Washington, Harvey became a featured player—he averaged nearly 20 points per game and was touted as the league's most improved player in 1990–91.

"I'd just once like to get that many shots," Horace would say, "just to see what would happen." Horace averaged about 8 shots per game for the Bulls, about a third of Jordan's total, while Harvey was getting 16 to 18 per game in Washington. "I know I'll never get the chance to find out what kind of player I can be here," said Grant.

And it was getting to him. He'd brought his scoring average up to 13.4 in 1989–90 and his rebounding to about 8 per game, including a fierce playoff run against Detroit in which he had six straight games with 10 or more rebounds. But he also wanted to share in the offense. He felt he worked so hard that he deserved a chance. Instead, Bach prepared him an edited tape of Buck Williams's play. Williams was not a big scorer, but a hard worker who did the dirty work inside. The message was clear to Grant: You rebound and play defense and let others run the show.

Grant had thought everything would be okay when he signed a three-year contract extension at $2 million per year after the 1989–90 season. During the 1989–90 season, he was among the lowest-paid Bulls because he was still bound by his rookie contract, which he had signed when he was a backup to Oakley. But when he became a starter, he began to believe he was underpaid, and his frustration led to a late-season demand to be traded.

Grant is perhaps the least egomaniacal of the Bulls' players and certainly the most popular. These were traits Jackson would use later in the season, for he knew the players always would rally around Grant.

Grant offered fans little of the fake celebrity of sport and much of the earnest reward. He truly stood for what the Wheaties box suggested: hard work, loyalty, trust, support, and modesty. He has remarkably soft features, with honest brown eyes and an open smile. He's the most likely to say what he feels and react to what he hears or sees. That was especially true as the 1990–91 season unfolded.

When Grant came to the Bulls he was something of a wild colt. The team had to hire a cook for him during his rookie season to get him to add weight, for he was eating most of his meals at fast-food restaurants. But it was the late-night menu that frustrated the team the most. He was what's called "a runner" in the NBA, a player who hits the night spots regularly in every city. The Bulls grew anxious about Grant's habits and eventually would trade Sedale Threatt because they believed he was poisoning both Grant and Scottie Pippen with his late-night adventures.

Grant and Pippen had a bond that appeared unbreakable. They met at the NBA draft in New York in 1987, and when both were selected by the Bulls they became friends, if only for protection. Rookies still endure hazing in the NBA, even though Bulls coach Phil Jackson curtailed the practice when he replaced Doug Collins. Rookies no longer had to carry other players' bags, but the veterans still played pranks on the rookies, and Grant and Pippen closed ranks after the veterans charged almost $1000 in food and gifts to their rooms one night.

The two became like Castor and Pollux, the twin heroes in Greek and Roman religion; they were giants in battle on the court, and patrons of adventure afterward.

They'd call one another up to a dozen times a day, even on game days. They purchased identical Mercedes SELs, Grant's white and Pippen's black. They drove the same demonstration cars for the same local sponsor. They lived within a few hundred yards of one another in the same North Shore neighborhood of Chicago. They were married within weeks of each other and were each other's best man. They both have sons (this was not planned). They bought the same breed of dog. They share the same agent and they vacation together in the summer. They went out together at every road stop, and in the Bulls' yearbook, when Pippen was asked, "Who would you take with you if you were going to the moon?" he responded: "Horace Grant."

But Grant was undergoing some personal changes, and while the pair remained good friends, they drifted apart somewhat. Pippen got divorced and Grant began to fear he was next. "My wife and I were having a lot of problems," he admitted. "And a lot was my fault. I wasn't treating people right, especially my wife."

So with her help, Grant began a conversion to Christianity.

"I was sliding spiritually," said Grant, who would become a regular at pregame chapel services, which are available to all NBA players before games. "I knew I had to do something, so I personally gave myself to the Lord. I realized He gave me so much, but I wasn't really giving back to Him all that I should. He gave me this talent to play professional basketball. He could have given it to so many others, but He gave it to me. I was abusing this talent and my body and that was not what He gave it to me for. The reason was to praise His name and be a positive role model for young people.''

For Grant that meant staying home. He quit the local nightclub scene populated by several of his teammates and began staying in his room on the road and reading the Bible. Pippen's agenda was somewhat different, so they began to spend less time together. And Grant also began to look at his friend more critically. One question in particular kept arising in Grant's mind: ''Why was Scottie trying to be so much like Michael?'' he wondered.

Pippen had become closer to Jordan, moving into his private berth on the team plane along with Cliff Levingston, who'd attached himself to Jordan like a fly to glue as soon as he joined the Bulls. But Pippen also had his contract on his mind, and after his near holdout he had decided he needed to produce statistics, for that's what the Bulls would measure him by. ''They talk about winning,'' said Pippen, ''but if I don't score more, they won't pay me. I've got to go for statistics this year.''

Pippen would begin to imitate Jordan's play, as Winter had noticed, thus removing opportunities for others and setting up a developing conflict with Jordan over just who should be taking the shots.

''This team has got to move the ball,'' Grant told reporters in Cleveland without mentioning any names, although the message was clear to his teammates. ''We'll have a lot to learn from championship teams like Boston, the Lakers, and Detroit until we do that.''

•

THE BULLS ROMPED through an easy 155–127 win over the Suns on December 4. It was their sixth straight win, all by wide margins, and it left Suns coach Cotton Fitzsimmons to remark, ''At least it took them longer to blow us out than their last few opponents.''

The starters sat out most of the fourth quarter, leaving the action to reserves like Craig Hodges, Will Perdue, Scott Williams, and Cliff Levingston. But Jordan's tongue was a little too sharp after the game. He had played part of the fourth quarter with Dennis Hopson, Stacey King, and B. J. Armstrong, and he complained to

Pippen, "I hate being out there with those garbagemen. They don't get you the ball."

Hodges overheard the exchange. Though not a great overall talent, he took pride in his role.

"Hey, I ain't no garbage player," he told Jordan. "I was playing in this league when you were still trying to figure out how to put your pants on."

"Hey, I wasn't talking about you, Hodg," Jordan interrupted, quick to extinguish Hodges's fire.

The tension broke, but it remained close to the surface despite the winning streak.

The Knicks were next, and this suggested another easy win. The Bulls matched up well with the Knicks. They'd knocked them out of the 1989 playoffs when the Knicks were at their best, and now the Knicks were faltering in a halfcourt game with players developed for former coach Rick Pitino's pressing style. They had little depth, the first two players off the bench this night being rookie Jerrod Mustaf and Brian Quinnett. And it was against Mustaf that Jordan would electrify the Stadium crowd again en route to a 108–98 Bulls victory.

Gerald Wilkins posted Jordan up for a jump shot, which usually infuriates Jordan. He hates to be isolated for a score and almost always comes back to go one-on-one with the player who does this to him. This annoys the coaches, because it means Jordan is going to ignore the offense, but they let it go because he usually scores. It's most aggravating to his teammates.

"The difference," says B. J. Armstrong, "is that in our offense, if your man goes at you, you can't go back at him—you have to run the offense. But Michael doesn't. Sure, he's better than everyone else, but you just hate to watch him get to do that without anything being said, and then if you try, watch out."

Jordan started dribbling near the three-point circle to the right of the free-throw line. He went through his legs once, twice, three times and back again, Wilkins trying to watch not the ball but Jordan's eyes. Quickly, Jordan moved the ball to his left hand and flashed by Wilkins. It's one of the moves that makes Jordan unstoppable. "He can get through cracks in the defense that other players don't even see," marvels John Bach. And with his explosive quickness off the dribble, few players can move their feet quickly enough to get in front of Jordan.

In his way was Mustaf, the athletic six-foot-ten-inch rookie. Mustaf jumped. Jordan jumped over him and slammed the ball, sending the Stadium fans into a frenzy.

On the bench, coach Phil Jackson smiled.

It's difficult to read Jackson sometimes. He has an impish sense of humor and can be found sometimes drawing hangman's nooses in his office before games while he watches "The McLaughlin Group" or "The MacNeil/Lehrer Newshour." He knows there's no play in his scheme that calls for Jordan to dribble for ten seconds and then fly down the lane against four players and slam. But it was hard not to appreciate the spectacular athletic move, and as a former player he had some understanding of the imperative of payback.

Jackson has a great fondness for the Knicks—by which he means the old Knicks, the team he was part of. He owns perhaps the only reversible leather coat in the world with a Bulls logo on one side and a Knicks emblem on the other. His days with the Knicks represent a kind of basketball nirvana for him: the unselfish play, the bonding among the guys. Jackson even had a chance to return to the Knicks as an assistant coach when Rick Pitino was hired; he was still stuck in the CBA when Pitino offered him a spot, but he was too wary of the Knicks' corporate ownership to sign on. He had clashed with management after Gulf + Western bought the Knicks and the personnel moves became more and more capricious. "These guys didn't know anything about basketball, about men coming together and bonding their talents," he said. "They'd say, 'Let's go get us Spencer Haywood. Uh-oh, he's not working. So we'll get ourselves a Bob McAdoo.' We had built a team with Frazier and Reed and [Mike] Riordan and Jackson, basically unheralded basketball players. And from this unlikely group of players, second-round draft picks, you have a team. You don't build a team by going out and getting stars."

Jackson may have avoided corporate pressure, but the Bulls management had its own quirks. His name was Jerry Krause.

Jackson has dealt with Krause's paranoia far better than any of the recent Bulls coaches. He's sometimes had to leave his office to take phone calls at a public phone because Krause was concerned someone might overhear the conversation. He's registered under false names at a Chicago hotel during the draft so only Krause could find him. He's listened to Krause threaten to fire anyone on the staff who talked to reporters after supposed "inside" information appeared in newspapers, including one memorable occasion when the leak was something Krause himself had inadvertently let slip.

"Jerry Krause sees the NBA as a covert operation," says one general manager. One of the team's minority owners adds, "He goes into a closet to change his mind."

So, despite having to handle the most dominant offensive force since Wilt Chamberlain, while working for the NBA's version of Professor Moriarty, Jackson's generally thrilled to have the job. "I'm having a great time," he'd tell friends. "This is fun."

And Jackson felt no different the next night, even though the Bulls lost for the first time at home in eighteen games through the regular season and playoffs, a 109–101 loss to Portland, as the Trail Blazers continued the hot streak that had put them out ahead of the league. It didn't help that the Bulls' bench faltered; Hopson scored just 1 basket while the Trail Blazers turned a 3-point lead into a 12-point margin in the second quarter when the reserves were playing. The Bulls led by a point late in the fourth quarter, but a weary Jordan, who put up 28 shots, committed a turnover and drove wildly into three Trail Blazers, his shot missing the mark. Clyde Drexler then beat Jordan downcourt for an easy basket from which the Bulls could not recover.

Jackson was diplomatic. It was a test, he said, and now the Bulls had an idea how much farther they had to go to play with the league's best. Danny Ainge's words were more direct: "We're just a balanced team. Every night someone different steps up to carry us. We had more weapons."

The next loss, against Milwaukee, would be harder. The Bulls had dominated the Bucks the last three years, eliminating them from the playoffs in 1990 and winning fifteen of the last seventeen games between them in the regular season. It drove Bucks coach Del Harris nuts. He almost always drew technical fouls in Bulls games, and although he tried to remain calm and diminish the game's importance in the pregame meetings, his neck would stiffen and his words became more clipped when he discussed the Bulls. Jackson did the same thing when the Bulls prepared for Detroit; he went over every play Detroit ran in detail and so often that the players felt they knew the plays too well and were thinking about what Detroit might do rather than reacting to what they actually did. The Bulls were to Milwaukee what the Pistons were to the Bulls.

But Milwaukee was healthy for the first time in several years and had won ten straight at home. And with Frank Brickowski rebounding and giving the Bucks second chances, Milwaukee held off the Bulls, 99–87. Jordan scored 31 points, but he was out for key stretches and, despite playing thirty-nine minutes, he was angry with Jackson for keeping him off the floor. During games, Jordan rarely wants to rest, and it takes all of Jackson's restraint to keep him off the floor; Jordan shouts out the names of players he wants to go in for. Jackson was certain that Jordan would wear down by the end of the playoffs as a result of the load he carried all season long, so Jackson had cut Jordan's playing time to thirty-six or thirty-seven minutes per game.

Some of Jordan's irritation flared after the game. A factor in the loss, Jackson told reporters, was the fact that the floor was slippery. When Jordan was asked about it, he denied it was any problem, and when someone started to ask B. J. Armstrong about it Jordan shouted across the locker room, "Don't make any excuses."

"I hate when P.J. does that," Jordan said afterward. "We stink. That's the problem."

Part of the problem, Jordan thought, was the Tex Winter–inspired offense. During the game, Winter had said pleadingly to Jackson, as both Jordan and Pippen went on mad dashes to the basket, "They're sabotaging the offense. They've got to pass the ball."

Cartwright, an increasingly strong presence on and off the court, had his own views on the subject. He believed in Winter's offense; Jackson was trying to get Cartwright the ball in a position where he could do something with it. But every Cartwright mistake was seized upon by Jordan. On this night, Cartwright took a pass down by the baseline in the third quarter and spun to the basket, but was called for traveling. The Bulls called time-out soon after, and as they walked back to the huddle, Jordan was furious with Cartwright.

"You've got to give me the ball," Jordan demanded.

"But M.J., you had two guys on you," snapped Cartwright.

"Yeah, but one was Fred Roberts," Jordan shot back.

Jordan and Cartwright had crossed swords before, although by this season, Cartwright's third with the Bulls, an uneasy truce had

developed. Jordan could even joke about Cartwright's flailing elbows, of which he'd been a victim in practice. Overhearing Cartwright talking about playing golf, Jordan once asked him if he'd
ever elbowed any of the players in his foursome.

Cartwright could laugh about such remarks now, but when he
first came to the Bulls, he didn't anticipate the problems that would
develop between him and Jordan, even though he quickly recognized
their differences. While Jordan is demonstrative, Cartwright is remote. Jordan is congenial, Cartwright is seclusive. Cartwright wears
a goatee stained with a splash of white and has a mysterious look
about him: sad, with gentle doe eyes and a tiny head that often is
enveloped in his large hands when he's working out a problem. One
such problem was how to deal with Jordan.

Cartwright was a star of some magnitude, the nation's leading
rebounder in his senior year at the University of San Francisco and
the No. 3 pick in the NBA draft, just like Jordan, only five years
earlier. He averaged 21.7 points and 8.9 rebounds and made the
All-Star team as a rookie and added 20.1 points and 7.5 rebounds
his second season. But it was his misfortune to join the NBA the
same season as Magic Johnson and Larry Bird, and greatness would
elude the seven-foot-one-inch Cartwright as if it were thick smoke:
He could see it, almost smell it, but he couldn't quite grab it. There
were no Olympics for Cartwright, no team promotional campaign
like the one the Bulls ran in Chicago for Jordan: "Here Comes Mr.
Jordan," the ads went, a takeoff on the classic 1941 film. New York
didn't exactly react that way for Cartwright, who has been described
as having the grace of a berserk crane. Centers are the rarest of
birds in the NBA, though, and Cartwright was one, even if he
reminded few of an athlete. Cartwright didn't even remind himself
of an athlete. Sometimes he'd find himself marveling at Jordan or
Scottie Pippen flying toward the basket for a slam and say to himself,
"Wouldn't it be something to be able to do that, to be an athlete?"
Cartwright, as the man said in the Dirty Harry movie, knew his
limitations. He also knew that his time would be short in New York
when Rick Pitino replaced Hubie Brown as coach.

"Rick wasn't looking for basketball players," said Cartwright after
leaving New York. "If you happened to be a basketball player, fine,
but Rick wanted guys who can run and jump, athletes."

Cartwright knew he didn't fit into that category. But don't tell him he's not a basketball player. There is no forge of athleticism in his movements, but rather the determined precision of a craftsman. Cartwright knows the game. He studied hard under Hubie Brown those years in New York when his Knick teams got close to being great, once taking the Celtics to a seventh game in the Eastern Conference semifinals. But Cartwright always had his critics. He rarely dunks the ball or blocks shots or dominates on rebounds. He's got an unorthodox jump shot in which he grabs the ball as if he's holding an axe, goes into a downward chopping motion, brings the ball up behind his ear while twisting away from the basket, and then squares up and leans in. It was good enough to make him among the league's best percentage shooters his first five seasons, when he averaged about 18 points per game. But he twice broke his foot, missed almost all of two seasons, and became a scapegoat for the Knicks' problems after being replaced by the superior Patrick Ewing. But he never lost his wry wit or keen sense of observation. He's a student of politics and government, a self-made philosopher whose father was a farm laborer and whose mother was a domestic, yet someone who espouses archconservative views. Not only does Cartwright favor capital punishment, for example, but he advocates public executions.

"Sure, it would be great for everyone," he says with just a hint of a smile so you're not exactly sure he's serious. But he is. "You'd have to have them on late after the kids went to sleep, maybe midnight. And you could show them on cable TV and make enough money to hire more police. It would be a great deterrent. Sure, it would be great. It would work."

And while Cartwright liked to play the remote tough guy, he was as softhearted as they came. Cartwright's home would often seem like a halfway house, with down-and-out friends staying for months at a time without a demand from Cartwright that they get a job.

But Cartwright didn't get much playing time in New York after returning from those foot injuries. Patrick Ewing had come along by then, and Brown tried a twin-towers approach with Cartwright and Ewing. That approach had come into vogue when Houston, with Akeem Olajuwon and Ralph Sampson, upset the Lakers in five games in the 1986 Western Conference finals; suddenly everyone wanted two centers. But Ewing didn't care to play forward, and when Brown was replaced, Cartwright took a seat on the bench behind Ewing. He didn't like it, but he started to get used to the idea.

"It was like being retired," Cartwright recalled. "I'd get eighteen, maybe twenty minutes against the backup center. It was hardly like playing." Cartwright did average 11 points and shot 54 percent in about twenty minutes per game that last season in New York (1987–88), but by then life had become particularly uncomfortable, although more for Cartwright's family than for him. He's a stoic man, quiet, almost impervious to criticism. "I know what I can do and the people I care most about know what I can do, so who cares what anyone else thinks?" he'd say.

His strength was tested often. New Yorkers railed at Cartwright for his fragility. Acerbic *New York Post* columnist Pete Vecsey nicknamed Cartwright "Medical Bill" and "Billy Idle" for his injuries and time spent on the disabled list. It didn't help that Cartwright's injuries came right after he signed a new contract. He was further tested by the health problems of his son, Justin, who had developed a rare heart condition and needed surgery to save his life. It would be successful and he would go on to have a normal childhood, but there were many terrifying moments for Cartwright then, none of which the public or media ever knew about.

One story, though, typifies that period for Cartwright. He was at the hospital waiting out the vigil of Justin's surgery. It was just after his own foot surgery and he was walking with crutches. He was standing outside the operating room with his wife, Sheri, when one crutch hit a wet spot and slipped out from under him. His gangly body collapsed under him and he went sprawling, one of the crutches catching Sheri, who collapsed on top of him. The two of them lay there struggling to get up while their son lay fighting for his life.

"This is typical of my life," Cartwright said to Sheri as she tried to help him up. "I've got to do everything the hard way."

Week after week there'd be another trade rumor once Cartwright recovered. Cartwright never complained, but he did tell a friend after being traded to the Bulls in 1988, "It's going to be interesting if New York doesn't win this year. It always seemed like if they could get somebody for me, they'd win. So who are they going to blame it on now?"

Rick Pitino? Al Bianchi? Ewing? Mark Jackson? Gulf + Western, which owned the Knicks? John Lindsay? Ed Koch? Take your choice.

The night Cartwright was traded to the Bulls for Charles Oakley, Michael Jordan was at the Mike Tyson–Michael Spinks fight in Atlantic City. Reporters started coming up to him: What do you think of the trade?

"What trade?" asked Jordan. When he was told, Jordan was stunned. He had adopted Oakley, the big, strong kid from Division II Virginia Union University, as sort of a little brother, albeit a little brother with broad shoulders and massive arms that gave Jordan a sense of security he felt with few other players. Oakley had become his bodyguard. In those days Jordan was making his points principally by hurtling toward the basket; the understanding around the league was, knock him down and you were going to get a shot sooner or later from Oakley. It gave an opponent pause. Jordan took Oakley under his powerful wing, brought him to the All-Star game as his guest in Oakley's first season, and began riding to home games with him. Oakley would occasionally complain about a lack of shots, which many viewed as jealousy of Jordan, although that wasn't totally the case; Oakley wanted to be an All-Star himself, and he knew in the NBA that meant scoring. He was frustrated by being left out of the offense. But even as he remained close to Jordan, Oakley realized what management was doing to the team, with its promotional campaigns for Jordan and the succession of coaches who relied completely on the game's greatest individual player. "You can't expect the rest of us to score all of a sudden when they shut down Michael and we haven't had shots all season," Oakley would tell Doug Collins. Oakley also didn't keep his feelings from the media, and when he was traded, several players felt the message was clear: Speak out about Jordan, even obliquely, and you were gone.

Still, Oakley's outbursts never affected his relationship with Jordan, for Jordan probably needed Oakley more than Oakley needed Jordan. The two often talked by telephone after the trade, and it was Jordan whom Oakley called the next season when he thought he had a chance to make the All-Star team and didn't.

And traded for whom? Jordan thought. Bill Cartwright? Jordan never cared much for Cartwright's play and wondered immediately who would be his policeman now. Not the bumbling Cartwright, or the then-210-pound Grant, who would take Oakley's place in the starting lineup. "I don't know about trading a twenty-four-year-old guy for a thirty-four-year-old guy [Cartwright was actually thirty-one then]," Jordan said at the time.

The big question was Cartwright's knee. "It was always 'I'm okay' when I asked him how he was," said Phil Jackson. "He'd always say he was ready to go. You couldn't even get him out of practice. He'd say he needed to keep in condition for the game." But by playoff time of 1990, Cartwright's knee was so wretched he couldn't sit in a car for more than a few minutes with his knee bent. On the team bus to games, he'd have to lie flat in his seat. But he never talked to anyone about it or complained. He just went out and played, often poorly because of his limited mobility, but even in that condition he was so much better than the team's backup centers, Will Perdue and Stacey King, that he had to be out there.

Meanwhile, Jordan, as if to emphasize Cartwright's clumsiness, began to lay out banana peels for Cartwright to slip on. He'd already proclaimed before the season that he would have to concentrate more on rebounding with Oakley gone. Knowing Cartwright was not a reflexively sharp athlete, he'd dart into the lane and shoot Cartwright a no-look pass. Invariably, it would bounce off Cartwright's hands and go out of bounds. "He's causing me too many turnovers," Jordan would tell reporters, always making sure Cartwright could hear. And Jordan would shake his head and look toward Collins disgustedly after a Cartwright mistake, stretching his arms out with his palms upward, as if saying, "What more can I do?"

Cartwright refused to break. He might never truly earn the fans' respect, but he did come to gain the respect of the players. Around the Bulls, they began to call Cartwright "Teach," as in teacher. In recognition of this, Jackson named Cartwright cocaptain (with Jordan) when the team returned home from its western swing this year.

"The coaches would always say that if you want to know how to get things done, you watch Bill Cartwright," said Jackson. "He's a skilled, veteran player in a clumsy body, but with good skills. He's got the best footwork on the team. We'd tell them to watch how he moves, how he gets position, how he moves his feet, his recognition of the offense. Everyone calls him 'Teach.' I don't think I've ever heard Michael call him that, though."

Not likely. Jordan didn't feel Cartwright could score a basket in an empty gym.

Cartwright didn't actually much care what Jordan thought. Winning was all he thought about. He was no different if he scored 30 points or 3: He believed in working hard, keeping your mouth shut, and doing what you could for your team. He couldn't understand why Jordan's fits of pique were always excused in the media as merely a competitor's desire to win. Did it mean the rest of them weren't trying as hard to win, didn't want to win as much, or perhaps didn't deserve to win because they weren't as talented?

Jordan liked to belittle Cartwright in the locker room. He'd imitate Cartwright's unorthodox shooting style with wild exaggerated moves that left many of his teammates trying to contain laughter when Cartwright was nearby. Cartwright would just look away and blame immaturity.

But Jordan went one step too far in the 1988–89 season. He was angry over the Bulls' slow start and had already gone to Krause during the western trip in November to ask that he make some trades. "I need help," he told Krause. Krause explained the Bulls had salary-cap problems, which Jordan neither understood nor cared to hear about. So Jordan made some decisions. One was that he would have to do just that much more himself. And to do that, he couldn't have Cartwright fouling things up, especially late in the game.

So he told Grant, Vincent, and Pippen—three players who were usually on the floor at the end of games with him—that they were not to pass Cartwright the ball in the last four minutes of a game. "If you do that," Jordan said, "you'll never get the ball from me." And suddenly, plays called by Collins were being ignored as Jordan took the ball to the basket. But who could really complain, since the Bulls had started to win? Eventually, though, word got back to Cartwright. He didn't do or say anything to anybody until late that season, when he told Jordan he needed to talk to him.

There was little small talk exchanged. "I don't like the things I've heard you saying about me," Cartwright told Jordan.

Jordan stared at him.

"If I ever hear again that you're telling guys not to pass me the ball," Cartwright continued, "you will never play basketball again."

That was it. But as Cartwright began to move better after surgery following the 1989–90 season, Jordan began to accept him more. He realized that neither Will Perdue nor Stacey King could adequately play center for the Bulls, and perhaps Cartwright could do some things to help the team. He didn't block shots or rebound that well, Jordan thought, but he appeared to be able to score. And opposing centers, whether they feared his mad elbows or not, seemed not to exert themselves that much against Cartwright.

Jackson had offered Jordan a piece of advice, for as much as Jackson liked Cartwright, he realized one problem was that Jordan was too quick and too good an athlete to play easily with Cartwright. "When you pass him the ball," Jackson told Jordan, "throw it at his nose. He'll catch it then. You've got to try to hit him in the face or he's not going to get it."

"I think Michael can accept the job Bill does out there," Jackson said in naming Cartwright cocaptain.

And Jordan did make a peace offering: He no longer throws Cartwright passes he doesn't believe Cartwright can handle. He does throw them at his nose when he can think of it. But Jackson also knows he must tread carefully with the two, and as a rule he never places Jordan on a team against Cartwright in a scrimmage.

"Phil knows I'll take him down if I have to," Cartwright says.

•

THE BULLS STARTED a new winning streak after the losses to Portland and Milwaukee, but no one was fooled. They beat the Clippers, who were playing without Benoit Benjamin and Charles Smith, by 40. They beat Cleveland by 18 after taking a 36–5 first-quarter lead in an astonishing display of ineptitude by the Cavaliers, whose starting backcourt of Darnell Valentine and Gerald Paddio went scoreless in the game. They beat Miami, which was playing without center Rony Seikaly, by 9.

The only real amusement was in the Miami game. Rookie Willie Burton blocked a Jordan shot and started taunting Jordan, who was bothered by the flu and was to some extent coasting through the game. Sophomore Glen Rice chimed in, saying the Heat were going to embarrass Jordan on his home court. This was not smart. It seemed to revive him. Jordan stole the ball from Burton and dunked after the Heat had pulled to within 1, 96–95. Then Jordan blocked an Alec Kessler shot and hit Pippen for a breakaway lay-up. Jordan then stole the ball from Sherman Douglas, was fouled, and hit two free throws. Suddenly the Bulls were ahead by 7 with two minutes to go and the game was over.

Miami coach Ron Rothstein told Burton and Rice after the game never to say anything to Jordan again.

•

DESPITE THE THREE wins, everyone knew there were problems. "We're not winning because of talent," said Jordan after the Miami game. "We're just beating bad teams."

The coaches met and talked about the bench, which had given up lead after lead. Jackson couldn't find a suitable combination; he had been playing the reserves as a separate unit, but he decided to start playing them more with starters.

King remained overweight after coming to camp some 30 pounds over his 245-pound playing weight; the players were calling him everything from "Juicy Juice" to "Doughboy." He looked as if he were wearing a coat under his uniform. Armstrong, too, was growing frustrated with his role on the second team. He had worked and improved during the summer, but Jackson liked the way John Paxson ran his offense and complemented Jordan. He felt Armstrong was too loose with the ball. So Armstrong sulked and his performance faltered. Dennis Hopson and Cliff Levingston continued to struggle in the offense, as Hopson tried to hide his slow return from off-season knee surgery. And Jackson was still wondering how to get five guards into the game. He wanted to play Craig Hodges more, but he was committed to trying to use Hopson and worried about Hodges's defense.

"They start posting him up as soon as he gets off the bus," Jackson joked in the meeting. The coaches called him "Highway Fourteen," as in "Everyone comes down Highway Fourteen." Fourteen was Hodges's uniform number.

Tex Winter said they should release him and let him catch on somewhere where he could play.

"Hey, we may need him sometime," said Bach. "You've got to remember, these are Hessians, hired soldiers. He's a piece that may win a game for us someday. You just don't give that away."

But there was a more important matter ahead: the Pistons in the Palace of Auburn Hills.

THE PLAYERS WERE loose in the locker room before the game, much as they were before the seventh game of the conference finals last June, when they were pummeled by the Pistons. Armstrong was throwing his hands around in an exaggerated manner in front of the blackboard in the dressing room, saying, "Who's this?" Everyone laughed.

It was an imitation of Krause, who after that seventh-game loss last June had told the team he never again wanted to be in such a position, as he threw papers down and slammed the blackboard. Krause had been coughing madly and trying to clear his throat and the players weren't quite sure what he was saying.

Sometimes the coaches worried that the Bulls were too loose. They were young and liked to joke with one another, although the humor often had a hard, cutting edge. They teased about everything from girlfriends and wives to their long noses and funny ears with an often roguish insouciance. Before the New York game earlier in the month, Jordan, Pippen, and Grant, all of whom had boys under three at the time, had debated for a half hour about whose child had the biggest penis. They eventually agreed it was Pippen's.

Before games, one of the coaches charts all the opponents' plays on a blackboard. NBA scouting has become so sophisticated—and assistant coaches John Bach and Jim Cleamons, the third and youngest of the assistants, were primarily responsible for this with the Bulls—that as soon as the opposing coach signals a play, the Bulls staff can relay it to the players on the floor. Once, when Miami's Sherman Douglas paused to hear his coach's instructions, Jordan yelled, "He wants a high screen roll."

Tapes of opponents' games are also edited and left rolling on a television in the locker room before the game, but Bulls players aren't always very studious. Cartwright and Paxson usually watch carefully, and Jordan does more often than most. But the younger players rarely do, and on this night it showed.

The game went as so many have in the Palace. The Bulls hung on for a quarter, but the pace was slow, which always worked in the Pistons' favor. The Bulls need to run and scatter the game against Detroit, but they can't because the Pistons dominate the rebounding. When that happens, it's just a matter of time before the Pistons pull away. In this game, the Bulls got dismantled in the second quarter and eventually lost by 21. Jordan scored 33, but no one else hit double figures. Pippen shot 2 for 16 and Hodges, Hopson, and Levingston combined to shoot 1 for 15. The entire bench was scoreless on 15 shots through three quarters.

Grant attempted 8 shots and was outraged again about the failure of Jordan and Pippen to pass the ball to anyone or run the offense. "We'll never beat good teams that way," he said as he walked briskly to the waiting team bus. The reserves felt they were being blamed for the team's failures, and the new rotation in which the all-reserve unit was broken up made things tougher. They were getting less time and even fewer shots because neither Jordan nor Pippen would pass any of them the ball, then when they did miss, they were singled out for the losses. "How are you supposed to average fifteen a game when you get three shots?" wondered Hopson.

Afterward, Jackson talked about changes in personnel and in the lineup if the Bulls could not come back a week later on Christmas Day to defeat the Pistons.

It was a quiet trip home, filled with glassy eyes and glum looks. Jordan unfurled the stat sheet on the bus and offered: "Headache tonight, Scottie?"

•

THE LAKERS WERE next, but the Bulls were still stewing about the Pistons. After the coaches watched the films, a regular postgame practice in the NBA now, they became even further enraged by Detroit's bullying tactics. Cliff Levingston had been kicked in the groin by Vinnie Johnson, and the Pistons again were allowed more latitude by the referees than other teams, the coaches felt.

"It's their style," fumed Jackson. "The referees get accustomed to the way you play and allow you to play within those parameters. So Detroit is allowed to play more physically."

The Bulls were so frustrated that they felt they had to do something. They decided to complain to the league, as the Pistons had years ago, a tactic that had resulted in fewer trips to the foul line for Jordan. Krause and Jackson complained intensely to operations director Rod Thorn that they could not compete with Detroit if the Pistons were allowed to play this way. They would send tapes.

At the same time, Jackson tried to encourage the team to get more physical. "You've got to hit someone," Jackson counseled Grant after the Detroit game. "When we play Detroit, you've just got to hit guys, anyone. Punch someone. Get thrown out of the game. Just do some damage."

Grant listened, but he was hesitant; that wasn't his game. Bach agreed. "Sure, we need to hit someone, but who's going to do it?"

The Bulls could fly, but they could also be as harmless as birds.

•

THE GAME AGAINST the Lakers showed just how magnificent the Bulls could be in full flight. The Bulls were too quick and athletic for the Lakers; both Jordan and Pippen missed triple doubles by just 1 assist. They forced turnovers, slashed to the offensive boards, and grabbed most of the loose balls. In Jordan, Pippen, and Grant, they had perhaps the quickest "two-three-four" trio in the league. It was their ultimate strength. But Bill Cartwright also bullied Vlade Divac out of the way, and in the fourth quarter, when the Lakers pulled within 3, it was Jordan, Pippen, and Grant scoring 22 of the team's 24 points.

The next night, the Bulls blew by the Pacers to take a 14-point first-quarter lead, this time with John Paxson hitting his shots; he would get 23 points for the game. The Bulls led by 20 before halftime and relaxed. The Pacers made a run, but the Bulls regrouped behind Pippen and Jordan, who scored 7 straight after the Pacers got within 1, 104–103, in the fourth quarter. The Bulls coasted to a 10-point victory.

But all thoughts were still on the Pistons, who were coming in next, on Christmas Day. And Jackson had an idea.

The Bulls, especially Jordan, knew they needed more scoring to defeat Detroit. They once had hopes that either Hopson or Walter Davis would come to the rescue. But Davis had decided to stay in Denver, although he was now on the market and the Bulls were talking about trading for him. And Hopson couldn't seem to find his way in the Bulls' system and seemed almost to resent the coaching at times; a wall was going up between him and Jackson that would only grow bigger as the season progressed. Jackson had toyed the previous year with the idea of starting King in hopes of getting him into the offense and bringing Grant off the bench. But Grant was in a fragile emotional state for much of that season because of his contract negotiations, and Jackson feared Grant would read the move as an attempt to lessen his bargaining power, so he stayed with him.

But now Grant had a new three-year deal and Jackson felt it was time to make the change. Perhaps Grant could score more coming off the bench, and Jackson liked the matchup of Grant coming in to play John Salley, who gave the Bulls trouble. Jackson also thought a start might jump-start King's game, which had been drowning under his massive ego. He'd already had a pair of scoreless games—King said he'd never had one in his life—and a third of his shots were being blocked. King seemed to be getting desperate; he told Bach he was going to change his number to change his luck, but Bach informed him he couldn't do that during the season. He got a trendy haircut in which several geometric designs were shaved into his head above his ears; Jackson, seeing one was triangle-shaped, asked him if he was trying to learn the offense by osmosis. But Jackson felt he needed King, and always believed if he left King on the court long enough he would score, maybe 14 to 16 points per game. So he decided to let King start against the Pistons.

Word began to circulate on the players' grapevine. King was upset about playing little, even if he'd rarely played well. The talk was that King's agent, the powerful David Falk of ProServ, had threatened the team: Play King or we are going to blast the Bulls in the press. Actually, Falk had merely talked to Krause about King's status. But there were rumors. And Grant believed the rumors.

And with good reason. When King first came to the Bulls, he was all confidence and swagger. He loved to talk. He made up nicknames for himself, like "Sky" and "the Pearl." He was a journalism major and he had a great story: He was an Oklahoma kid whose father had served two tours of duty in Vietnam and was decorated for drenching himself in water in order to put out a fire threatening a munitions dump. His mother was tough and demanded a good education for her son; when Oklahoma tried some questionable recruiting tactics, she told the newspapers, "I don't want my baby to go to Oklahoma. I want him to be able to read a stop sign."

King did have academic problems—yes, even at Oklahoma—when he started; he lost his eligibility as a freshman and struggled somewhat as a sophomore. But with opposing defenses geared to stopping Harvey Grant, he blossomed and became a big-time scorer. The knock on him was that he was "soft," in the pro scouts' vernacular—that he didn't rebound well despite that 10-per-game average, and he didn't guard the middle. He played in an offense suited to his quick style, so he didn't have to power to the basket as he would in the pros. But all that was forgotten as the draft drew near; he was projected as the Bulls' power forward of the future, but for now he would play behind Horace Grant.

This was made clear when King arrived, and King said all the right things. But privately he boasted about becoming a starter, and King's girlfriend, when she met Grant's wife, Donna, boldly said, "My boyfriend's going to take your husband's job."

Donna, a shy, sensitive South Side Chicago girl who'd met Horace at a local club when he was a rookie, was devastated. She cried about the meeting, and would again when the starters were introduced on Christmas Day with King at power forward and the girlfriend in the stands taunting her. "Told you, told you," King's girlfriend, Lisa, shouted from about six rows behind Donna in the wives' section. "My boyfriend is the starter and Horace is never going to get it back." Eventually, Jackson would have to call both players in and tell them to tell the women to cool it.

The Bulls beat the Pistons on Christmas Day and they even got rough; Grant pushed Joe Dumars in the fourth quarter and was ejected. Bullies? By then, though, the Bulls were ahead by 12 and the game was pretty much decided. They shot well, 52 percent, which they didn't do against Detroit in Auburn Hills; Grant did hold Salley down, although Salley tends to coast in the regular season and play harder in the playoffs. But King was a bust, shooting 2 for 7 and scoring 6 points. Mostly, the Bulls won with an aggressive third quarter. Since they have no shot blocker and aren't an exceptionally strong rebounding team, they rely on their defense to create opportunities and their quickness to stymie shooters. They held Detroit to 4-of-17 shooting and 14 points in the third quarter and went from 5 down at halftime to 9 ahead. They pretty much controlled the game afterward.

The win didn't exactly trigger a celebration. They had defeated the Pistons at home before, three straight in Chicago in the 1990 conference finals; what had they proven?

"We're *supposed* to win at home," said Hodges. "It's like Eddie Murphy said, 'Show me something. Here, Stevie [Wonder], you take the wheel and drive.' Now that's something. We haven't shown anything."

And the Bulls marketing staff was disappointed. For the big national-TV Christmas Day game they had hoped to put the Bulls in red uniforms, but the league had rejected the request. They had wanted the team to wear green uniforms for Saint Patrick's Day the year before, but Jackson had squelched that. They were hoping to revive an indoor fireworks display they had tried earlier in the season, but the players complained about being hit by falling debris from the rafters of the elderly hulk that was Chicago Stadium. It was a constant battle Jackson would fight with management. "What's all this stuff with mascots and dancing Blues Brothers and blimps floating all over the place?" he'd say. "Why can't it be just basketball? They seem to do all right with that in Boston."

It's the NBA, he was told. It's Fan-Tastic.

•

THE BULLS HAD little trouble with Golden State two nights later, although the game became something of a spectator event for everyone but Jordan and Pippen.

The latest results in the All-Star voting had come out and Pippen was fifth in the fan balloting for the two Eastern Conference forward positions. He studied his statistics before the game, and while they were good, he knew Bernard King was having an All-Star season after knee surgery and Dominique Wilkins and Kevin McHale were always coaches' favorites for the team. Charles Barkley and Larry

Bird were sure to be selected by the fans as starters and it was unlikely more than three more forwards would be selected by the coaches. "I've got to get myself up there in the voting," he said.

So he started taking the ball to the basket, and by halftime he had 15 points and 11 shots, 1 more than Jordan. "The General's not going to like that," Hodges whispered to Paxson as the teams left the court at halftime with the Bulls ahead by 14.

Sure enough, Jordan took 6 of the Bulls' first 7 shots of the second half and scored 18 points in the third quarter, although Pippen would not quit: He added 14 as the Bulls went ahead 105–85.

"It's just two guys," Grant said later, having scored 1 point off the bench. "Two guys are doing what they want and the rest of us don't seem to matter."

On the bench, Winter was threatening to quit. "They won't run the offense," he told Jackson. "If we don't want to run the offense, I'll just leave."

Were Jordan and Pippen being selfish? Jackson was asked afterward.

"We like to call them scorers, not selfish," Jackson offered.

Jackson finally gave Pippen a long rest in the fourth quarter, and he would finish with a career-high 34. But Jordan had 42, and an AP wire-service reporter summed up every writer's defense for not featuring Pippen in the game story: "You've usually got to lead with the high scorer," he explained.

King had started again, and after he scored only 2 points and shot 1 of 4, Jackson had to admit the experiment was a failure. With Seattle coming in, Jackson decided to go back to Grant as a starter to face Shawn Kemp. "He'll be jumping over Stacey and standing on his shoulders," Jackson told his coaches.

Again, the game was no problem. The starters gave the Bulls a 38–27 lead after one quarter. Seattle pulled within 8 at the half, then the Bulls took a 17-point lead after three quarters and had it up to 29 before calling in the end of the bench. But there wasn't enough time to get Scott Williams into the game.

The rookie free agent had been the surprise of the training camp and the early season. He hadn't been drafted because of shoulder problems—the pros had figured he'd need surgery. But the Bulls signed him, and despite several excruciating episodes in which his shoulder popped out of place, Williams insisted on playing through the season. And he would play so well at times later in the season that Jackson would use him ahead of King and even Grant.

Jackson, though, generally believes in seniority, so Williams had to wait his turn. He was doing that on the bench as the Bulls stretched their lead to almost 30 against the SuperSonics in that last game of December 1990. Finally, Jackson called for him to go in, but as he waited at the scorer's table no fouls were called, the clock didn't stop, and the game ended.

In the locker room afterward, Williams sat crying.

Jordan whispered something to him. They'd put the rookie next to Jordan because Jordan had helped recruit him for North Carolina and had wanted him with the Bulls. Rookies can get lost sitting next to Jordan. It was harder on 1989 rookie Jeff Sanders, whom Jordan didn't care for because of his lazy attitude. Jordan often demeaned the slow-moving, slow-talking Sanders as he sat not three feet away. Once when Sanders rebounded and slammed in practice, Jordan shouted, "Hey, the No Doz must have worn off." Before the season, the Bulls traded Sanders to Miami, which later released him. He went to the CBA and got called up on a ten-day contract by the Charlotte Hornets; "It's probably a twelve-day," Jordan said when he heard about it. "He needs two days to wake up."

But Jordan liked Williams and sympathized with him. He knew what the problem was, and it wasn't just that Williams had become frustrated by not getting into a blowout game.

"It's worst for him around the holidays," said Jordan. "I don't say much to him, but I'll usually ask him home for dinner or try to do something with him."

Three years earlier, on October 15, 1987, Williams's father, Al, estranged from his wife, Rita, waited for her in the garage of her California home. Rita was on the way home from work as an insurance executive. Al, a department-store manager, shot her dead before she could get out of the car, and then turned the gun on himself.

Scott Williams, at 6-10 and 240 pounds, had been a high school star in Hacienda Heights, California. Bill Cosby called him on behalf of UCLA, as did Tommy Lasorda, Kareem Abdul-Jabbar, and John Wooden. UCLA didn't want to let this big local talent get away.

But Dean Smith and North Carolina won, with the help of alumni such as Jordan, James Worthy, and Sam Perkins. Williams became Dean Smith's first West Coast recruit. He performed below expectations in college, though satisfactorily, as he was overshadowed by J. R. Reid. Scott Williams was just preparing for his sophomore season in North Carolina's senior-dominated scheme when the murder-suicide occurred.

"Obviously, it had an effect on him," Dean Smith said. "No one could ever be the same after something like that."

Williams never averaged more than the 14.5 points and 7.9 rebounds he reached in his senior season, and went from being a sure first-rounder to being undrafted. His brother would move to North Carolina after the tragedy so the two could comfort each other. Williams, a powerfully built kid with a fast smile and hard eyes, grew remote and often wandered the campus pensively.

Williams doesn't talk about the deaths of his parents. He prefers to remember how his father raised money so his high school team could have state championship rings, and how his mother would miss work to get to his games and pitch batting practice to the two boys when they were trying to make the Little League team.

He just plays through pain and disappointment. He says that he knows now he can handle any sort of adversity, that no matter what he has to face it cannot overshadow what has happened to him. He doesn't say anything about it. There's no need to.

Williams wiped his eyes as the other Bulls dressed. It was December 29 and the team would not play again until January 3; they'd have the next two days off and return for a light practice on New Year's Day. They were 20–9, the same record they'd had last year after twenty-nine games, when they went on to win fifty-five, the second-most in team history. Grant made fun of Pippen's shoes and Pippen joked about Armstrong's cologne. Hodges had departed quickly while Hopson slowly pulled his clothes on. He had taken the corner locker, the one Dave Corzine always had, where Corzine would sit for an hour after the game. Hopson, for some reason, was often the last out of the locker room, too. "Noon, Jan. 1" was scribbled on the blackboard. The Bulls' locker room is cramped and the players don't linger much other than Hopson and Jordan, who usually plows patiently through twenty minutes of interviews. Reporters and TV technicians jockey for position. Paxson swept out quickly with his son, Ryan, who attended the game, and Jackson finished a beer and a cigarette, a postgame ritual. The interviews over, Jordan turned to the still red-eyed rookie.

"Come on, Scott, let's go get something to eat," Jordan said softly.

6

JANUARY 1991

1/3 at Houston; 1/5 v. Cleveland; 1/8 v. New Jersey; 1/9 at
Philadelphia; 1/11 v. Atlanta; 1/12 at Charlotte; 1/14 v. Milwaukee;
1/16 at Orlando; 1/18 at Atlanta; 1/21 at Miami; 1/23 at New
Jersey; 1/25 v. Miami; 1/31 at San Antonio

WHAT IS IT about Houston and pro athletes?

Earlier in the 1990–91 season, that's where James Worthy was
arrested for soliciting prostitutes. A few years back in the playoffs,
Seattle's Dale Ellis and Kevin Williams were hauled in after a bar
fight. It's also where several baseball players from the New York
Mets and Boston Red Sox have gone down on strikes to the local
police at late-night clubs in recent years, and in early 1991 Ricky
Sanders of the Washington Redskins was cleared of hit-and-run
charges relating to a trip to another Houston nightclub.

Houston has an inordinate number of night spots that attract pro
athletes, and many in professional sports believe that the Houston
police single them out for persecution and prosecution. The Bulls
management warns players to avoid the Houston night scene, cau-
tioning that they are targets to be picked off. The players quickly

135

learn that there is a different culture in Texas, where someone once said the people think Hanukkah is a duck call.

The Bulls arrived in Houston late on Wednesday, January 2, for Thursday's game, the rule in the NBA being that teams always travel into a city the night before a game when they aren't playing. Everyone managed to stay out of trouble—at least until the game was under way.

In the 1989–90 season, Jackson's first, the Bulls took one of their worst beatings in Houston, falling behind by 20 points in the first quarter. It wouldn't be that much different this time as the Bulls got swept up by a half-dozen straight Rockets' fast breaks to fall behind by 8 at halftime and then 20 after three quarters. In the Bulls' defensive scheme, either Jordan or Pippen has to drop back to pick up the fast break, but neither did in the second quarter against the Rockets. Both drove to the basket and left the rear unprotected.

Jackson was unusually angry afterward. When he saw Jimmy Sexton, Pippen and Grant's agent, walk into the locker room after the game, Jackson exploded. "Media only!" Jackson demanded. "Out of there."

Sexton looked around somewhat stunned, trying to explain that he just wanted to tell Grant and Pippen where to meet him after the game. Across the locker room, Jordan was sitting in front of his stall talking with heavyweight champion Evander Holyfield; Jackson issued no such demands to either of them.

Later, Grant simmered while having dinner with former Houston great Calvin Murphy. Grant had taken 10 shots in the game; Jordan and Pippen had combined for 40. Murphy told Grant he'd never reach his potential playing with someone like Jordan. And that was like throwing gas on a smoldering fire; Grant said he had tried, but it was difficult watching Jordan and Pippen score so much while he was denied the opportunity. Early in the season, he'd tried to score more and drawn Jackson's wrath. "I understand my role," Grant explained, "and it's not like I have a big ego or anything. But with the talent and skills I have, I'd like to score a little more. People look at numbers and stuff like that and don't understand about good defense and running the floor and setting screens. I feel like I can help this team with more chances to score."

During the game, when Grant had cut under, toward the baseline, in front of a man who was screening him, instead of over, behind the man, Jordan had screamed that Grant was going the wrong way. "Get out of my way," he yelled. Grant, weary of Jordan's outbursts, demanded, "Why don't you shut up for a change and play?" It wasn't much of a comeback, but it was probably a declaration of independence from Grant, who rarely talks on the court.

"What can I do now?" Grant would ask Murphy later. "I already asked to be traded and they signed me to a new contract. Why would I be asking to be traded now?"

The Bulls, though, still had Grant's contract on their minds. His importance grew as King's promise faded, and since his new three-year deal was his second contract, he would be a free agent—and the Bulls would have no claim on his services—as he approached his twenty-ninth birthday after the 1993–94 season. So even as Sexton and his partner, Kyle Rote, Jr., talked with Reinsdorf regularly that season about extending Pippen's contract, Reinsdorf would invariably bring up Grant. "You know," he'd say, "we've got to do something with Grant's contract."

Sexton, though, knew Grant's feelings. "Don't even tell me what they offer," Grant had said. "I just want to get out of here in three years."

But the real fury on that frosty January night was coming from the Houston side. The Rockets' star center, Akeem Olajuwon (soon to change the spelling of his first name to *Hakeem*), had been taken to the hospital after colliding with Bill Cartwright's elbow. This was not a rare occurrence around the NBA; two seasons earlier, Cartwright had been fined—although the fine was later rescinded when none of the acts were determined to be intentional—after putting Greg Kite and Fred Roberts out of action with elbows to the face and delivering lesser blows to Robert Parish and Isiah Thomas. Thomas was so enraged that he began strangling assistant coach Brendan Malone when Malone tried to keep Thomas from going after Cartwright on the court during the game.

Cartwright plays with his elbows away from his body. As he drives to the basket, he'll often lead with his elbows. It's not an uncommon practice, but because Cartwright is awkward opponents find it difficult to get out of the way. It was one of the hidden advantages the Bulls believed they had with Cartwright, who had already held fifteen of twenty centers under their season scoring average. "Guys don't want to go in there against him because they don't know what to expect," said Jackson. Although the injury to Olajuwon's eye would result in his missing two months, the blow clearly was from incidental contact. But given Olajuwon's importance to the team and Cartwright's reputation, the Houston management was enraged.

Houston's general manager, Steve Patterson, called the league's director of operations, Rod Thorn, to demand that Cartwright be suspended, and Patterson later released a series of tapes to the national media showing Cartwright knocking out several players. After Roberts had been KO'd by Cartwright, Bucks coach Del Harris had compiled such a series of tapes; the Bulls figured that's where Patterson was getting his material, since Harris had coached in Houston and now saw himself in a blood feud with the team ninety miles to his south. Later in the month, Kite would again take a blow from Cartwright and would need stitches in his chin, and the Bucks' Jack Sikma would miss the fourth quarter of a Bulls win with a bloody nose.

"Guess Who's elbow?" Sikma offered after the game.

That would lead to more outraged calls to Thorn. Thorn called Cartwright.

"This has to stop," Thorn said. "Would you consider wearing elbow pads?"

Cartwright was astounded. He'd played the same way his entire career, and he believed pads would inhibit his game as well as send up a red flag for the referee.

"I'll give it all the consideration it deserves," Cartwright told Thorn.

Thorn called Jackson. Would Jackson ask Cartwright to wear elbow pads? No, Jackson said, Cartwright didn't want to and the Bulls were not going to ask him to. And anyway, Jackson added, it seemed as if players were trying to undercut Cartwright to gain an advantage and were walking into these accidents themselves. Thorn said he'd be watching because the outcry was getting louder and louder.

"What's the big deal?" offered Grant. "He gets us like that in practice all the time."

In the fourth quarter of that loss to Houston, John Bach began doodling on the board the coaches use to draw plays during time-outs. He drew a series of headstones with the names "Olajuwon," "Kite," "Roberts," "Parish," and "Thomas."

On top, he labeled it "Cartwright National Cemetery."

•

THE BULLS RETURNED home to face the decimated Cavaliers next for the third time in just over a month. It was getting so bad in Cleveland that the Cavaliers had picked up a CBA player named Henry James and he led them in scoring. "Who are you?" Jordan asked him during one break in the play. The Bulls scored just 14 points in the first quarter and trailed by 5, but were ahead by 11 before the second quarter was over and sailed to a win that was largely due to 18 points and 8 assists from B. J. Armstrong off the bench. But the performance only served to frustrate the baby-faced kid further.

A month earlier, Armstrong had gone to Krause asking to be traded. It wasn't quite a demand, but he said he was vastly outplaying John Paxson in practice, so he deserved to start. If the Bulls didn't care for his play, they should trade him.

Krause told Jackson, who bawled out the sensitive Armstrong, sending him into a depression that lasted several weeks. Jackson told Armstrong there was more to the game than what you did in practice, that he was missing the whole point. He was supposed to provide leadership and scoring for the second team. "I'm not going to turn this team over to your game," Jackson told him. "You dribble too much and you're mostly looking for your own shot. John knows how to get us into our offense. You want to start, but you're not even close. You don't play the defense we want and you don't want to help others get their shots. That's why Jordan and Pippen don't want to play with you."

Armstrong figured that was it for him with the Bulls. He'd lost considerable confidence as a rookie as he found himself, for the first time in his point-guard life, without the ball; it was hard enough to try to run the complicated offense without being run off the ball by Jordan, who didn't care much for rookies. "I never knew where I was supposed to be or what I was supposed to do," Armstrong said. "I wondered, 'Could I play in this league?' " But he'd run the Bulls' summer-league team and made the all-league squad, and he felt he was ready to take over. It wasn't happening, though, and he thought he'd be better off elsewhere.

He'd have to get in line, it seemed.

Perdue went to talk to Jackson. He wasn't playing much, a few minutes per game between DNPs (did not play—coach's decision), so he finally decided to talk to Jackson. Jackson told him that it was a case of improper matchups and that he'd get his chance.

"They must think I'm stupid," said Perdue, who wasn't. He's mostly known for having the biggest feet in the league. He moves slowly and one expects him to sound like Gomer Pyle, but he's got a quick wit. Later in the season, as fortunes changed for him, a Bulls' minority owner told him he was making Krause look good. "And don't you think I'm sick about it," Perdue quipped. But Perdue figured he had time on his side. He'd heard Cartwright talk more often lately about getting out after the 1990–91 season, about finishing his career back home in California now that he was about to become a free agent.

"Then they'll have to use me," said Perdue. "Meanwhile, I figure there are worse ways to make a living."

Even Michael Jordan was beginning to get tired of his role.

A reporter had stopped him at practice. Rod Thorn had called and wondered if the reporter would ask Jordan to call him. He wanted to find out if Jordan was going to participate in the slam-dunk contest at the All-Star game in Charlotte, and Thorn couldn't reach Jordan. Of course, this wasn't unusual. When Jordan won the league's Most Valuable Player award in 1988 for the first time, he ignored dozens of phone calls from the league about attending the awards ceremony. He was playing golf.

"I've been getting his messages," said Jordan, "but I'm not going to call him. I know what he's up to."

Thorn wanted Jordan for the contest because the game was in Charlotte, and, of course, because Jordan was the premier symbol of not only the NBA but its high-flying, acrobatic game. But Jordan had long ago decided his dunking-contest days were over. He'd won in 1988 in Chicago and figured all he could do now was lose, since he was expected to win and do it more spectacularly each year. He'd rather play golf.

He'd gone through a dance like this with the league in 1989. Jordan didn't want to compete in the contest, so he told Thorn when he called—as a way to get him to stop bothering him—to raise the prize money to $20,000; it had been $12,500. Thorn called back a few days later and said, "Done." Jordan was stunned. "I'll think about it," he said. Besides the possibility of a fall from his dunking throne, Jordan had always found himself weary after the All-Star weekend, and had not played well in the succeeding games. It was time to let some kids come out of the bullpen and have a start, Jordan felt. But the league announced that Jordan had agreed to participate. Jordan called the Bulls; he needed the team to say he was injured so he couldn't compete. No problem. Within a few days of the All-Star game, Jordan turned up with a minor injury and the Bulls said they didn't want to risk Jordan exacerbating the problem.

The league compromised in 1990. Would Jordan come to the three-point-shooting contest? Sure, he'd try. He thought that might be fun, and certainly less pressure. He would find out differently. Jordan had been shooting more threes that season and hitting them, but he was nervous for the contest and posted an all-time low score of five points. He'd had it with All-Star-weekend contests.

In many ways, Jordan had had it with basketball.

"Five more years," he eagerly told teammates early in January. "Five more years and I'm out of here. I'm marking these days on a calendar, like I'm in jail. I'm tired of being used by this organization, by the league, by the writers, by everyone."

Being a pro basketball player wasn't much fun for him anymore. Everyone wanted something. He had so much, everything but time to get away and do as he pleased. He was handsome, rich, and personable. Picasso had once said they could take his spit and frame it as great art; Jordan was viewed the same way on the basketball court. Every time he moved, people stared. But the sweet life was seeming all too sour suddenly. He was kicking ass across the NBA landscape, but also hauling boxcars full of doubt and resentment.

This was no longer the Michael Jordan who had a "love of the game" clause in his contract that allowed him to play any time he wanted without club permission. It had long disappeared in collective bargaining, and Jordan didn't play much basketball out of season anymore—just a few charity games for other players so they'd come to his, and for his shoe sponsor. A few incidents early in his career began to change his love for the game. "I quickly learned it's just a business and you get as much money out of it as you can and then you get out," Jordan found himself saying this January. He was feeling like one of Bach's mercenaries. Also, he was feeling more and more embittered toward management. "They're not interested in winning," he would say. "They just want to sell tickets, which they can do because of me. They won't make any deals to make us better. And this [Toni] Kukoc thing. I hate that. They're spending all their time chasing this guy." Jordan felt the media were demanding too much of his time and sniping at him. He felt his teammates were becoming too heavy a load to carry. And now he had two children at home. It all was becoming just too much. All he wanted to do was play golf.

Sidney Moncrief understood. He was one of the great NBA players in the 1980s, but he had retired after the 1988–89 season. Now he was back, playing for the Atlanta Hawks, whom the Bulls would meet in a few days. He'd seen some tapes of Jordan and could see a lot of himself in the look in Jordan's eyes.

"You play ten years and the games mount up, the travel, the winning, the losing, everything," said Moncrief, regarded during his prime as not only a perennial All-Star but an eloquent spokesman for the game. "I would say it hit me after year eight. Especially if you're playing a lot, you start to feel it. You keep playing. You deny you don't have the desire anymore. But you find yourself becoming more critical of everything around you, your teammates, the coaches, the front-office people, the press. You're probably not as mentally focused for the entire year as you need to be. You tend to go in and out mentally, and everything around you seems to distract you a little more. I took that year off and I didn't watch any basketball. I played tennis and golf and I was on my own schedule for the first time in ten years. I had knee problems, so I'm not the player I was, and I have a lesser role and I can't say I don't miss playing thirty-five, forty minutes per game and scoring twenty, twenty-five points. But I feel totally different about everything after a year away. I realize what a privilege it is to play in the NBA and how really nice it is. I think now I'll stay around three or four more years."

Jordan wasn't feeling nearly so sanguine about life in the NBA, and his talk about five more years masked even deeper doubts. He had gone so far as to discuss with David Falk whether he could quit after the 1990–91 season, at least for a year. "There are two problems, though," he said. "One is my endorsements. I told him I'd do it if he could find a way to keep my endorsement money coming. Of course, the Bulls would probably sue. But I'm more worried that if I quit for a year, I'll never want to come back."

•

THE GAME AGAINST the Nets at home on January 8, a win in which the Bulls led by 24 in the third quarter, wasn't very pretty. The excitement came afterward. Jordan had scored 41 points and former Bull Jack Haley, who mostly waved a towel on the bench for a season in Chicago, said, "Michael always seems to get up for me."

But Jordan would create a new bench insurrection with his comments after the game. The Nets had cut a 24-point deficit to 10, and Jackson had to put Jordan back in the game to stanch the bleeding. Jordan was seeing red.

"Our bench guys are not going out there looking to improve on the game," Jordan complained to reporters afterward. "They're mostly looking to improve on their statistics instead of learning to play with each other and get some kind of continuity. They're playing as individuals and that's something they need to change."

The principal reserves, Armstrong, King, Hopson, Levingston, and Hodges, saw it otherwise. When they were on the floor, they felt, they ran the system, but Jordan and Pippen wouldn't. They played 12 to 15 minutes, but in two or three shifts that was just a few minutes on the court at a time, and hardly enough chance to get into the flow. And all they got for it was criticism.

But they didn't like what they heard from Jackson, either, when they demanded a meeting with the coach after Jordan's outburst. Jackson told Levingston and Hopson (the loudest complainer in the meeting), "You guys are either stupid or just incapable of being on the floor together. Because nothing happens when you two are out there together.

"And life," Jackson continued, "just isn't meant to be fair. There are different rules for you guys and Jordan and Pippen. They are here to take the shots and you're not. You're here to fill roles and that's what you're expected to do."

Jackson didn't understand, Armstrong thought as he sat there. He liked the coach, thought him intelligent and funny. He liked playing for him. But he also knew his friends. Hopson, to whom Armstrong had grown closest, had a big ego; he had been Big Ten Player of the Year and was the leading scorer with the Nets. King had been a big college star who thought he should have been the No. 1 pick in the 1989 draft. Levingston had even clashed in Atlanta with Dominique Wilkins because he wanted more of Wilkins's shots. These guys were all high first-round draft choices and believed themselves capable of starting—capable, in fact, of being stars. Jackson had to see that, if not in their play, then at least in their pleas. Armstrong saw that no good was to come from the meeting.

Jackson, for his part, understood only too well how large a percentage of the league's players saw themselves as stars. All of them had been stars before joining the NBA, but on this level you had to accept your role. He saw Armstrong as salvageable, but he wasn't sure about Hopson and King. He worried that the three spent considerable time together, on the team plane and bus and on the road. A few weeks later, Jackson approached Armstrong. "There's too much negativity going on with those guys and it's going to poison you," he warned. "You might want to join another group." Armstrong would stay friendly with both, but on the team plane he began to move in an open area with some of the other players, and would continue to for the remainder of the season.

THE BREAKS CERTAINLY were coming the Bulls' way as the team headed for Philadelphia, the 76ers being another team with injuries when they met the Bulls. The Bulls hadn't played well on the road, going just 2–6 against winning teams. But Rick Mahorn was out with an injury, and the 76ers had just traded Mike Gminski for Armon Gilliam. Jackson thought this was to the Bulls' advantage because Gilliam was what the players called a black hole: Once you threw the ball in to him, nothing ever came back out. Barkley likely would have to play more power forward, which he liked less.

The Bulls' own good health—they hadn't lost a starter to injury yet, they would have a league-low four player-games missed through the All-Star break and just twenty at the end of the regular season—was partly due to their youth, but Jackson felt it was also partly due to the offense. It left less room for the out-of-control rushes to the

Young Michael Jordan, in his first year with the Bulls. (*Chicago Tribune*)

The 1990s-model Jordan drives to the basket. (Chicago Bulls)

The late-1990s-model Jordan (?) watches his tee shot with pro golfer Raymond Floyd. (*Chicago Tribune*)

Pippen flies high against Indiana in 1991. (*Chicago Tribune*)

Scottie Pippen tries to relieve his migraine headache during game seven against Detroit in 1990. (*Chicago Tribune*)

New head coach Phil Jackson talks with Bill Cartwright before practice in 1989. (*Chicago Tribune*)

Jackson, flanked by assistant John Bach (left) and Tex Winter (right), enjoys an easy moment during the 1991 season. (*Chicago Tribune*)

Phil Jackson signals for the triangle. (*Chicago Tribune*)

John Paxson releases a jumper against Orlando. (Chicago Bulls)

Bill Cartwright's elbow finds Patrick Ewing's ribs in a 1989 game against the Knicks. (*Chicago Tribune*)

Horace Grant grabs a re-
bound against Minne-
sota. (*Chicago Tribune*)

B. J. Armstrong brings
the ball up against New
Jersey.
(*Chicago Tribune*)

Craig Hodges. (Chicago Bulls)

Stacey King maneuvers against the Knicks. (*Chicago Tribune*)

Will Perdue gets off the ground on defense against San Antonio. (*Chicago Tribune*)

Jerry Reinsdorf. (Chicago Bulls)

Scott Williams. (Chicago Bulls)

Dennis Hopson dunks while
Cliff Levingston looks on.
(*Chicago Tribune*)

Jerry Krause hugs the Larry O'Brien Trophy during the Bulls' victory parade. (*Chicago Tribune*)

Michael Jordan, with his wife Juanita, reaches out to his fans along the parade route. (*Chicago Tribune*)

basket that can cause injury. Jordan laughed when this theory was relayed to him. "P.J. comes up with some wild stuff," he said.

The Bulls had finished their pregame shooting and were returning for the regular pregame meeting to go over the scouting report on the 76ers when Charles Barkley walked into the Bulls' locker room wearing his coat. It was about 6:40. Game time was 7:30. Barkley had just arrived and hadn't gone to his own locker room yet. The Bulls required all players to be at a home game by 6:00 P.M. or be fined. Philadelphia coach Jim Lynam had dropped a similar rule because Barkley never adhered to it.

"A great, great player, maybe unstoppable," Jackson said as he watched Barkley talking with Jordan. "But he's got no discipline, none. You can't win with a player like that."

This night, Jordan most certainly was a player you could win with, scoring 40 for the third time in the last six games. Philadelphia drew within 1 late in the game, but Armstrong hit a jump shot to put the Bulls ahead by 3 and then Bill Cartwright hit two straight jumpers to hold off the 76ers. It was an important win, almost a crucial one, the coaches felt. The Bulls needed to defeat a good team on the road, something they hadn't done since the Utah and Boston games two months earlier. Philadelphia may have been hurting, but it counted.

The Bulls then went home and defeated the Hawks, with all five starters scoring in double figures. Grant, Pippen, and Cartwright each got 10 rebounds, and Paxson and Cartwright hit the crucial shots in the last two minutes when Atlanta closed a 16-point deficit to 1.

A trip to Charlotte was next and was relatively easy for all but Jordan, who was always greeted there like a returning war hero. He rarely got his afternoon nap before the game because he had to receive old friends, much as the pope might. In the game, the Bulls pulled steadily away and led by 19 early in the third quarter before letting the Hornets close to within 7 with nine minutes to go. So Jordan put on a show, scoring 12 of the Bulls' last 14 points.

Then the Bucks came down to Chicago for the Bulls' last home game before going on the road for nine of their next ten over the twenty-five days leading into the All-Star break. Milwaukee had defeated Chicago at home in December, but the Bucks were struggling now and a little beaten up. They'd surrendered first place after almost a month atop the Central Division; they were now a half game behind the Bulls and in third place.

Jordan and Pippen applied their own kind of accelerant, stealing the ball and feeding one another for slams. They pretty much just looked for one another on the court these days, as neither much trusted Cartwright and they only viewed Paxson as a bailout in case of emergency. They combined for 19 points in the third quarter as the Bulls went up by 10 and never led by fewer than 6 in winning 110–97.

The Bulls had now won six straight and would face teams with losing records in four of the next five before another western trip. They weren't playing that well, the coaches knew, but their defense and overall team athleticism was enabling them to escape with wins after those impressive spurts. It was still early in the season and still a time for development. They were in good position as the race headed toward the halfway point.

But Jerry Krause, for reasons that were unclear to the team, insisted on dumping gasoline onto the fire.

There was a growing tide of resentment on the team about the Bulls' pursuit of Yugoslav Toni Kukoc. Everyone had heard the stories about what a super player he could be, but they saw Krause's obsession with him as a pipe dream, and one that was costing them money. The Bulls had offered Kukoc a firm $15.3 million for six years. They were being careful to keep about $1.8 million available under the salary cap so they could sign him if he decided to come to the NBA. This left the Bulls with one of the lowest payrolls in the league. Pippen was demanding a new contract and Jordan, too, wanted more money, although he was not sure how he could get it. Paxson and Cartwright were unsigned. The players naturally weren't thrilled that the Bulls were offering millions to an untried European who might take one of their jobs.

The team sent Jordan a half-dozen tapes of Kukoc so Jordan might see how talented Kukoc was. Jordan refused to watch them.

Krause traveled to Yugoslavia in December to meet with Kukoc and give him a deadline, the first of Krause's three trips overseas and the first of at least five "final" deadlines for Kukoc to make a decision. The Bulls said he must make a decision by the end of January.

But the 6-10, 200-pound Kukoc could not be persuaded to make up his mind, and the January deadline would pass without a decision. Pippen could barely be contained as reports circulated regularly in the media about offers to Kukoc while his own negotiations weren't moving. Jordan remained displeased, even telling Falk to try to work out a trade if the Bulls signed Kukoc. Jordan also believed Kukoc would fail because of the incredible pressure that would fall on him the way the Bulls had built up his ability, and the promise he'd heard that Kukoc would be made the starting point guard; he told Reinsdorf the Bulls should trade Kukoc's rights and get something for them. But Jordan also doubted Kukoc would come to the Bulls, especially after Krause's visit.

"What a guy to send if you're trying to get a guy to come here," Jordan said laughingly in the locker room. "He's gonna think everyone over here has doughnut crumbs on their face."

To Jackson, though, it wasn't a joke. He saw the resentment growing on his team, not only toward Kukoc, who he felt could be a solid player someday, but toward the organization. And he began to think Kukoc was just using the Bulls to increase his bargaining power with teams in Italy and Spain. Krause asked Jackson to call Kukoc and assure him that he would get a fair chance for playing time. Jackson reluctantly agreed, but Krause was having paroxysms after the call.

The translation wasn't exact, but Jackson, after listening to Kukoc hesitate in his intentions, got fed up. "Listen, kid," he said. "Enough of this. Either shit or get off the pot."

•

THE BULLS WENT to Orlando on January 16 to open a four-game, eight-day trip, but the game would matter little. It was sunny and the evening was balmy as the team bus rolled up to the arena, but it would be the desert everyone would soon be thinking about. Some thirty minutes before the game was to begin, word flashed that the United States had begun bombing Iraq. The Persian Gulf War had begun. The usual pregame tape of that night's opponent was slipped out and everyone watched the TV news reports. Jordan has an older brother, Ronnie, stationed in Germany, and he figured Ronnie might be called. "We're gonna kick their asses," Jordan said as the first reports of the beginning of hostilities passed on the screen.

"We're gonna show them they can't mess with us." It wasn't a unique response, and his thoughts clearly continued as his words trailed off. Emotions were stampeding away everyone's concentration on the game.

It would be a period of ambivalence for Craig Hodges. He's a Muslim and was sympathetic to elements of the Iraqi cause, but he knew he had to remain quiet to protect his family. Actually, he was quite popular on the team, and he often debated religion and politics with Paxson and Grant. He believed this was Armageddon. "We've been in it for a while, but this is just the physical manifestation," he told Grant. He said he was ready to die if necessary and wasn't worried because he knew he had lived a good life. Hodges was a student of black history and often tried to rally his teammates, but he found it wasn't easy to gain sympathy among blacks who were doing so well.

Hodges had become a follower of the controversial minister Louis Farrakhan. When Hodges was playing in Milwaukee, he had tried to get his teammates to attend a Farrakhan rally. He was the only one who attended. Less than a week later, Hodges was traded to Phoenix, and word got back to Hodges sometime thereafter that the Bucks were worried he might try to start some kind of black-nationalist movement among the players. Hodges wasn't sure what to believe.

Although Hodges shielded his politics from public view, there was concern, too, in the league office as plans were made for the All-Star weekend. Hodges's appearance as defending three-point-shooting champion was being greeted with very little enthusiasm. League officials were worried that with the nation at war with a Muslim nation, Hodges might say something embarrassing if he won. There was talk of asking Hodges not to mention Allah in any postgame speech if he won.

Hodges was very tolerant and was a source of enthusiasm for the team. Jackson thought long about working him into the lineup more to take advantage of his passion and drive. He could be encouraging while remaining a good sport, so he was often the subject of kindly ridicule for his beliefs. Some players called him "the Sheikh," and one time on the team bus after the war had started, a player farted and Jordan, militantly chauvinistic throughout the campaign, yelled, "Hey, Hodg, that's a bad one. Is that one of them Muslim farts?"

Hodges thought his detractors foolish, for he had studied the Koran and believed the end was near; he said the Koran offered symbols of the end that were evident in this struggle. He believed Ronald Reagan was the devil, noting that there were six letters in his first, middle, and last names, and that the address of his California home had been changed because it was 666. But Hodges preached nonviolence and respect, often leaving teammates to wonder whether he made more sense than the government, which was at war.

•

IT WAS UNDENIABLY hard for anyone to concentrate on the game. Orlando led by 7 late in the third quarter and the game was tied with about nine minutes left when former Bull Sam Vincent completed one of the most extraordinary sequences for a point guard anyone could remember: He went seven straight possessions without letting anyone else on his team touch the ball. After Vincent missed three shots and committed four turnovers, the Bulls were ahead by 10, and they would win 98–88. Soon, Vincent would lose his starting job for the rest of the season to Scott Skiles, his college teammate.

The outbreak of hostilities in the Middle East and what it could mean remained in the players' thoughts throughout. Before the war, Saddam Hussein had threatened to send out assassination squads if the United States attacked his country. During the first time-out, Hodges looked around the stands and said to Grant, "You know, the General [Jordan] is considered a national treasure. If they're going to try to get anyone it would be him." Grant and Hodges moved a few steps away from Jordan. The word spread in later time-outs, and by the time the game was over Jackson was standing next to Jordan shouting plays and advice while the other players leaned away.

The Bulls moved on to Atlanta the next day; thanks to their charter plane, they were unaffected by the newly tightened airport restrictions that would force most teams to spend hours in airports before their flights. Jackson, an antiwar activist from the sixties, wanted to make a statement, but felt he had been blackballed once for his activism and couldn't take the chance again, especially when this was the last guaranteed year of his contract. "I'm trying to figure

out how to do something without it being too public," he said. He
was frustrated and angry. He felt it was no more possible to win a
war these days than to win an earthquake. For now, though, he'd
concern himself with the Hawks.

Some of Jackson's players had the war on their minds, too, after
an off-day in Atlanta. Several of them went to see the Martin Luther
King, Jr. Center, and Cartwright said later his palms were sweating
when he got to meet Mrs. Coretta King. "The first time I've ever
been nervous like that meeting someone," he said. The visit had
been set up by the TNT cable network as a media event, but the
media and team officials were cleared out and only the few players
who went, including Cartwright and Hodges, got to see Mrs. King.
She wanted to talk with them about the state of black America and
the war. Why, Mrs. King wondered, did the U.S. government pick
January 15, Martin Luther King Day, as its deadline to begin a war
in the Persian Gulf, a war in which, she noted, more than 50 percent
of the combat troops—those most vulnerable—were black. It was
a question Craig Hodges had raised, too.

•

FOR MOST OF the team, a day off in Atlanta meant far less lofty
thoughts. Atlanta is one of the players' favorite towns for its night
spots, especially some of the X-rated kind. Knowing this, Tim Hallam, the team's PR director, thought he'd have some fun. He knew
Cliff Levingston wanted to go to one of the strip bars so popular
among the players here. He also knew Jim Durham, the Bulls'
longtime play-by-play announcer, was a devout Southern Baptist
who usually adjourned to his room early to meditate and read the
Bible.

"Cliff," Hallam said as the bus rolled toward the downtown Mar-
riott, "I think J.D. would like to go tonight."

"Great," said the gregarious Levingston, and he turned across
the aisle to Durham. "Hey, J.D.," said Levingston, "we're going
to the Gold Club tonight. Want to come?"

"Uhhhh, no, I don't think so, Cliff," said Durham.

"Aw, c'mon, you'll love it," said Levingston, flashing his char-
acteristic inviting grin. "They stick their titties right up there in your
face."

"Well, no," protested Durham. "I'm kind of retired from that kind of stuff."

Behind the pair, fellow broadcaster John Kerr, Durham's best friend, and Hallam were holding their sides trying to keep from bursting out hysterically.

"Okay," said Levingston. "But it's gonna be great."

The game turned out not to be so great for the Bulls, who were up by 10 midway through the second quarter, but were overwhelmed by Atlanta's fast break and led by just 1 at halftime. Jackson admired the job Bob Weiss was doing as coach of the Hawks, a team of disparate parts Weiss was somehow getting to play together. As Collins had with Jordan, Weiss's predecessor, Mike Fratello, had told team management they'd never win with Dominique Wilkins because he was too selfish. Fratello was fired after the 1989–90 season and replaced by Weiss, who had Wilkins rebounding more, had turned Moses Malone into a reasonably agreeable role player to the surprise of everyone in the league, and had gotten Spud Webb to become an offensive threat at point guard. Weiss used perhaps the only system of leverage left to men who coach athletes who earn three times their salary or more: If the players wouldn't do what he asked, he'd cut their playing time. "The two most important things to athletes," agreed John Paxson: "playing time and money."

The Hawks gradually took over the game in the third quarter and then blew out the Bulls early in the fourth to win 114–105. Jordan scored 30 and Grant had 10 rebounds again, but the bench was outscored 47–20, and Jackson grew more and more frustrated as the game went on at the 29–15 disparity in free throws. And even though Jordan took 28 shots, lead referee Darell Garretson and his crew sent Jordan to the free-throw line just twice in the forty-one minutes Jordan played.

The Bulls trailed by 13 points with fifty-nine seconds left; still, Jackson called three time-outs. Jackson resented Garretson's sometimes abusive behavior toward Jordan on the court, and he told his assistants, "I'm going to make him stay out as long as I can."

At the broadcasting table, Kerr, a former NBA coach, joked about the coach who was about to die and uttered his last words: "Hey, I've got one time-out left."

Garretson was considered something of a little dictator and seemed to resent star players like Jordan, although Jackson admired his ability to call a solid professional game. But Jackson hated to see Garretson get a Bulls game because of Garretson's conflicts with Jordan. It was the second Bulls game this season for Garretson, and the Bulls had lost both. The first one had been in Milwaukee in December and that one, too, had angered Jackson because Garretson's son was on the crew and Garretson spent much of the game telling his son where to stand. Jackson was among the most quarrelsome coaches in the league, spending much of the game debating calls, but often with a sense of humor that kept him from getting assessed too many technical fouls. When Wally Rooney called a foul on B. J. Armstrong for bumping John Salley in a Pistons game, Jackson leaped up and yelled: "For God's sake, Wally, he's a hundred and six pounds."

Jackson told the players that the signs of slippage were apparent to the coaches, but the team wasn't actually convinced. After all, they'd just won seven straight. Jackson wouldn't sleep that night, tossing and turning over the signs he was seeing.

•

JORDAN WOULDN'T SLEEP much, either. Jordan never slept much, which was one reason Adolph Shiver was on the trip. He was an old friend of Jordan's from North Carolina, and Jordan remained close to him and to Fred Whitfield and Fred Kearns, both North Carolina businessmen who would often join Jordan on the road. Jordan has incredible stores of energy, and it would be Shiver or one of the Freds who could be found playing cards with him late into the night on the road. Jordan doesn't bear idleness well. This is not uncommon among great athletes, one thing that explains their desire to drive fast. Charles Barkley has always told friends he expects to die someday going 150 miles per hour down the road, and friends who have driven with Jordan are amazed he has avoided such a fate. He would come screeching to a halt in front of the Chicago Stadium parking lot after going 70 miles per hour down the side streets, and observers would say they'd often see Jordan gunning through stop signs at intersections, almost testing whether his reflexes were fast enough to get him past approaching cars. Athletes of such ability, it seems, need constant challenge.

Jordan had few friends on the Bulls since Rod Higgins and Charles

Oakley had been traded, so he imported his own company, people who could adhere to his schedule and his manias. It wasn't surprising that Jordan didn't socialize much with his teammates, for it was particularly hard on them. Going out with Jordan can be like a trip through a high school with Mick Jagger. "It's like being with a rock star," a Bulls rookie, Anthony Jones, had noted during an exhibition trip in 1988. Earlier in the 1990–91 season, Cartwright and Hodges were sitting in a restaurant when a boy came over and said, "Mr. Cartwright, I've been waiting five years." He handed Cartwright a piece of paper. "Could you get Michael Jordan's autograph for me?"

Autographs were a sore subject among the players. Jordan wouldn't often sign autographs for his teammates, and when he did, he expected a favor in return. It's why the coaches had to stop asking him. Like everyone else involved with the Bulls, they were bombarded with requests for Jordan's autograph from friends, but Jordan would eventually expect some kind of repayment. Stopping the requests was "one big thing that helped my relationship with him," explained Jackson. "He couldn't look at me as someone asking him for favors." It would allow Jackson to tell Jordan no when Jordan wanted friends on the team plane or bus, a practice that others before Jackson were unable to stop. Likewise, Bach, though the person in the organization closest to Jordan, had also stopped asking for his autograph once he'd seen how Jordan had used the privilege.

"I used to sign [Jordan's name] myself," Pippen said, "but now I've stopped that, too. I've got some pride, too, and I'm not going to beg him. I tell them now, 'I'm not asking him.' I just don't get them anymore."

Jordan is a star unlike any other in sports, both in his skill and in his earning power. Estimates of his actual income vary because of speculation that ProServ, his marketing representative, may inflate the amounts to help solicit other clients. But Jordan probably earned as much as $10 million from outside sources during 1990–91; he issued several videos which became record sellers, and he moved past the likes of Arnold Palmer and Jack Nicklaus as the most profitable commercial spokesman in America. It was why Jordan could turn down $18,000 for a one-hour store-opening appearance, or $250,000 for a business seminar weekend, because he had a golf trip planned. All this, too, tended to distance Jordan from his teammates, because no other Bull earned any significant money in commercial endorsements. Paxson had gotten a razor-blade commercial because the company was looking for a brother trio, and Pippen had finally gotten a $200,000-per-year shoe deal after becoming an All-Star. But Hodges never received an offer after winning consecutive three-point-shooting contests at the All-Star break, and Cartwright was mostly asked to do public service announcements, which he graciously accepted. Jordan was different, everyone knew, and sometimes it was hard for teammates to accept.

Stacey King was bright enough to see what had happened. "They created a monster," he observed.

And there was this thing about "the Jordan Rules." Newspaper and magazine articles used the term to refer to the supposedly secret way the Pistons had of stopping Jordan. But to the players, "the Jordan Rules" were something very different.

Take the time Jordan picked up the flu in December. He called in to say he was sick and wouldn't be at practice. Jackson sent trainer Chip Schaefer to Jordan's house to bring him medication.

A week later, John Paxson called in to say he was sick with the flu. He had been vomiting all night. Jackson told him to come to practice and then they'd make an assessment. There was a rule that if you were sick, the trainer had to see you. Paxson was sent right home. The trainer was not asked to go to his house.

It was nothing new on the Bulls, this separate set of rules for Jordan and the other players. Why then, some would ask, *wouldn't* Jordan think he had special rights to go solo instead of joining the ensemble in the game? If it was a mosaic of the air he wanted to create, what signal was there that he shouldn't? If Jordan was given the impression by management that he was special off the court, why should he think things were any different on the court?

The stories, meanwhile, were legion, and the dilemma remained. Jordan was the best. He did so much more for the team. Didn't he deserve special treatment? Don't all superstars in all sports get special treatment?

Jordan was always the last player on the team bus. He didn't like to sit there and wait for others while fans crowded around the bus. The bus always waited. One time he climbed on, but then-Bull Rory Sparrow was stuck in the lobby. As Sparrow got to the front door of the hotel, the bus pulled away. When Jordan suffered a groin pull in the 1988–89 season and had to miss a game, the team set him up at home with a machine for treatment; other players are usually asked to accompany the team if they want to get treatment when they are hurt.

Perhaps the most famous incident involving Jordan's rules occurred during the 1988–89 season. The Bulls were in Charlotte just before Christmas. Coach Doug Collins had said there probably wouldn't be practice the next day, Christmas Eve. But when the Bulls lost to the lowly Hornets, Collins wrote on the blackboard after the game: "Practice at the Multiplex 11 A.M."

"No way," Jordan said.

The next morning, the players sat wearily on the team bus waiting for the trip to the airport and a commercial flight home in holiday chaos. No Jordan. Collins was frantic. He sent then-trainer Mark Pfeil to knock on Jordan's door; Jordan wouldn't answer the telephone. Jordan told Pfeil he wasn't going back to Chicago for practice just because Collins was angry, because he would then have to travel all the way back to North Carolina for Christmas as he'd planned. Pfeil could tell Collins that.

Pfeil did and Collins sent him back. He was horrified. Tell Jordan, Collins instructed, that if he'd just come to the airport, Collins would cancel practice.

"I'll be there for five minutes," Jordan said. "That's all."

The bus left, and shortly after the players arrived at the gate Jordan showed up and Collins gathered the team. It was Christmas Eve, Collins said with anxious eyes, so as a reward he was calling off practice.

Jordan turned and started walking away. Paxson noticed he was not wearing socks. No socks? Going to Chicago in December? The players knew immediately why practice had been canceled.

Collins never did figure out how to deal with Jordan. During that 1989–90 season, Jordan's friends rode the team bus and the team made reservations for them on the road in the team hotel. Other players were told they couldn't even have friends or family with them on the road, let alone have the team handle the accommodations. Jackson stopped much of that when he became coach after the 1988–89 season. But when the players showed up in Atlanta and were handed rooming lists, they saw that Shiver was back with the team, as was Tim Grover.

Grover is Jordan's personal weight trainer. Again, the separation, the Jordan Rules; the other eleven Bulls work out with strength coaches Al Vermeil and Erik Helland. Helland even goes on long road trips with the team to help keep players on their weight-lifting and workout routines and to find a gym. Jordan and Grover always find a different one.

Jordan started working out on his own during the 1989–90 season. He purchased a weight set for the basement of his home and eventually hooked up with Grover through the team doctor. Jordan had never worked out and always joked that his pre-training-camp routine involved walking on the golf course. He had long been a junk-food addict who probably took in more grease a year than a squeaky joint, although in recent years he'd stopped eating fast foods. Jordan is just a natural, says the Bulls' team doctor, John Hefferon, and that allowed him to ignore most of the prescribed regimens for athletes.

But Jordan was finding himself getting worn down in the latter stages of the playoffs, and he wanted to work more on a post-up move, so he decided he'd need to get stronger to battle for position. He started lifting weights and got his weight over 210 during the 1990–91 season.

Why not with the team strength coach?

The official reason was that Jordan would draw crowds that were too large at the team's practice facility.

The real reason? No one was quite sure, but there was considerable speculation that it had to do with the competitive fires that raged within Jordan.

Teams take on their own personality in the locker room. Some are serious, others are into hotfoots and juvenile antics. The Bulls, taking their cue from Jordan, like to harass one another verbally. Often, the abuse can get ugly and personal. Jordan derided Grant regularly during his contract negotiations about how lousy his contract was and how he would be willing to buy a pencil from him to support his family. When rumors spread that Pippen was in line for a contract that might equal or surpass Jordan's, Grant told Jordan that Pippen would now have to take all the shots and that they'd be glad to help Jordan out with a loan if he needed one. Perhaps for a hair weave?

So the concern was that weight lifting would become a competition and Jordan would lose. Grant, according to Vermeil, already was bench-pressing the weight a football defensive lineman can lift. And even Will Perdue, whom Jordan didn't respect, had been lifting weights for so long that Vermeil felt it would take Jordan a few years to reach the levels Perdue had now attained.

"Wouldn't the team just love it if he got a hernia trying to lift more than me?" said Perdue. "They'd probably blame me."

So the team's own Jordan rules sent a definite message: Michael Jordan *is* different from the rest of the team. But not so different that, as the team moved on to Miami on Saturday, Jordan would be permitted to bring his entourage on the team charter. Shiver and Grover would have to meet him in Miami.

·

PRACTICE WENT BADLY on Sunday. Jackson blew up at Armstrong several times as the young guard showed little enthusiasm and played out of control. Jackson was now desperately urging Krause daily to make a deal with Dallas. He wanted point guard Derek Harper. He was telling Krause to trade King and Armstrong and Hopson, too, if possible, and Krause had offered Paxson to Milwaukee, hoping to get a first-round draft pick to deal to Dallas in a package for Harper.

But it was a dilemma for Krause. He was calling around, but the value of King, Armstrong, and Hopson had plummeted. "I can't trade anybody if you don't play them," Krause told Jackson. "You want them traded. Play them."

Meanwhile, Armstrong was feeling he had become a target of Jackson's through no fault of his own. Sometimes he was right. For example, Jordan likes to try to sneak in on occasion to slam in a missed free throw. It had worked a few times earlier in the season and was a crowd-pleasing move. When Jordan wanted to try it, he'd tell Armstrong to drop back to protect, which was Jordan's job. Armstrong's job was to meet the opposing point guard at halfcourt or sooner, but he'd drop back to protect for Jordan. Then Jackson would scream from the bench, "Up, B.J., up, get up. What the hell are you doing?"

Jordan would tell him not to worry about Jackson. Jackson would tell him to do as he said.

Armstrong was losing confidence quickly. Finally, he had his agent, Arn Tellem, call Jerry Reinsdorf. "B.J. is confused," Tellem told Reinsdorf. "He doesn't know who to listen to. The superstar of the team tells him one thing and the coach tells him another. What should he do?"

"You tell him to listen to the coach," Reinsdorf instructed.

Armstrong wasn't so sure.

•

JACKSON WAS AWAKENED at 7:00 A.M. Monday by a call from Krause. "Did you see the newspaper?" Krause asked. Even if Jackson did read the sports section, he certainly wouldn't have seen the Chicago newspapers in Miami. Krause studied the stories about the Bulls, living in mortal fear of negative reports. This one was horrible. Stacey King was blasting the team. If the Bulls didn't think he could play, fine, then trade him somewhere he could. He wasn't getting a chance when others in his rookie class were, and it was time to stop blaming every loss on the bench. The story went on and on. Krause wanted to talk to King. Jackson said he would do the talking; he knew that Krause would just make things worse.

"Would you really rather be playing for a team like New Jersey or the Clippers?" Jackson asked King.

"Sure," King replied.

Jackson understood, but he was disappointed. "The only way you make money in the pro game today is to get statistics," Jackson told a friend later. And he even tried to help his players in that quest. It was why he ignored Pippen's often-selfish play. He knew Pippen was trying to get a new deal, and he could not in all good conscience counsel him otherwise. But he also felt King could prove himself on a winning team like the Bulls. King obviously felt otherwise.

The game against the Heat on January 21 proved to be the easy part. The inexperienced Heat players were hanging in, but committed 5 turnovers in 7 possessions in the third quarter, allowing the Bulls, who rarely made any mistakes, to take a 14-point lead and walk away with the game.

King played twenty-two minutes, the second-most he'd played in a month. And he performed reasonably well, getting 9 points and even 5 assists, which only infuriated backup center Will Perdue, who played two minutes.

Perdue was in his third season and was waiting patiently. He'd rarely played in his first season; Collins and Krause feuded over his use and he became a pawn in their battle for control. Jackson had used Perdue more, but thought he was too weak defensively to play for extended periods of time. And it didn't help that Jordan had once felt inclined to punch him around in a practice.

It was during the 1989–90 season. Perdue was setting a screen, which usually resembled a seven-foot piece of spaghetti, but this time he dug in. Jordan came by, expecting Perdue to give way as usual, when *Bang!* Jordan slammed into Perdue and stopped, almost sliding down to the floor like some life-size cartoon character. Jordan stopped, looked hard at Perdue, and swung. *One! Two!* Right to the side of the head. Perdue's knees wobbled, but he remained upright.

"Why the hell don't you ever set a pick like that in a game?" Jordan screamed.

Everyone stopped, and since this was early in practice no one was watching from outside the glass-enclosed gym in the Multiplex. The incident would lead to Jackson's demand that the team install a curtain so practice could be private. Explanation: The players need to concentrate. Reality: We can't have people seeing this stuff.

Perdue's playing time was continuing to decrease, and he'd talked to Jackson about it at the end of December. He was ready to press his case in the media, but his parents were in town for a few weeks and he didn't want to upset them. He'd wait. But now King had complained and his playing time had gone up. So Perdue went to the newspapers.

He wasn't playing and didn't believe that was right; King had spoken out and got to play more. "That seems to be the way it is around here," Perdue told Kent McDill of the *Daily Herald*. "And I don't want to be playing in the last minute and a half of blowouts." Perdue also wondered why Cartwright was playing so much—forty-four minutes in one recent game—since he clearly was wearing down. What was the team thinking of? "I'm treading water here," Perdue said. "My skills are deteriorating, no doubt about it."

The bench problems didn't stop there. Hopson was proving dif-

ficult to coach. Jackson had sent him into the game almost two
weeks earlier against Philadelphia, and Hopson had sauntered over
to the scorers' table to check in, moving as if it were a chore,
although Hopson often walked like that. Before he got there, Jackson yelled to him, "Show like you care." The Bulls started offering
him around, but no one wanted to touch his $930,000-per-year con-
tract. He was hesitant and lost on the court, Jackson felt, and he
blamed the team. "They say I'm supposed to score and I get two
shots a game," Hopson complained to close friend, Armstrong.
"Now they say I'm a defensive player. First I was a guard, now I'm
a forward. Before I was a scorer, now I'm a defender. Who knows
what the hell's going on here?"

And nobody seemed to know what was happening with the rookie
Scott Williams, even though the coaches were impressed with his
play at times. Bach had even stunned Reinsdorf at the team's Christmas party by telling him that Williams would be a better player than
King. Reinsdorf, paying King $8 million over six years, was not at
all pleased to hear this, although he was pleased with the way Krause
had finagled getting Williams as a free agent. But Williams had
stopped showering after games, apparently in a protest over a lack
of playing time. He was saying that he was better than King and
Perdue and should be playing. He'd often stare long and hard at
Jackson or Bach without saying anything, and Jackson began to
worry. He started to ask the players if something was wrong with
Williams, whether he needed professional counseling. He had no
feel for the kid. Bach did. He called his son, a California state
trooper. "Get me a gun," he said. "We've got a kid here who's
gonna walk into the coach's office one day and go off and I want
to be ready."

The Bulls were starting to hit bottom, and it wouldn't be a quick
climb back out.

•

WORD HAD BEEN circulating around the league the last several days
that the Bulls and Denver Nuggets had agreed to a deal for Walter
Davis. With the Denver season turning into a disaster, Davis wanted
out and had been calling Jordan every few days to ask what he'd
heard. The Bulls had sent a scout to each of Denver's last four

games. Many believed Davis could be the final piece of the championship puzzle for the Bulls, including Jordan, who argued regularly that the Bulls needed more scoring off the bench and it was clear that Hopson couldn't provide it.

The Nuggets called as the Bulls were heading to New Jersey Tuesday, January 22, for Wednesday's game against the Nets. A deal was close, but not with the Bulls. It would involve Portland giving up Drazen Petrovic and the Nets giving up a future first-round draft pick. The Nuggets wanted a pick now, but they'd wait for New Jersey's, which could be a high selection. What did the Bulls want to do?

Krause contacted Reinsdorf. They might need to clear a roster space for Davis. Reinsdorf was unwilling to release Hopson because he would also have to pay Hopson more than $900,000 for the 1991–92 season. Hodges was signed through the same season at $700,000, and the team didn't want to give up on Williams quite yet. Everyone else but Paxson and Cartwright had long-term deals, and those two were starters. But all the Bulls owed Cliff Levingston was a buyout of about $400,000 after the 1990–91 season. "Go ahead," Reinsdorf said. "Tell Phil we'll release Levingston if he wants Davis."

Krause called Jackson when the team arrived in New Jersey. The deal had to be done now, Krause said, because Denver was about to move. We should be able to do it for a first-round pick, so if you want Davis, let's go.

Jackson met with his coaches and discussed the relative merits of Davis and Levingston. The verdict: Let the deal pass. Jackson said Levingston would be helpful in the playoffs. He felt the same way about Hopson. There were too many questions about Davis's defense: Whom could he guard in the last minute of a game with Detroit?

The announcement came just as the Bulls were arriving at Byrne Arena. Jordan was standing in a rampway to the main arena, waiting to go out for his pregame shooting drill, while two teams of teenagers finished a game. He'd heard the report of the deal and was furious. As two of the boys rushed by, one bumped Jordan and exulted, "I touched Michael Jordan."

"As soon as we get back, I'm calling Reinsdorf," Jordan fumed. "Krause has messed everything up again. He can't do anything. We don't get Walter Davis and we won't get LaSalle [Thompson, the

Indiana forward rumored to be coming to the Bulls]. You'll see, we won't do anything. He's too scared and nobody wants to deal with him. We can't get anything done because of him. I'm going to tell Reinsdorf when I get back that it's either me or him. If he wants to keep Krause, fine, I'll tell him to trade me. But this is it. It's got to stop here."

The game didn't do much to change Jordan's mood. The Bulls lost, 99–95, to the 13–26 Nets. But the knife went deeper and twisted for Jordan. It was Reggie Theus who scored 8 of the Nets' last 10 points after the Bulls had taken a 90–88 lead. Jordan missed a pair of jumpers and Theus stole a pass intended for Jordan and scored, all in the last ninety-five seconds.

Jordan hated Theus as much as he did any player in the league. Jordan disliked hot dogs like New York's Mark Jackson, but his face always turned hard and cold against Theus. He'd angrily slap Theus's hands away hard, with a short, chopping slap, when Theus tried a hand check. It was a common defensive move against Jordan and he'd usually just push the defender's hand away. Against Theus, his response was more like a karate blow.

"He tried to undercut me in Kansas City my first year in the league," Jordan said once when asked about why he disliked Theus so.

"I hate his game," Jordan said another time. "He's so selfish, always berating the referees and yelling out there."

None of the reasons made sense. The story around the Bulls, though, was that Theus had briefly dated Jordan's wife, Juanita, before Jordan met her. Whatever the reason, Jordan went home from New Jersey angry, and when the team met for practice Thursday in the Multiplex, he hadn't cooled down.

Stopped by a reporter and asked about the Davis deal, Jordan took off after Krause again. "If I were general manager," he said, "we'd be a better team."

The newspapers were full of stories of the latest Jordan–Krause rift. It wasn't a fair fight. Jordan was beloved; Krause was loathed. Krause was in tears when he talked to Reinsdorf. The owner had to do something. This could not be allowed to happen. Players could not speak like this. Reinsdorf would have to blast Jordan in the newspapers. Reinsdorf told Krause he was not about to get into a war with Jordan, that he would handle it his own way.

The game the next night against Miami was almost an after-thought. The Bulls led by 17 points ten minutes into the game and started emptying the bench. The only concern was the nine minutes played by Cartwright after he hurt his hip in a fall. It would even-tually necessitate his sitting out a few games, but the Bulls' run of mostly good fortune continued: This was their third game against Miami, and while the Heat were not formidable at full strength, their best player, Rony Seikaly, had missed all three games. The Bulls already had played Philadelphia without Johnny Dawkins and Rick Mahorn, Cleveland without Mark Price and John Williams, the Clippers without Benoit Benjamin, the Bullets without Darrell Walker, and the list was getting longer. Teams seemed to be coming into the Stadium injured or at the end of long road trips. Isiah Thomas was now out for most of the rest of the regular season after wrist surgery; Larry Bird's back was acting up and he was still out. Maybe this would be one of those years when everything just broke right and the Bulls took advantage. Good fortune was smiling on the Bulls, but nobody was smiling back.

Before the game against the Heat, Jackson issued a gag order of sorts. If players had something to say about the way they were treated or about the team, they should come to him first. A little rebellion now and then was fine, Jackson knew—Jefferson had called it the medicine for the sound health of government—but this was becoming an overdose.

Later in the season, Jackson would be asked about the period of late January and early February. "We did have some rough times," he admitted, "but every team goes through periods like that." But he also knew that greatness rarely comes easily. He'd referred once to the Graham Greene quote from *The Third Man*, about the Bor-gias' rule in Italy in the fifteenth and sixteenth centuries and how it had resulted in war, murder, and terrorism, yet from that era came Michelangelo, da Vinci, and the Renaissance. In Switzerland, where they lived brotherly love, peace, and democracy for eight centuries, all they could claim was the cuckoo clock.

It was left to John Paxson to sum up the craziness. Paxson, perhaps more than anybody on the team, had a truly serious grievance and had been treated as heartlessly by the Bulls as anyone. Only Scott Williams earned less than he did. He'd been a loyal team player, but it was beginning to be apparent that the Bulls wouldn't even make a serious offer to keep him after the season. And Krause was still telling the coaches that Toni Kukoc could be a starting point guard in the NBA by next season.

"I've never seen anything like this," Paxson said. "Here we are winning [the Bulls were now 29–12, on course to break the team record of fifty-seven wins, and tied for first in the Central Division with the Pistons] and nobody's happy. I was with the Spurs and we went from winning the division to winning thirty-seven games and guys still enjoyed playing. They enjoyed the game and had a good time. But nobody wants to be here, except maybe me, and they don't want me. Everyone wants to play somewhere else; nobody's happy or having any fun. Guys want more minutes or more shots or more money. They want guys traded and management guys fired. And what if we weren't winning? It's just not supposed to be like this. Is it?"

7

FEBRUARY 1991

2/1 at Dallas; 2/3 at L.A. Lakers; 2/4 at Sacramento; 2/7 at Detroit; 2/12 v. Atlanta; 2/14 at New York; 2/16 v. New Jersey; 2/18 at Cleveland; 2/19 v. Washington; 2/22 v. Sacramento; 2/23 v. Charlotte; 2/26 v. Boston

NINETY MINUTES BEFORE the January 31 game against the San Antonio Spurs that opened a four-game Western Conference trip, Michael Jordan was sitting in front of his locker stall in the cramped visitors' locker room. He felt like one of the last defenders of the Alamo who had trod this ground 155 years before. He'd rarely felt lower. Jordan was holding the portable disc player he carries everywhere, and had on his headphones. He might have been sleeping, though it was hard to tell because he was wearing dark sunglasses. He wasn't going out to shoot before the game for the first time in more than two months. He hadn't said anything earlier in the day at shoot-around.

"What's wrong with the General?" Hodges asked Grant, the two eyeing Jordan from across the room. "He's been in a big-time pout all day."

165

"I don't know," Grant responded. "Must be some problems at home."

In a sense, Grant was right; Jordan's dark mood stemmed from a conversation he'd had back home in Chicago—not with any family member, but with Bulls owner Jerry Reinsdorf.

The talk was triggered by Jordan's outburst about Krause in New Jersey. Reinsdorf had been obligated to respond publicly, and the situation clearly made him uncomfortable, though his support for Krause was unequivocal. "Michael Jordan," said Reinsdorf, "is undoubtedly the greatest player that ever lived. He's probably one of the three greatest competitors of all time in any sport, the other two being Jake LaMotta and Muhammad Ali. Guys you had to kill to beat. Michael's like that. But he's still a player and, quite frankly, players don't know a whole lot about coaching and they don't know a whole lot about what it takes to make a deal. If Michael knew what we tried to accomplish and the pitfalls and problems we ran into [trying to obtain Walter Davis], he probably wouldn't feel as frustrated. But he doesn't, and we can't sit and explain to every player what moves we are trying to make. And we cannot single out one player and make him a consultant to the general manager."

Jordan wasn't all that surprised by Reinsdorf's attitude. He liked Reinsdorf and respected him for his ability to make money; that and a low golf score ranked highest in qualities Jordan generally admired. In fact, Jordan had just gone into a partnership with Reinsdorf in a sports paraphernalia business, putting up his own money, something he didn't do casually. Reinsdorf was trying to put off renegotiating Jordan's contract by cutting him in on some investments, but the league got wind of the plans and said that any such profits Jordan received would count under the Bulls' salary cap unless Jordan had invested his own money.

Nonetheless, Jordan still didn't care for Reinsdorf's choice of general managers, and his outburst after the Davis deal, he told friends, was not merely out of frustration and emotion.

Several of Reinsdorf's minority partners in the Bulls had approached Jordan about getting Krause out. Reinsdorf was the team's managing partner under the original agreement, so he had total say on basketball operations. No case could be made for mismanagement or violation of fiduciary responsibility since the Bulls were one of the most profitable teams in the league. So the partners went to

Jordan. They, too, wanted Krause out, and they thought only Jordan's outrage could get him removed.

"I figured I'd try to put the pressure on him to do something about Krause," Jordan said about his first volley of remarks after the team returned from New Jersey in late January. His eyes were hard and cold as he spoke. "This thing isn't over. I'm gonna get that guy fired yet."

Reinsdorf called Jordan and asked him to come over to his North Shore home just before the team left for San Antonio. It was the first time Reinsdorf ever had invited a player to his home. Reinsdorf recognized that Krause had weaknesses, he told Jordan, but he believed Krause had done an adequate job. "We are in first place," he said. "Jerry's done some good things. He got Scottie [Pippen] and Horace in the draft and he got us a center [Cartwright]." Reinsdorf knew Krause could be annoying with his secretive ways, and he knew he wasn't the ideal person to represent the team in public. But he liked Krause's moxie. And the team was winning. So what was the problem?

Jordan insisted that Krause was incapable of making any but the draft-choice deals he'd made, that his lack of personal skills kept him from making serious deals and getting players who could already have helped the Bulls win a title. He wasn't a good judge of talent, Jordan said. The Bulls should have a former player as general manager.

"Someone perhaps like Elgin Baylor?" Reinsdorf asked. Baylor was one of the game's all-time greats, but the Clippers continued to sputter under his direction despite years of top draft picks.

"I play golf with these general managers all summer," Jordan said, "and they all tell me they don't want to deal with Krause because he's always trying to rip them off, get something for nothing. It's why we don't do anything."

"Jerry likes to get value," Reinsdorf explained.

Despite the team's success, Jordan said he still believed the team Krause had put together lacked the ability to win a title. Krause's recent first-round picks of Perdue, Armstrong, and King weren't helping much; Grant was playing well, but he couldn't be trusted, and neither could Pippen. "You know he hasn't shown up for our two biggest games yet," Jordan pointed out, referring to Pippen's famous injury and migraine in those final playoff games against

Detroit. Jordan said he'd warned them about Hopson—even given up money at their request—and why was all this time being spent on Toni Kukoc? The Bulls didn't need him and he wasn't going to be any good anyway. And Jordan thought the coaches were wrong about not needing Walter Davis. They needed the scoring off the bench, and come playoff time everyone would notice. And if not Davis, what about Tony Campbell or LaSalle Thompson? The Bulls also needed another frontcourt player.

"Well," Reinsdorf pointed out to Jordan, "you're not helping any. We're working on several deals, but every time you come out criticizing the general manager, it makes it look like Jerry has to do something and that makes it harder on us. People start thinking we're desperate and want to take advantage of us."

Reinsdorf hoped he wasn't being too hard on Jordan. He always felt they had a good relationship, even if he sometimes had to take a hard line. A few years ago Jordan had come in to talk to him, upset about the team's play and demanding trades. He wanted Horace Grant out, among others. He was going to go public with his complaints. "Do you want people to start thinking of you like they do Isiah Thomas?" Reinsdorf said.

It stopped Jordan in his tracks. Thomas had recently been blamed for getting Adrian Dantley traded for Mark Aguirre. Thomas was being reviled in the media as a spoiled, meddling player. Reinsdorf knew the effect of his comments immediately. He knew Jordan's feelings about Thomas and knew Jordan could see how Thomas was being condemned. Jordan backed off.

"Imagine how this makes your teammates feel," Reinsdorf continued. "What are they supposed to think when their captain says we're not good enough? How are we supposed to get the most out of them? And then how are we supposed to make a deal when you're knocking your players? Are other teams going to want them when you say they're not good enough?"

Jordan was baffled and speechless. He knew Reinsdorf was right, and he didn't know what to say. He believed the Bulls were going about this all wrong, but Reinsdorf made sense. As he always does. Jordan felt small, like a kid in the principal's office. The conversation eventually turned to lighter topics and Jordan soon left to go home. His little speech had had little impact. Things would remain as they were. They weren't going to make a deal, Jordan thought. Krause was too scared and Reinsdorf was too satisfied. Jordan called Falk. Had he checked any further on whether Jordan could get out of his contract for next year?

•

THE BULLS' ROAD problems continued in San Antonio. They knew they couldn't hope to stop David Robinson with Cartwright, since Robinson is so much quicker and a better jumper. But the Bulls' strength is their overall quickness, and they're very effective at sending the double-team at the other team's best player from different directions. The Bulls pounced on Robinson from all over, taking a reasonably comfortable 82–75 lead going into the fourth quarter. But with the reserves in, Robinson looked like Santa Anna's army to the Bulls. He came from everywhere and led the Spurs on a 13–2 run in the first four minutes of the quarter that put the Spurs back ahead. Jordan was fuming on the bench. Jackson had fallen into a rotation in which the reserves started the fourth quarter. Jordan felt the Bulls were being beaten too often at that point in the game. "We get the lead and they let it go and then we have to get it back," he told Bach on the bench. "We're not going to be able to do that all the time. Tell him to get me back in there."

It was 88–84 Spurs when Jordan returned. He scored on three straight possessions and the Bulls tied the game, but the Bulls couldn't control Rod Strickland, who got loose for a pair of drives. The Spurs held on for a 106–102 victory as Jordan fouled out trying to steal the ball with two seconds left and the Spurs ahead by 2.

Jackson said Jordan had tired at the end. Jordan, who led the Bulls with 36 points despite hitting just 9 of 22 shots, said he wasn't tired and wished he'd been in the game earlier in the fourth quarter. Robinson had 31 points and 17 rebounds.

To many, Robinson was already the league's most valuable player. He wasn't as dominant as Jordan, but the consensus around the league seemed to be that he was the better teammate, even if he couldn't carry a team for as long as Jordan. Robinson had touched on this in an interview when the Bulls were in town. He didn't mean to discredit Jordan, but the message was clear.

"Michael is more of a non-basketball-fan type of player," Robinson said. "He always looks great out there hanging, jumping, dribbling around. But if you know a lot about the game, you appreciate what I do more. It's more basic.''

The talk about Robinson versus Jordan reminded some among the Bulls of a story Rod Thorn had once told about his time with Julius Erving. Larry Kenon, then Erving's teammate on the ABA Nets, was having some problems with his game and not feeling too good about his play. He was a scorer, and the team needed him badly. Erving went to Thorn, who was an assistant coach, and said he was going to take care of the problem that night.

Every time Erving got the ball and the double-team closed in, he hit Kenon for a close-in jumper or a dunk. Kenon scored 30 points and afterward the reporters had crowded around him to ask him about breaking out of his slump. Kenon was ebullient, telling writers about how he'd gotten his game back and how he knew he was on the way to many more games like this. Erving had 12 points in the win, and the few writers who went to talk with him were directed by Erving to the evening's star.

"Can you see M.J. doing something like that?" wondered Grant.

The Bulls moved on to Dallas the next night to play the Mavericks, a game they figured to win easily. Dallas was staggering; Fat Lever and Roy Tarpley had been out the entire season with knee injuries, and the Mavericks were going to miss the playoffs.

Again, Jordan wouldn't go out and shoot before the game; this time he sat no more than a foot from the TV screen, watching the endlessly rolling pregame tape of a previous Mavericks game, again wearing his dark glasses. He hadn't joked with anyone, hadn't talked to anyone.

"I know something's bothering you," said Bach. No one had talked to Jordan all day, and finally Bach had come up behind him, ready to listen if Jordan had a problem. Bach also knew the team needed a win with the Lakers coming up next, and Jackson, too, was concerned about Jordan. "You've got to come out into the world."

Jordan kept looking at the screen.

"I don't want to see the world," he whispered, never turning his head back to Bach.

What Jordan did see was another failure of the reserves to hold a lead at the start of the fourth quarter. The Bulls regrouped enough to pull away for an 11-point win, but the fact remained that they had struggled against a weak team. Jordan remained distant from his teammates, Pippen was worrying about his contract negotiations, and Grant, Cartwright, and Paxson were getting few shots. There were a good many slouching backbones as the players filed out of the arena. The days in Texas had been soft and mild, but the nights, for the Bulls, had been filled with anger and resentment.

As the team moved on to Los Angeles to play the Lakers, the coaches talked about what could be done. They talked about the complete absence of team unity, and Jackson decided he'd talk to the team on Sunday morning before the game. Bach said they needed to be awakened by something. "Shoot a hostage," he told Jackson in his colorful, military-laced dialogue. "Trade someone and get their attention."

Krause had been in Dallas to look at Derek Harper. And Bach had been dispatched after the game to feel out Mavericks assistant coach Bob Zuffelato, a longtime friend and former assistant with Bach in Golden State. Krause told Bach he'd be on a reconnaissance mission, but Bach said he wouldn't betray his friend; he'd talk to Zuffelato, but wouldn't undermine him.

What he heard from Zuffelato was not encouraging. The Mavericks wanted to give it one more try when Tarpley and Lever returned from injuries, and it would take more than Stacey King, B. J. Armstrong, and draft picks, which the Bulls were offering, to get Harper. So that deal didn't look promising.

The trade talk was unsettling to the players. "I wish the [NBA's February 21 trading] deadline were past," said Paxson as the team prepared to play a February 3 game against the Lakers. "Even if I lost my starting job, I'd just like to know." Armstrong met again with his agent, Arn Tellem, after the team arrived in Los Angeles on Saturday, February 2; Tellem assured Armstrong several teams were interested in him, including the Clippers, Lakers, Pacers, Bullets, Kings, 76ers, and Hawks. It was important for Armstrong to get to a team on which he'd be a starter. This was the second year of his four-year deal, and if he were to get another good contract, he'd have to become a starter by next season. Somewhere.

"I'm not the same player I was when I came here," Armstrong told his agent. "All I want is a chance. Stacey got a chance when Horace was out and now Will is going to get a chance [Cartwright's hip was acting up and Jackson had decided to start Perdue against the Lakers]. But they won't give me a chance here. I know I can lead a team. It's what I've always done, but they keep telling me I don't fit in. I've just got to get out of here."

King, meanwhile, was doing little to lose weight since his diatribe against the team. He was back to playing sparingly and had decided he'd be better off elsewhere. Jordan's anger toward him continued to grow; the two ProServ clients barely spoke. Falk would call Jordan and ask what was wrong with King, and Jordan would tell him that King stinks. Falk, though, told King that several teams were pursuing him and it was time to get him out of Chicago. He'd do all he could to get him traded, but he wasn't sure Krause could pull off a deal.

With all of this in the air, Jackson's words to them on Sunday were hardly surprising.

"You guys are not bonding," Jackson told the team at a breakfast meeting before the afternoon game. "It's midway through the season and you're not playing like a team. You're not coming together as a team. You're still looking out for yourselves."

The game with the Lakers showed clearly what Jackson meant. The Lakers would win 99–86 even after Magic Johnson went out with a concussion late in the third quarter; Johnson, backpedaling against a Bulls rush, had gotten kicked in the head as he was falling over teammate Terry Teagle's leg, and his head bounced as it hit the floor.

Pippen scored 18 points in the first half. He always does well against the Lakers since he's much too quick for James Worthy, and he hit 9 of 15 shots for the half, but got just 5 more opportunities the rest of the game and was fuming afterward. "I guess my teammates didn't realize how good I was playing," he said. "The ball didn't come my way and I wasn't too happy about it. The ball gets in certain people's hands and doesn't get moved." Jordan had moved to point guard in the second half, but rarely passed to Pippen, who had outscored him 18–9 in the first half. Jordan was angry, too; he'd been out at the start of the fourth quarter again when the Lakers went on an 11–4 run to retake control of the game. He was trying to be a good soldier, but Jackson kept calling for his triangle/motion offense and Jordan wanted to drive. The offense was costing the team the game, he felt. The Bulls got the score back to 89–86, but rookie Tony Smith, replacing Johnson, drove for a score, and then

Cliff Levingston missed a wild outside jumper and the game slipped away. "We don't seem to get the right people the right shots," Jordan said afterward. He yelled at Paxson for passing to Perdue, who shot 2 of 11. "He can't do anything with the ball. Don't give it to him," Jordan demanded of Paxson during the game. The bench had scored a combined total of 4 points in sixty minutes among six players. Perdue had done reasonably well as a starter with 11 rebounds, although he hadn't blocked the middle like Cartwright, and opposing center Vlade Divac had gotten loose for 12 points and 13 rebounds.

The team headed right for the plane and left for Sacramento, where everyone knew they'd get a win and make it a 2–2 trip. At Sacramento, the Bulls led by 17 points in the first quarter and 22 by halftime. Ralph Sampson, pretty much given up on by the Kings because of his bad knees, gave the team and the crowd a lift with an aggressive performance to open up the second half as the Kings cut the Bulls lead to 4, but Chicago went on to win by 11.

Jordan was still angry from his meeting with Reinsdorf and remained in his shell. Bach finally told him, "The team needs your energy. You've got to be happy. You're sending the wrong message."

"I just can't be, coach," Jordan replied.

Bach, too, had gotten angry earlier. He was a devoted military man and a patriot and the nation was in a patriotic fever with the war in the Persian Gulf going so well. Teams began to celebrate with a wide variety of national anthems. This night, a man came out and whistled the anthem. The veins in Bach's neck began to tighten, and although he stood at attention, it was clear he was growing angrier and angrier at the disrespect being shown. His eyes drilled holes in the whistler and his nostrils flared.

"I suppose they'll have five guys come out and fart it the next time," he spat after it was finished.

But the fireworks were just beginning.

Levingston, having played just ten minutes against the Lakers and averaging little more than that on the season, was angry because he was warned again about taking bad shots—during the film session before the Kings game. He was having trouble fitting in with the team; he was a poor passer and Jackson had lost faith in him quickly. Levingston's passes to the wingman in the offense would either be stolen or end up in the stands—fans were said to have caught more of his passes than his teammates. The frustration finally boiled over in Sacramento.

"Why did they bring me here?" he exploded on the bench during the game. "If they weren't going to play me, why'd they get me? What the hell am I doing here?"

Teammates turned as Levingston continued his monologue.

"What the hell's going on here? Put me in the game. I'm not getting to play. What's going on? Why am I here? Who's running this show? I want out. Get me out of here, get me the hell out of here."

"Cliff," whispered Hopson, "P.J.'s gonna hear you."

"Fuck him," yelled Levingston. "Who cares? He's not playing me. Fuck him. Let him kick me out of here."

The discourse continued for almost thirty minutes.

Then, during a time-out, Jackson counseled the players, "Let's hit the open man, let's move the ball and get it to the open guy."

"I'm open," said Pippen, still seething over his 5-shot second half against the Lakers.

"You can't hit your shots when somebody throws it to you," Jackson shot back at Pippen.

Pippen lunged at Jackson and Grant jumped in between.

"Okay, okay," Grant said to Pippen. "Let's just play ball. Let's just go out and play ball."

"Who the hell does he think he is saying that to me?" Pippen shouted at Grant. "He better not say that to me again or I'm gonna go after him. What's he saying that for?"

At that point, Cartwright, who was not in the game, leaned over to assistant strength coach Erik Helland. "I like our team unity," Cartwright said. "How about you?"

On the bench, Jordan took a seat at the end and didn't talk to anyone. That wasn't a comment on this particular evening; even at home, Jordan sits at the end of the Bulls' bench with a space between him and the rest of the team. In many ways it's symbolic of the gap between Jordan and the rest of the Bulls in talent and communication.

When Jackson calls for Hodges or Hopson to get up and replace Jordan, the Bulls' bench sometimes resembles a game of musical chairs, with players scrambling away from the end of the bench. "Nobody likes to sit next to him and listen to him complain and scream to get back in the game," Cartwright explained.

Were they having fun yet?

Next would be the rematch with the Pistons in Detroit. The reporters wanted to know afterward not about the Kings, but about the Pistons. Could the Bulls win in the Palace?

Reinsdorf checked the box scores and the schedule at home the next morning. "The season is over," he thought, "if we can't beat the Pistons in Detroit without Isiah."

•

JACKSON THOUGHT THE time was right to beat Detroit. Thomas's absence would help, because he was a great clutch performer who had changed his game to help his team win. Although he clearly was the better player, he had given up some of his shots to accommodate Joe Dumars and others; the Pistons had improved and become champions. But Thomas still ranked among the best guards in the game and he could break down the Bulls' guards any time. But now Dumars would be playing point guard, and Jackson could have his guards attack Dumars, taking away his offense and forcing the ball to Vinnie Johnson, who was not an All-Star performer and whom the Bulls felt they could handle.

Jackson hoped his outburst after the last game in Detroit in December had finally gotten the attention of the league; perhaps the Bulls would get a break with the officiating. But one thing concerned him: the basket in front of the Pistons' bench.

The Bulls coaches had inspected that basket and believed the Pistons had tinkered with it. A rubber-and-foam piece usually found behind the rim appeared to be missing. Jackson had studied tapes of the Pistons games and noticed that whenever the Pistons were shooting at that basket, they had their best rebounders in the game and crashed hardest for offensive rebounds. Jackson knew the Pistons were one of the greatest teams ever at screening and hitting the boards, but this was different. It was almost as if they expected to miss more on this particular basket. The visiting team gets its choice of baskets to shoot at and Jackson, like most coaches, liked to have his team playing defense in the second half in front of his bench. But he changed this time. He wanted the Pistons shooting at the basket in front of their own bench to close the game.

Actually, such tactics are not all that uncommon around the NBA. It's why Jackson always carries an air-pressure gauge with him.

"I used to laugh at him," said Bach. "But we've seen it necessary more and more the last few years."

Like that night in Miami in the 1989–90 season. Jackson always tests the poundage in the game balls before the game. The balls this night in Miami were well below the required 7½ to 8½ pounds. An innocent oversight? Unlikely. With a softer ball players can't dribble as fast and the game slows. It was what a less talented team like Miami wanted against a running team like the Bulls. Jackson got the balls pumped up and the Heat were deflated. It works the other way, too; Jackson has caught the Lakers trying to sneak balls with 15 to 17 pounds of air into the game. Why? Magic Johnson likes a high dribble, and a livelier ball results in long rebounds that key the kind of fast break the Lakers love to use, especially at home.

It was no coincidence that Jackson knew what to look for. He had played on the 1973 championship Knicks, regarded as one of the smartest teams ever to play the game, and such tactics were not beyond their ken.

"We used to deflate the ball because we were a short team and didn't want long rebounds," Jackson said, adding that most of his teammates carried pins in their belts to deflate the ball when they'd get a chance. "It also helped our offense because we liked to pass the ball, and other teams couldn't run on us as well because the ball wouldn't come up so fast when they dribbled." The nice word for it all is *gamesmanship*.

Jackson knew these were some of the hidden reasons it was so hard to win on the road. When the Bulls were in Portland, they found the balls softer. Why, since the Trail Blazers liked to run? Because they crash the boards, and soft balls will stay on the rim longer for offensive rebounds, which was an advantage they had over the Bulls, who also liked to run. The lighting is usually poor in Washington, where the Bulls always shoot poorly, and the back-boards are suspended in an awkward way in the L.A. Sports Arena, causing unusual bounces that favor the familiar home players. And the Celtics are notorious for overheating the opponents' locker room to make them more tired. You had to be prepared for the enemy in pro sports, especially when you were in hostile territory.

.

THE GAME COULDN'T have gone better for the Bulls. They rarely shoot well in Detroit against the Pistons' quickly rotating defenses; Dennis Rodman bumps and battles against Pippen and refuses to give him the lanes, and Dumars and Laimbeer or Thomas drop off against Jordan and quickly hurry back. But even with Jordan missing 5 of 8 shots in the first quarter, the Bulls trailed just 26–25 by hitting half their attempts, and Rodman drew 2 early fouls and had to leave the game. By halftime, the Bulls had climbed ahead 44–41 as Detroit hit just 5 of 17 shots in the second quarter. The first test had been passed. The Bulls now would be shooting at the softer, more forgiving basket.

Laimbeer, the cur who seemed more suited to the World Wrestling Federation, pulled off a classic in the third quarter, grabbing his face and falling after Cartwright hit him with an elbow in the chest. The referees missed the exchange, and when Cartwright started to complain about the call, he was ejected. It was rare for a player to be ejected without a warning or two technical-foul calls, but the referees had been warned about Cartwright since he'd knocked Olajuwon out for two months with that inadvertent elbow. This was exactly what Jackson was worried about when Thorn asked Cartwright to wear elbow pads. But the bench wasn't playing scared this time, especially Armstrong. With no Thomas there to harass him, Armstrong started breaking toward the basket with confidence and converting clutch jumpers. Despite the concerns about his play and his status, Armstrong could still carry himself with pride and defiance, and this time his confidence was justified by his play; he found himself still in there at the end of the game—crunch time, as the players like to call it.

The Pistons, though, took control in the fourth quarter. Rodman and Laimbeer rebounded missed jumpers and scored. "There they go," Jackson thought, "hitting the boards on that basket." The Pistons took a 5-point lead with five minutes left. It looked like their game.

Armstrong hit a jumper, but after James Edwards missed two

free throws, Pippen missed a jumper when Detroit sent two defenders at Jordan and he had to pass off. Laimbeer then rebounded
a miss for another basket: 87–82 Detroit with four minutes left.

But Pippen came back with a smart, leaning jumper and then one
of two free throws on the next possession after Aguirre missed a
jumper. Pippen had 20 and had begun to shake some demons. The
Bulls had narrowed the Detroit lead to 87–85. But Detroit crashed
the boards again and Laimbeer was fouled going for a rebound. He
converted two free throws for an 89–85 Detroit lead. With just over
two minutes left, Grant rebounded a Jordan miss and got it back
to Jordan. Jordan drove and scored while being fouled for a three-
point play to bring the Bulls to within 1, 89–88. And then strange
things started happening.

Edwards missed and Aguirre was called for going over the back
on a long rebound. Close call. Two free throws for Jordan: 90–89
Bulls. John Salley was called for an offensive foul against Armstrong
as Salley tried to get around the small guard. Pippen then threw the
ball away. Laimbeer launched a three-pointer that went halfway
down and spun out. "Hey, maybe," Jackson thought. Jordan appeared to push off on Dumars getting the inbounds pass, but Dumars
was called for the foul. Chuck Daly was dancing halfway down the
court on the sideline; his dance would remind no one of Fred Astaire,
though there was some Bobby Knight in it. Jordan made both free
throws and the Bulls led 92–89 with fifty-five seconds left. "We're
home!" Daly was yelling to the referees. "What's going on?" Vinnie
Johnson then hit a jumper to get the Pistons to within 1, 92–91.
Jordan followed with a seventeen-footer with thirty-seven seconds
left and the Bulls led 94–91. But Edwards put in a Johnson miss to
get Detroit back to within 1. "Damned offensive rebounds," Jackson
muttered. Jordan again appeared to push off against Dumars.
Foul—on Dumars! Jordan made one of two free throws for a 95–
93 lead. He was as exhausted as a laborer after digging ditches all
day. This time it wouldn't be a grave for the Bulls, though. The
Pistons missed three attempts at the basket as time ran out.

"A monkey is off our back," Jordan exulted. "We'd seemed
snakebitten there," Jackson agreed. "Eye of the tiger," yelled Pippen. It was a happy ride to the airport for a change. "I can't remember many from here," Paxson would recall. Jordan had finished
with 30, including the Bulls' last 10 points in the final 2:13. "That's

when we want to go to him," said Jackson. "He's the best closer in the game." Pippen's 20 enabled him to forget about last year's migraine, and Armstrong was the third Bull in double figures with 12. He'd converted three clutch baskets without a miss in the fourth quarter and had helped in bothering Johnson and Dumars into 10-for-27 shooting. He said his good-byes as the players headed back to Chicago for the four-day All-Star break. Jordan would be going to Charlotte, and Armstrong would be staying in Detroit, his hometown. His high school, Brother Rice in Birmingham, was going to retire his number the next day.

•

IT WAS ALWAYS the discussion around the kitchen table in the Armstrong household that B.J. most cherished. It's where he learned about life, where he considered his mistakes and set about to repair them. He was the only child of Barbara and Benjamin Roy. He was Benjamin Roy Armstrong, Jr.—B.J. to the kids, to everyone. *Baby-faced* had become a cliché to him by the time he was becoming a star at the University of Iowa. When he came to the Bulls, he looked no more than sixteen. When he went to visit the Sears Tower that year, the attendant charged him the children's price. The players liked his toughness, though, because he played hard, even if he was somewhat sensitive, perhaps because he was an only child. His brown eyes were soft and comforting, and his high cheekbones framed an expressive face.

It was to the kitchen table that B.J. came for insight and counseling, as when he didn't understand why he wasn't starting at Iowa as a freshman, even though he was outplaying the senior point guard in practice every day.

"You've got to be patient," Barbara counseled. "Your turn will come."

He understood, for from his mother B.J. learned the patience to be strong. She had been stricken with multiple sclerosis when he was a high school sophomore and she was now confined to a wheelchair, but she continued to work for the doctor she had been with before. And it was at that table again, the night before the Pistons game, where B.J. listened and learned some more.

He wasn't playing the way he had in college, or even in high school. He was tentative and almost afraid. He used to penetrate, he used to be aggressive. He wasn't doing what had made him a star at Iowa, what had made him a first-round draft choice in the NBA. Where was that player, Benjamin Roy and Barbara wondered?

Friends had warned Armstrong about coming to the Bulls. Isiah Thomas, whom Armstrong had admired since he was in high school, had tried to tell him gently that playing with Jordan would not be as easy as it seemed. The Bulls had told Armstrong they wanted him because he was also such a good shooter. "A guard playing opposite Jordan gets so many opportunities," Krause had said. "Look at John Paxson. And you can take the ball to the basket."

But Sam Vincent, a friend from his time at Michigan State, also counseled Armstrong. It was hard to play with Jordan. There's a reason the Bulls have had more than a half-dozen point guards and only Paxson, perhaps the slowest and least like a point guard, remained. "You can't play point guard with him," Vincent said.

But Armstrong wasn't concerned. Here was the greatest player in the game and he'd be opposite him, perhaps not as a rookie, but surely by the time he was in his second season. He could see Paxson was too slow even to play him, and Armstrong knew he wasn't the quickest of point guards. It would be he and Jordan, surely, by his second season.

His first season was tough, Armstrong admitted. He'd never played for a team where he was waved off by the scoring guard. Every time he'd get the ball, Jordan would be yelling for it and demanding he get out of the way. He started spotting up on the perimeter like Paxson and Craig Hodges. The coaches were angry; he didn't have to do that, they told him. He could go to the basket and they couldn't. Why didn't he?

"I didn't know where I was supposed to be," Armstrong told friends after the season. "I didn't know what I was supposed to be. I was hesitant to play my game. I'd never played without the ball and I couldn't get it. It was tough."

He'd also found the guards so much bigger and stronger and knew he had to get stronger. He began lifting weights. The pro game always looked so easy—guys scored seemingly at will. He found that was because the players were so great. Defenses really played hard, and it was only because the players were truly great offensive machines that their scoring looked easy. He would have to work harder.

And he did. He played the entire schedule for the Bulls team in the summer league while his rookie friend, Stacey King, showed up for just a few games. He liked King for his brash manner and good humor, but he worried about him. "He won't work on his game," B.J. thought. "He has to learn different moves."

Armstrong, though, had gone back to Detroit after his rookie season and worked out with Thomas and Joe Dumars, and they'd urged him to find something new. Thomas had told him that no matter how good you believe you are, you have to add something to your game every year; otherwise, the league starts catching up with you. Armstrong worked hard and impressed in the summer league, leading the Bulls team and averaging about 25 points per game.

But that was not all. He knew that his fate, like that of his teammates, was tied to Jordan. He saw Jordan not only as the greatest player in the game, but as a man perhaps too good for the game. "Everything comes so easy for him," Armstrong marveled. "He can do anything anyone does and do it better than them. In a way, I think he's too good." Jordan was a genius of the hardwood, so Armstrong went to the doctor his mother worked for and borrowed some books on genius. He took some out of the library. He read about geniuses in different professions, how they felt about themselves and viewed the world, how they related with others and how others got along with them.

"I felt if I could understand him better I could play with him better," Armstrong said.

But it wasn't happening. Donnie Walsh, the Indiana Pacers general manager, saw it in the few Bulls games he watched. He liked Armstrong and told the Bulls he'd be interested in him, for he saw how Armstrong struggled. It reminded him of when he had played in college with Doug Moe, a high-scoring guard more talented than he.

"I'd say, 'Moe, where do you want me to go?' " recalled Walsh. "You see Pippen and Jordan taking the ball and going and you can see B.J. doesn't know where to go or what he should do. It used to drive me crazy. You know what you're supposed to do, but these guys are so good you get to the point where you're just trying to figure out how to get out of their way."

Armstrong was trying to learn and had taken to studying Cartwright, who he felt was the most professional among the players in the way he approached games. He began to watch film and tried to concentrate harder before games. But again, he'd find Jordan waving him out of the way. He was stuck in a revolving door of confusion.

But the meeting with his parents seemed to relax and revive him. He had been feeling sorry for himself, he knew, and letting that claim his game. He told Jackson he was ready to do what he asked. Jackson told him he would not start this season; Armstrong said that was fine with him. And he was a different player against the Pistons. Twice in the second quarter, he split the Pistons' defense for driving baskets. The coaches looked at one another on the bench. Armstrong did it again early in the fourth quarter and then knocked in jumpers later when the Bulls trailed by 4 and 5. Missing either could have meant the game would be lost.

Armstrong went back to his high school on Friday a hero. And when he returned to the team after the All-Star break, he scored 17 or more points in three of his next six games and was averaging 5 assists in less than twenty-five minutes per game.

The coaches weren't convinced, yet, that he was the team's point guard of the future, and Krause was still lusting after Toni Kukoc. Nevertheless, he was starting to help and feeling better about himself.

"I've got it back, the fire," Armstrong told a friend after the All-Star weekend. "I thought I'd lost it, but I didn't and it feels good. I care again and I'm emotional. That's me. It's the first time since college that I feel like I'm helping, that I feel good about myself. I'm gonna be okay."

•

THE BULLS PLAYERS split for the All-Star break. Paxson went into the hospital to have some old cysts removed and Perdue went to Las Vegas; Cartwright's wife dragged him off on a weekend with the kids. Jordan and Hodges went to Charlotte, Hodges for the three-point-shooting contest and Jordan for the All-Star game. The

All-Stars are supposed to meet with the media Friday afternoon of All-Star weekend, but Jordan hadn't shown since his first season in the league. The media often excused his behavior because he was usually so gracious before games, and when he did interviews he was open and helpful. The league also had to excuse his behavior because it had little control over him. But this time the league had a plan. The players get tickets for family and friends, and the league decreed they would be handed out only at those Friday afternoon interview sessions. Jordan had to attend.

The highlight of the Saturday night activities was usually the slam-dunk contest, but Hodges stole the show with a run of 19 straight three-point field goals that helped win him his second straight shooting title and the awe of many. Hodges had aimed all season for the three-point-shoot-out crown since he was playing so little; he hoped this would help him get some more playing time. Most of the All-Stars had come to watch the dunk contest; they found themselves counting along with the fans as Hodges hit one after another. Conspicuous by his absence was Jordan. He said he had a headache.

The All-Star game on Sunday was not particularly interesting. Without the injured Thomas, the East had no point guard and Jordan had to play the position much of the game. He scored a game-high 26 points, but committed 10 turnovers. Jackson saw some of the game back home and wasn't surprised. Jordan, he felt, had lost his point-guard vision. He didn't seem to find the shooters running the perimeter the way he used to. But Jackson still was amazed at his ability to score any time he wanted against even the best in the game. It was a curse in some ways, he thought, to be so good, to be a comet racing across the game with everyone light-years in your wake.

•

THE GAMES RESUMED, and the Bulls resumed their roll. They trailed Atlanta by 10 in the first quarter but took the lead by halftime and won by 9. Grant wouldn't miss and scored 23, and Armstrong had 18, although Spud Webb cut up the Bulls' guards for a career-high 30. The middle remained vulnerable, especially when Perdue or King played, but the Bulls were overwhelming teams with speed and defense. They would go on to take New York on the road, the

Nets at home, the Cavaliers on the road, and Washington at home
to bring their winning streak to seven as the trading deadline of
February 21 loomed. Were they playing well enough that management didn't feel it had to make a move? Jordan was beginning to
think that beating Detroit might have been the worst thing the team
could have done.

"They're really afraid to do anything now," Jordan said before
the Washington game. "We're beating a lot of poor teams. So what?
We won a lot of games last year, too. Will Horace and Bill still be
playing at this level in the playoffs? Maybe, and if they are, we can
do something. But what if they're not? What do we do then? Can
Pip keep it up? And that guy over there [Jordan pointed toward
Paxson]. He's loyal. He doesn't say anything and what does he want,
maybe seven hundred thousand, eight hundred thousand dollars,
and they're going to screw him. I just hate that. This is going to be
our last chance to win. I just know it. There's this Kukoc thing and
these guys becoming free agents after this season and the rookies
not doing anything. They'll change everything again after this year.
Reinsdorf seems like a smart guy and he seems like he knows what's
going on, but he won't do anything. I don't understand. I know
what's gonna happen. We'll wait until the last minute and then they'll
say something like they couldn't get a deal done because of the cap
or somebody pulled out at the last minute. It happens here all the
time. I don't know why I'm surprised every year."

Jordan was wrong if he thought the Bulls weren't seriously pursuing deals. They were talking with the Bucks about Ricky Pierce
and the Hawks about Glenn "Doc" Rivers, and they were even
exploring the possibility of getting Reggie Theus from the Nets.
(Jordan told Jackson when this was brought up that he would retire
if the Bulls got Theus.) And Krause had had a bizarre conversation
with his old friend Bob Whitsitt, general manager of the Seattle
SuperSonics, telling Whitsitt about the pressure Jordan was putting
him under to make a deal and trying to appeal to Whitsitt's friendship
to get Whitsitt to trade him Eddie Johnson, another potential
shooter off the bench, to save his job. Krause had spoken to the
Bullets about Mark Alarie or Darrell Walker, and to the Spurs about
Paul Pressey, and he still hoped the Bulls might get a shot at Derek
Harper. Jackson wanted Benoit Benjamin. There seemed to be as
many players under discussion to come to the Bulls as there were

players talking about leaving. And on the morning of the trading deadline, one more name would be added to the latter list.

The Bulls were now 37–14 and starting to pull away from the Pistons, with a three-game edge in the loss column. They'd broken the team record with their sixteenth consecutive home-court win and had lost just once in February—on the road against the Lakers— as they moved toward an all-time club-best month. It was a time to savor the aroma of winning as if it were fresh-baked bread. It was also a time for Scottie Pippen to demand to be traded.

Jackson hadn't seen the newspaper story until he arrived at his office the morning of the trading deadline.

"Ain't winning great?" he said to Winter.

Pippen had grown increasingly frustrated about the slow pace of negotiations for his new contract. It had taken the Bulls almost a year to agree finally to a new deal with Jordan, and Reinsdorf believed there was no such hurry with Pippen, especially since he had two years left, both option years at the club's discretion. Pippen had taken out a $3 million disability insurance policy from Lloyd's to protect himself, but he was growing unsettled and nervous.

He was talking almost daily with his agents and Grant about wanting to be traded, and he had even started wearing a back warmer. His back was fine, but he was thinking he could further pressure the team by feigning a back injury. After all, he thought, he'd had disk surgery a few years ago and who really knows about a back injury? He started to tell trainer Chip Schaefer his back was bothering him and he was getting treatment, but he was playing and performing extraordinarily well. The coaches saw that he was becoming a star, something the public wouldn't notice until the play-offs. Since being left off the All-Star team, Pippen was averaging 18.3 points, 7.9 rebounds, and 5.9 assists per game and shooting 54.6 percent. To Jackson, he was the key to the Bulls' fortune. "The big reason we weren't playing well on the road earlier this season was Scottie wasn't playing well on the road," said Jackson. Pippen had been shooting under 40 percent on the road through January, averaging 8 fewer points per game than at home. "He has to play well for us to win, to rebound and pass and run the floor," Jackson said. Pippen believed he was doing all of that, but he didn't see any rewards.

Jimmy Sexton, Pippen's agent, was always amazed at just how

poor Pippen was. Sexton's firm represents about fifty professional
athletes, but he said he'd never encountered real poverty until his
first visit to Pippen's Arkansas home. It was just a little shack, really,
and Sexton thought to himself, "Twelve kids live here?" Pippen
was now in his fourth season and was facing two more in which if
he were hurt he'd get "only" $600,000 as a buyout. He was growing
ever more nervous. "People look at Scottie and see a wild kid,"
said Sexton. "They see a guy who runs around and doesn't seem
stable. But the first thing he did when he got his money was buy
his mother a house, and that's where he stays all summer. He wants
annuities and insurance policies and every kind of protection imaginable. I've never had a client quite like him."

Pippen had grown angry with Krause, the negotiating bad cop.
Krause had earlier told Pippen, "We never negotiate with anyone
with more than two seasons left." Pippen hadn't forgotten and had
focused his resentment on him, even while Reinsdorf and Sexton's
partner, Kyle Rote, Jr., moved ever closer to a deal. Finally, Pippen's impatience could be caged no longer.

He said the Bulls had broken their promise. They'd promised him
a new deal by Christmas and here it was the end of February. He'd
watched all this negotiating going on with Toni Kukoc and what
about him? He was the one helping the Bulls win.

"I've been patient," Pippen said. "I haven't said anything. Our
team is winning. I'm keeping my part of the bargain, but they aren't.
I'm the sixth-highest-paid player on the team. If they don't want to
treat me fair, then they should trade me."

The players, of course, and even Tex Winter, would have some
fun with Pippen, for even words spoken in anger are fair game on
the Bulls. Pippen worked some with the second team in practice the
next day, and Winter began taunting him, "Keep talking to the
newspapers, and it's third team for you tomorrow."

But Krause panicked when he heard that Pippen had talked to
the newspapers. He called Reinsdorf, who was in Arizona with his
family before heading for Florida to see his White Sox in spring
training. Reinsdorf told him just to go on with business.

So even the passing of the trading deadline wouldn't bring calm.
King had wanted out, but he knew where he'd be now. He'd heard
how close the Bulls had come to dealing him to Golden State earlier
in the season for Sarunas Marciulionis, and about the recent talks

with Atlanta, Milwaukee, and Seattle. But most of the players were more relaxed at practice on February 22 as the deadline had gone by with no changes in the roster, and several would later credit that as a key point in helping stabilize the team. King, too, was light-hearted; he pasted the number 23 on his practice jersey and taped his forehead to look bald. "Now can I get some extra socks, Chip?" he yelled at trainer Schaefer. "That's the only way you get anything around here. You've got to look like him."

The Bulls played Sacramento and it was apparent Dick Motta knew this would be bad. He'd appeared at a speaking engagement the night before in Chicago, but didn't show for the game, claiming to be ill. Rookie Duane Causwell shouldn't have; he ended up in Cartwright's elbow trophy case with a broken nose, as Bach drew more tombstones on the bench. The Kings lost by 47. Jordan put up 34 points in twenty-eight minutes and Pippen missed a triple double by 1 assist. The next night, Charlotte came into the Stadium and Pippen was magnificent, playing to standing ovations no one but Jordan had heard there before. Pippen scored a career-high 43 points as the Bulls won by 21. He was 16 of 17 from the field, the best shooting performance in the league during the season for so many attempts. He became the first player ever to score 40 or more points while playing with Michael Jordan in a professional game.

Jordan was gracious afterward, sitting in his locker stall for a long time and congratulating Pippen for his effort. Grant was almost forgotten despite 20 points and 17 rebounds, more boards than the entire Hornets' starting front line. Pippen told him he thought Jordan was looking away from him on the court and that's why he got just 17 shots (to 22 for Jordan) despite being so hot. It didn't seem that way to him this time, Grant thought.

The next game wouldn't be quite so easy. The quarry was the Boston Celtics. The Pistons were wounded and falling back and the Celtics were just a half game ahead of the Bulls in the race for the best record in the Eastern Conference and home-court advantage throughout the conference playoffs. The Celtics were starting to feel their age, as Jackson had expected. Larry Bird had been out much of January with a bad back. Kevin McHale was now out with an ankle injury, and he probably wouldn't play against the Bulls. Another break in a season of breaks, it seemed. McHale, Bach thought, was the greatest post man in the history of the game. His long arms could snatch a ball out from a defender with position, and his moves were nearly unstoppable. Grant feared Karl Malone the most, perhaps, because of his physical play, but he was baffled by McHale. "There's no way to play him," he said.

It was being billed as a clash of styles, the tradition-bound, aging Celtics against the speedy, nineties Bulls in the Stadium.

Grant sprained his ankle early, but it would not matter. Bird could barely bend over and the Bulls used Cliff Levingston to attack him. The Bulls went on a 21–2 run in the first quarter and the game was all but over. And they did it in their style. Jordan blocked shots and stole the ball to create fast breaks and Pippen got in for three straight slam dunks, leaning out and seeming to fly over grounded Celtic defenders. It was the greatest margin of victory ever for a Bulls team over the Celtics, and Jordan reminisced afterward about how when he came into the league there was no way the Bulls could hope to beat Boston and now they were doing it with relative ease.

The Bulls led by 26 at halftime and by 36 after three quarters. Jordan and Pippen each had 33 points after the third quarter. Jordan told Jackson he wanted to go back into the game, so he started the fourth quarter with King, Perdue, Craig Hodges, and Armstrong and took 6 of the first 7 Bulls shots. He left five minutes into the fourth quarter with 39 points—Pippen would stay on the bench for the remainder of the game with 33—and with the Bulls ahead by 39.

"He wasn't going to let me outscore him two straight games," Pippen said to Grant as the team left the floor. They both laughed.

Pippen's success the last two games should have given him some pleasure. Instead it gave him an idea, and not a good one. Practice was scheduled for 11:30 A.M. the next morning, about forty-five minutes later than usual. At about 11:35 A.M., Pippen called in. He said he was sick and was staying home. He had been asked by reporters all during the past few days about his trade demands and he'd said he was sticking to his word of wanting to be dealt. Jackson asked him whether he was trying to make a point when he called saying he was sick. He was too ill to come in, Pippen said. Jackson told him he would be fined.

"I'm sick, Phil," Pippen said. "Guys are sick all the time. Why can't I be sick?"

But Pippen wasn't. He'd decided to skip a few practices as a way of putting more pressure on the team in his negotiations. He felt he could panic Krause into going to Reinsdorf and saying he had to cut a deal quickly with Pippen or all would be lost. The newspapers and TV the next day would be full of speculation, quoting "friends" and "business associates" of Pippen as saying he was trying to send a message to the team.

Reinsdorf got the message that day. He heard Pippen had missed practice the morning after scoring 33 against Boston and after having no apparent signs of any illness the night before. And word was that Pippen had gone out after the game to celebrate.

Reinsdorf called Rote.

"I'm sure Scottie is sick," Reinsdorf told him. "But if he isn't and he doesn't come to practice tomorrow or if he says he has a back injury, we're done. He plays out his contract and we don't talk again, not a word, until after the 1992–93 season. And then we just match whatever offer he gets. He doesn't get a penny more for two years and you tell him that."

The next morning, Pippen showed up for practice. Pippen privately told teammates he'd planned to miss practice again until Rote's midnight call. Pippen said no, the media misunderstood. He was sick and he didn't know why everyone was making such a big deal out of it. Guys got sick all the time. He could see where people might get the wrong idea since he was upset about his deal, but he'd never do anything like that.

Negotiations between Reinsdorf and Rote continued.

The Bulls finished the month 11–1 and had now won ten straight. They led the East and suddenly were within reach of Portland for the best record in the league. Were they that good? They hadn't made a deal. Hopson hadn't played since hurting his toe in the Detroit game before the All-Star break, and the coaches felt he was babying himself too much. Levingston had yet to assume a role with the team, despite his strong game against the Celtics. Perdue was playing better, but the coaches were still of a mind to get a center. They wanted to trade both King and Armstrong and they didn't believe a team could win with a starting point guard like Paxson. Just what was going on? Jackson wondered. "Sometimes," he said, "I look at this team and who we're playing and wonder just how we're winning." But Jackson also was starting to think that this Bulls team was like the old Celtics teams he remembered dominating the

NBA: They were greater than the sum of their parts. Their on-court harmony was tremendous, even though those Boston players and star Bill Russell shared nothing in common and rarely spent any time together. This Bulls team seemed to be able to relate on the court, which was enough. Basketball was a team game, and even if Jordan did dominate the offense, the Bulls were playing like a team, winning games with their defense and speed. There was definitely something happening here.

8

MARCH 1991

3/1 v. Dallas; 3/2 at Indiana; 3/5 v. Milwaukee; 3/8 v. Utah; 3/10 at Atlanta; 3/12 v. Minnesota; 3/13 at Milwaukee; 3/15 at Charlotte; 3/16 at Cleveland; 3/18 v. Denver; 3/20 v. Atlanta; 3/22 at Philadelphia; 3/23 v. Indiana; 3/25 v. Houston; 3/28 at New Jersey; 3/29 at Washington; 3/31 at Boston

PRACTICE ENDED THE last day of February with as much of a punctuation mark as the Bulls' victory over the Celtics a few days earlier.

The Bulls were just two short of the all-time franchise record for consecutive wins, but Jackson warned the players as they prepared for a March 1 game with Dallas—and certainly an eleventh straight win—that they were not 30 points better than Boston and shouldn't get too cocky. Jackson had grown into his job well. Bach, who was close to Collins, had developed deep respect for Jackson. He marveled at Jackson's ease in handling Krause with a joke or a deflected statement. "Don't take life too seriously, Jerry," Jackson would say. "You'll never get out of it alive." And Jackson was equally adept at the delicate balancing act of broncobusting the Bulls' young stallions while keeping them eager to run.

Jackson liked to test the players, and Jordan as well. Sometimes what was mistaken as an inability to recognize time-out situations was an intentional effort by Jackson to challenge the players to work through a difficult time. So many of the games the Bulls were playing were not close that he could afford to experiment in games with fatigued players or when the momentum was working against his team.

This day at practice, he decided upon a special challenge for Jordan: He stopped keeping score in the scrimmage.

Jordan hated this as much as anything. He only played to win. What was the point of playing, he believed, if you didn't keep score? A winner had to be determined and Jordan insisted upon winning. He'd make bets with players and assistants throughout practice on free throws, shots from odd positions, just about anything. Sometimes, before games, he'd sit on the bench and attempt shots sitting for $5 each. And he'd always collect. "Sometimes he'll come to me," says Bach, "and he'll say, 'Coach, you know you still owe me two dollars.' And it would be from some free throws he'd hit in practice a month ago."

Jackson was willing to draw Jordan's anger if it would keep him motivated. Any emotion, even fury at his coach, was better than the listlessness he'd shown in Texas. And Jordan cooperated. As practice was about to end, he grabbed the ball, ran toward the basket and launched a vicious tomahawk slam and then glared at Jackson.

Jackson smiled.

•

DESPITE THE WINNING streak, Jordan remained angry over the team's failure to make a move and his inability to sway Krause or Reinsdorf. Jordan hadn't talked to Krause since his outburst after the Davis trade to Portland in January, and had grown even angrier when he'd heard that Krause had gone to Cartwright to ask his opinions on some potential personnel matters, including, perhaps, the pickup of free agent Adrian Dantley.

"I'll ask Cartwright or Brad Davis [a Mavericks player drafted by Krause and longtime favorite] before I'll talk to him," Krause had said.

Krause also wanted to assure Cartwright that the Bulls wanted him back, but they couldn't make him an offer just yet because of other matters, namely the working deals for Kukoc and Pippen and the fact that they'd given him $400,000 up front this season to help create room for Kukoc under the salary cap. League rules didn't allow a new offer until a year from the change in the previous contract. Cartwright, typically, offered little of his thinking, and mostly listened. It's why some on the staff thought Krause liked Cartwright so much—he was less likely to contradict Krause's repetitive stories from his scouting days. He listened and sorted them out, but wouldn't challenge Krause like the others.

Cartwright intended to ask for three more guaranteed years at $2 million or more per season. If the Bulls went for it, he'd probably stay. He had mixed feelings. It was easier not to move and start over with new teammates, but the sands were running out for him, and if the Bulls didn't win this season they might never.

"There's not a lot of instant gratification involved for me on this team," he admitted. "The most instant gratification is in scoring, and we have a lot of scorers, so I've got to do what we need for a championship. A lot of times I don't like it, but with the chance for the best record dangling in front of you, the sacrifices become more tolerable."

But there was something else he didn't talk much about. Oh, Cartwright talked vaguely of finishing his career back home in California, but never much explained why. "Sheri [his wife] would like that," he once told a friend, but went no further.

The Cartwrights, with their four children, live in Highland Park, a wealthy suburb near Lake Michigan on Chicago's North Shore. It's a hamlet of multimillion-dollar homes and much less expansive minds and attitudes.

Sheri Cartwright is white, a pert blonde who had dated Bill since high school. One day, a neighbor met Sheri when she was with two of her four children. "Oh," the neighbor exclaimed, "you mean those are your children?"

Although she'd grown comfortable in the Chicago area and had become close friends with June Jackson, Phil's wife, Sheri Cartwright had never truly felt her mixed marriage was accepted in the conservative, snobby North Shore neighborhoods where all the Bulls lived. Once, when she'd gone to the local library, the librarian had asked her if she was the guardian of the children. She had once told Bill she'd be more comfortable back in California, where their marriage would be accepted more easily. Chicago could be a cold place, she felt, in more ways than the weather.

Isiah Thomas would understand. The Pistons star grew up on Chicago's West Side, but his family had insisted he attend St. Joseph's High School in Westchester, a blue-collar bedroom community about fifteen miles west of Chicago. It would improve Thomas's chances of getting a good education, since the Chicago inner-city schools had become dens for drug use and violence. Mary Thomas wanted her son to have a chance if his basketball skills proved not good enough. Of course, they were, but when Isiah sought to buy his mother a house, he found out his color mattered; advisers to Thomas said they were told as they searched for a location around Westchester that the family wouldn't be welcomed. Thomas eventually had a home built for his mother in nearby Clarendon Hills—ironically, across the street from the house where Bill Laimbeer was reared.

Thomas, having grown up in Chicago, long known for its separatist battles among ethnic groups, was perhaps more accustomed to overt racism. Michael Jordan had never experienced it much growing up in rural North Carolina and then attending the University of North Carolina. He'd decided to stay near home for college and almost attended the University of South Carolina or Clemson because they'd said he could play baseball, too, and Jordan mostly thought of himself as a baseball player then.

"Even now, when people talk about my greatest thrill being the shot against Georgetown to win the NCAA title, I still think to myself that my greatest accomplishment really is the Most Valuable Player award I got when my Babe Ruth League team won the state baseball championship," says Jordan. "That was the first big thing I accomplished in my life, and you always remember the first. I batted something like .500 and hit five home runs in seven games and pitched a one-hitter to get us to the championship game."

Jordan was thinking about other such athletic feats as he sat in his locker stall before the March 1 game against the visiting Dallas Mavericks. It had just been announced that he'd been appointed to the board of the Western Golf Association, which runs the Western Open on the PGA tour. Someone wondered what it meant to Jordan, whose passion for golf had become widely known, to be the first NBA player ever appointed to the board of a pro golf tournament.

"What it means is I get to play every PGA tour course in the country for free," Jordan noted.

Jordan considered this a great plum, for he loved great golf courses and spent his summers trying out as many new ones as possible. But his friends who played golf knew he could play just about anywhere he wanted to anyway. They called him "America's Guest." He'd have someone call for him, saying Michael Jordan wants to play your course today, and there would always be an opening. "But now I won't have to play with a member," Jordan explained. "And they always put me with the worst members. And, anyway, I'm just a token."

Professional golf, the summer before in 1990, had been embarrassed when a member of the Shoal Creek club in Alabama, where the PGA Championship was being held, had said the club wouldn't have blacks as members. The remarks caused a firestorm of protest and the PGA launched an expeditious campaign to remove racial barriers from its tour. That was a problem, since virtually all the golf clubs at which the PGA held its tournaments had exclusionary policies. As a result, the Western Open, held in Chicago at the Butler National Golf Club, would eventually be moved to a public course. Jordan had become friends with a member of the Western Golf Association, and he'd asked Jordan to join the board. Jordan agreed, even though he knew the true intent.

In the last few years, particularly because of his growing love for golf, Jordan had come to experience racism as he never had before. In his special place as an American icon and folk hero, he'd been able to transcend racial hatred and divisiveness. In the NBA, the way had been cleared for him by the likes of Julius Erving, and now a black superstar could be admired and adored as a national hero and treasure. Jordan was welcomed where black men didn't tread, namely on the country-club circuit. He played on all the exclusive golf courses on Chicago's North Shore and his appearances were cause for celebration.

Word would sweep the course that Jordan was playing that day, and when he'd arrive, the pro was usually there to watch his swing on the driving range and offer a free lesson; on the course, members would encourage him to play through to get a chance to see his much-talked-about game. Jordan had become a solid amateur, about a 6 handicap by 1990, meaning he'd shoot in the mid to high 70s. It wasn't nearly good enough for him to become a pro, but Jordan liked to consider doing so as a fantasy and a goal. He was like a Moses on the course, the members parting as his group would come up behind them.

But actual membership was a different story. He had thought about joining a Jewish club near his home, and friends made private inquiries on his behalf. They were politely informed that, no, Jordan wouldn't be welcomed as a member. Of course he could play any time he wanted but, well, there just weren't any immediate openings. You know.

The realization had never really struck Jordan before: He couldn't go somewhere because he was black. He never pursued the matter, but he clearly was hurt.

It was why he'd responded to a friend the way he did when the Illinois state lottery jackpot had grown to over $40 million in early 1990, and the players were laughing and joking in the locker room about what they'd do if they won.

"I'd retire at halftime," he said with a smile. "I'd take my uniform off and just leave the court. And then I'd go open up a country club and post a sign that said, 'No Jews Allowed.' "

.

THE MAVERICKS TRIED to play the Bulls the way the Pistons do: They slowed the game to one of those traffic-jam paces in which the movement is bumper-to-bumper slow and the frustration level is high. At halftime, the Bulls were trailing 43–39 after scoring just 12 points in the second quarter. But there was no Rodman or Thomas or Dumars to continue the frustration. The Bulls hustled their transition game into gear and let Jordan begin to attack. He scored 15 third-quarter points and the Bulls pulled away to an easy 109–86 win, now just one short of the longest winning streak in team history.

But Indianapolis, their next stop, hadn't been an easy place for the Bulls to speed through. They'd lost five straight there, mostly because they never could figure out how to defense Detlef Schrempf, and because Reggie Miller usually got hot against the Bulls at home. (He once said that all the NBA looked excitedly on Bulls–Pacers matchups because it was Air against Hollywood. No one was quite sure who Hollywood was, but everyone assumed it was the swaggering Miller.) Not having Horace Grant would hurt the Bulls. He was missing his second straight game with a sprained ankle and this would be a more difficult test for Stacey King. Dallas's front line couldn't score much, but the Pacers would go right at him.

Before the game, the locker room was lively with talk about Bobby Knight, the famous Indiana University coach. Some of the players were talking about NBA players now being permitted to play in the Olympics, and Pippen asked Jordan if he wanted to participate again.

"Why would I?" he responded.

"For your country and all that, I guess," Pippen said.

"After playing a whole season you're gonna be awful tired to start again with qualifying tournaments and exhibition games and all of that," Jordan said.

And, Jordan said, his first Olympic experience, a gold medal in 1984, while exciting, had been difficult because of Knight.

"I don't know if I would have done it if I knew what Knight was going to be like," Jordan told the players, who were leaning in like kids around a campfire to hear a ghost story. "I'd heard about Coach Knight when I was at North Carolina, so I asked Coach Smith and he advised me to do it. I think all the coaches did because after playing for Coach Knight they knew you'd appreciate them more."

Jordan said that time after time the team would be blowing out the opponent and Knight would come in raving at halftime. "It was like we were losing by thirty every game," Jordan recalled. "And this one time with [assistant coach] George Raveling was unbelievable. Patrick [Ewing] was getting a little homesick and Raveling said he'd take him to see John Thompson [Ewing's college coach] one night. Patrick gets in late that night and the next day in the game he's not playing well and Knight's screaming to Raveling on the bench and saying Patrick wasn't playing well because of Raveling.

"He's saying, 'You MF [Jordan cannot get himself to say the words], it's your fault he's playing like shit. You kept him out late, you MF.' And Raveling's yelling, 'F you, it ain't my fault that he can't hit a shot. F you.' And the two of them, they're cursing and yelling at each other on the bench all game and we're winning, killing the other team, and they're yelling at each other. I don't think they talked for the next two or three days."

It was also at the Olympics that Jordan became friendly with Charles Barkley, the Eddie Haskell to Jordan's Wally Cleaver.

"We're getting ready for the team picture," Jordan went on, "and Knight comes out wearing these old wing-tip shoes and Barkley starts getting on him and asking him where he got his granddaddy's shoes. Everyone falls over and Knight's not laughing and Barkley's still going on about those shoes. Knight said something about Charles being a jackass and started cussing. I've never heard anyone talk to Coach Knight like that. The next day was when he was cut."

Assistant coach Bach had joined the group. As a student of military history and former naval officer, Bach was a great admirer of Knight. They had become friends when Bach coached at Fordham in New York City and Knight was coaching at West Point. Bach particularly reveled in Knight's independence, even though it ran somewhat contrary to military protocol. It seems, Bach said, that every time some major or colonel would get on Knight at West Point, Knight would call General William Westmoreland in the Pentagon. Westmoreland was a big fan of Knight's and a devotee of the sports teams at the academy and pretty soon there'd be a call from Westmoreland, the four-star general, to the colonel about his behavior and orders to leave Knight alone. "Finally, he'd pissed off too many colonels and Westmoreland couldn't save him," says Bach.

But one incident with Knight struck Bach. He'd gone to Knight's house for a visit, and when he sat down Knight jumped up like the good host.

"John," he said, "how about some coffee?"

Before Bach had a chance to answer, Knight was yelling for his wife to get Bach some coffee. But she was bathing the children at the time and said she couldn't.

"It was amazing," recalled Bach, who also had been something of a disciplinarian with his children, once dumping milk on his baby son when his son had spilled milk on him to teach the boy what it felt like. "He ran up to her and started shouting that he had a guest there and she damn well better get him coffee and he's screaming and the kids are crying and she's running for coffee.

"The thing was," said Bach, the players grabbing their sides in laughter by now, "I didn't want any coffee. But after that I figured I damn well better drink it."

•

THE GAME WENT about as well for the Bulls as the Olympic trials did for Barkley. As the Bulls expected, the Pacers attacked King right away with LaSalle Thompson, who exceeded his per-game average in the first quarter with 11 points. Grant, after a slow start, had become as important to the Bulls as Jordan or Pippen. He was desperately missed against the Pacers, who were playing better under coach Bob Hill. They were now using Rik Smits and Vern Fleming off the bench along with Schrempf, and it was difficult for the Bulls to match up.

"We're running to an early defeat," Bach whispered to Jackson on the bench as the Pacers were on the way to a 24-point lead after three quarters. But Jackson believed in learning experiences. He wanted to see his team under duress and he wanted Jordan to remember Miller loading him up for 40 points. He wanted Jordan ready for the rematch in Chicago three weeks later.

Despite the 135–114 loss, the Bulls were six games up on staggering Detroit in the Central Division and in a virtual tie with Boston for the best record in the Eastern Conference. They were on a pace to win more than sixty games and would start a new streak against Milwaukee, winning at home by 18.

The day before the game, though, Jackson had a different battle in mind. The war in the Persian Gulf was close to being over, as the coalition troops had gained clear dominance over the Iraqis. The only question now was how much devastation would be brought upon Iraq. Jackson decried the entire war machine, for he remembered Vietnam well and knew that in war, truth becomes the first casualty, but Jackson had never found a good way to demonstrate his distaste for war. In his position, it would have been impolitic to oppose such a popular effort. Like Hemingway, he believed that no matter how apparently necessary or justified, war remained a crime. He argued long about it with Bach, who relished the allies' strategy and happily drew attack patterns on the blackboard where opposing plays were usually drawn.

As the team sat ready to go over the Bucks' plays and scouting report, Jackson decided the team was his only true forum left.

"Who wants the troops to go into Baghdad and go after Hussein?" he asked.

The hands of most of the younger players went up. Jordan, Pippen, and Grant particularly said the troops should go in and get Hussein.

In the corner, Hodges could barely contain his anger. Jackson, in a way, agreed.

Do you understand, he explained, that these are people who will never forget, the people who lose their father or a brother or a relative? They or their children or even their children's children. Do you want to see, Jackson wondered, your son killed someday in an airplane explosion because we've made Iraq a terrorist nation from what we've done? Consider the terrorism that could be done in this nation. A guy with a bomb can just drive into the Lincoln Tunnel or walk into the Sears Tower and kill thousands. Is this what you want to see and have it affect your children or their children?

Jackson wanted them to think a little more about the consequences of war. Everyone did.

.

THERE WERE TWO things, perhaps more than anything, that united the Bulls. They were hardly a close group; they brought to mind the old Boston Red Sox motto "Twenty-five men, twenty-five cabs."

But they also had talent and played exceptional halfcourt defense that produced a transition game that allowed Pippen, Jordan, and Grant to run and overcome the team's weaknesses. They shot the ball extremely well, and they retained strong continuity, with Jordan, Pippen, and Paxson three of the four league leaders in consecutive starts.

And there were two major areas of agreement: The players disliked general manager Krause, and they mostly distrusted the team's medical staff, not because they felt the staff was incompetent, but because, as they saw it, the staff favored management over players.

This conflict had already resulted in the departure of ten-year trainer Mark Pfeil to the Bucks after the 1989–90 season and had caused lingering resentment among several players. Hodges had complained almost the entire 1989–90 season about foot pain, and it wasn't until after the season that the team asked him to be operated on. The same with Cartwright—he'd complained about knee problems, diagnosed as tendinitis, until he, too, had surgery after the season. Pippen had complained regularly in his rookie season about back pain, and it wasn't until after the season that he had disk surgery. None of the tests administered by the medical staff ever revealed a problem until after the season, and the players grew increasingly concerned about the pattern. So when the team told Dennis Hopson to practice despite a painful toe injury, several players advised him to stay off his foot and get a second opinion.

And then there was former trainer Pfeil, viewed as another tool of management for his gruff ways. After ten years in the league, Pfeil had grown suspicious of the players and their perceived injuries. He generally believed the players to be malingerers and the players felt he refused to take their injuries seriously enough. It got so bad that for two seasons the players refused to vote him a playoff share.

"I remember the first year I was here I was thinking, 'How could these guys be so cheap?' " recalled Bill Cartwright about the postseason playoff share meeting in 1989. " 'That guy's with us all season and we're going to shut him out?' But these guys were saying he didn't deserve anything and finally we all agreed to chip in a few hundred dollars for him." By the next season, after his knee miseries, Cartwright was among the majority in efforts to deny Pfeil a playoff share. Cartwright had been in intense pain down the stretch and into the playoffs. He couldn't sit with his knee bent for more than a few minutes. He couldn't drive a car, and when he was in one he had to lie down in the backseat. Pfeil told him to take some pills and he'd be fine.

It was against this backdrop that Grant was being asked to return to play the Utah Jazz on Friday, March 8.

His left ankle remained swollen and he was concerned about the future. "I've seen a lot of guys go out with ankle injuries like this and come back too soon and make it worse," said Grant. "I want it to heal completely." The coaches, though, felt Grant was babying himself too much, particularly Bach, who had become Grant's confidant on the staff.

But it was more than pushing Grant to get him to play though pain—a requisite, the coaches thought, for playoff toughness. The coaches feared the consequences of playing King against Karl Malone. In his three starts with Grant out, King had gotten 1 defensive rebound. The coaches were amazed as they watched the film. One defensive rebound in eighty-four minutes on the floor! "A two-year-old could get hit in the head with more rebounds than that," Bach said.

This wasn't lost on the players, either, especially Jordan. The day before the Utah game, some of the office staff came to practice with a carload of souvenir items for the players to sign. It was a twice-a-year routine; after practice, the players would gather in a circle, pass around balls and pennants, and sign each. The team would then auction off the items for charity. As the players sat signing, Jordan started talking.

"Listen to this," he said. "You ever hear of a guy, six-eleven maybe and two hundred sixty pounds, a guy big and fat like that and he can't get but two rebounds, if that many, running all over the damn court and he gets two rebounds?"

The players began trying to muffle laughter because it was clear whom Jordan was talking about.

"Big guy like that," Jordan continued, "and he gets one rebound. Can't even stick his ass into people and get more than that."

"Fuck you, M.J.," King finally said. "All you're interested in is scoring and taking every shot. Maybe if you passed the ball to somebody else for a change instead of worrying about winning the scoring title, somebody else on this team could do something."

"Big, fat, fat guy," Jordan went on. "One rebound in three games. Power forward. Maybe they should call it powerless forward."

Finally, King got up, muttering and cursing . He stormed into the trainer's room and said to no one in particular, "I'm gonna kick his ass one day. You wait. My time will come and I'll get him. I'll shut his mouth."

Both Jackson and Bach worked Grant over before the Utah game. "You don't want a kid to get hurt," said Jackson later, "but with this kid you need to push him to play through it." Bach gave him a version of a Vince Lombardi speech on courage and Jackson told him at least to try it. If the ankle felt bad, he'd come out right away, promise. Good cop–bad cop in reverse. Grant didn't know what to think. He said he'd play. Bach spliced into a game tape scenes of

bodies lying dead on the beach from the TV show "China Beach."
It's going to be a war, he wrote on the blackboard. Not again, coach,
Paxson thought.

The Bulls couldn't get much going early, falling behind by 2 points
after a quarter, by 5 at halftime, and then by 16 midway through
the third quarter as John Stockton found Jeff Malone and Thurl
Bailey for open jumpers and Mark Eaton for dunks every time the
Bulls dropped off them. Little was going right for the Bulls, and
even what appeared good in the crowd's view wasn't. Early in the
second quarter, Jackson moved B. J. Armstrong in at point guard
and Stockton drove him to the basket and scored for a three-point
play. Armstrong then came right back at Stockton and hit two jumpers, but the Bulls players were going berserk. The fans were cheering
Armstrong while the players were screaming for Jackson to get him
out of the game. "What the hell's he doing, Phil?" Pippen yelled
as he went past the bench. "Give up the ball," Jordan screamed at
him on the court. "Get him out of there," Pippen was yelling. It
was chaos. The Jazz went on a 10–1 run and Jackson finally lifted
Armstrong.

"He goes back to the old playground Detroit," Jordan lamented
afterward. "He was scared in there and panicking. He just lost
it when Stockton scored. That's why John works better with us
down the stretch. It's the same thing in practice. Paxson hits a few
jumpers on him and he goes right at him and gets away from what
the team is doing. You can get away with it in practice, but not in
the game."

Grant, meanwhile, was brilliantly bothering Karl Malone into an
8-for-21 shooting game, and suddenly it was Jordan time. He drew
Jeff Malone into a key fourth foul and then took over offensively.
Jordan at his best was electric and exciting, a human alchemy where
action became art and effort hardened into brilliance. He moved
toward the middle of the floor and was unstoppable in his passion
and delight. He blew by defenders as if they were moving in slow
motion. It was the kind of moment players occasionally talked about,
a time when they were going at full speed and everything around
them seemed to be moving in slow motion. Some called it "the
zone." It was a time when they could see defenders coming from
all angles and be out of the way before the defenders got there,
when they could move to the basket as if they were alone on the

court or shoot the ball as if it were on a string attached to the basket. It only happened to the great ones, and only rarely, though more often to Jordan. He scored 8 points on driving baskets in the third quarter and 17 in the fourth quarter as the Bulls overwhelmed the Jazz and pulled away for a 99–89 win, finishing the game with a 22–7 run.

The Bulls' defense was sharp down the stretch, too, and bothered Utah into several turnovers and the fast breaks the Bulls rely upon to put up their point spurts. It was a close game the Bulls had won and one in which they'd come from behind. But the real significance was the way it happened. To Jordan, it was a playoff preview, and after the game he stood up in the locker room and thanked Jackson in front of the team "for sticking with me."

To Jordan, it was an escape from the jail he called the triangle offense. He was as happy as a baby in a tub and as anxious to recount the events of the evening as a kid coming home from the circus. Jordan's eyes sparkled when he talked about the game.

"The triangle's killing me," Jordan insisted. "All I can do in it is take jump shots, but he finally gave me the freedom. This was the first time all season I kind of felt free of the triangle. He gave me the option to drive and boom, screen roll, everything was working. I had space and could move. I don't think we'll go back to an open court game in the regular season, but it's what you've got to go to in the playoffs. I think he's just trying to lift everyone's confidence a little and this (tonight) is not the game Bill can play because it's too quick. Horace is going to get his points off the boards and Paxson will get his spotting up. This is the type of game we need for Scottie and me and I think he'll keep it under wraps until the playoffs. But we'll have to go with it then or we won't have any chance."

The game with the Jazz was frightening to the Bulls in another way. Although they'd won, they had to resort to massive use of Jordan and the starters against the team with the worst bench in the league. And there was the specter of what the Jazz had to endure. Coach Jerry Sloan was saying that only in the last few weeks—after the All-Star break—had the team started to recover from the season-opening trip to Japan. Sloan said he had actually gone weeks without any kind of practice at all because the players were so tired from the trip and then returning to the arduous NBA schedule. The entire Bulls organization feared they'd be next.

They steadfastly tried to ignore the probability, like a kid in class who doesn't know the answer and figures if he doesn't look up he might not get picked. No NBA team that had gone to Europe to the preseason McDonald's tournament had finished that season with a better record than the season before, and the Japan trip was far tougher. The Bulls were a natural attraction with Jordan, but more than that they believed NBA commissioner David Stern would soon send them as punishment. For what? For beating him.

The Bulls had switched their televised games to WGN, a so-called superstation capable of carrying Bulls games to cable systems throughout the country. The league was outraged because of the potential competition in smaller markets. Would Indiana fans want to watch their Pacers or Michael Jordan? The league ordered the Bulls to cut down on their TV games each season and go off WGN within five years. The Bulls sued and won. This left them both thrilled and worried. Stern, the powerful commissioner, had never been beaten in a public arena like that before. In many ways, he'd shaped the current success of the NBA and had been rewarded by the owners with a contract worth millions of dollars a year.

Stern has been credited as a marketing and promotional genius, but he is more than that. He is a behind-the-scenes power, manipulating ownerships in different cities and even helping sign players. Clippers' owner Don Sterling says a call to Stern enabled him to break what he considered a hopeless impasse in the negotiations with then–No. 1 draft pick Danny Manning. Stern had arranged for black ownership in Denver to help the league's image, and he'd forced out weak owners when he had to and come up with stronger groups. Bach had always heard rumors that Stern's fingerprints were all over Franklin Mieuli's sale of the Golden State Warriors. And when Reinsdorf was once asked why he's not more involved in the NBA, as he is in baseball, he responded, "Stern won't let the owners get involved."

No one was complaining about Stern, though. He was the NBA's kingmaker, and could also cause a team problems if he wanted. The Bulls were sure he'd soon be sending them on some awful preseason or season-opening trip that would ruin their year or try to catch them in some sort of minor rules infraction and fine them or take away a draft choice. They didn't believe he'd take his loss on the WGN case quietly. Krause had more reasons for paranoia.

•

THE GAMES ARE Olympian any time Michael Jordan comes to town, even after all these years. Atlanta Hawks president Stan Kasten said his son had asked that his birthday party be postponed because he didn't want to miss seeing Jordan for the final time this season when the Bulls came into Atlanta March 10. The Hawks, perhaps, could have done without seeing Jordan again; recently winners of twenty-two straight at home and conquerors of the Bulls in Atlanta in January, the Hawks surrendered as if Sherman were back in town. They were down 15 by halftime and by 31 midway through the third quarter on the way to a 122–87 loss. After the game, Hawks coach Bob Weiss, seeing Phil Jackson, said, "Hey, we didn't even finish second out there today."

The scene in the locker room before the game was heart-wrenching. Almost weekly, Jordan meets a kid from the Make-a-Wish Foundation, a group that tries to grant last wishes to dying children. There's nothing sadder. But Jordan has seen so many in his seven years and the Bulls have processed so many requests, the senses become numbed. Jordan is gracious with the kids, who usually are frightened and thrilled and invariably speechless. He'll ask them their names and about basketball and about getting a win. He'll sign some things and sometimes the kids will want to meet other players. Basically, they're there for Jordan. But the little girl who came in this afternoon was special. Sweet, blond, wearing a frilly dress, she was glowing. Public-relations man Tim Hallam stood nearby. He'd processed dozens of these requests, but he was near tears. The girl started crying, she was so excited to be near Jordan. "Relax, take it easy," Jordan said comfortingly. His voice was breaking. She sniffled and smiled. It was heartbreaking and uplifting at the same time. Jordan didn't want her to go. He sat with her and talked and laughed and she smiled some more, fighting away tears. Finally, it was time for Jordan to get taped. The little girl stood, and as she walked away she kept looking back over her shoulder. Tears were in Jordan's eyes.

"How do they expect me to play basketball now?" he wondered aloud.

Earlier, there had been big business for the team. Krause had flown down from New York with scout Jim Stack to meet with the coaches. Scott Williams, the mercurial rookie, had cracked, they thought. He was demanding an operation on his shoulder. All season, he had fought even the suggestion when friends saw him in pain. Although he could barely lift his right arm, which severely hampered his rebounding ability, he wouldn't hear or talk of an operation. "I'm going to finish the season," he'd say. Now, he had demanded immediate surgery. He'd aggravated his shoulder injury in the Indiana game ten days earlier and had grown dark and remote, slipping into a personal dungeon in which he was all but unreachable. The coaches suspected his representatives had talked to him about going to Europe next season, and if he could get the Bulls to operate now he'd be ready. He might not have time to recuperate from off-season surgery before the European season began, or, worse, he'd have to pay for the surgery himself. Jackson would eventually call him in and tell him the Bulls had taken a chance on him when no one else wanted him, they'd offered him an opportunity, and now he wanted to walk out on them. Williams would relent and say he was ready to finish the season. But a roster spot was looming.

The coaches agreed it might be worth it to give still-unsigned free agent Adrian Dantley a look. They'd had a chance the year before, but Jackson had believed Dantley wouldn't fit into the Bulls' style of play. He was a 6-4 post player; he needed the ball and space to operate. His game would not fit Jackson's triangle and movement concepts. And he was not noted for his defense.

Perhaps rejecting Dantley had been a mistake, Jackson thought. Dantley had been with Detroit, his fifth team, as the Pistons made their climb to get past Boston, but midway through their first championship season he was traded for Mark Aguirre. Dantley blamed Isiah Thomas, with whom he'd never gotten along. Dantley went to Dallas, and the first time Dallas came to Detroit and the two met, Dantley walked up to Thomas and whispered in his ear, "I know it was you who got me." He had grabbed a piece of Thomas's leg and squeezed it in an exaggerated pinch. "I'm not going to forget, and the first chance I get I'm going to mess you up."

Maybe Dantley could help the Bulls. He might even have helped them get past Detroit in 1990. Who would have been more willing to break down the Pistons' physical tactics than Dantley? And he could score. He always could score. The triangle really didn't work

well among the Bulls reserves. Jackson had hoped to develop a
second unit, but they couldn't play together. King had disappointed
as the designated scorer and Hopson wasn't getting many opportunities. Perhaps Dantley could help.

There were doubts, though. Dantley's agent was David Falk, and
Krause disliked Falk intensely for his habit of bypassing Krause and
talking to Reinsdorf. The Bulls might look at Dantley, but they'd
make it hard; they'd bring him in for a physical and a mental exam,
they'd question him hard, and they'd pay him little. It was typical
Krause, Jackson thought: Go after a guy and then belittle him in
the process. The Bulls had done that in their bitter negotiations with
Levingston and Krause wondered why the players said the team
wasn't fair. "We're fair to everyone," Krause told Jackson. "Have
you been fair to John Paxson?" Jackson shot back.

Jackson asked Bach to talk to Frank Layden, Dantley's old coach
in Utah, who once said Dantley had driven him out of coaching.
Layden was at the Atlanta game for the NBA radio network. He
had nothing good to say, but he did say Dantley would score for
the Bulls. That he could do. The Bulls would think about it some
more.

Tuesday's game against Minnesota figured to be easy and it was.
The Timberwolves were the drying paint of the NBA. They played
like a leftover fly from January, moving more and more slowly and
then trying to buzz for a shot. The Bulls simply had too much talent
for them: They led by 23 at halftime and put the lead into the 30s
by the third quarter before Jackson emptied his bench in a 131–99
laugher. Jordan and Grant were sitting with 20 points and Armstrong
had 19 with about five minutes to go when Jackson put Paxson back
in. The players razzed Armstrong because they knew his career high
was 20 and now he wouldn't be in the lead paragraph of the stories
as the leading scorer. Armstrong was not amused. He called his
agent, who later called Reinsdorf to find out why Armstrong had
been pulled at that point. Jackson had no idea, actually, how many
points Armstrong had or what his career high was. He told Reinsdorf
he thought Armstrong was playing selfishly.

Armstrong had one other discussion that had some effect on the
team. Pooh Richardson, the Minnesota point guard, told him he'd
rejected a new contract offer from the Timberwolves of $3.5 million
per year. Armstrong told Pippen. The pace of negotiations between

Pippen and the Bulls had quickened and the two sides were close to a five-year extension that would pay Pippen almost $3.5 million per season. But now Pippen was worried. Was Richardson telling the truth? His agents had told him he might be better off to wait until summer, but Pippen was growing ever more nervous.

Bo Jackson, the two-sport star, was said to be through for his career because of a hip injury, although he would eventually sign with Reinsdorf's White Sox with the hope of returning for the 1991 or 1992 baseball season. "What if something happens to me? I've got nothing," Pippen told Rote in a desperate late-night call. But Pippen's teammates told him the market would be going up, that he'd be crazy to lock himself up through 1998, as he would if he accepted this deal. Rote thought Pippen's teammates were using him, trying to keep him from signing a deal so there might be more money left for them. The salary cap had made the players vultures, Rote thought, preying on one another over the scraps of cash that were allotted. Paxson and Cartwright were free agents and Jordan wanted more. And the Bulls remained in pursuit of Kukoc. There was only so much under the cap and everyone knew it wasn't going much higher without a new TV deal and expansion. But, Pippen wondered, what if he signed and two years from now the cap doubled? And what if he got hurt? He was desperately confused.

Meanwhile, the Bulls were racking up milestones in this historic twenty-fifth anniversary season. The win over Timberwolves coach Bill Musselman, Jackson's old CBA coaching foe, was Jackson's hundredth—he'd had the quickest hundred wins for a coach in team history. The Bulls had just won the thousandth game in franchise history and were on a pace to break the all-time team win record for a season, and would certainly win just the second division title in team history. The newspaper reporters already were writing about magic numbers. And the Bulls had simply been dismantling teams. They'd won more games by at least 10 points than any team in the league and had the biggest winning margin per game, averaging 9 more points scored than yielded. They were the league's hottest team.

How crazy would things be if we were losing? Jackson thought.

And even when they should have lost, they wouldn't, or couldn't. The Bulls went to Milwaukee, where the Bucks usually played them closer, although with just slightly more success. But this time it appeared the Bucks would carry away a win in a wild game. Milwaukee had a 5-point lead with less than five minutes left, only to unravel late this time. Fred Roberts and Dan Schayes committed turnovers against the Bulls' slapping hands and Paxson hit two big three-point field goals off the transition breaks. Jordan hit two free throws with five seconds left to give the Bulls a 102–99 lead, and the Bucks threw in to Frank Brickowski, who stepped close to the three-point line and fired. It was good and referee Ted Bernhardt, standing a few feet from Brickowski, signaled a three-pointer while Dan Crawford from across the court was waving him off. The lead official in the crew was Hue Hollins. He was at the lower right baseline and too far away to see the play.

There's an informal rule among those close to the NBA: To ascertain the quality of a game, add up the numbers on the backs of the officials. If the three total less than 100, it should be a well-officiated game. If the total is between 100 and 120, there could be problems of consistency. Over 120? Tell your team to foul every time because no one knows what will happen. The numbers for Hollins, Crawford, and Bernhardt are 42, 43, and 63. Ugh, 148! This was a disaster waiting to happen.

The Bulls started to leave the court. "I was always told to take your team off the court," explained Jackson, "because they're reluctant to bring you back."

But there was no hesitation from Crawford. Replays were inconclusive, although it appeared Brickowski had a toe on the three-point stripe, which would negate the extra point and end the game. The Bucks, though, claimed they had a replay that showed Brickowski's foot behind the line. Referees are not permitted to speak to reporters after games in the NBA, but it was clear what Crawford was telling Bernhardt: His foot was on the line. Bernhardt had been just two feet away, but he backed off and it was a two-pointer. The game was over. Bucks coach Del Harris went berserk. He'd lost almost every way imaginable to the Bulls, but this one was unimaginable: A guy who'd made one three-pointer in his career hits one and it gets waved off to prevent overtime.

Charlotte on March 15 proved stubborn, but the 105–92 win was inevitable as Jordan put on a show for the folks back in North Carolina yet again with 34 points. The Bulls moved on to Cleveland, where the Cavaliers led by 11 shortly after halftime, but the Bulls hung a 23–6 spurt in eight minutes to take control of the game and win 102–98.

"Another brick in the wall," Jim Cleamons said afterward—it was becoming a regular postgame comment for the young assistant coach. Bach was more direct: After a win, he'd draw an ace of spades on the blackboard. It was the military sign of death; soldiers would leave one between the toes of a fallen enemy in battle. Another one bites the dust. Aces of spades were turning up everywhere the Bulls went.

Despite the Bulls' gaudy record, respect was hard to come by. Opposing players and coaches doubted the Bulls' chances all season, even after losing to them by 20 and 30 points. Reggie Miller's comments after the Pacers' win in Indianapolis were typical: "We're just as good as they are. Take Michael Jordan off that team and who the hell do they have? Who the hell do they have over there? Nobody."

Pooh Richardson echoed that after the Timberwolves game, saying the Bulls were no better than a half-dozen teams in the West. A few days later, after the Hawks defeated Boston, Glenn "Doc" Rivers would say that while the Bulls had the best record, the Celtics were the best team. And Milwaukee assistant coach Mack Calvin said after that controversial ending March 13 that the Bulls would not win the East because they didn't shoot free throws well enough. Cleveland coach Lenny Wilkens added that he thought with McHale and Bird healthy the Celtics would defeat the Bulls.

The Bulls were battling a lot of resentment. Earlier in the season, it was suggested that they were winning because of injuries to all the other teams. "We get good and now the league's bad, right?" Jordan protested one day. "Well, there are some great teams in the league and we're one of them."

There were some very good reasons for the team's success, especially the defense, like the terrorizing fireman's drill the Bulls had become adept at. Jackson, who pieced it together from the teachings of Bill Fitch, Red Holzman, and Hubie Brown, is a great teacher, and the Bulls worked on it in almost every practice. Four players go against four, with four waiting on defense up the court each time to pick up the players who have penetrated the first group. It's a scramble to get to the basket, and players learn about fighting pressure, but even more about playing midcourt defense. And midcourt is where the Bulls beat teams. The area from the free-throw line to midcourt is where plays begin, and that's where the Bulls take teams out of their offense, often turning the mistakes into transition slam dunks by Pippen, Jordan, or Grant. Grant's speed allows him to double and then retreat to his man, and Jordan and Pippen are the riverboat gamblers of the NBA, sharp dudes who will steal your underwear off you, but carefully. Jordan gambles in games the way he gambles off the court—on everything—and Pippen, though more conservative off the court, has a mean streak in him and likes the challenge of the chase. Together, they look like an octopus coming at a ball handler. And Cartwright is inside, if not to block any shots, then to create fear and loathing with his flailing elbows and bruising body, while Paxson is deadly spotting up for his shot. And while there seemed to be resentment of the Bulls around the Eastern Conference, some of the players saw something else.

"Teams are quitting on us, they're afraid," Cartwright noted after the Cleveland game. "You can see it in their eyes. They made a run and they quit. They were satisfied to do that. They don't think they can beat us. We haven't been playing that well, but these teams are scared. It's like when teams used to play the Celtics."

•

MACK CALVIN WAS right. The Bulls are not a good free-throw-shooting team. The entire front line was averaging less than 70 percent from the free-throw line. In comparison, no one on the entire Celtics team shot less than 76 pecent from the free-throw line. Jackson knew the Bulls were not a good free-throw-shooting team. "Bad mechanics," he explained. He had set a preseason team goal of 78 percent, but had lowered that to 75 percent, and the Bulls had just reached that level. But Reinsdorf had watched that Bucks game on TV from Florida and seen the Bulls miss 7 free throws in 23 attempts, 70 percent for the game. Reinsdorf couldn't understand how the Bulls could shoot better than 50 percent from the field and not much better than that from the free-throw line. He'd called Jackson again and wondered.

Jackson knew full well the team's free-throw-shooting problems were due in large part to the poor form of Pippen, who was not a good outside shooter, either, but had a good shooting percentage because he dunked so often, as did Grant, although Grant was a better straight-on shooter from fifteen feet. Also, Jackson knew that Cartwright, a 79 percent career free-throw shooter, didn't get many shooting opportunities in the Bulls' offense, so it was hard for him to be in rhythm when he did get to the free-throw line.

"But short guys don't understand this," Jackson explained about Reinsdorf. "They can't understand how guys cannot make free throws. That's because they had to make free throws to play. Otherwise, they wouldn't get in the game. If they couldn't make 'em, they'd be sitting at home. It's not that way with the big guys. They played no matter how they shot and nobody worried about the free throws."

Until they became pros, that is, and small guys paid their salaries.

Wilt Chamberlain, of course, had problems at the foul line. The great scoring machine of NBA history was a 51 percent career free-throw shooter. He never liked to talk about his free-throw shooting because it was a failure and the big menacing Wilt wouldn't hear of such things. He was an angry giant when he played. Once asked by a fan, "How's the weather up there?" Chamberlain said, "It's raining," and then he spit on him. But the week of the Bulls–Hornets game, Chamberlain had finally agreed to have his number retired in Philadelphia. And he was feeling self-deprecating, a posture unfamiliar to many who knew Wilt, who was living mostly in record books these days. "I went to a psychiatrist once about my free-throw shooting," Chamberlain deadpanned to reporters. "After six months I was still all screwed up, but the psychiatrist could make ten of ten."

Jackson wasn't aware of Chamberlain's little joke, but he wasn't joking when he went to Grant, Pippen, and King and asked them all to begin seeing a psychologist. He felt all had poor concentration on the court, and he'd made appointments for each one.

"He's the one who's got to be nuts," Grant later said as he and Pippen canceled their appointments. King simply didn't show.

•

ON MARCH 18, AFTER a slow start, the Bulls ran away from Denver in the third quarter to a 13-point win in which Jackson got some substantial bench production, particularly from Will Perdue. Perdue was now something of a folk hero to the Stadium crowd, sort of a pet they wildly applauded every time he came into the game. It was a kind of derisive applause, much like that reserved for Harthorne Nathaniel Wingo in Madison Square Garden in the 1970s. Perdue was a clumsy white man who was not a total bumbler after all. He still played mechanically, thinking about shots before taking them, so he got few. But under Vermeil's program he'd gained strength, and with that confidence he could now rebound without bending his knees to jump. His jump with his arms up was stronger, and he had become a really useful rebounding engine. His hands and feet would never be quick and his defense was still poor; opponents attacked the lane when he was in the game. But he could help, though not yet as much as Cartwright and perhaps not ever. Cartwright didn't look pretty playing, but no one liked to drive into the paint against Cartwright. If he could knock out Akeem Olajuwon for two months, what might he do with some 6-3 guard? In practice, the players yelled "Incoming" or "Scud missile attack" when Cartwright started winging his elbows as he revved up for a drive to the basket. "Get those Scuds away from me," Pippen would taunt Cartwright in the locker room in the Stadium, where Cartwright sat next to Pippen. Even the best centers, like Olajuwon and Patrick Ewing, routinely were held under their scoring average by Cartwright.

The Bulls pounced on Atlanta again on March 20 and won by 22. It was their fiftieth win—they'd won fifty faster than any team in franchise history—and they had gone 18–1 since the All-Star break. The Hawks were starting to slip now, but many felt Bob Weiss should be Coach of the Year. "For a team that would rather pass a stone than the ball, it's amazing the way they've been playing," he joked. For the first time in years they had been playing basketball instead of 'Nique ball when Dominique Wilkins had the ball, and Doc ball when Glenn Rivers had the ball, and Mo ball when Moses Malone had the ball and so on.

Cliff Levingston had another good game against the Hawks. He'd had few good efforts this season, mostly because he simply could not figure out the Bulls' offense and Jackson was afraid to leave him on the court. But he could be active on the boards—scrumming up the game, Jackson liked to call it—and he scored 12 points against the Hawks. Levingston was desperately disliked by some of the Hawks, and during the game Levingston took down John Battle hard on a drive to the basket. With just a few seconds left and the Hawks trailing by 24, the Hawks were yelling for Weiss to call a time-out. They wanted to run a play so they could try to get Levingston. Weiss said there'd be another time.

Earlier, another little drama played itself out at courtside. Kevin Loughery, the Bulls coach when Reinsdorf purchased the team, was now a Hawks assistant. He was sitting on the Hawks' bench when Krause walked by. Krause usually sits there before the game to watch the Bulls players shooting, but when he saw Loughery he kept going without a word.

"I knew I was fired the day he got the job," Loughery recalled. "I knew all about Jerry Krause and he knew that I knew, so he couldn't have me around."

Loughery didn't have much success with the Bulls and was never considered a great tactician, but he remained bitter nevertheless.

"You see," Loughery was telling a reporter, "I was in Baltimore [as a high-scoring guard] way back when Jerry Krause was there and I knew he had nothing to do with signing Wes Unseld and Earl Monroe and all these guys he takes credit for discovering. And he knows I know and that he couldn't con me. He was just a gofer."

"Me and Murph haven't talked in years," Krause said to the reporter after he'd left Loughery. "Some guys never forget. He have anything to say?"

•

A DISTURBING PATTERN was developing for the Bulls as they went into Philadelphia and had their nine-game winning streak broken March 22. Jackson had begun to rely less and less on the bench players in important games. Only Perdue and Armstrong were getting any significant playing time, and Grant was feeling the fatigue as he went forty-two minutes and grabbed 10 rebounds, but slowed at the end as Charles Barkley climbed all over the Bulls and Philadelphia ran off a closing 15–4 streak to win 95–90. Jordan hit just 8 of 23 shots, and even though the rest of the starters combined to shoot 58 percent, it was hard to overcome a poor Jordan shooting game. In the team's other loss in March—to the Pacers—Jordan had also shot 8 of 23. Pippen tried to be diplomatic in his postgame comments. "They forced Michael into taking some shots he doesn't normally take," said Pippen about Jordan missing 3 of his last 4 shots against double- and triple-teams. Despite that, Jordan had attempted 4 of the Bulls' last 6 shots.

Grant, 8 of 10 from the field, had hit his only 2 fourth-quarter attempts and was exasperated. Cartwright, 5 for 9, hadn't gotten a shot in the fourth quarter; neither had Paxson. They'd seen it before. "If Michael had just shot .500, well . . . ," observed Paxson. The victories were almost shrugged off while the losses gnawed and rankled.

· Jackson had played all twelve players for some time to try to keep harmony and find a rotation. It hadn't worked and the starters were now being stretched, including Cartwright, who could least afford it. Jackson was worried about him breaking down since he'd had trouble with his hip and calf. Cartwright told friends he was feeling tired, but he wouldn't tell Jackson. Jackson talked to him about sitting out a week in April if the races were decided to rest for the playoffs, but Cartwright didn't like the idea. He felt that for the sake of his timing and game conditioning he needed to play. And, in any case, he felt he needed to be more involved in the offense as playoffs approached, not less. Jackson said they would talk about it again.

But if the Bulls were looking ahead a little, it was hard to blame them. Much had been made in the newspapers and on TV about the rematch with the Pacers because of Reggie Miller's comments. Copies of the quotes about the Bulls' lack of talent beyond Jordan had been pasted above the players' locker stalls. Everyone was asked before the game about them. Miller felt his remarks had been taken out of context and stopped talking to reporters even before the team got to Chicago. In the game, he was heartily booed every time he touched the ball, but he played well and scored 34 points. He had plenty to say in the game, however.

The Pacers are a team known for what the players like to call "talking trash." Talking trash is the on-court banter and brinkmanship some players use to motivate themselves or harass teammates. Not much goes on among Bulls players, but in Miller and Chuck Person the Pacers have two of the boldest trash talkers in the league.

Early in the game, Pippen went down against a Miller rush to the basket, trying to draw a charging foul. "Get up, you punk-ass motherfucker," Miller screamed at Pippen. Pippen got the ball the next trip down, drove at Miller, and lost the ball trying to elbow Miller in the head. Pippen would be so annoyed he'd get into early foul trouble, commit 6 turnovers, and score just 10 points. "I should have waited to get him later in the game," Pippen decided afterward. The taunts and cursing continued throughout the game, but the Bulls could not shake the Pacers until late even after an 11–3 start.

"We got too carried away with all that stuff," lamented Cartwright. "We expended too much energy early."

But the game became a riot. Detlef Schrempf got ejected for arguing after being called for a foul. He had previously been elbowed in the head by Cartwright and he was called for pushing with his elbow to ward off Cartwright. And Chuck Person was ejected late and drop-kicked the basketball thirty rows up into the stands in a wild display of emotion that had referee Bill Oakes screaming at him as he left the court.

With three of the six Pacers' starters gone—Vern Fleming having already left with a back injury—the Bulls took control and won 133–119. It was their twenty-sixth straight home win, and it gave them the second-best all-time NBA home win streak. It would turn out to be good playoff practice for the Bulls, both physically and verbally. But another potentially explosive game was coming up: Olajuwon and the Rockets were coming into the Stadium Monday for the first time since Olajuwon's injury.

Rockets management had gone near berserk after the injury and had done everything short of posting a bounty on Cartwright's head. But Cartwright remained cool, and before the game he met Olajuwon on the court and thanked him for his restraint. In Houston, they were now talking about Cartwright as the Rockets' most valuable player. The Rockets had run off eleven straight wins and had gone 15–10 without Olajuwon. They'd found they had players who could perform and not just watch while Olajuwon spun and drove and shot. And those players, the guards particularly, sliced up the Bulls. Kenny Smith, Vernon Maxwell, and Sleepy Floyd blew by Bulls defenders. The Cartwright–Olajuwon matchup would quickly be forgotten as both seemed timid in trying to avoid another controversy. Olajuwon shot 5 of 17 and Cartwright 2 of 9.

Jordan scored 34 points, thanks mostly to abandoning the offense after halftime and driving to the basket, but he, too, was frustrated. He was hardly satisfied the Bulls were a championship-caliber team yet. "Every time I'd switch guys, then they'd go to the other guy and he'd score," he complained afterward. "I switch to Kenny and then they go to Maxwell and then B.J.'s in there at the end short-arming shots. Where was Hodges to spread the floor? And they played off Pippen [who went 4 for 17] and he couldn't do anything. We're going to see more of that in the playoffs."

The media celebrated Jordan afterward for playing heroically despite a head cold. Jordan had slept in the trainers' room before the game and wore a towel around his head at halftime. Both stunts amused the team, since Jordan had gotten sick because he had gone out to play golf Sunday on a cold, windy day after an all-night card session at home with friends. "I asked him why," said Cartwright, "and he said he doesn't sleep much. I've never seen a guy sick so much in my life."

The players thought Jordan made much of his illnesses to impress the media, and they were especially appalled when he came out to shoot after halftime wearing a towel like a turban. "Maybe he thought someone in the building didn't know he was sick," said Grant.

Earlier, while Jordan slept, Levingston, who had gotten a nasty reputation on the team for sticking by Jordan and becoming something of a cloying toady, lay down next to Jordan and slept. He, too, claimed he was sick. "Cliff play golf, too?" Paxson wondered. "Don't think so," said Hodges. "I think it's sympathy pains."

The Rockets won by 10 and, more distressing, the Bulls scored 90 points for the second time in three games in playoff-style defensive ball. The Bulls' bench came up short again, although Armstrong did score 15 points despite a couple of late misses when Houston went on a 9–0 run to assure the victory. Hopson didn't even get in the game; Levingston played only five minutes and Stacey King, eight. Perdue had now taken King's time at backup center and King was being used behind Grant, although Jackson felt he didn't rebound enough to play power forward and threw off the team's offense when he was in the game.

The Rockets were now the hottest team in the NBA with their twelfth straight win. The Bulls' twenty-six game home winning streak was over. They were just 12–12 against the top ten teams in the NBA and 4–7 against the top six in the Western Conference after having been swept in the season series with Houston. Jackson, though, had a way of keeping the team on track, and with a matchup against Boston looming at the end of the month, he knew he had to keep the team from looking ahead.

"Unless we win the next two games [against New Jersey and Washington], playing Boston isn't going to mean anything," said Jackson. The Boston game would be the last stand for the Celtics in their effort to overtake the Bulls for best record in the Eastern Conference and home-court advantage should the two teams meet in the playoffs. Kevin McHale hadn't played in two weeks because of an ankle injury, but the Bulls expected to see him. Larry Bird was laboring like an elderly man with his back problem. Reggie Lewis had sustained back spasms, and Brian Shaw was playing on a bad ankle. The red-shirted Bulls would be the big bad redcoats coming into New England. But before that, there were the Nets and the Bullets.

"Those are the most important games we have coming up," Jackson insisted. No one believed him.

•

JACKSON WAS THINKING about his offense. He was thinking about the playoffs and isolating Jordan on top of the floor. "It's the offense everyone fears," he agreed. But doing so ran counter to the principles preached by Winter and Krause. Jackson was a disciple of the team game, but he recognized the weapon he had in Jordan. And he knew Jordan's distaste for the offense tended to sabotage it because he refused to cut without the ball.

For about a month or so, Jackson had been able to implement his plan to get Jordan to run upcourt ahead of the ball, bringing defenders with him and making the ball handler's job easier. But that, too, had been a struggle. "We had to try to trick him," Jackson acknowledged. So he persuaded Jordan that he could get easier scoring opportunities as a post-up player. Jordan, unsurprisingly, quickly became the best post-up player on the team, scoring easily against smaller guards, especially now that he had built himself up to around 210 pounds. But Jordan eventually caught on to the ploy, and the Bulls were able to run that way less and less as the season progressed.

The trouble with putting Jordan on the top of the floor was that when he gave up the ball he'd often step back instead of cutting through. "He could make the offense so much more effective," Jackson lamented. Yet Jackson needed a happy Jordan to win, and he knew how Jordan chafed under the so-called equal-opportunity triangle offense. But tonight against the Nets would be a good time to experiment.

Jackson had one of his tips about the Meadowlands baskets. In watching the tapes, he had seen too many balls rattle out on the rim in front of the Bulls' bench. The Bulls would be shooting at that basket first. "Everything comes out of that basket," Jackson instructed the team before the game. "Let's stay with every shot even if it looks like it's going down."

By halftime, the Bulls had 18 offensive rebounds on the way to a season-high 29. Horace Grant had 9 in the first half. The Bulls had a 69–56 lead and were pulling away. It had been a Jordan show; when the cat's away, Perdue joked, Michael gets to play.

Winter was at the NCAA Final Four, a perk the Bulls annually allowed him as a veteran college coach, while Krause was out of the country with Reinsdorf on yet another trip to Yugoslavia. Jackson spread the floor, put Jordan on top, and he went left, right, left, dancing all over the Nets on the way to a 28-point first half. He scored 19 points in the last five minutes of the second quarter. Everybody else could have taken a seat. Jordan was thrilled; he took 26 shots in thirty minutes. His teammates weren't as happy, even though the Bulls pulled away to an easy 128–94 win. It was the kind of game that tended to corrode the relationship between Jordan and his teammates further because it was a game in which he could have deferred to the other players, but didn't.

"He didn't have to score that many," noted Cartwright about Jordan's 42 points. Yet even Jordan wasn't thrilled, since Jackson took him out after three quarters.

"He's not going to let me get fifty this season," he would say afterward.

But Cartwright couldn't understand. "We're going to beat this team anyway," he said. "This was a game we all could have gotten twenty [no other Bull scored more than fourteen]. That's the thing that gets me."

"Hey, Hodg," Grant yelled across the room as about two dozen reporters made a thick circle around Jordan. Hodges had been calling Jordan's act "the show" for some time and the term had caught on. "What were you doing during the show?" Grant asked. "I went out and got some popcorn. Did anyone miss me?"

The Bulls moved into the Washington, D.C., area the next day, a stormy Good Friday. When they left for the Capital Centre from their suburban Maryland motel, Stacey King wasn't on the bus. He arrived in the locker room about forty-five minutes later and said he'd been stuck in traffic, that he'd gone to see his agent on a promotional deal and traffic was bad. It was; Washingtonians handled rain-slicked highways about the way a lady in high heels navigates an icy driveway. Jackson took King aside and warned him about such violations of team rules.

What Jackson didn't know was that King hadn't gone to see his agent, who wasn't even in Washington. King had begun his own little campaign. He pretty much figured his days with the Bulls were over—or should be—and he decided he'd help them end. He'd outlined the plan to a friend. He'd force the Bulls into trading him by coming late for meetings, games, team buses, and so on. He'd become too much of a distraction. He felt his plan was validated that night when Horace Grant played forty-one minutes (and King eight) even though Grant had a painful stiff neck and could barely hold his head straight. "Now I know I'm finished with this team when I can't even play when Horace is hurt," King would tell teammates later.

The Bulls won by 18 even though the Bullets, playing without leading scorer Bernard King, made one hard run in the second quarter, cutting a 17-point Bulls lead to 1. Jackson had instructed the Bulls before the game to pack in their defense. "This is the worst three-point-shooting team in the league," he said. The Bullets hit 4 straight three-pointers in the second quarter in their run. Oh, well, Jackson thought.

Despite the stiff neck that had him running like a scarecrow, Grant scored 22 points and grabbed 13 rebounds, and Pippen performed an impressive Jordan act, swooping down the lane for 22 points while Darrell Walker was harassing Jordan into a 7-for-17 shooting effort.

The Bulls could now enjoy Sunday's last-day-of-March national-TV game. They'd won the easy two and Boston had even lost in Miami to fall two and one-half games behind with twelve to go. The

Celtics had to have this one. Jackson watched the NCAA Final Four UNLV–Duke game in the hotel-lobby bar in Boston with some reporters. He admired UNLV coach Jerry Tarkanian for his methods, if not for his reputation. "He gets those kids to play hard," Jackson marveled. That was what coaching was still all about. He thought UNLV's Stacey Augmon would be another Scottie Pippen. He had some Sam Adams on tap, smoked a cigarette, and fended off a request from the bartender for two tickets to Sunday's game. "For me and my kid," the bartender said in his flat New England accent.

"How old is your kid?" Jackson asked.

"Twelve," the bartender replied.

"I can't help you," Jackson said softly, staring hard at the man. "But it's nice that you thought of your son."

•

CHIP SCHAEFER, THE young rookie trainer of the Bulls, still marveled at the Boston Garden. The famed parquet floor looked like a collection of lumberyard throwaways to him. "If you bought a new house," Schaefer was remarking before the game, "and you had this floor, you'd say the house was great, all except for the floor, that you needed new hardwood. This thing's a mess. It's got cracks and bumps and even looks old."

The visitors' locker room in the Boston Garden was equally appalling. Foil-covered pipes snaked around overhead so the players could barely straighten up, and the heat was turned up so high you had to run in place to keep from falling asleep. "Same old stuff every time you come here," said Craig Hodges.

"This is great compared to the way it used to be," said Bach, who played for the Celtics in the late 1940s. "At least you've got a urinal in here now. We used to have to go out in the hall with the fans and they'd be yelling at us, 'You piece of shit, you motherfucker.' It was unbelievable. At least you get to stay in here until the game starts."

But if the accoutrements were intolerable, somehow the games played here always seemed special. And this one would be ever so special. It was one of those games that you might want to hang a banner for, like Jordan's 63-point explosion that forced a double-overtime playoff game a few years back. Again, the teams would play overtime and again the Celtics would win. But it was a memorable day on national TV for both teams.

The NBA provides a sort of itinerary of the game's events to visiting teams. On it are listed the pregame presentation, the celebrities expected, and halftime events. On the one distributed by the Celtics, all the categories were empty except the one that read, "Halftime events." It read: "A ballboy rolls the ball cart to center court."

But these were not the mighty, feared Celtics anymore. Larry Bird would probably have been retiring after this season if he didn't have a $7 million contract for next season under a salary-cap quirk. McHale, as the Bulls expected, suited up after missing six games, but was limping. Brian Shaw and Reggie Lewis were also hurt, but all the players would forget the pain and strain every breath out of themselves and the hot, stuffy arena before the afternoon was over.

Chris Ford had done a terrific job remaking the Celtics with Shaw back after a year in Italy and Dee Brown providing help despite being a rookie. In this game, Brown would be remarkable, hitting 10 of 12 shots for 21 points. The Bulls, though, felt they could collapse on the Celtics because they didn't believe the guards posed enough of an outside-shooting threat.

Bird's balky jumper—this year's version, anyway—was falling early, and when the Bulls gave Grant a break and brought in Cliff Levingston, Bird posted him up and went to the hoop for a pair of easy baskets. The Celtics held a 53–47 lead at halftime. King hadn't played and was restless at halftime, looking around the locker room as Jackson was going over some of the team's first-half breakdowns. "Pay attention, Stacey," Jackson snapped. "We're going to need you in the second half."

Bird kept firing and Jordan started answering back, but the Celtics weren't missing much, 16 of 22 in the third quarter, as they went ahead 86–78. They led 96–82 early in the fourth quarter when a three-point shot by McHale danced all around the flexible Garden rim and fell in. Both the rats and the leprechauns were still around the old building. The Bulls cut the Celtics' lead to 10 and Jackson called a time-out.

"It's only five baskets," he said coolly. "We can attack this team."

And that's what the Bulls set about doing. Jordan and Pippen took a cue from Raymond Chandler: When in doubt, have two guys come through the door with guns blazing. They drove and jumped and pierced the Celtics with their deadeye marksmanship and daring élan. The Bulls knew their strength remained in their youthful alacrity and the Celtics weren't quick enough to handle their slashes to the basket. John Paxson hit the third of his 5 three-pointers of the day with 5:19 left to make the score 103–97, and that sent the Bulls on a 13–2 run that gave them a 3-point lead with fifty-five seconds left. Lewis missed a jumper, and then Jordan missed a drive that could have ended the whole thing. Bird missed a three-pointer, but the ball was tipped back to Lewis, who tied the game at 110 with a three-pointer with nineteen seconds remaining. It was his first of the season. It was just one game, but it was becoming a special day, filling with golden moments as the tension grew. Boston basketball fans were considered the most sophisticated in the NBA, but they were as loud and excited as a high school crowd by now.

Cartwright, standing in the right corner, flipped the ball to Jordan, but Lewis had a hold on him. No call, and the ball dribbled out of bounds off Jordan's fingertips with three seconds left. "You don't get that call in Boston Garden," Cartwright agreed later. With three seconds left, Bird flipped the ball in to McHale and then stepped gently on the court. The Bulls inexplicably collapsed on McHale, who dropped the ball back to Bird for an open three-pointer. The ball hit the back of the rim, bounced straight up and headed back down to the basket. Behind Bird, the cameras caught several Boston newspaper writers jumping up and using their own body English to try to wriggle the ball in. One more wonderfully beguiling moment for the great Larry was all they were asking, even the ones who weren't supposed to care. The ball refused to cooperate and leaked off. Overtime.

Robert Parish hit two jumpers and a drive before fouling out in the first overtime as the Celtics took a 118–113 lead. But Jordan got two back with free throws and Paxson spotted up for another three-pointer to tie it at 118 with thirty-two seconds left. Grant then blocked a Bird shot, but Jordan drove and threw a wild runner off the rim. Boston had the ball with 1.1 seconds left. Bird threw a lob that was intercepted by the Bulls. Time-out.

It was miracle time. It was Jordan time. Cartwright found him deep in the right corner. Jordan knew he had to be quick, but he also had to square up and see the basket. He grabbed the ball, leaned back, hung, and shot falling away. The Garden crowd froze. Jordan had made such moments delicious and painful before. As the ball nestled softly through the net he was colliding out of bounds with Ford and celebrating an apparent Bulls victory. "No good, no good," screamed referee Mike Mathis, waving off the basket. "Good, good, yeah," Jordan screamed, "yeah." The clock had expired before Jordan had released the ball, Mathis said. Jordan ran immediately to the press table to watch the replay on TV. Mathis was right. "Damn," he said. It was one time that hang time had betrayed Jordan. If only he had shot it more quickly, he counseled himself. The game would head for a second overtime, and with Grant, Pippen, and Jordan each playing more than fifty minutes, the troops of energy looked as if they would reinforce the Celtics' side.

The Celtics again went ahead by 5 in the second overtime, but back came the Bulls. Jordan hit two free throws after rebounding a Cartwright miss and was fouled by McHale, his sixth. But Bird drove for a three-point play to keep the Celtics lead at 5, 127–122. Bird had summoned all of this up from somewhere, and he was "Larry Legend" again. Bird's painful back problems would require surgery after the season, putting his career in jeopardy. He had missed most of the 1988–89 season after heel surgery and his return in 1989–90 had been painful as he tried to adjust to diminishing skills. He shot a career-low 47 percent and rumors abounded of conflicts with angry teammates, some of whom began to resent Bird's preeminent position, which was based on his prior skills. But he was no less a competitor than Jordan, and despite the searing pain he snaked his way through the defenses and lofted his deft fallaway jumper as if he'd gone back in a time machine. And his teammates, grown used to his absence, had begun to look for him again and to expect the moments he so often had produced. On this day he was back up front leading the way, rolling imaginary dice after baskets and even taunting the youngsters again. One sign of age, it has been said, is a passing from passion to compassion. The fire of passion was back this day in Larry Bird.

Jordan answered back with an off-balance runner that went in as he was fouled. The Bulls were back within 2. Bird then hit a jumper for his final points of the game, giving him 34, including 9 in the

final overtime, and Brown drove for a basket after a Jordan jumper
rimmed in and out. The Celtics led 131–125 with 1:17 left. Paxson
then floated into place above the three-point circle on the left side
and fired. The shot was good and he was fouled by Lewis for a rare
four-point play, the free throw giving him a career-high 28 points.
There was still more than a minute left and the Bulls were within
2. The Boston Garden was a well of emotion now, a geyser, flooded
with a fury of excitement. Shaw hit a jumper and Jordan missed.
Celtics by 4 with twenty-eight seconds left. Lewis was fouled, but
he made just one. From the deep right corner, Pippen hit a three-
pointer. Wouldn't this ever end? Boston led 134–132 with twenty-
one seconds remaining.

The Bulls fouled Lewis again with fifteen seconds left and again
he made just one. One more chance. The Bulls trailed by 3. The
play was for Jordan to pull up for a three. He weaved his way toward
the basket and stopped, the defense falling back, and he shot. The
ball rimmed in and out. But Grant rose up from the crowd like a
giant beanstalk and grabbed it. As he came down, he flipped back
to Jordan. The Celtics had collapsed toward Jordan and the ball as
it went back. They had overloaded Jordan's side of the court. Paxson
was wide open on the left, the area from which he'd hit his last 3
three-pointers. "Here! Here!" he screamed. "Here!"

Jordan had to know Paxson was there, but there wasn't much
time. In the huddle, Jackson had told Paxson to stay near the circle
on the left side, but Paxson wasn't too upset or surprised. "I would
love to have had that shot," he would agree later, "but mostly good
things happen when Michael's got the ball, so what can you say?"

Bach would agree. It was what he called "Red October time."
The Bulls shout "Red" for the last five seconds of a possession, a
time when it's difficult to get off a shot and Jordan usually steps
forward to take one. "His shooting percentage would be maybe
thirty points more if he didn't have to take all those shots," acknowledged Bach, "but he somehow finds a way to get those shots
off, and his teammates are always running to throw the ball back
to him then anyway."

Shaw ran at Jordan and Jordan ducked below, hanging and then
leaning in and shooting. It was not a good shot, sort of a liner, as
Jordan leaned forward. The ball caromed off the side of the back-
board like a billiard ball and out of bounds. It was over. The Celtics

had won 135–132 and had kept alive their slim hopes to overtake the Bulls in the East.

Everyone around the Bulls felt drained from the game, but not empty, because of its meaning. They still maintained the advantage in the East. Jordan, Grant, and Pippen had played more than fifty minutes and Paxson and Cartwright more than forty. Jackson was asked about the bench, and he said that Levingston was having trouble handling Bird and King didn't appear to be into it. It was the first game King didn't play when not injured in his short pro career. But on the whole, Jackson was as satisfied as you could be without winning. If this was a playoff preview, the Bulls had to feel good about pushing the Celtics to double overtime on their home court in a game that Bird would be hard-pressed to repeat in his condition.

9

APRIL 1991

4/2 v. Orlando; 4/4 at New York; 4/5 v. San Antonio; 4/7 v. Philadelphia; 4/9 v. New York; 4/10 at Indiana; 4/12 at Detroit; 4/15 v. Milwaukee; 4/17 at Miami; 4/19 at Charlotte; 4/21 v. Detroit

WERE THOSE APRIL showers or a man crying out for discipline?

That's what Phil Jackson was wondering about Stacey King.

Monday's workout on April Fool's Day had been light. The team had a mandatory semiannual league meeting on the dangers of drugs and alcohol, and Jackson had scheduled a workout for only the seven reserves, most of whom had played little or not at all the day before against Boston.

"I'm out of here," King muttered during the meeting. "I'm not dressing. I'm leaving."

"Sure, sure, Stacey," taunted Pippen. "You better be getting taped."

"I'm leaving, you watch and see," said King. He looked hard at Pippen. "I'm not staying."

After the session, true to his word, King walked out of practice. Failure had indeed gone to his head.

228

Jackson called King at home. His answering machine was on, and later even that would be disconnected. Jackson called King's girlfriend; she claimed she didn't know where he was.

"It's a soldier gone AWOL," Jackson told reporters.

It seemed to the Bulls staff that the last chance to save King was now gone. The team had tried to move him before the February 21 trading deadline, but Krause had held out for the value of a No. 6 pick in the draft, more than King was worth now. After the season, the Warriors again would try to get King, offering forward Tyrone Hill, their No. 11 pick in 1990, but the Bulls were uncertain about whether they could sign free agent Cartwright, so they decided to keep King, who also could play some center. They felt his upside remained substantial, even if his backside did, too. The players would taunt King about staying under the "calorie cap." "Calorie cap problems," someone would invariably say to him during practice.

As his game continued to slide, King became desperate; he finally concluded the problem had to be Al Vermeil, the Bulls' trainer. King announced that he needed a private trainer, someone who would give him more weight-lifting work and less of the power jumping Vermeil preached.

The Bulls weren't so sure, but they did bring in a dietitian for King: If he was going to eat, they decided, he should eat right. King sat with the dietitian for almost two hours, taking notes and listening to a lecture on nutrition. He said he would follow the program.

After the lesson, King went to get a rubdown. During the rubdown, he ate two bags of Doritos.

But he was trying to retain his sense of humor, even if no one was laughing along.

"I set a screen roll, and these guys," said King at practice, loudly mocking Jordan and Pippen, "they're out there dancing around and waving you off." King went into a maniacal mambo, flailing his feet and arms. "They're dancing around like this and not even looking at you." But then he would turn somber. "This is not the place for me," he'd say, "although I don't know if I'll be able to get out— the line at Jerry Krause's door to get traded after this season is going to be so long."

If anything was going to put King at the front of that line, it was his walkout. Jackson called Krause, who had just returned from seeing Kukoc. Krause told Jackson to find King $250 for missing practice and suspend him from the Orlando game on Tuesday, which meant docking his salary about $12,000.

King ducked reporters all day, but he did show up that night at the local TV station where he did a weekly show. He had walked out, he suggested, because Jackson had publicly criticized him with the "King wasn't into it" comment after the Celtics game. Jackson was a hypocrite, King said, because he had told the players not to take their complaints to the media, and here he was doing it himself and embarrassing a player. The coach didn't have the guts to face him, King said.

Jackson didn't hear the comments. Later he said that if he had, the suspension would have been for more than one game.

The next day things would get worse.

King came to practice, but only to meet with Jackson, since he wasn't going to play. The meeting quickly turned ugly. "Look," King demanded, "I don't give a shit if you play me or don't play me. Just get off my fucking back."

It takes quite a bit to make Jackson angry. This was quite a bit. Jackson's jaw muscles tightened, and then he erupted, like a long-dormant volcano.

"I've had to sit in this room and watch tapes of seventy games," he blasted, "and for seventy games I've had to watch your fat ass make mistake after mistake and screw up just about everything we've tried to do. And I'm sick of it."

King started cursing Jackson and, as Jackson would say later, "the epithets were flying pretty good after that." King got up and left, cursing Jackson more as he stormed out.

Everyone who didn't hear the outburst heard about it fast. Jordan said if it were up to him he would just suspend King for the year, but he wasn't about to get involved. "Then everyone will go running around saying, 'Michael Jordan got him traded.' I'd just sit his ass. He's of no use to us anyway, and you don't treat a coach like that no matter what your problem is. I always told them the guy was a problem. But they never want to listen to anything I've got to say."

Paxson shook his head. King's outburst was the talk of the team.

"We've got so many guys on this team going in different directions," he acknowledged. "That's the kind of thing that kills you."

If anything good came out of the King controversy, it was that it was overshadowing a new chapter in the Pippen controversy. There had been a story by Lacy Banks in the *Chicago Sun-Times* that day saying that Pippen was annoyed that Reinsdorf and Krause had gone to Yugoslavia to woo Kukoc, while Pippen still didn't have a new contract. The story quoted Pippen as saying he didn't see why he should play hard the rest of the season if the team was going to treat him that way.

Meanwhile, a process server wandered through the Multiplex to serve Levingston with papers about some credit-card debt.

As Jackson tried to cool down, team photographer Bill Smith stood by anxiously. It was time to take the 1990–91 Chicago Bulls team picture, a task that had been planned for several months and rescheduled several times. This was the final time it could be done.

"Everyone smile," said Smith.

•

REINSDORF SAT IN the White Sox offices in Sarasota, Florida, feeling pretty good. His baseball team was finally getting some respect. Just a year earlier, most free agents—even bad ones—wouldn't even consider signing with the team; Reinsdorf couldn't even overpay for one. Now the team had surprised baseball in 1990 with a second-place finish behind Oakland, the new Comiskey Park was about to open, and season-ticket sales were at an all-time high.

And the team was about to announce it had agreed to terms with Bo Jackson. Jerry Reinsdorf now employed the two most popular athletes in the United States—Jackson and Jordan. What more could an owner ask for?

Then his secretary came in and handed him the newspaper article about Pippen.

Reinsdorf was shocked. Had Pippen gone nuts?

"We're going to stop giving physicals to these guys," he thought to himself. "From now on we're only going to have psychological testing."

What had happened? he wondered incredulously. The day before he left for Yugoslavia to see Kukoc, he had talked to Pippen and Kyle Rote, Jr., in a three-way conversation. They had essentially agreed upon a new deal for Pippen, a contract extension of five years for almost $18 million. Everyone agreed it was fair, and Reinsdorf even admitted it was his fault the deal hadn't been negotiated sooner; he had stalled because of the Kukoc situation.

He wanted to make one more strong pitch for Kukoc. If the Bulls could sign him, they'd need the approximately $1.8 million they had left under the salary cap this year; if they couldn't, part of that would go to Pippen. In either case, Pippen would get the full amount of his extension. But Reinsdorf needed time. So he told Pippen, "I'll guarantee your deal myself. Even if you get hurt now, we'll be obligated to pay you. No matter what happens to you, consider that deal done.

"Do you understand, Scottie?" Reinsdorf had repeated. "Is that okay with you? We'll get this done, probably after the season is over, but you can consider the deal done. Okay?"

Pippen had agreed.

So Reinsdorf took the nineteen-hour trip to Split, Yugoslavia. For months, the consistent report was that Kukoc was about to sign with Benetton, the Italian-league team, for upwards of $4 million per season. The Bulls wouldn't match that, having offered Kukoc a $15.3 million, six-year package. But every time Reinsdorf asked, Kukoc's representatives said there was no deal. Was he being suckered? Reports circulated in Europe that the Bulls could not sign Kukoc because of Pippen's contract status. Finally, Reinsdorf had decided to see Kukoc and his family himself.

Krause had also made the trip to talk with Kukoc about basketball, how he'd be featured in the Bulls' offense and how it worked. Reinsdorf sat for two days with Kukoc's worried parents. They knew nothing of the United States but what they'd read in controlled press reports, and Reinsdorf sought to assure them that there was a substantial Yugoslavian community in Chicago with access to the Belgrade newspapers. He told them about his four children, ages twenty-one to twenty-eight, and how he'd treat Toni as one of his own.

Only Kukoc's girlfriend seemed to be a problem. She didn't want to go to the United States and was openly hostile toward Reinsdorf. Still, he was feeling better about the Bulls' chances of getting Kukoc, and he was back in Sarasota three days later. He believed he had done what he could and now it was up to Kukoc to decide. Both Reinsdorf and Krause saw the Yugoslav as the final piece in the

Bulls' championship puzzle; Reinsdorf was also looking at him as the player who could fill Jordan's shoes—and any empty seats—after Jordan retired.

The reports of Reinsdorf's trip were all over the newspapers when the Bulls returned to practice Monday after the Boston game. Pippen hadn't thought much about it until several teammates began taunting him about how much more the team wanted Kukoc than him. And Krause, ever the fingernails on the blackboard, hadn't helped. The week before, he had told Pippen he wouldn't even have been a Bull if Krause hadn't traded up in the draft to get him; Pippen owed everything to him, he said.

And if Pippen had been anxious, he was downright panic-stricken when he now heard that Charles Barkley had hurt a knee; all he could think about was what could happen if he was injured, spoken guarantee or not. Krause and Reinsdorf had shown Cliff Levingston last summer what their assurances were worth, he felt. Pippen called Rote, nearly hysterical. "I want to sign a contract, now. I've got to sign something now," Pippen repeated over and over. Rote understood. He knew that Pippen remained deathly afraid of dying young, as his father had just a year ago, or being crippled like his brother. He played with a constant fear of a crippling injury.

Still, even Rote was astounded by Pippen's public threat to play at less than his best, as was the furious Reinsdorf, who wasted no time in calling the agent.

"You get this straightened out or we're through," Reinsdorf said. "Scottie Pippen has a contract with this organization and he has every legal and moral right to live up to it. We've been fair, but we're not going to be made fools of. I don't feel the least bit sorry for Scottie Pippen."

Rote called Pippen and told him there had better be some statements in the newspaper the next day saying that there had been a misunderstanding, that he would always play hard no matter what. It would also be nice, said the agent, if he said he wanted to stay with the Bulls. Pippen agreed.

Krause also had something to say.

"You ain't going anywhere, Scottie," he told Pippen as the team got ready to play Orlando on April 2. "We got you and this is where you're staying. No matter what you do and no matter what you say. So get used to it."

•

WHILE THE PIPPEN story would quiet down, the King blowup had everyone talking, analyzing, and deciding how the Bulls should handle the situation. John Bach and his old friend Frank Layden had gone to lunch at Ditka's restaurant in Chicago one afternoon, shortly after King's walkout, where they ran into the Bears coach himself. He pulled Bach aside.

"This thing with King really bothers me," Ditka said, stopping by their table. "Now, here's a guy who forgot about the team. Sometimes, you have to make that clear. What I would have done is ripped his locker out of the wall and thrown it out in the street and said, 'There. That's where you can go.' Who the hell does that kid think he is?"

•

THE STRAIN OF seventeen games in March was beginning to show on the Bulls in April; they seemed to have lost a step. Their shooting eyes were still holding up, but they weren't executing the harassing defense that so frustrated opponents; teams were getting to the basket more easily. The Orlando Magic shot 55 percent in the April 2 game and even pulled ahead by 3 points with three minutes left. But the Bulls turned up the defense for a few minutes and made the Magic disappear; Orlando went five straight possessions without scoring while Jordan and Grant combined for 6 free throws in the last forty seconds for the 106–102 Bulls' win.

But Grant would get just 5 shots while even the coaches were screaming for somebody to get him the ball. Worse, Grant had 12 points on those 5 shots, underscoring the Magic's inability to cover him. "First, I've got [6-6, 210-pound] Nick Anderson on me in the post and then [6-8, 195-pound] Jerry Reynolds, and I can't get the ball. It's ridiculous," said Grant, noting that Jordan attempted 26 shots and scored 44 points.

Also unhappy was Armstrong, whom Jackson had pulled with just a few minutes left in the game. The coach was keeping both point guards on a short chain and neither was too happy about it, although Paxson would show his displeasure less. Make a turnover, B.J., and you're out. Miss a shot, John, and you're out. Both would invariably come muttering back to the bench.

For Armstrong, it would carry over to practice the next day as the team prepared to go to New York. Jackson watched him for a while, and then finally shouted at him to sit down. "You're not into it," he yelled. Later, Jackson made it clear: "Michael is taking the shots," he said.

Armstrong knew what he had to do. "When I get it," he told Grant, "I'm shooting it. Jordan doesn't get it from me."

"Me, too," said Grant. "Watch me against New York. I'll shoot it every time I get it."

It was a little game the two played. They knew it wouldn't happen. Like Paxson, who made the threat before almost every game, they were too programmed to pass off. They'd feel too guilty about being that selfish.

•

WHEN THE TEAM pulled into New York Wednesday night, April 3, NBC was waiting. The Bulls would be on national TV Sunday against Philadelphia and the network wanted some interviews. Jackson, Pippen, and Grant showed up to meet with former Lakers coach turned broadcaster Pat Riley, but Jordan refused. He had substantially cut down on his media appearances in the 1990–91 season. The demands on his time were intolerable; he was convinced that he was merely being used by others, and he resented it. Instead, he went to his room to meet up with comedians Dan Aykroyd and Bill Murray.

Grant had been carrying a touch of the flu and had tried to get out of the pregame shootaround Thursday, but Jackson told trainer Schaefer to make sure Grant was there. Grant fumed.

"When Michael's sick, he just calls off practice," he told Schaefer.

The Bulls all looked sick against the Knicks, who were without Charles Oakley and Gerald Wilkins. If they had heard the line about New York leading the nation in people around whom you shouldn't make sudden moves, the Bulls had paid close attention. They were in slow motion.

Blitzed by Mark Jackson and Brian Quinnett, they fell behind by 24 late in the first half and would trail by 18 at the end of the second quarter. Phil Jackson kept the coaches out of the Bulls' locker room at halftime.

"Let them sit and think about it," he said. "Let them look at the guys responsible."

Jordan was pretty sure he knew who was responsible: Jackson and the triangle offense. He had 9 points on 4-of-12 shooting, and he was enraged. "No more triangle," he promised himself.

In the second half, Jordan came out on the attack and Jackson cooperated; he went into the new open offense the team had been working on to isolate Jordan on top of the floor, and within ten minutes the Bulls had tied the game as the Knicks collapsed like the city's economy. They committed 9 turnovers in the third quarter and were outscored 30–12. It was an impressive display of Bulls strength. The Knicks held on to a tie after three, but the result was as inevitable as death, taxes, and bobbing corpses in the East River: The Bulls won by 10. They still could turn it on, but they knew it was getting hard to keep it on.

"We knew we could be tired by this point," Jackson said.

The main topic of conversation after the game was Patrick Ewing. He had seemed content to take fallaway jumpers along the baseline, even against Will Perdue, who could have done little to stop Ewing if he'd tried to drive. And Ewing certainly would have gotten the foul call against the young Bulls backup center if he had.

Knicks insiders believed that Ewing, frustrated over the constant swirl of controversy in New York, the collapse of the team, and some failed renegotiations of his own, had pretty much quit for the season, or at least until the playoffs. Thinking about it after the game, John Bach just shook his head. The Bulls had turmoil, too, he knew, but the players always competed hard. It was a tribute to both them and Jackson, he thought.

•

IN THE TWENTY-FIVE-YEAR history of the Bulls, there had been just one division title. It came in the 1974–75 season, in what would signal the end of the great Dick Motta defensive club of those early 1970s. The Bulls were then in the Western Conference, and they had never been able to get past Kareem Abdul-Jabbar's Milwaukee Bucks teams in their division—and if the Bucks didn't take care of them, the Lakers and Wilt Chamberlain did. But Abdul-Jabbar broke his hand in the exhibition season in 1974; Milwaukee would collapse and finish last in the division, and Chamberlain had left the Lakers. The Bulls' 47–35 record wasn't their best ever—they'd won fifty-seven games in 1971–72—but they had the second-best record in the conference, one game behind Golden State. It would be thirteen years and nine coaches before the Bulls would win as many games again.

Jackson admired Motta's Bulls for their team play as much as he disliked the Bucks and their one-man approach to the game. "It seems that [Bucks coach Larry] Costello consistently overcoaches his teams," Jackson wrote in his 1975 book, *Maverick*. "Knowing that only Kareem will take the important shot, no matter what number may be called, allows a defense to do a lot of double-teaming and forcing. This can make the Bucks have to go somewhere else for their offense and that disrupts their flow. . . . The fact is that Milwaukee's predictability makes them lose too many close games. I personally don't particularly like the kind of games the Bucks play. There's just a limited number of things the other four players can be doing when Kareem has the ball. Milwaukee can certainly come out and kill you on any given night, but they really can't function as a team, and a smart club can take advantage of this. I don't believe that basketball can be anything but a team game."

At the same time, Jackson revered those Bulls for their defense— they still hold the all-time league record for most games in a season in which opponents scored under 100 points. They controlled the court by forcing opponents to alter their offense, a technique Jackson would later adopt for his own Bulls; it would become their most successful tactic.

Describing Motta's team, Jackson wrote, "Chicago stops the ball from moving by taking away the passing lanes. They literally isolate the man with the ball and force a team into playing baseline basketball. . . . Norm Van Lier, for example, can pick off a laterally thrown pass just by outrunning the ball. Playing against the Bulls makes a team slow down and make sure of their passes. It's like playing against an octopus."

Fifteen years later these words would describe his own team.

If Motta inspired Jackson, he also inspired future NBA coaches Jerry Sloan, Rick Adelman, and Matt Guokas, all of whom played

on that 1974–75 team, and Bob Weiss, who was traded by the Bulls
before the season. Motta's 1974–75 division winner lost in the conference finals to eventual champion Golden State, although the Warriors actually trailed the Bulls three games to two at one point.
Motta later blamed holdouts Bob Love and Norm Van Lier; he
demanded that they not get full playoff shares and created a near
mutiny among the players.

When the Bulls won only twenty-four games the following season
with their aging cast, Motta left Chicago to coach the Bullets, who
had lost to the Warriors in the championship series the previous
year. It wasn't until Jordan arrived in 1984 that the Bulls began to
regain any credibility. The Chicago Bulls had come a long way in
twenty-five years, from 1966–67, when coach Johnny "Red" Kerr
had to call the newspapers after games to report the score and spell
the players' names, to 1990–91, when every kid in America could
spell *Jordan*.

(And how well Jordan knew it. One day, a reporter was baby-
sitting his one-year-old son. Jordan, who gravitated toward kids,
kept trying to get a response, but the boy ignored Jordan and fiddled
with his father's mini–tape recorder. The reporter joked, "Guess
he's not impressed with the superstar."

"Give him six months," Jordan shot back.)

•

THE BULLS WERE moving inexorably toward that second division title.
One more win would clinch it, and they were prepared to get it from
San Antonio at the Stadium.

But they would have to wait a little longer. The Spurs pushed
them all over the court, outrebounding the Bulls 50–29 and taking
a 21-point lead late in the third quarter before Jackson switched to
a small, quick lineup and began relying on some three-point bombing
from Craig Hodges in a fireman's drill exercise. The oft-forgotten
Hodges hit 3 three-pointers in about two minutes, and within ten
minutes the Bulls had sliced a 21-point deficit to 1. They appeared
to be on the brink of yet another impossible comeback, but San
Antonio beat their pressure and went on to win 110–107. Afterward,
Spurs coach Larry Brown said the Bulls could be awesome if they
could get the entire bench scoring the way Hodges had.

Dennis Hopson only wished he could get the chance. For the third time in the last four games, he didn't make it into the game, and he wasn't happy about it. When the Bulls traded with the Nets for him in June 1990, he was a career 13-point scorer after three NBA seasons. But now he was the eleventh man, ahead of only Scott Williams on the depth chart. And despite his $900,000 + -per-season contract, he was actually wishing he were back in New Jersey, which he had hated. Hopson wasn't playing much, and he'd drawn Jordan's wrath quickly.

"I know he doesn't like me, but he never says anything to me," Hopson was telling a friend one day. "You hear all the things he says behind your back and then he comes up to me the other day and asks if I'd heard from Brad Sellers [Hopson's teammate at Ohio State], and how was Brad doing. Can you believe it? The guy tries to run him out, and now he wants to know how he's doing. Like he cares. I just said he was fine."

Hopson, with his hard, sharp features and tight skin that looked as if it had been stretched over his face and gave him an angry look, had feuded angrily with Nets coach Bill Fitch. "Get off my back," Hopson had once yelled at Fitch during a game. "If you don't like the way I play, get me out of here."

"Dennis," the usually stormy Fitch said mildly, "I'll do my best to accommodate you."

Fitch told Jackson that Hopson merely needed a change of scenery and could blossom with the Bulls. But Hopson chafed at the reduced role; he couldn't adjust to the idea of coming off the bench. He was the kind of player who needed to get into the flow of a game, and needed more than four- or five-minute intervals to do it. The Bulls were now saying he really was a defensive specialist. Hopson wasn't buying it.

"When I first came here, they told me I'd be a scorer off the bench," Hopson recalled about his conversation with Krause after the trade, in which the Bulls gave the Nets their 1990 first-round pick and two future second-round selections. "Defense never came up, which makes it look sometimes like I'm crazy. People look at me and say, 'Here's a guy they brought here to score, so what's the problem? Why isn't he scoring?' "

So Hopson was actually thinking about being back in New Jersey. "Hey, I averaged nine point six my first year, twelve point seven

my second year and then fifteen point eight, and I was learning and
getting the shots and the opportunities," he said. The Nets were a
veteran team in the process of disintegrating when he arrived as the
No. 3 pick in the 1987 draft, a kid who was supposed to breathe
new life into a dying franchise. But Hopson was alone in that role.
"I had nobody," he recalled about that lonely first year. "Here,
Horace had Scottie, and Stacey and B.J. were together, but in New
Jersey they had guys like Mike Gminski and Buck Williams and
Roy Hinson and Mike O'Koren, and I was always alone. And there's
nothing to do in New Jersey."

Hopson missed home and wanted to play in Cleveland, mostly
because he liked Lenny Wilkens's coaching style and felt the Cavaliers needed a shooting guard. Hopson, a muscular 6-5, 200-poun-
der who occasionally stunned the Bulls coaches in practice with
athletic moves they'd only seen from Jordan and Pippen, told his
agent to talk to the Bulls about dealing him to the Cavaliers after
the 1990–91 season; he'd already made some inquiries on his own
and had found the Cavaliers to be receptive.

Hopson had once looked forward to coming to the Bulls, although
he'd been warned that Chicago was a tough place to play. His best
friend in college was Sellers, the former Bull who had gone to Greece
to play in 1990–91. Sellers told Hopson what it was like to play with
Jordan, but Hopson thought it was just a bad match since the fans
and Jordan had wanted Johnny Dawkins and Sellers had never had
a chance. But then he talked to another friend, Seattle's Sedale
Threatt.

"I feel sorry for you," Threatt told him. "There's a reason there
have been so many guards through there. You're not going to get
the ball. You play with Jordan, you watch. Sometimes you play
more than other times, but mostly you watch."

Hopson insisted he'd been assured otherwise. The Bulls were
looking for him to play twenty to twenty-five minutes and score in
double figures off the bench. They'd told him that Paxson, Hodges,
and Armstrong were all inadequate because they were small, that
teams like the Pistons took advantage of them, and that the Bulls
needed a big guard to play with Jordan. He'd get eight to ten minutes
behind Jordan and at least another ten beside him and perhaps even
more at small forward.

"No way," his friend Ron Harper, the big guard now with the

Clippers, told him. "You're not going to get any minutes there. Just look how they play. Where are the minutes going to come from? Man, it's going to be bad for you."

The same words had come from another Ohio friend and former Bull, Charles Oakley. Oakley said he liked Jordan, but forget it, man, you weren't going to get to score.

Hopson was starting to get worried, and by training camp he was in a near panic. He and Armstrong had become close friends, and Armstrong told him right away: "You're going to wish you were back in New Jersey. You're going to look back and think it was better."

"No way," said Hopson. "You're crazy. You know what it's like there? People booing you, the few that do come to games. Losing every time. No, I just want to get a chance to win some games again."

After the Bulls won their NBA title, he was asked jokingly whether he'd rather be in New Jersey. He answered "Yes" without hesitation. And he wasn't joking.

•

DESPITE THE LOSS to San Antonio, the Bulls found themselves division champions when the Pistons lost to New York on Saturday night. There wasn't much celebrating; Pippen didn't even know. "I wondered why we had these division-championship T-shirts in the locker room," he would say later. Jordan hadn't celebrated, either; he had a 7:00 A.M. tee time. After all, game time Sunday against Philadelphia was 2:30 P.M., and that gave him plenty of time for a round of golf. His golfing mania had become nearly insatiable and he was now playing often during the season.

Jordan had even found a way to use his golf as a psychological ploy against the 76ers. Jordan made a point of telling Sixers assistant coach Fred Carter about his game, knowing Carter would try to use it to motivate Hersey Hawkins, who'd be playing Jordan. The Sixers, Jordan hoped, would be driven to distraction by the notion that he was so confident about playing them that he actually spent the morning on the golf course. A few days later, Barkley would complain about Jordan's early-morning golf game on his Philadelphia radio show, saying the Bulls hadn't taken the 76ers seriously. "If

I had done that," observed bad boy Barkley, "I'd have been killed."

Despite the golf flap, which left Jordan's teammates predictably annoyed, Jordan managed to score 41 and steal 4. If Jordan had indeed intended to distract Hawkins, he succeeded: Hawkins shot just 3 of 10 in the first half for 6 points. But the 76ers were proving stubborn, even though Barkley wasn't playing because of a knee injury; he had come to Chicago to watch the nationally televised game, however, and he was clearly enjoying himself.

"Hey, Stacey," he yelled at King, who was being booed by the fans during a rare game appearance, "what time's practice tomorrow?

"These guys ain't winnin' no title. They're too soft," he'd shout occasionally, and when lead referee Jess Kersey would call a foul, Barkley would continue, "Don't help these guys out, Jess. They're soft."

Of course, there was some truth to Barkley's assertion; many around the league still questioned how long the Bulls could last in the playoffs with guys like Grant and Cartwright as their power players. And the 76ers were whacking the Bulls around on the boards in this game, just as San Antonio had done a few days earlier. The Bulls' weaknesses were beginning to show. They could be pushed around, as Detroit knew, and sometimes you could get them out of their game that way. Rick Mahorn was doing just that, as he went on to grab 14 rebounds, and even Armon Gilliam, who was being called "Charmin " Gilliam by his teammates because *he* was so soft, was muscling inside for offensive rebounds.

There was plenty of theater in the game: Pippen dunked over 7-7 center Manute Bol, sending the 76ers' bench into convulsions of laughter, and Bol entertained them further by dribbling between his legs after a rebound. But the game got serious down the stretch, and the 76ers would force it into overtime. The street-clothed Barkley grabbed Hawkins in the huddle and shouted at him as the overtime period was about to begin, "If you want to be an All-Star [which Hawkins was that season for the first time], now's the time you've got to take over." And he did, scoring 6 straight 76ers points, including 2 baskets on brilliant drives against Jordan. The 76ers refused to surrender the lead, and won 114–111 when Armstrong came up short on a last-second jumper.

John Paxson watched from the bench, shaking his head. Armstrong had played the last twenty minutes of the game, almost the entire second half. He seemed tired and, predictably, his shots were short at the end. Jackson told the coaches he was leaving Armstrong in to see how he would finish a game; the Bulls would need Armstrong in the playoffs, and Jackson wanted to see how he fared in a pressure situation. It wasn't the best strategy, given Armstrong's obvious weariness, and the coaches also knew it, but they understood: It was another experiment out of Jackson's behavioral laboratory.

But Paxson didn't understand. He sat on the bench, examining both the game and his life. He thought about the technical foul he'd drawn against Orlando in the Stadium a few days before, and the disapproving look his four-year-old son had given him for it. Ryan Paxson had become a big basketball fan, watching his dad on TV, turning off the lights to introduce himself when the pregame introductions came on, and playing his own game with a small basket set up in front of the TV during Bulls games. Paxson would use the game as a means of communication and discipline. When Ryan was naughty, John would call a time-out, and Ryan would have to go sit down. And when he'd really get out of control, John would call a technical on him, to teach him a lesson. But, he asked himself, what lesson was the father learning? Paxson, though slower than most guards he faced, was a tough competitor. It was one reason he stayed in the starting lineup. Armstrong was quicker, yet he couldn't pressure the ball as well as Paxson. "He plays defense better than he's got any right to," marveled Bach. Paxson did things out of sheer will, and despite chronically aching knees and ankles he had the fourth-best streak of starts in the league. But his fiery desire could bring with it a nasty temper in games. And his ensuing arguments with referees had gotten him labeled a complainer and probably cost him some calls. Paxson vowed to get more control of himself.

But watching Armstrong play the final twenty minutes of the Philadelphia game began to convince Paxson that his Bulls career was at an end. The team hadn't talked to him at all about a new contract. Paxson figured Armstrong would start in 1991–92, but he didn't really mind. "I'm the perfect backup point guard for this team," he would say. "I can run the offense, I can play with Michael, and I can shoot. I can play both guard positions and I wouldn't mind being a backup. I just want to get paid." But there were always doubts about guards after they hit thirty, especially white guards. This game, Paxson believed, only showed that his career in Chicago was over, no matter what the Bulls said.

Caroline Paxson was angry about the team's treatment of her husband. She's a delicate blonde, quiet, shy, and loyal to John, who always arranges for a friend to drive her to and from the Stadium for games—he doesn't want her going alone. Krause told associates that she would screw up her face and eye him angrily whenever she saw him. And Bach, whom she liked, said he hated to look at her these days. She would look at him with pleading eyes, as if to say, "Isn't there anything you can do?"

As Caroline and John drove home in silence after the 76ers game, John finally made a decision. "Let's sell the house," he said.

"I'll call the realtor tomorrow morning," Caroline said quickly.

•

JACKSON WAS EXPERIMENTING again. Jordan had pretty much abandoned the offense, and was scoring in droves. In the last five games, he'd averaged 29 shots per game and 39 points. Pippen, too, was spending considerable time free-lancing, and in the 76ers game the two had scored 51 of the starters' 55 points in the second half. Armstrong was the only reserve to score in the last two quarters. So Jackson was trying to figure out how to restrain Jordan without his knowledge. He tried putting him in the corner of the triangle offense where it would be hard for him to get the ball, but when that failed, Jackson just took him out of the game, twice after he'd hit a pair of jumpers.

"Hey, don't take me out after I hit a couple of shots," Jordan complained. "At least let me miss a few." He was angry after the April 9 Knicks game in the Stadium, and he was offering unusually curt answers to reporters' questions. The Bulls had managed to survive the Knicks, 108–106, on a Paxson jumper with twenty-two seconds left (the Armstrong experiment had ended) and a Cartwright steal as the Knicks tried to get the tying basket. It truly was one of those games in which victory went to the team making the next-to-last mistake. It wasn't a particularly good performance, but the Bulls were overconfident against the Knicks. They'd beaten them in the playoffs in six games in 1989, and had only lost once to them since in the regular season, when Trent Tucker took an inbounds pass and hit a three-point basket, all in one tenth of a second; the league later ruled that the shot should have been waved off for lack of time but refused to change the outcome of the game. That disputed field goal had become the source of immediate controversy. "You can't shoot the ball in a tenth of a second," Jackson had complained afterward. The incident reminded Bach of a 76ers–Portland game in which Archie Clark dribbled and dribbled with just a few seconds on the clock and finally put up the game winner. Portland officials tried to find the timekeeper later, only to be told they couldn't talk to him. "I don't want to talk to him," said one Trail Blazers executive. "We just want him to time the rest of our lives."

Bill Cartwright thought the team was tired, both physically and mentally. It was a long season and most of the team's goals had already been accomplished; the games just seemed to drone on and the Bulls, Cartwright felt, needed the playoffs to revive them. He was worried, too, about players like King, who was still blaming everyone but himself for his problems. Horace Grant had come in and worked hard to earn his position and respect with the team, but King seemed to expect it to be given to him. Cartwright had also listened to Armstrong complain about his lack of opportunity, as had Perdue and Hopson. And he had grown weary of Levingston, who was often late for practice and complained often and loudly about his lack of playing time. Levingston would sit around telling the other players about the big parties he was throwing and purchases he was making, even though everyone knew about his financial problems.

Cartwright felt some of the veterans on the second unit did little to help the younger players, which accounted somewhat for King's drift. "The kid's all screwed up now and we're going to need him," Cartwright lamented.

Jackson thought the same thing, and despite King's felonious behavior, he was receiving an amnesty of sorts. Jackson felt he had to try to get King ready for the playoffs, even if King continued to play poorly. Krause had also warned Jackson that the less King played, the lower his value would be and the harder it would be for the Bulls to trade him after the season.

The Bulls moved into Indianapolis for a game the Pacers were treating like a grudge match, after that wild affair in the Stadium a few weeks earlier. This was a possible first-round playoff matchup, and it was a game the Bulls wanted badly to win, having lost six straight in Market Square Arena. The Pacers, a good three-point-shooting team with Reggie Miller, fell behind quickly, but regained the lead and went ahead 57–51 at halftime as they ran and fired long. It appeared that the Pacers had fiddled with the nets: They were shorter than most, which allowed the ball to come through faster for quick outlet passes and fast breaks. The Bulls had to extend their halfcourt defense to the three-point line, which put pressure on their rebounders. The Pacers had a 27–13 rebounding margin at halftime.

The Bulls needed to slow the game down and get it into a halfcourt pace, which they finally did in the third quarter, showing some versatility that would prove useful at playoff time. The Pacers went cold, shooting jumpers from a set offense and falling behind by 7. Indiana started to charge back in the fourth quarter, but Jordan decided to take over, if not in scoring then on the floor. He told Jackson he wanted to play point guard, so Jackson shifted him to the top of the floor. Jordan said Armstrong was pushing the ball too much, and he wanted him out of the game; Jackson obliged. This was a game for pace and patience, and Armstrong wasn't adept at either quite yet. Paxson dropped into the corner and Jordan started to work on top of the floor.

The Bulls, trailing by 1 with six minutes left, scored 12 of the next 16 points, taking a 7-point lead with two minutes left, and held on the rest of the way to win 101–96. Jordan had scored under 30 for the second straight game, but his leadership on the floor had been crucial.

It was an encouraging victory for the Bulls, since they were out-rebounded but still managed to win. It would be essential for them to be able to control a game like that, particularly because they lacked a shot blocker. Bach felt it was a breakthrough of sorts. "They seem to be coming together as a team again," he said. And just in time: The Bulls were heading to Auburn Hills to play Detroit and Isiah Thomas was back in the lineup.

·

TWO NIGHTS LATER, Jackson was smoldering, and it wasn't from the smoke of his postgame cigarette. "I've got a stupid team, a stupid team," he repeated furiously after the Bulls' loss, as he looked for a place to finish his cigarette and have a beer after talking with reporters. "I don't know what they were thinking about," Jackson raged. The staff had never seen him like this.

The Bulls had shot 51 percent in the first half to trail 50–49 behind 24 points from Jordan. But the team shot only 40 percent in the second half, and 29 percent in the fourth quarter, which they entered tied, to lose 95–91. It had been an important game, Jackson felt, because Isiah Thomas was back from his wrist surgery and the Bulls' only win in the Palace had been when Thomas was out.

But what upset Jackson the most was this: *The Bulls had taken the wrong basket.* After pregame shooting drills, the players said they wanted to shoot at the basket in front of the Pistons' bench in the second half. That was the basket, the coaches believed, that had been "adjusted." Jordan said the team didn't want to get a complex about that basket, so they would try it in the second half.

But in the fourth quarter, Jordan would be the only Bull to hit even half of his shots, on the way to finishing with 40 points. It was a typical Pistons win. Thomas was brilliant, zipping a nifty pass to John Salley down the lane in the last seconds for a three-point play and the victory. Thomas finished with 26 points and 16 assists—and the Bulls' wrath. With five minutes left and the Pistons ahead by 1 point, Paxson was cutting across the court with the ball when he tripped over Thomas's foot, stumbled, and fell into Joe Dumars's knee. Paxson was dazed with a mild concussion and had to leave the game, and Armstrong would replace him and miss all 4 of his fourth-quarter shots. Paxson would recover in time for Monday's game against Milwaukee, but the Bulls knew that Paxson's fall over Thomas was no accident. Bach liked to call Thomas "Assassin"; he had that angelic smile, but he was known as a vicious player who would try anything to rally his team. Like Bill Laimbeer, he was

not popular around the league, but they admittedly were the kind
of players you'd pick for your team if you were choosing up sides
for a game. The Bulls coaches respected Thomas, but Jordan just
thought he was a phony. Thomas had recently blistered his teammates and even coach Chuck Daly about the Pistons' poor play since
his return, and Jordan believed it was just an act. "He loves the
stage," Jordan said. "That's why he's back now. He's all ham."

Maybe, but he was no turkey. Thomas was bred on the ugly West
Side streets of Chicago near the Chicago Stadium and learned that
those who attack first survive. That lesson had shaped his game,
and now it had led to Paxson's concussion. Thomas was known to
move up close to the opposing guard and step on his foot or kick
him on the side of the foot—anything to throw off his rhythm. The
Bucks' point guard, Jay Humphries, had become particularly adept
at beating Thomas at this game: Before Thomas could try to kick
Humphries's foot or step on it, Humphries would anticipate the
move and, even while he was dribbling, kick Thomas in the shin
and knock him back. It would allow the Bucks the sort of penetration
few teams could get against the Pistons.

The Bulls were only too aware of Thomas's guerrilla tactics and
had warned their guards, but the tactics were hard to monitor.
Armstrong was especially bothered by them, and although Paxson
was used to them, he wasn't strong enough to keep them from
hurting his timing. So this time, as Paxson tried to cut across the
floor, Thomas simply stuck out his foot and tripped him.

It wasn't the only Bulls casualty. Pippen had left the game mentally in the first few minutes. He wanted so badly to do well here—
too badly, really. On the first play of the game, Pippen was called
for a foul against Dumars, and midway through the first quarter he
drew his second, a questionable offensive foul. The pair of calls so
distracted Pippen that he scored just 2 points in the first half, and
spent the rest of the time arguing with the referees and cursing at
Jackson. "Give me the fuckin' ball," he yelled to the bench after a
time-out. "Fuck you," he screamed later at Jackson when the coach
yelled at him to "push the ball" after one rebound. After three
quarters, Pippen had only 6 points, although he would finish with
13 after a sharper fourth quarter.

The Bulls were again coming apart against the Pistons. Jordan,
seeing his teammates crumbling, took it upon himself to do all the

scoring, and refused even to look at Grant or Cartwright on screen rolls. Kent McDill of the *Daily Herald* counted Jordan missing on nine possible open passes to Cartwright. "Well, at least he was under double figures," Jackson would joke a few days later. Between them, Grant (who had scored 8 of the Bulls' first 10 points) and Cartwright would get just 1 shot in the fourth quarter. It had been the last test of the regular season, and the Bulls had failed.

Meanwhile, there was euphoria in the Pistons' locker room. The Pistons had been squabbling much of the season, but only when they weren't counting their many injuries. Thomas had missed more than two months with his wrist surgery, Dumars had limped around on a bad toe much of the season, and James Edwards, Mark Aguirre, and John Salley had missed sustained periods with various ailments. A third championship had seemed remote; anti-Thomas and anti-Laimbeer cliques had developed and there were arguments over playing time and shots. But with the victory over the Bulls, there was suddenly a feeling that perhaps they could do it one more time, especially if Chicago was to be the main obstacle in their path.

A few days later, Cartwright sat watching a tape of that Pistons game as the Bulls prepared to end the regular season with a game against the Pistons in Chicago. He watched himself spring loose on screen rolls time after time without a pass. "Hey, Bill, you're open," Grant would say from his locker stall next to Cartwright's. "Phil's got to say something to him. If we're going to do anything we've got to stop playing Michaelball."

Cartwright's tiny head was engulfed in his huge hands, the way it always was when he was perplexed. He rarely grew angry like the younger players. He was just sad.

"He's the greatest athlete I've ever seen," he said of Jordan. "Maybe the greatest athlete ever to play any sport. He can do whatever he wants. It all comes so easy to him. He's just not a basketball player."

•

THE BULLS NEEDED two more wins to clinch the best record in the conference, which would mean home-court advantage throughout the Eastern Conference playoffs and the team's best chance ever at a trip to the Finals. And with a game against Milwaukee coming up

in the Stadium on April 15 followed by a trip south to face expansion
Miami and Charlotte—the Bulls had not lost to an expansion team
all season—home-court advantage seemed guaranteed. In effect,
the Bulls would have a week to rest before that closing game against
Detroit, and then the playoffs would follow.

The Bucks proved to be as fragile as a house of cards again. They
blew out to a big first-quarter lead, but a collapse in the Stadium
was inevitable. It came in the third quarter as Jackson sent his team
into its fireman's drill, a risky ploy because it leaves a smaller player
under the basket; earlier in April against Philadelphia it had failed
miserably as Grant was overwhelmed by the 76ers' forwards. But
the Bucks were caught by surprise. They committed 7 straight turnovers and fell behind by 10 after three quarters. The Bulls held on
to chalk up their fifty-eighth win, 103–94, a new team record.

Despite the victory, Pippen was furious. He had taken just 6 shots,
and he was blaming both the triangle offense and Jordan's reversion
to a one-man game. Afterward, he was so incensed he threw his
shoes in the garbage. And when he left the locker room that night,
he promised Grant, "I'm shootin' against Miami."

Jordan had scored 46, but the real hero of the game had once
again been the pressure defense.

"Earlier in the season, people asked me if I thought the Bulls
were better," said Brendan Malone, the Pistons' chief advance scout
and astute bench assistant. "I really didn't think so, but they are.
Their defensive intensity has picked up. They're probably now the
best pressing team in the league."

Of course, Jordan was a major part of that, as was Pippen. But
they had the best jobs. Cartwright's role was to stay back and zone
the area under the basket while Jordan and Pippen crept into the
passing lanes for steals. This strategy leads to breakaways and crowd-
pleasing slams, but they're often made possible by Paxson, whose
job it is to turn the guard to one side so Jordan can jump in and
force a bad pass, or Grant can come from behind as he's racing
downcourt, bothering the man with the ball.

"He's the intrepid one," said Bach of Grant. "He's the one who
has to meet the ball on the double-team and then sometimes a second
time as he goes downcourt, and then he has to find a man to guard
and rebound. He's the one who's really made our press. We always
had the ability to trap a ball handler with two guards, but he's given

us the addition of a big man able to do that. So now you've got Pippen at about six-eight and Horace at six-ten and Michael at six-six, and they're roaring around the court in a triangle of defenders and interceptors, anchored by Paxson in the guard position and Cartwright in the back. And it works by the boldness of Phil in his calls."

But Jackson's demands were unnerving the intrepid Grant. He had been brilliant against the Bucks, stealing the ball, forcing mistakes, scoring 19 points (despite just 9 shots) and grabbing 11 rebounds. But when Frank Brickowski flashed by for a lay-up, Jackson was all over Grant. Grant was used to it—he knew he was Jackson's so-called whipping boy—but he still didn't like it. He complained to Pippen on the bench that he was going to tell Jackson off next time.

"He's pushed me up to here," Grant said, putting a hand on top of his head. "I'm working so hard and he's yelling at me all the time and Michael throws the ball away and he doesn't say anything. He's going to push me too far and then that's it."

Pippen had heard this from his buddy before. "Oh, 'G,' you always say that," chided Pippen. B. J. Armstrong came by and patted Grant on the rear end, and Hodges told him to "be cool."

Bach watched it all with bemusement. He had doubted Jackson's psychological ploys at first, but eventually realized how well they worked. Jackson had identified Grant early as a player who could take the abuse. Jordan and Pippen might pout, but Grant would remain strong and not let it affect his play. And it also served as a rallying point for the team. Jackson knew that the other players would come to Grant's aid and defense, and this united them as a group. His goal was to develop an all-for-one attitude on the team, and picking on Grant was one way that worked.

•

THE TEAM ARRIVED in Miami early on April 16, leaving about thirty hours to game time. The first two seasons the team had visited Miami, they had stayed at an airport hotel. But then they found a little hideaway in Coconut Grove that Jackson loved. The Mayfair House was a five-star European-style luxury hotel, and the Bulls had managed to get discounted rates. Directly across from the hotel was a three-story outdoor mall with one corner of the upper level devoted to a restaurant-bar called Hooters, sort of a Playboy Club for fraternity guys. The waitresses weren't allowed to socialize with the patrons, but they wore skimpy outfits and it was a loud, fun place. For the next two days, it drew every Bull but Cartwright, who went to the movies. It was the closest the players had been since Jordan's first few seasons in the league, when the players gathered nightly in someone's room for card games, food fights, and all-night movies. But then Jordan became a star in his own constellation and didn't spend much time with his teammates anymore.

But this time Jordan was just one of the boys. He hooted at Hooters along with everyone else and even joked with Hopson when Hopson bought a Hooters T-shirt. The players never drank much, just a few beers each, but they were enjoying the balmy weather, the light zephyr off the bay and the coming close of the long regular season. This was as far from Chicago and the NBA season as one could get. "No tickets for the Hooters girls," Jordan announced loudly after seeing one of the single players offer a waitress a pair of tickets. Under their NBA contract, the players received two tickets to every game and would generally trade them back and forth. "Hey, I need thirteen for tonight," Jordan bubbled. Everyone laughed as the festivities continued Tuesday night and again at lunchtime Wednesday before the game.

The Bulls clinched the best record in the Eastern Conference with a 111–101 victory over the Heat, but John Paxson wasn't celebrating. In fact, he was smashing soda cans off the wall in the locker room. He had been ejected from the game in the third quarter during a Heat comeback from a 16-point deficit. Miami would take a 3-point lead, but the Bulls pulled away in the fourth quarter behind a stingy defense that allowed Miami just 15 fourth-quarter points, while Pippen, still upset by the Milwaukee game, scored 21 with 11 rebounds, 9 assists, and 6 steals, including a three-pointer to end the third quarter that gave the Bulls a lead they would hold to the end.

Paxson couldn't believe he had been ejected. The whole thing started when Sherman Douglas held him, and Paxson tried to push his hand away. But it was Paxson who was called for an offensive foul. He slammed the ball down. *Bam!* Technical foul. He started to argue. *Bam!* He was gone. It was an unusually quick hook from referee Bernie Fryer, and Paxson still hadn't cooled down by the time reporters arrived in the locker room after the game.

"It's a double standard," Paxson complained. "I can guarantee that if Michael Jordan had done what I did, he never would have gotten tossed. I'm tired of seeing other guys get away with stuff that I get penalized for."

It was that fiery Paxson temper; his brother had it, too. In his final pro game, Jim Paxson was ejected by referee Ed T. Rush and, walking off the court, yelled, "Hey, Ed," and pointed to his groin.

"What a way to go," John marveled.

Tonight, when he got back to his room after the game, Paxson called home.

"Caroline," he said, "was Ryan up? Was he watching the game?"

The boy wasn't. Paxson breathed a sigh of relief. At least Ryan didn't see him getting thrown out of the game.

•

THE TEAM FLEW into Charlotte late Thursday for the last game of the season. At the shootaround before the game, King hit a three-pointer and was boasting of his long-distance shooting prowess, as if nothing had happened earlier in the month. He had played reasonably well against the Heat with 8 points in sixteen minutes and was feeling loose. "Must have hit forty, maybe fifty, in college," he was saying. "Always took the trey."

His teammates were doubtful, but B.J. thought it could have been possible. "The way [coach Billy] Tubbs played that game down there at Oklahoma, who knows?" Armstrong said. "Maybe he did."

King still wasn't playing particularly well, and come the last game of the season against Detroit, with nothing at stake and mostly reserves on the floor, Jackson would send Grant back into the game with two minutes left for King. Grant had been on the end of the bench, joking with Jordan and Pippen and certain his day's work was over. He'd put away his black goggles, which looked like 3-D glasses and had lenses that looked like soda bottles. "Sorry, Horace," Jackson would say, "but he can't get a rebound. You've got to go back in." But King was trying to put it all aside. He was sure he'd be traded after the season and now figured he'd joke his way through the last few months.

On the bus ride back to the hotel after the pregame shootaround, Armstrong said to PR director Tim Hallam, "Find out what Stacey shot in college on threes."

Hallam investigated, and reported that King had been 0 for 2 in his college career. Armstrong wouldn't leave him alone before the game. "You didn't even hit one, King," he shouted in the locker room. "Man, you can't even dunk. I knew you couldn't hit no three-pointers."

The shouting would continue later even though the Bulls picked up their sixtieth win over the Hornets. It was Charlotte's last game of the season, which they dubbed Teal Night, after their uniform color. They had asked the Bulls to wear their white home uniforms so the Hornets could wear their teal road uniforms. The Bulls declined.

The Bulls led Charlotte by 20 in the first quarter and held a big lead until Charlotte pulled within 4 in the fourth quarter. But the Bulls pulled away for a 115–99 win. Jordan scored more than 40 for the fifth time in ten games. He told reporters it was because some of his teammates were relaxing and it was up to him to take over.

He was particularly angry with Hopson, who had played just four minutes in the game, the fewest on the team. Hopson's playing time had been decreasing steadily, and by now he'd fallen to twelfth man on the roster. Some of that was due to Hopson, some to Jackson. Hopson had never adjusted to the triangle offense, but Jackson also didn't care for Hopson's emotionless look, which looked like arrogance to Jackson. The coach liked emotional, tough players, and Hopson was too much like Brad Sellers. For whatever reason, the Bulls found Ohio State players to be lacking toughness. So Hopson got almost no playing time behind Jordan, who would yell at Jackson during games, "Put me in for Hop." Jackson usually would.

After a scramble in the fourth quarter in which Hopson lost the ball, Jackson called time-out. Hopson had played his four minutes and figured that was it for him. He was always pulled after a mistake. The Charlotte crowd was the only one in the NBA that was perhaps as loud as Chicago's, and as the Hornets hovered within 4 points there was chaos. Hopson wandered to the edge of the huddle and stared up in the stands.

"Dennis," Jackson shouted, but Hopson didn't hear. Jackson saw it as indifference, as did Jordan. "Your boy doesn't want to play," Jordan yelled at assistant Jim Cleamons, an Ohio State graduate who had been assigned to work with Hopson that season. "I'm tired of bailing his ass out."

Jordan went back into the game for Hopson and the Bulls recovered, but Jackson was angry. He thought Hopson didn't want to go back in the game. As a result, Hopson would be the only Bull not to make an appearance in Sunday's finale against Detroit; Jackson explained, "I owed him one."

Hopson was supposed to be one of the final pieces the Bulls would need to get past Detroit. Levingston was the other piece, an active rebounder to back up both Grant and Pippen and run the court. He played fourteen minutes in the Charlotte game, mostly in the first half, and when he was removed after a short first-half stint, he began cursing Jackson. "Screw him," he shouted to teammates as he came to the bench. "If he ain't gonna play me, screw him." He finally composed himself after the game and admitted he had let his emotions get the best of him, but he was still unhappy that he didn't have a role, the tenth man at a time when teams rarely go more than nine deep into the bench.

The anger wasn't limited to those two. Armstrong was disappointed with his 1-of-6 shooting. Recent late-game failures against Philadelphia and Detroit seemed to have drained his confidence and demoralized him again. It was the seventh straight game he'd failed to shoot at least 50 percent.

Armstrong was complaining after the game about not getting any opportunities, when Jordan began shouting at him.

"Hey," Jordan yelled, "we've had a great season. I'm tired of this. We won sixty games and you should be happy about that."

"Screw you," Armstrong shot back. "You don't tell me what I can and can't say."

As Jackson had said earlier, "Ain't winning great?"

But by Sunday's final game, Jordan couldn't have been nicer to Armstrong. He joked with him endearingly as if nothing had happened, and displayed an interest he'd never shown before, asking him how he was doing and including him in his inside jokes with Pippen. Armstrong was absolutely charmed, for Jordan could radiate like the rings of Saturn when he chose to.

Grant just watched. "That's the way it is with him," Grant said. "You've got to stand up to him or he'll never respect you. Brad Sellers never would and he killed him, just killed him. Same with

Hop now. We get along a little better now, but that's only because I told him what he could do with himself. He still pushes me, but he knows when to stop now."

·

THE FINAL GAME of the regular season was against Detroit on national TV, but nothing was at stake except pride. Playoff pairings had already been clinched and the Bulls would open against bottom-seed New York. The Bucks had collapsed down the stretch to fall behind the Pistons into fourth place in the East, so the Pistons were in the opposite playoff bracket. The teams wouldn't meet again until the conference finals, assuming both won their first two playoff rounds.

It was a time of celebration for the Bulls, and on this Fan Appreciation Day the adoring crowd rained bouquets of applause all over the team. The Bulls would win their sixty-first game that day, 108–100. They had the most blowout wins and the biggest margin of victory per game in the league; they tied the franchise record for most road wins and had won twenty-six straight at home to tie for second place in the league's all-time list. They were the highest-scoring Bulls team in twenty years; at 51 percent on the season, they were the best-shooting Bulls team ever. They also set team records for assists and three-point shooting and were the best Bulls defensive team since the Dick Motta era.

And still Phil Jackson was livid. For a game that was seemingly unimportant, the players were playing rough. Isiah Thomas got smacked on his sore wrist by Armstrong; Thomas slapped Paxson in the face after a hard foul and the two began shoving each other. Late in the game, chief referee Darell Garretson decided he wanted the rough stuff to stop, so he called for both captains. But when cocaptain Cartwright approached along with Thomas, Garretson waved Cartwright back. He wanted Jordan and Thomas.

Jackson started screaming at Garretson, "You dickhead. You dickhead."

Bach tried to keep Jackson from running to midcourt, and Jordan, having left the game after three quarters, went to meet with Thomas and Garretson. Cartwright, who tagged along anyway, told Paxson when he got back to the bench that he thought the sullen Garretson just wanted to be on national TV with Jordan.

But Jackson remained angry long after the game, saying that Cartwright was a cocaptain, which he was. Garretson had explained that since Jordan had come out as captain with Thomas before the game, Jordan was the only Bulls captain he would accept. Jackson wouldn't accept the argument, but he never would when it came to Garretson.

Jackson and Garretson had a history dating back to Jackson's playing days; he had once purposely run over Garretson in a game and been fined. Although generally depicted as an even-tempered intellectual, Jackson was a ferocious competitor and was known as a dirty player in his days. His reputation was somewhat similar to Cartwright's, actually—he was considered clumsy and dirty, although he lacked Cartwright's offensive ability. Former Knicks teammate Walt Frazier remembered how the Knicks tried to avoid Jackson and his lethal flying elbows in practice, and how Jackson broke Jerry West's jaw once, though not in a game. "He was waving to someone after the game and just clocked Jerry," laughed Frazier. "Broke his jaw and nearly knocked him out. Couldn't catch him in the game, though."

When the Bulls–Pistons game—and the regular season—finally ended, Krause was walking around the locker room trying to pump hands. "Jumping on the bandwagon," someone mumbled.

Krause had just returned from watching the European Final Four, where he had made one last pitch for Kukoc. It was the third European trip for Krause in four months, and to the players that seemed to be all the front office cared about. Jordan was still refusing to call Kukoc, as Krause asked, and was instead swiping at Krause over his failure to deal with Paxson's contract situation. "I'm surprised by the Bulls' treatment of him," Jordan said. "They talk about loyalty all the time here, so this is a good opportunity for them to prove themselves."

Meanwhile, Pippen remained annoyed that his new deal wasn't signed yet. Owner Reinsdorf had by now given him a written assurance that he would extend his contract for five years, but Pippen knew he was still on hold because of Kukoc. Paxson had yet to hear anything from the Bulls and Cartwright, too, was being stalled. Scott

Williams, the rookie, felt his playing time was being minimized so he would have less bargaining power and the Bulls could re-sign him cheaply. Maybe he'd go to Europe, he thought. Levingston was thinking about Europe, too, having heard talk that the Bulls were not about to pick up his one-year option. Hopson just felt as if he'd been lied to; Krause had told him he would be the sixth or seventh man, and now he was the only one not playing against the Pistons. He was embarrassed and angry.

Jackson watched his unhappy players after the game, and realized that their mutual problems with Krause were actually uniting them as teammates—and just at the right time. It was like a pickup game in the schoolyard, he thought, where you could play hard and play well, even with guys you didn't like, and then go your separate ways later and rip each other. It didn't matter, Jackson felt, as long as the group would come together in games and use their talent to win. They just needed to be united.

10

WARMING UP

4/25 v. New York; 4/28 v. New York; 4/30 at New York; 5/2 at
New York*; 5/4 v. New York*

*If necessary.

BY THE END of the first day of practice for the playoffs, Scottie Pippen
was ready to kill Dennis Hopson. It wasn't really Hopson that Pippen
was upset with; he was still thinking about an afternoon almost
eleven months ago.

He looked out at the assembled media beyond the glass wall from
the court the Bulls used for practice in the Deerfield Multiplex. The
first-round playoff series against the Knicks would begin Thursday
night in the Stadium. He knew they'd be waiting to talk to him. He
knew the reporters would be there from the national publications
and they would be coming. Everyone would want to know about
"the migraine."

Pippen now knew he wasn't dying. On that frustrating afternoon
in Auburn Hills early last June and during the next few frightening
days in Chicago, he hadn't been so sure. He'd even gone to the
hospital to get a CAT scan. His head throbbed for days and the

259

pain would grow worse at times. Sometimes he felt a numbing sensation around his skull. It couldn't be just a headache. "I thought it was a brain tumor," he said.

The Bulls had overwhelmed the Pistons in Chicago in Game 6 to knot the Eastern Conference championship series at 3–3. But as the Bulls gathered by their bench for the start of the deciding game, Pippen started blinking his eyes madly. "The lights look dim to you?" he asked Horace Grant. "No," Grant said. "I'm having trouble focusing," Pippen said. The introductions were beginning and some twenty thousand fans were screaming. The public address system was blaring a song from the movie *Animal House*. "Hey, Mark," Pippen yelled to Bulls' trainer Mark Pfeil, "I got to have some aspirin." Pfeil handed him two and Pippen swallowed them down.

Boom! Pippen's head felt as if it had exploded.

"That seemed to energize it," Pippen recalled. "It got worse and worse and when the game started I couldn't focus. I thought I'd been poisoned."

It was a migraine headache at the worst possible time for an athlete. It was the Bulls' moment of truth, their crucible. And Pippen couldn't go. Oh, he stayed in the game after a quick rest a few minutes into the game. Jackson had asked him to stay out there and try it. But it would have been better for the team if he hadn't. He played forty minutes, but he scored just 2 points, hitting 1 of the 10 shots he attempted as the Bulls lost big.

Pippen thought back many times to that day and the night before. He'd gone to a movie. He was fine at breakfast and wasn't nervous. "We'd had a successful season and nobody really expected us to get to the seventh game against Detroit after we lost the first two," said Pippen. "There really wasn't anything to be nervous about."

But it was a headache. And that's associated with nerves, even though Dr. Lawrence Robbins, the neurologist the Bulls sent Pippen to, told the team afterward that the symptoms could be physical and there were various possibilities other than stress that could have caused it, even food. Pippen was given new instructions on his diet, started wearing glasses off the court, and never had a recurrence. Sometimes he actually wished for another migraine, just to show people that he hadn't choked, that he really did have a headache. He had been told later it can happen just once in a lifetime, but how, he wondered, and why then? There is nothing worse that can be said about a top athlete: Pippen had cracked under pressure.

Pippen's voice doesn't trail off when he talks about that day anymore. Although he was savaged by the newspaper columnists and national NBA writers afterward, he was greeted sympathetically that summer by fans. "People would say they were sorry about what happened in the playoffs," said Pippen. "And then they'd say they got those all the time and they couldn't understand how I could even be on the court. But I know people are going to be looking at me, especially in big games. It's always going to be there for me, even if we win the championship. I know people will always say, 'Well, if Pippen had played last year, the Bulls would have had two in a row.'

"Now," said Pippen, his voice firm and hard, "I just want to get a chance to get back to that final game again, and whether we win or lose, I just want to be there and play and say I was there for the team. I know it's in my past and it will always be there and people will be looking at what I do. But if we can get back there and I can have a chance to play and help the team, well, that's what I feel I have to do this year."

Dennis Hopson found himself in the way of Pippen's determination at that first practice. Pippen hit Hopson with an elbow and the two squared off before being separated by teammates. Hopson had been guarding Pippen tightly and hooking Pippen when he tried to move; Pippen didn't like it and Hopson didn't like the elbow. Bach was closest and jumped in quickly. Pippen was feeling a little anxious. He was ready to go. That final conference game couldn't come fast enough.

•

THE BULLS WERE not terribly concerned about the Knicks, though there was always some anxiety about an opening series. The Knicks just couldn't play the Bulls anymore. Nonetheless, Jackson was at practice early. "No one in our business sleeps much this time of year," he said. "You're always wondering what you could do or should have done. So you get up and go to work."

Jackson had been reading more lately, and had come upon a passage he liked in Rudyard Kipling's *The Second Jungle Book*.

Now this is the Law of the Jungle—as old and as true as the sky;
And the Wolf that shall keep it may prosper, but the Wolf that shall
  break it must die.

As the creeper that girdles the tree-trunk, the Law runneth forward
  and back—
For the strength of the Pack is the Wolf, and the strength of the Wolf
  is the Pack.

Jackson sometimes saw his team as a pack of wolves; the way
they picked over one another with their biting verbal exchanges,
the way they sparred with each other over money, playing time, and
shots. Jackson selected the passage because he wanted to make a
point about staying together. Only in the pack was the wolf strong;
the Bulls must play that way and be that way, despite their dis-
agreements, to survive the playoff jungle. It was time to come together.

The quote was at the top of the scouting report on the Knicks
that was handed out to each player.

Jordan told Hodges they ought to have a team meeting. "No
coaches," Jordan said. "Just players. Just to make sure everyone's
focused on the same thing." Hodges agreed and began to tell some
of the other players. Although he wasn't a pivotal contributor like
Jordan or Pippen, Hodges was respected by everyone, a rarity on
the Bulls. In one of the team's rituals, after every Bulls win in the
Stadium, he'd race down ahead of the rest of the players to the
landing at the bottom of the steps from the court. There he'd greet
every player and coach with a handshake as they turned toward the
corridor to head for the locker room.

The players-only meeting never occurred. The weather cleared,
and Jordan decided to play golf after practice instead.

Oh, well, few on the team really thought of Jordan as their leader
anyway. "Michael wants to win, really bad, but he doesn't want to
win," Pippen would tell friends. "You know what I mean? He's
trying to win, but doesn't always do it the best way."

Pippen, though, had started to grow into a position of some respect. "Every time you go on the court wearing a Bull uniform if
you're not Michael Jordan, you have to work for respect," Pippen
knew. "We know everyone says the Bulls would be nothing without
Michael, so there really isn't much respect for the other eleven guys,

even after I made the All-Star team. You take Michael off this team and give us a consistent two [shooting] guard and we'd still be a top, contending team. I wouldn't say we'd be in the position we are now, but we could be like Milwaukee or Philadelphia, win forty-five to fifty games and play a round or two in the playoffs. But people are never gonna think much of us. And why is it that if Larry Bird gets fifty points, the Celtics are a team, but if Michael Jordan does, the Bulls are a one-man team?" Still, Pippen felt reasonably comfortable in Jordan's shadow. "As long as we keep winning," he said. "If we aren't, well, I don't know. It would be harder to take."

Jordan was the greatest scorer in the game. But could he win? The Bulls knew that the public notion that their offense relied less and less on Jordan this season was not quite correct. Jordan still dominated the offense; his percentage of the offense was the same as it had been the last two seasons, including in Doug Collins's last as coach, when he was accused of catering too much to Jordan. Jordan's shots per game were about the same; his scoring total was down to 31.5 per game only because he was attempting fewer free throws. The Bulls had concluded the season with just three players averaging in double figures, and no team in modern NBA history had won a title with so few; only the 1957–58 Hawks, the 1974–75 Warriors, and the 1982–83 76ers had won titles with just four players averaging in double figures during the season.

Jackson publicly protested that if Jordan scoring was what it took to win, then so be it. The aim was to win. But it was Jackson who tried desperately before the season to make Jordan realize that only once had a team won a title with the league's leading scorer. He knew the feeling around the league was that Jordan would have to adjust once his supporting cast improved. It had this season with the development of Pippen and Grant.

Walt Frazier, now a Knicks broadcaster, had wondered about Jordan in his autobiography a few years earlier: "He's a terrific player who can do everything, but I wonder as his teams get better and better if he'll be able to adjust to playing a smaller role and scoring less. Will he be just as happy when he's scoring 25 instead of 35? How will he react when he's taking only 20 shots a game instead of 30?"

Jackson knew what Frazier was talking about. But Jordan had not gone down to 25 points, nor had he substantially cut his number of shots. Jackson had thought he could vary the offense by making the Bulls a running team that would score more points; then Jordan could score his 30-plus and others would increase their scoring. But the increase was only marginal and was mostly gobbled up by Pippen.

The questions that were there at the start of the season hadn't gone away. Only the playoffs would provide an answer.

•

JUNE JACKSON, PHIL'S wife of almost twenty years, couldn't recall Phil being this confident before a playoff game. But Jackson knew that the Bulls had the overall matchup advantage against the Knicks; Bill Cartwright played Patrick Ewing well and the Bulls had the advantage at almost every other position. Jackson felt good, even if it didn't stop the nightmares. For there were still the games to be played and sometimes they could be as hard to predict as honest dice.

"Should I play Hopson?" Jackson thought. "Can Levingston play? Is he big enough? And what about King? Should I forget about him and go with Scott Williams and we'll worry about King this summer? Horace has to have some help from somebody. Bill seems to be slowing down a little. He doesn't seem to be moving like he was a few weeks ago."

Horace Grant wasn't aware of what Jackson was thinking, but he was a little annoyed about the practice session, about ninety minutes of films and then almost a two-hour practice.

"More than an hour of film," he said. "And then running like this. We know this team [the Knicks]. Coaches get crazy this time of year. It happens to all of them, even the good ones, like Phil." Later, Grant would be told that Del Harris in Milwaukee had put his team through a combined six-hour film-and-practice session during the Bucks' opening-round three-game loss to the 76ers. "See, see, just what I told you," Grant would say. "The playoffs make them crazy."

Jackson's first impulses were correct. The Knicks were no match for the Bulls and wouldn't be. They were a team in turmoil, about to lose their fifth coach in five years (John MacLeod would leave to become coach at Notre Dame, a job he interviewed for in Chicago between Games 1 and 2 of the series). They were, undoubtedly, the most mismanaged team in the NBA. All around, the players talked about changes. "I guess I'm gone," Charles Oakley told a friend before Game 1. "This whole thing is a mess. The guys here don't like one another and everyone's pointing fingers and they worry about what's in the papers and let it bother them. It's a mess."

Like that first game. The Knicks would hang in for eleven minutes as they slowed the pace, worked the ball around, and hit a few open jumpers. But Jordan made a steal and hit a three-pointer with ten seconds left in the first quarter and then B. J. Armstrong made a steal and hit another three; suddenly, after trailing by 1 point with two minutes to go, the Knicks were down 10 after one quarter. Jackson knew the psychological impact this had on a team. "They think they've played a great quarter, done everything the coaches wanted them to do, and they're still behind by ten," he sympathized. The Bulls then sprang their defensive trap and the Knicks fell right into it, piling up turnovers as if they were running a bakery. New York fell behind by 23 points six minutes into the second quarter and trailed by a whopping 65–36 by halftime. The game was over. They would go on to lose 126–85.

The Knicks pounded away in Game 2, slowing the game, taking better care of the ball, and getting Patrick Ewing, who scored just 6 points on 7 shots in Game 1, involved; he had 11 shots and 14 points in the first quarter, even if he would go on to miss 10 of 11 shots thereafter. It would be the Knicks' best chance in the series. Jackson called his team into a time-out in the third quarter and shouted, "Do you guys want to win this game? No matter what we try, it's not working." The Knicks hung tight and the score was tied with eight minutes left, but the Knicks' energy was gone and they let go. They would be held to 4 points in the next five minutes as the Bulls pulled away to an 89–79 victory and a sweep of their two home games, thus all but guaranteeing a first-round victory. Publicly, the Bulls were saying things about how the Knicks came back from 0–2 the previous year to defeat the Celtics in the opening round, but they doubted it was possible. And, frankly, so did the Knicks. They seemed beaten mentally and physically. Rookie Jerrod Mustaf had gotten his nose broken, and Mark Jackson was wearing a bandage over a seven-stitch cut. He said Cartwright had bitten him.

•

BUT THERE WAS trouble in the Bulls camp as they prepared to head to New York for Game 3. The trouble was coming from the Bulls' wives. They wanted to go to New York and they were angry. Jackson had issued an edict: The wives wouldn't travel until the Finals, if the team got that far. And several were furious. "I don't care who Phil Jackson thinks he is," said Donna Grant. "He can't stop me from going to New York." In the end, she wouldn't go. But she would require some soothing from Jackson's wife, June.

June Jackson had raised four kids and had participated in almost a dozen moves with Phil over the years, but life at last seemed to be settling down. She's an energetic, petite brunette with a small, turned-up nose and dancing eyes who looks ten years younger than she is. She had met Phil back in New York after Jackson's first marriage dissolved. She'd been committed to raising a family, and now that her kids were growing, she went back to school, working on her master's in social work. In many ways, she helped Jackson maintain his sixties consciousness; she often wondered how they could be making so much money. Jackson would sardonically tell her to call him to discuss it from her car phone.

But she remained a devoted basketball fan and had inherited the distaff-side problems. She planned a meeting with the wives. It was time, she said, to support the men. No arguments, no pettiness. Let's not create problems about going to New York, she said.

It was an attitude recently expounded by 76ers' forward Rick Mahorn. "You've got to let your family sit back this time of year and let you play basketball," Mahorn explained. "It's no time for the little nitpicking things, for, 'Oh, honey, you've got to cut the grass or pick up so-and-so.' Nothing against your family, but this is when you have to be selfish and when the summer comes and you're champions people will be saying, 'There's so-and-so's wife. She's a champion.' We're champions, they're champions. Everyone's a champion. That's when you reap the benefits."

The wives watched Game 3 on TV.

.

THE BULLS COULD see the end coming quickly. Game 3 was set for Tuesday, April 30, in New York. Game 4, if necessary, would be Thursday. Jordan scheduled a tee time back in Chicago for Thursday morning.

"How are you feeling?" someone asked Jordan after Game 2.

"I'm fine as long as the weather stays nice," he answered.

Translation: golf weather.

Cartwright decided to pack for just one night.

"They're a team without emotion," Bach told Jackson. "They've got no soul, no anger, no hatred. They just seem dead. It's funny, but only Mark Jackson seemed to have that, but he's not doing anything. You get the right coach in there, and I think Pat Riley would be a huge success, and they could do some things. But now they can't seem to come together."

The Knicks had one last cartridge left and they squeezed it off in the first quarter, taking a 31–25 lead behind 11 points from Gerald Wilkins. The Knicks went ahead by 12 midway through the second quarter, but the Bulls sent a calling card that would ultimately signal the end of the series. First, Pippen came down the lane and rose and slammed over Ewing, and then Jordan, deking and wriggling along the baseline, split two defenders and also powered over Ewing, almost throwing himself through the basket with the ball. The Bulls had made their point: They had attacked Ewing and he had retreated, a beaten man who symbolized the fate of his team. The Knicks were backing off from the challenge. The Knicks led by a point at halftime, but the game was already decided, an eventual 103–94 Bulls win. By the end of the third quarter, the Bulls were ahead by 12 points and were watching the scoreboard for Philadelphia's sweep over the Bucks. They'd meet the 76ers again in the second round, just as they had last season.

There would be no celebrating. There was a long way to go and this was to be expected. It was almost like an exhibition-season version of the playoffs. It was time for the real games to begin.

When Phil Jackson left the locker room and walked into the narrow hall outside to answer reporters questions, he saw the Reverend Jesse Jackson. The former presidential candidate, lately a talk-show host, made a habit of showing up at such events. Reporters, cameras, action! Phil Jackson knew that the Reverend Jackson had called Bulls players in their rooms during the playoffs the last few seasons to pray with them and occasionally to suggest plays. Two years earlier, in the playoff series against New York, he'd started giving interviews about game strategy. He'd try to jockey close to the bench before games and get into the locker room and say a prayer with Jordan. Jordan confided to friends that he never quite knew what to make of Jackson; he was fearful of offending him because of Reverend Jackson's clout in the black community, but he was wary of the reverend's motives. Phil Jackson had stopped all of that, and this year the Reverend Jackson would be getting no free publicity from Phil Jackson's team.

"Only accredited media in the locker room, and that includes you, Jesse Jackson," Phil Jackson shouted in the tight corridor off the Madison Square Garden floor as he walked out of the locker room.

The Reverend Jackson looked hard at the coach and then away, as if no one had heard. Next to the Reverend Jackson stood filmmaker Spike Lee, who'd done Nike commercials with Jordan. He had started to hang around with the players, and Grant and Pippen were wearing T-shirts that read, "Give Us Our 40 Acres and a Mule," a reference to the promise made to freed slaves, and also to the name of Lee's production company. Lee, too, was waiting to get into the Bulls' locker room. Jackson looked at Lee. Lee started to back away, as if saying, "If he ain't letting Jesse Jackson in, no way I'm gettin' in." The Reverend Jackson left unobtrusively, but a few days later he would show up in Chicago at the opening game of the series with the 76ers. After Game 1, he would be seen sitting next to Charles Barkley and whispering in Barkley's ear while dozens of reporters tried to get at Barkley for postgame comments.

5/4 v. Philadelphia; 5/6 v. Philadelphia; 5/10 at Philadelphia; 5/12 at Philadelphia; 5/14 v. Philadelphia*; 5/17 at Philadelphia*; 5/19 v. Philadelphia*

*If necessary.

The Bulls were more worried about the 76ers than the Knicks, particularly because of Charles Barkley and Philadelphia's physical upfront play. Jackson had felt the team would need mental toughness for this series, and had taken a quote he said he found from Thomas Jefferson to lead into the scouting report on Philadelphia: "Nothing can stop the man with the right attitude from achieving his goal," Jackson wrote, "but nothing on earth can help the man with the wrong attitude." But there also was the question of the 76ers' unpredictability, which Jefferson did not address. "The players call 'em 'One Flew Over the Cuckoo's Nest,' " Jackson noted. "Jimmy Lynam [the 76ers coach] has done a great job with that bunch, not only because of injuries, but because you never know what's going to happen with those guys."

So Jackson wasn't surprised when, early in the opening game, 76ers' center Manute Bol, the seven-foot-seven-inch African tribesman, started screaming at him. "Zone, zone," Jackson started yelling as Bol stood near the free-throw line on defense. Jackson had complained going into the series that the referees allowed Bol to play in a zone without guarding his man, and he was going to point this out.

"Mother fuck, mother fuck, mother fuck," Bol shouted at Jackson in a sort of soprano hyena form of broken English. "Why you pick on me, you mother fuck?"

Jackson could only laugh.

But there were other reasons to laugh, for Jackson's five, as the Bulls management liked to advertise the team, was having itself a laugher over the 76ers. Barkley was magnificent, virtually unstoppable, as he bulled past Bulls to the basket—he scored 34 points and had 11 rebounds—but the other four 76ers' starters combined for 17 points in a performance the Bulls players recognized only too well.

"It was a total reversal of what we used to be," Jordan agreed afterward. "I'm familiar with that, because you want to be a competitor and try to carry the load. But sometimes you'll come up short. If Charles continues to score almost half their points, we'll win. You're bound to get tired when you have to score and rebound and play defense. I know. I've been there. Our main focus was to contain Barkley, let him have his points, and shut down the other guys."

It seemed to his teammates that Jordan was finally beginning to understand. He scored 29 points in the game as the Bulls took a 20-

point lead in the first quarter and never allowed the 76ers to bring
the deficit under double figures. The Bulls' smothering team defense
limited Armon Gilliam to 2-of-10 shooting as Grant drove him away
from the basket, while Pippen closed down Ron Anderson in a
tummy-to-tummy bump session that held him to 3-of-11 shooting;
by the end of the game it seemed as if Anderson had "Bulls" written
backward on his chest. Jordan's man, Hersey Hawkins, could do
little in a 2-for-9 shooting effort; Jordan was so wrapped up in his
defense that when he came out at the start of the second quarter,
he demanded of Jackson as Craig Hodges took his place, "I've
stopped him. Now don't let somebody else get on him and let him
get off!" Jordan would be back in the game four minutes later after
Hawkins got free for a three-pointer, and the 76ers' All-Star guard
from Chicago wouldn't score the rest of the quarter.

But perhaps more than anything, one Jordan play call signaled
the apparent change in Jordan's attitude. "Five-three, five-three,"
Jordan hollered as he stood near the top of the floor, dribbling the
ball.

"Five-three?" Bill Cartwright thought to himself. Jordan had
never called that play before. It was a screen play for Pippen with
Cartwright blocking out Manute Bol. Pippen had the advantage
because of Bol's lack of lateral quickness, but Jordan rarely called
plays for others, especially when he had the ball on the top of the
floor. He'd either dump off the ball and step back, or take it up the
middle, trying to score and then fanning the ball out on the wing
or inside when the defense collapsed.

Cartwright nodded to himself and smiled. And Pippen scored.

Jordan would end the game with just 15 shots, 1 fewer than Pippen.

Cartwright and the others didn't know about a conversation Jackson and Jordan had had as the playoffs were getting started. Jackson
wanted to talk with Jordan about the postseason. And Jordan said
that since his history was to come out smoking offensively—he held
the scoring records for three- and five-game opening-round series—
he'd hold off. "I'm going to lay in the weeds because they'll be
expecting me not to," Jordan told Jackson.

This was just what Jackson wanted to hear. That it came from
Jordan only made it better. The Bulls would have their best chance
if Jordan played that way and then pounced when it was his time,

in the last five minutes of games. Jackson especially knew that Philadelphia would be looking for an explosion from Jordan because of
the way he'd scored against the 76ers in the 1990 playoffs, averaging
43 points and more than 30 shots per game in the Bulls' 4–1 victory.
The 76ers hadn't played much double-team on Jordan then, but
they'd certainly watch him more closely this year. That would make
his passing off all the more effective.

The Bulls were already beginning to look ahead after their 105–
92 opening-game win over the 76ers. Jordan had watched the Trail
Blazers, considered to be the best team in the Western Conference,
and he wasn't impressed, even though they'd beaten the Bulls twice
in the regular season.

"They play stupid," he was saying in the locker room before Game
2. "They take all kinds of stupid shots and then think they can get
every rebound. I thought [Danny] Ainge would make them smarter,
but he hasn't helped in that way that much, I guess."

The Bulls had little trouble in Game 2 Monday. After an up-and-
down first quarter in which both teams ran and scored, the Bulls
clamped down on defense again and took a 9-point halftime lead.
Pippen again worked hard to deny Ron Anderson the ball. Jordan
forced Hawkins into a series of tough shots, and Grant continued
to grapple with Armon Gilliam, pushing him out of the inside position he'd used to score easily against the Bulls during the season.
They were rotating quickly on Barkley and then dropping back to
protect when the ball was reversed. The Bulls were working hard
and were seeing the payoff. The 76ers did make one late surge, but
Horace Grant grabbed 3 consecutive offensive rebounds, 2 of which
the Bulls turned into baskets, in the last three minutes to keep the
76ers from ever getting closer than 3. The Bulls would win 112–
100; it would turn out to be just one of three times in seventeen
playoff games when the Bulls would allow 100 points or more.

Jackson was not satisfied. Although the Bulls won, he knew it
was due to their relentless effort on the boards. Grant had grabbed
7 offensive rebounds, Cartwright had had 3 while shutting down
Mahorn again, and the Bulls had outrebounded the supposedly
tougher 76ers by 15. But Jordan had shot 12 of 26. Despite his 9
assists, he'd also taken 5 three-point shots, all of which missed badly,
while Hodges had hit his only 2, but didn't get any other passes
even though he'd popped wide open on the wing several times. It

was a worrisome sign. Jackson had watched Jordan studying the playoff statistics before the game.

"Is he worried about not being the leading scorer in the playoffs?" he thought.

"MJ Under Control." Jackson wrote those words on his game notes as the Bulls prepared to play the 76ers in Philadelphia in Game 3 on Friday. The words would be prophetic, but would be among the least of Jackson's concerns.

•

ED T. RUSH, Hue Hollins, and Jack Nies. They would be the referees for Game 3 in Philadelphia. Jackson knew what that meant: It meant the Bulls had problems.

Pro basketball is probably the hardest game to officiate because so much judgment is called for. Theoretically, no contact is allowed. But that is unreasonable the way the game has evolved, so the notion is that play out of the ordinary is penalized. Referees make scores of judgment calls in every game, a Gordian knot to be cut day after day.

The Bulls felt the NBA had sent the 76ers a message in Game 2 with the presence of chief of referees Darell Garretson: The 76ers had better cut back on their rough tactics. It was a message the Bulls had long sought. Jackson had complained during the season that Jordan, who is generally thought to be "protected" by referees and sent to the free-throw line often because he is a star, wasn't getting his fair share of foul calls. The referees were assuming Jordan would make the shot and then when he was fouled, Jackson charged, it was too late to make the call. Jordan's free-throw totals were his lowest in five years. Jackson's remarks were generally disregarded publicly, but Jackson felt he had to continue to pound away to get the attention of the league. Rough, physical play was the one thing that could stop the Bulls. Jackson knew his team was too quick and athletic for anyone in the Eastern Conference as long as the game didn't become a wrestling match.

The referees refused to allow rough play in the first two games of the series, but Jackson was worried about the Game 3 crew. Garretson and Jake O'Donnell were considered among the best officials for a visiting team because they were least likely to be intimidated into making calls for the home team. But this crew, though competent regarding the rules, would be vulnerable. And Charles Barkley didn't help any. The referees had popped out of their dressing room and were just passing the 76ers' dressing room when the insouciant Barkley stuck his head out.

"Hey, Ed," he yelled at Rush. "I hope you've got some Vaseline. I know you're planning to fuck us, so maybe you'll at least make it feel better."

The Bulls were already on their way to the court and heard Barkley's comment. "Great," Jackson thought. "This crew and now this from Barkley. We're not going to get any calls tonight."

But, in some ways, the Bulls were not surprised. The league couldn't want another Bulls sweep. It was too costly. The league had a TV contract with NBC to honor and ticket revenues to consider for owners like Philadelphia's Harold Katz, whose team didn't regularly draw sellouts like the Bulls. If the 76ers could win two games, they'd be assured of at least one more home game. No one believed the league was trying to manipulate games for any untoward purposes. But a Bulls sweep would help only the Bulls. NBC and the TNT cable network needed the games for valuable programming, especially since Michael Jordan always drew impressive ratings and would help produce one of the highest-rated Finals in league history. Nobody would tell anyone to make sure the Bulls lost, but . . . The assignment of referees did come from the league office. It was too much of a coincidence, the Bulls coaches and players thought, that this crew would show up now, now that the Bulls were on the verge of putting the 76ers away.

They wouldn't, at least not tonight. The 76ers would shoot 40 free throws to 19 for the Bulls. It would be enough for a 2-point victory.

But the Bulls nearly upset all the carefully laid plans, leading by 3 points with just over a minute left. Jordan would have a chance to make it 4 points as Manute Bol was thrown out of the game for firing the ball at Rush after being called for a foul that resulted in a Jordan three-point play. But Jordan missed the technical, Andre Turner hit a jumper, and then Jordan hit just one of two free throws, missing his third in the last two minutes—a rarity for Jordan, an 85 percent free-throw shooter. Hersey Hawkins took a pass from Barkley, who was double-teamed by Jordan, and hit a three-point field goal with ten seconds left to give the 76ers a 1-point lead.

Jordan time, right? Wrong. Jordan had already scored 46 points, hitting 20 of 34 shots, including two brilliant, acrobatic drives in the last two minutes. But he was suffering a recurrence of some tendinitis in his left knee that was making it difficult for him to bend and follow through on his shots, including his free throws. So he began driving to the basket, often slicing through two or three defenders for a little stunt flying, and he would then be limping back on defense. Because of those missed free throws, Jackson called the last play for Pippen, who drove right, appeared to be fouled, and let go a wild jumper. It missed, there was no foul called, and the 76ers had some life. And a 99–97 win.

Jackson would later admit that if he had to do it over again, he'd go to Jordan. But Jackson wasn't all that happy with Jordan anyway. He'd confronted him before the game about his knee. The teams had three days off between games, so Jackson gave the team the day off Tuesday after Game 2. On Wednesday, Jordan showed up at practice complaining of tendinitis in his knee and began treatments. He had played thirty-six holes of golf on the day off. Jackson said the problem was related to his golfing, but Jordan demurred. "It's something I've had before. No way," he said.

And perhaps to show Jackson, or to steal that third win and effectively kill the 76ers and get some rest before the next series, or because he'd had so much scoring success against the 76ers in last season's playoffs, Jordan reverted to his scoring ways. Jackson wasn't quite sure what triggered the explosion for Jordan, but he knew it didn't benefit the team. And Jackson was sure it was no coincidence that it would be the Bulls' first loss of the playoffs and Jordan's biggest scoring game.

But Jordan seemed to be enjoying himself. Hawkins later said he'd talked to Jordan about one of his assaults on the basket.

"I asked him how he made one shot," Hawkins said, "and he says, 'When you get up, you hang for three seconds and let the defender fly by and then you release it.' He's explaining gravity to me while I'm trying to get a straight answer on how to do that."

Later, though, Hawkins would have his own fun, doubting Jordan's knee problem. Jordan had attempted 34 shots, after all.

"Fifteen points—that's tendinitis," said Hawkins. "I'll take forty-six points and tendinitis anytime."

"I don't know about his knee," offered Barkley, "but I imagine his arm is tired."

The game had been a physical affair, as Jackson had feared. Barkley and Rick Mahorn were banging around with more impunity and Armon Gilliam, who had 1 defensive rebound in sixty-two minutes in the first two games, was getting low post position, scoring, and playing his own tune on Horace Grant's head. Grant had saved Game 2 with those 3 late offensive rebounds, but now he was getting beaten to the punch and Jackson was growing upset. It was nothing new, but Grant was feeling particularly raw emotionally. For one thing, he was tired. Jackson was barely using Stacey King anymore, and he was afraid to put rookie Scott Williams in. Grant felt he was being asked to carry too big a load against the likes of Oakley and Barkley. He felt up to the challenge, but he felt he needed support from the coach rather than criticism. Didn't anybody notice how much he was doing? he wondered.

The night before, after the team's practice, Grant had spotted a homeless man sleeping in front of the Catholic church across from the team's fashionable Philadelphia hotel. Grant, an innocent in many ways, had wandered over and asked the man if he was scared. The man said that he wasn't, that he had faith, and pointed to the statue of Jesus above his head. Grant was overwhelmed by the man's faith and decided to get him a room for the night and give him a few hundred dollars of spending money. Yet that just made Grant feel even more guilty. He knew by his renewed religious teachings that he should be helping all men, but he couldn't do it himself. So why didn't the government? Why didn't somebody? Why did it have to be like this? he wondered.

He thought of the man, Tony, often the next day. Tony was there Friday afternoon after the team returned from the noon shootaround to thank Grant. Grant could barely speak. He now felt himself guilty for all the good he hadn't done.

With just over three minutes left in the third quarter and the Bulls ahead 69–64, Gilliam elbowed Grant hard in the back, knocking him off his position. Grant turned and hit Gilliam and was caught; officials in most sports usually detect the retaliation. Gilliam went to shoot two free throws and Jackson yanked Grant from the game and called a time-out.

"Don't let him do that to you," Jackson bellowed at Grant. "You've got to rebound and hold your position. You can't let him do that."

But Grant would have none of it as he rested on an emotional precipice. He said he was fed up with Jackson's abuse of him alone. Jackson had finally pushed him too hard. "I'm tired of being your whipping boy," Grant yelled at Jackson, pushing Jackson's arm away when he tried to grab Grant to talk to him. "Get over here," Jackson demanded. "Fuck you, fuck you, fuck you," Grant screamed. He was in tears. He was angry, hurt, and now embarrassed. He never cursed. He hated Jackson for yelling at him again, for making him curse. He hated crying in front of the team and in the middle of the game. He just wanted to get out of there.

On the bench, Grant's teammates were trying to console him.

"Fuck him, fuck him," Grant repeated.

"Tell him to shut up," said Jackson. "Let's go."

Jackson tried to grab Grant and Grant pulled angrily away. Jordan moved over and Grant grabbed at his hand. Later he would tell teammates he was trying to break it.

It was the longest time-out anyone had ever experienced. Paxson tried to talk to Grant and then Cartwright came up to him. Grant was perhaps the most popular player on the team, a good-natured puppy dog of a man who often said what he felt and endeared himself to everyone other than Jordan. Jackson wondered if he had gone too far.

From the other end of the bench, outside the huddle, Jordan retreated to watch the incredible scene. He thought back to the seventh game of last season's playoff against Detroit and Pippen's headache. The scene seemed to be repeating itself. Jordan had long doubted Pippen and Grant—not their talent, which he saw was considerable, but their maturity and ability to realize what was important. He always felt they weren't serious enough and doubted they could perform consistently at crucial times.

"Now?" Jordan began to mumble himself. "Now he's losing it? What the hell is going on?"

The bus trip back to the hotel was silent, except for general manager Jerry Krause.

Earlier that day, he'd learned that Toni Kukoc had decided to sign a contract to play in Italy. Krause had taken the call in the team's Philadelphia hotel at 5:00 A.M. He began calling around. "A terrible thing has happened . . . ," he'd begin in a most lugubrious way. Everyone thought someone had died. To Krause, a dream had.

Krause had made every effort and had finally prevailed upon a Bulls player to call Kukoc. Krause had asked Cartwright. Kukoc, Krause said, was worried about TV reports he kept hearing that Bulls players like Jordan and Pippen didn't want him. Cartwright was to assure him otherwise.

Just before the end of the regular season, Cartwright made the call. Kukoc didn't say much as Cartwright explained that Kukoc would be welcome. Kukoc didn't have any questions. The Bulls said they'd get Jordan to call him. Kukoc said to forget it. Cartwright knew what that meant.

About that time, Krause did an NBC halftime interview with Mike Fratello about Kukoc. But when the cameras moved back to play-by-play announcer Marv Albert, Albert questioned Krause's credibility and said he'd heard the players didn't really want Kukoc. Kukoc would later hear the interview on a tape of the game shown in Europe.

It was Marv Albert's fault, Krause kept saying on the ride back to the hotel. This would hurt Albert's career, Krause was saying, because it wasn't true. He couldn't get away with this. He'd pay.

"Forget it, Jerry, it's over," Jackson finally told him.

Krause never understood. Before the game, reporters had asked Pippen and Jordan about Kukoc's decision. "Great," Jordan said, "now the guys who deserve the money will be getting it. I think you'll see some happy guys around here."

"Maybe I'll get my new contract now," said Pippen.

It was the last remaining distraction in a season full of them.

•

JACKSON DECIDED TO give the team Saturday off before Game 4 on Sunday, May 12, Mother's Day. It had been a year ago on Mother's Day—"the Mother's Day Massacre," the Bulls liked to call it—that the Bulls had taken Game 4 from the 76ers before going on to win the conference semifinals series in five games.

Jackson went for a long walk down to the river to watch the crew races. Although physical exertion remained difficult for him because of the hip surgery he'd had years earlier, it was important that he get some exercise. Jackson had a heart ailment, which he generally kept secret. It was not considered serious, but he did need exercise, so he usually ran on the treadmill or the Stairmaster at the Deerfield Multiplex. The heart ailment, known as atrial fibrillation, can be treated with drugs like digoxin and procainamide, which arrest irregular heartbeats. The only problem was that Jackson didn't believe in taking medication. He'd never had any growing up as the son of a Pentecostal minister and evangelical mother in Montana. The family believed in faith healing, as Jackson in many ways still did. When he was a child, he had what his family said was polio, and they told him he was healed by God. Jackson had agreed to take aspirin over the years for his heart ailment, but refused any other medication and wouldn't even discuss it with his family.

That weekend, President Bush was hospitalized with what was initially diagnosed as atrial fibrillation. June Jackson, back home in Bannockburn, Illinois, thought to herself, "Good." It wasn't that she disliked the president, although she was a liberal Democrat and didn't care much for the prospect of Vice-President Dan Quayle moving up, but she also knew what a hospitalization for a heart ailment would mean. The newspapers and TV would examine atrial fibrillation in great deal.

"Now we'll know better what Phil can do for treatment," she thought.

On his return from the walk to the river, Jackson encountered John Paxson. Paxson said he needed to get more shots after having just 3 in Game 3. Jackson agreed. Nobody pointed any fingers.

Jordan stayed in his room to get treatment on his knee. He had planned to go to Atlantic City with Barkley after Game 3; Jordan had gone last season after Game 3, had stayed all night, and had driven back directly to the team's practice the next morning. He and Barkley had been at the craps table for a while playing with $500 chips.

Jordan's knee was bothering him, but he would still go in for some gambling. Barkley came by his room with TV personality Ahmad Rashad for a long afternoon of blackjack. Jordan seemed happy the next morning about the results.

He would be no less happy about the game.

Jackson walked into the locker room, looked at Jordan and said simply, "Jake."

"All right," Jordan said, making a fist and thrusting it into the air. "We win."

Jake, of course, was Jake O'Donnell. There would be no rough stuff today, no great disparity in foul calls, no intimidation by the home crowd. The best team would win. Jordan was certain it would be the Bulls.

Jackson had convened an unusual pregame breakfast for the team. He'd done something similar back in February in Los Angeles when he'd felt the team was splintering, and the chaos of Game 3 was worrying him. Paxson would need to get more shots, Jackson said. And as for Horace, he'd broken the chain of the group, in Jackson's words.

It was a Native American expression. Growing up in Montana and North Dakota, Jackson's family had lived on Sioux land at times. As a child, Jackson had become envious of the Indian culture and heritage and often daydreamed about being an Indian, becoming involved in Indian crafts and woodworking. Jackson also read volumes about the Indians and remembers telling his parents once that he was an Indian child adopted by them. He became a great believer in tribal circles and often saw his team in tribal terms. He'd read *Hanta Yo* for psychological messages and spliced scenes of Indian villages and ceremonies into his game films. The Indians were warriors, the scenes would show, but they were also a group that stayed together and supported one another. The Bulls had to do this to remain successful, Jackson felt.

To conclude the meeting, since it was Sunday, Jackson asked Grant to read to the team from the Psalms. The chain was reforming.

•

GRANT STORMED OUT like an angry bull in Game 4 and the team followed. He grabbed 5 offensive rebounds in the first quarter as the Bulls pulled out to a 26–20 lead after one quarter; they were up 52–38 at halftime. The 76ers looked like a beaten team. Grant would score 22 points, Pippen 20, and Jordan 25 to go along with

12 assists. In the third quarter, Barkley would hit Cartwright and find the lumbering center chasing him. "What's his problem?" Barkley said to Jake O'Donnell as O'Donnell called technical fouls on both. "He have his period?" Cartwright overheard this and went at Barkley again. The Bulls would lead by 23 in the third quarter en route to a 101–85 win, just another Mother's Day Massacre.

But Bach, the veteran assistant, would see it as more. Bach was a student of military history and tactics and he saw the Game 4 effort as more than just the virtual elimination of the 76ers. Bach saw the Bulls finally responding to physical threats boldly. It could only bode well, he thought, if the Bulls had to face the Pistons in the conference finals. The Bulls were under fire, especially Grant, and he'd thrown himself on the hand grenade. The 76ers offered as much physical danger as the Pistons, as much verbal intimidation, and the Bulls had taken it and played well, even with Jordan not at his best in an 11-for-27 shooting performance in Game 4. It wouldn't be enough to get to the Finals, but it was a start.

Game 5 went mostly as expected, with the Bulls back in front of their adoring home crowd, assaulting the 76ers early behind 24 first-half points by Pippen. The Bulls would take a 10-point lead after three quarters and then weather a storm down the stretch as the 76ers pulled to within a point with less than a minute to go. But Jordan, who had a playoff career-high 19 rebounds in the game, drove for a basket—he was the game's best ever at that time of night—and Philadelphia would not score again as the Bulls won 100–95. Jordan would score the last 12 Bulls' points. "That's when we need him to attack," agreed Cartwright. "He seems to understand more," noted King, who'd suffered much from Jordan's wrath during the season. "Where he used to signal the coach to get you out, he's been coming over and patting you on the back when you make a mistake now." King was still making plenty of them, so he knew. Barkley was magnificent again with 30 points, but Mahorn would get only 2 and Ron Anderson only 4 while the Bulls grabbed 23 more rebounds. And rebounds win playoff games. It is written in stone in the NBA: Rebounding and defense equal rings. Effort and hard work. The Bulls had more talent, and they worked harder. It was a tough combination to beat.

The Bulls would get a five-day break now. Boston and Detroit were battling in the other bracket and would go for another few days. Boston would be the easier to defeat, everyone knew. But no one really wanted to play the Celtics.

Every move the Bulls had made the last three seasons, in both personnel and offensive and defensive development, had been aimed at defeating the Pistons. It was time.

"They're the albatross," said Bach. "We've really got to get them, kill them, and end this Detroit thing. That's the only thing that will really get us respect and make us feel like a winner."

11

FINAL EXAM

5/19 v. Detroit; 5/21 v. Detroit; 5/25 at Detroit; 5/27 at Detroit; 5/29 v. Detroit*; 5/31 at Detroit*; 6/2 v. Detroit*

*If necessary.

MARK AGUIRRE, WHO grew up just blocks west of the Chicago Stadium, had just hit a three-point field goal from downtown to give the Pistons a 59–58 lead in the third quarter, and Aguirre was having the convulsions of a madman.

"Get someone on me," he screamed at Jordan. "Nobody can guard me. Get someone on me."

No one really could that day. It was Game 1 of the Eastern Conference finals and the Bulls had gotten their wish: They were playing the defending champion Pistons. On Friday the Pistons had struggled past the Boston Celtics; this day, Sunday, was the date with destiny the Bulls had longed for all season.

The Pistons appeared on the verge of stealing the home-court advantage in the Chicago Stadium and sending the Bulls to another ignominious defeat. The Bulls had blown out to a 20–8 lead in front of a roaring crowd, but Aguirre came off the bench hot, getting 13 points in the first half and another 10 in the third quarter. The Pistons had regained some control in the second quarter, trailed by 8 at halftime, and then took the lead in the third quarter. And the Pistons were doing it as they always had: through intimidation.

The Bulls had, for years, been beaten and beaten up by the Pistons. When the emotional Doug Collins was coach, the Bulls often played directly into Detroit's claws—Collins once got involved in a fight and was tossed over a table by then-Piston Rick Mahorn, who smiled. Collins and the Bulls raged and lost. The Bulls, in those years, were living the emotional life of drug addicts; the highs, from wins, were exhilarating and impassioned, the losses so depressing and verging on the suicidal.

But Jackson's message all year was not that the Bulls shouldn't be emotional, nor that they should turn the other cheek. In fact, going into the Detroit series, Jackson had counseled the team to strike the first blow, not to allow the Pistons to hit them with three or four elbows every time they crossed the lane. Strike first, Jackson said; let strength grow out of weakness. But he also knew that his players needed to remain composed.

And, surprisingly, they would throughout the series.

"Phil taught us how to respond to Detroit's aggressive nature," John Paxson would say after the Bulls victory. "It's something we never had before."

And the Bulls were learning well. Jordan, of all people, took on the unfamiliar role of enforcer. In the early moments of the game, he popped Joe Dumars with a vicious elbow, a flagrant one really, to the chest, knocking Dumars down in front of the Pistons' bench. There would be no call. The Bulls also felt the league was sending another message: that it was going to let teams retaliate against the Pistons.

Pippen found himself being challenged, too. "You're dead, Pippen, you're dead," Aguirre yelled at him. "I'm getting you in the parking lot after the game. Don't turn your head, you cocksucker, because I'm gonna kill you. You're fuckin' dead. Dead, Pippen, you're fuckin' dead." The monologue continued almost all game.

"It actually got kind of funny," Paxson would say afterward.

"Aguirre was calling Scottie into the parking lot all game and Scottie was just laughing."

Laughing in the face of this kind of pressure was a new experience for the Bulls. It showed maturity, especially on the part of Pippen, who had surprised the coaches with his seriousness. He was watching game tapes now for the first time in his career. He was working hard in the gym and in games; on defense he was now less like a matador, with a wave and an olé, and more like a bull. He made a steal, one of his six in the game, and hit a jumper to give the Bulls a lead in the third quarter, but Isiah Thomas tied the game with a three-point field goal. Pippen would be fouled and hit a pair of free throws to get the Bulls the lead back, 68–65, after three quarters, but a Bulls win was by no means assured. And Jackson intended to stick with his plan, resting both Pippen and Jordan to open the fourth quarter; both had played virtually the entire third quarter, and Jackson didn't believe Detroit was capable of putting the game away in the next few minutes.

The Pistons clearly were tired from their Game 6 overtime victory over Boston less than two days earlier. Their weary starting five would combine for just 37 points in Game 1 as Aguirre would lead with 25 points off the bench while Vinnie Johnson came in and scored 21.

The Bulls reserves had performed reasonably well in the New York and Philadelphia series, but they had never done well against the Pistons. As he always does, Bach had put together an edited tape before the Detroit series on specific players. He had focused on the reserves and showed the tape to Jackson before the series started. It was horrific: missed shot after missed shot, rebounds dropped, turnovers, belly flops. Jackson had known the reserves had performed badly against Detroit, particularly remembering an 0–15 shooting run in an earlier game that season, but it hadn't seemed this bad.

"John, did you just pick their bad plays?" he asked Bach.

"No," Bach replied. "I tried to make it their highlights."

"We won't show it to them," Jackson decided.

The reserves would provide their own highlight film today. They entered the game and all of a sudden the Bulls led by 9 points, 81–72. B. J. Armstrong hit a couple of free throws and Craig Hodges a long jumper and later a three-pointer. Will Perdue hit a short jumper and Cliff Levingston a short jumper and a tip-in. They combined to hit 5 of 7 shots; the Pistons would miss 4 of 7 and the game would slip away, with the Bulls going on to win 94–83.

"The key to the game was when we took that nine-point lead," Jackson would agree later.

And a surprising key would be Levingston, the lost man. He'd played a little against New York and Philadelphia and was feeling he was done for the playoffs, if not also done with the Bulls. "I figured when I didn't get in against the Seventy-sixers, and those guys don't even box out, that was it," Levingston had admitted to a friend before the Detroit series began. But Jackson's methods are both sensible and instinctive. Jackson usually sits for a while at home on game days, trying to visualize what will happen in the game. He saw Levingston as someone aggressive and willing to match blows with Detroit, since he had played with the Pistons years before and had endured several physical series with them when he was with the Hawks. Jackson wasn't sure what the result would be, but he felt the enthusiastic Levingston could give the team the kind of emotional and physical lift it needed.

Jordan and Pippen returned to the game with just over six minutes left and Detroit would never get closer than 7 points.

It would not be a brilliant game for Jordan offensively, but it may have marked a turning point for the Bulls franchise. Jordan had led the Bulls with 22, but was just 6 of 15 from the field with a game-high 6 turnovers.

After the game, he slumped into his seat in front of his locker and said, aloud, "Thanks for picking me up."

No one said anything.

Afterward, Jordan dressed quietly and went to the mass interview session, the national media crowd now growing in anticipation of the Pistons' being dethroned. Jordan's comments there were a little less gracious.

"You have to give credit to my supporting cast," Jordan said about Pippen coming up with 18, Bill Cartwright 16, and 30 points from the bench. "I basically had a bad game today," Jordan added. "Maybe I had a headache."

Jordan's remarks seemed curious to some, insensitive to many. He seemed to be making sure the spotlight would shine on him, no matter what his effort. But it was not surprising to those around the team. He had taken shots at Pippen before, in part out of resentment and in part to motivate the kid some were calling "the Air apparent." And Jordan had started in recent weeks to call the rest of the team "my supporting cast."

"I wish I hadn't used that phrase," he told a friend later, "but, hell, everyone thinks that way, so why not?"

It had been an uncharacteristically emotional game for Jordan. He had always been a quiet player, not particularly animated on the court, except for his slams. He liked to joke with players some-times, but he always preferred to lead through his play. He often backed away from the traditional leadership role, and while he re-mained the team leader in the public's mind, he rarely spoke with his teammates other than to taunt them with his rapier wit.

But on this day he was in a curious emotional frenzy. There was that flagrant elbow early on that had even caught the referees by surprise, and late in the second quarter Jordan found himself jawing halfway down the court with Dennis Rodman.

"We're gonna kick your butts," Jordan bellowed into Rodman's face. "I'm comin' after you."

Jordan's reactions surprised even him, but he had been unusually somber leading up to the series and had told friends he was deter-mined to defeat Detroit this time.

"We're not winning any title," he said. "But I want to get by Detroit this time."

Even Jordan's teammates had never seen him rise up in this sort of volcanic fury, and the coaches, though unprepared for it, were pleased. They believed Jordan was behaving the way he was, in part, to embolden Pippen and Grant.

"Is he trying to make Horace braver?" Bach said. "Is he trying to make Scottie more confident? Sure. He's trying to make these guys better, but also braver. That's the difference in playing De-troit."

The Bulls believed a year ago they were more talented than the Pistons, but were not sure they were better.

"They knew we were more talented than they were a year ago," said Armstrong. "But they also knew they could beat us. This year, they talked and we talked, they hit and we hit. The big thing about the game was we answered some questions about our-selves."

•

THE RESPITE BETWEEN Games 1 and 2 would be brief, just a day, before the May 21 second game. Then the teams would wait four days, until Saturday May 25, Memorial Day weekend in Detroit. The TV networks chose the dates for playoff games to accommodate their schedules, and while players and coaches groused a little, Jackson tried to put the situation in perspective for the team.

"That's why you guys are earning as much money as you are," he said.

John Paxson wondered if that meant *his* games were being televised on local cable access. But things were looking up; Paxson was starting to believe he might be back, and unbeknownst to him, Reinsdorf had been thinking the same way with Kukoc now out of the picture.

"I always felt we hurt the White Sox when we let Jerry Koosman go," Reinsdorf told an associate. "There are these kind of chemistry-type guys who you just need around. I think Paxson may be one."

All of this led to an entertaining conversation with Cartwright, also a free agent. Cartwright had been telling Paxson about his experiences as a free agent when he was with the Knicks, and he said that if Paxson could get an offer in Chicago he probably was better off staying, for Cartwright was now also leaning that way.

Cartwright had had five successful seasons in New York, making the All-Star team as a rookie, and there had been some demand for his services, since centers remained a rare commodity. He was a restricted free agent, which meant the Knicks could match any offer made to him. But Cartwright thought he would test the market.

Cartwright, along with his agent, Bob Woolf, and an old friend and adviser, Dan Risley, went to meet with the Dallas Mavericks. The Mavericks prided themselves on their committee approach to personnel matters, so general manager Norm Sonju, basketball operations director Rick Sund, and owner Don Carter were there.

Carter, an iconoclastic owner, a garrulous man with a deeply religious side, spoke. Everyone else listened. For fifteen minutes Carter went on about the evils of free agency. He said his team would never sign a free agent, that it wasn't right for a man to sell his services like that, like a vagabond or prostitute, to the highest bidder. It wouldn't be done in a Don Carter organization. Free agency was going to kill sports and he wasn't going to have it. His voice rose and trembled. Finally he stopped and stared at Cartwright. No one but Carter had said a word the entire time.

"Son," Carter said to Cartwright, "do you love your mother?"

"Sure," Cartwright responded.

"Are you faithful to your wife?" Carter asked.

"Yes," Cartwright said, now beginning to wonder just what was going on.

"Do you believe in God?" Carter demanded. He stared into Cartwright's lazy, liquid brown eyes.

"Yes," Cartwright said.

Carter thought for a few moments. Then he turned to Sonju, said, "Sign him," and got up and left the room.

"You've got to be ready for free agency," Cartwright said. "It's crazy."

•

BOTH JORDAN AND Jackson had work to do between Games 1 and 2. For Jordan, it was a chance to expand his realm, as the league announced that he had won the Most Valuable Player award for the second time in his career. For Jackson, the effort was to limit Jordan's world and expand that of Jordan's teammates. Jackson was proud of Jordan's aggressive play in Game 1 as a signal to his teammates, but Jackson was also worried about some of Jordan's choices on offense. Paxson had gotten just 5 shots in Game 1 and Grant, 2. The distribution had to be better.

So Jackson put together a tape of Jordan, focusing on his choices when in the post and where his teammates were. Jackson remained subtle with Jordan, but the message was clear: Don't fight the double- and triple-teams. Pass out of them.

Jordan went to accept his MVP trophy Monday May 20 and took the occasion to both praise his teammates and bash the media about its voting for such awards in what some saw as an I-should-have-won-this-every-year vein. Jordan addressed the long-held belief that he doesn't make his teammates better, one reason given for why he didn't win the MVP award more often. "I'm no baby-sitter," he said sharply. "You've got to step up and get your own respect. They've got to want to play better." Brilliance could truly be a curse sometimes.

But Jordan dropped that angry edge and called for his teammates when NBA commissioner David Stern offered another MVP presentation at halfcourt before Game 2. Jordan seemed overcome by the moment, the loud ovation washing down on him while he was surrounded by his teammates. He was in the spotlight, which was fine with Jackson, but the coach knew it had to widen.

And one of those Jackson knew needed to see more light, reflected or refracted, was Horace Grant.

Grant had taken 2 shots in Game 1. He'd hit them both, but both were lay-ups. Grant had often complained during the season about his lack of participation in the offense, but the coaches noticed that Grant was starting to avoid the medium-range jumpers that were an important part of his game.

At home, David Orth was shaking his head and saying to himself, "I told you so."

Orth is the Bulls' ophthalmologist. Before the season began, he had fitted Grant with prescription goggles. Grant's vision was terrible; Bach had noticed that Grant would read a newspaper an inch or two from his nose, so he suggested Grant get an eye test. It turned out that Grant needed glasses to drive a car. He had tried contacts once in college, but had rejected them. He couldn't stand putting something in his eyes. It made his skin crawl. But he'd try the goggles. And they seemed to work. Grant developed more range on his jumper and shot a career-best 54.7 percent in 1990–91. But in the series against the Knicks, Grant discarded the goggles after Charles Oakley kept pulling them off when the officials weren't looking.

Grant shot an air ball in his first field-goal attempt against the 76ers in round two of the playoffs. Orth began to keep score. Grant missed 8 jumpers beyond fifteen feet at one point, although he would shoot a respectable 54 percent against the 76ers without the corrective lenses and almost 70 percent against Detroit. There didn't seem to be a need to change. But Orth thought otherwise.

"Without the glasses he has zero depth perception," Orth complained to Reinsdorf. "But the big concern is when he's under stress and the game's on the line. He's not going to be at maximum efficiency. He's been shooting a basketball long enough, so he can pick out a landmark and make a lot of shots. He might make ten or fifteen in a row in practice, but when he's under stress and pressure he won't have that maximum vision."

Orth went public with his observations and Krause went into fits, calling the doctor and berating him. But Orth believed the point had to be made. Reinsdorf agreed. Before Game 1 against the Pistons, Reinsdorf made a rare appearance in Jackson's office in the Bulls' locker room. "We've got to do something to get Horace to begin wearing his glasses," he told the coach.

•

DETROIT GOT JOE Dumars going in Game 2, as the smooth guard opened with 15 points in the first quarter. The Pistons are the kind of team that looks for a scab on defense and then probes and picks away at it. They found Dumars getting free by running Jordan through two or three screens, and they kept going to him. But by the end of the first quarter they trailed 27–22, as the Bulls spread the scoring around. Grant led with 9, Pippen had 6, Paxson had 4, Cartwright had 4, and Jordan had 4. The system Jackson had so often talked about appeared to be working, though with some important modifications.

Detroit was one of the best teams in the league at breaking down the so-called triangles that formed the Bulls' motion offense. Players were to form triangles on either side of the court to get the offense going, but Detroit could squeeze the triangles against the corners of the court and leave the players nowhere to run. So Jackson had done a little redecorating for this series, building on something he'd used against Philadelphia. The Pistons' strength had always been their three-guard rotation, and against the Bulls they were always able to run Paxson or Armstrong off the ball or force them to work harder to advance the ball up the court. As a result, Jordan would get the ball without enough time to run an offense, and he would make a one-man rush into the teeth of the defense or throw a return pass to another player with little time remaining.

So Jackson made a switch. He sent Paxson off on the wing, where he was best for his spot-up jumper anyway, and had Pippen carry the ball upcourt more. This removed the pressure from the ball— while also keeping it out of Jordan's hands—since the Pistons then had to try to contest the ball handler with a forward or leave themselves in a major mismatch against Pippen once the ball got upcourt. It was the culmination of the maturation process Jackson had long planned for Pippen.

The process had started earlier in the season when Jackson began leaving either Pippen or Jordan on the floor with the reserves. Ostensibly, Jackson did this to keep a scorer out with the bench players. But Jackson also wanted to push Pippen into developing on his own. He knew Pippen had difficulty taking charge and getting his shots when he played with Jordan.

"But now he was the guy," Jackson said. "He had to make the decisions and take charge and score."

Pippen would grow comfortably into the role; it had been a major factor against Philadelphia. And now, against Detroit, the pressure seemed to fall away from the Bulls' offense while on defense the Bulls continued to apply pressure of their own. They swarmed over Detroit, making it hard for the Pistons to run their deliberate offense. The Pistons always played ball-control basketball since they were not a great offensive team; they'd control the clock and the backboards, and a 4- or 6-point win by them was like a 15-point win by another team. But they never could get control of these games from the Bulls, no matter what they tried.

For Game 2, the Pistons tried their bully act. Early in the second quarter, Dumars took down Armstrong hard. Flagrant foul, called Darell Garretson. It was a good sign, the Bulls thought, that Garretson was in for the game and making the tough calls. It was a message directly from the league's supervisor of officials. The Bulls went on a 14–2 run and led 41–24. The Pistons then scored 9 straight before Pippen went down hard on a drive. Flagrant foul! It meant two free throws and the ball.

"The referees sent a message to the Pistons," Jackson would tell the media later. "They're saying, 'Enough of that rough stuff and let's get down to playing basketball.' "

The Bulls led 49–41 at halftime and began to open up the game behind 12 points from Jordan in the third quarter. Jordan had been quiet, with just 8 in the first half to 16 from Pippen, but then his jumper started falling. The Pistons were still being watched carefully; Tree Rollins, in for an ineffective James Edwards, was called for a pair of offensive fouls, and then, as the Bulls began to stretch out their lead in the fourth quarter, Jordan was knocked down hard; another flagrant foul call, this one on Thomas, the third of the game. It was time for the referees to begin counting over the Pistons. Like an aging fighter, they were starting to go more quickly than anyone had thought possible.

The Pistons hadn't lost a home game yet, and they still believed, despite being outplayed twice in a row, that they could intimidate the Bulls into a loss. But the Bulls' defense had taken away so many things the Pistons did well. The Bulls doubled quickly on Edwards, identifying him as a player who didn't pass well. They countered the Thomas-Laimbeer screen roll with Pippen's lightning-quick re-actions. And they shot twice as many free throws as the Pistons, which hadn't gone unnoticed.

"Phil Jackson complained about our defense when they were play-ing New York," noted John Salley. "They're on the foul line all the time. He's gotten everyone convinced we're dirty players."

The Bulls won Game 2 by 105–97 and made still another symbolic statement late in the game. Pippen got the ball out on the break, ahead of everyone and ready to go in for a slam, when he spotted Armstrong trailing alone. Pippen stopped, waited for Armstrong to catch up, and then handed off the ball for a lay-up. It was a nice statement: We're all going to be a part of this.

•

THE ANTICIPATION WAS high and the Bulls' mood buoyant as they entered their personal Palace of Horrors for Game 3 on Saturday. It was Memorial Day weekend and the Bulls had a barbecue in mind: hot dogs like Laimbeer, big ears from Rodman, and buns courtesy of Mark Aguirre. All the ingredients were there and the Bulls felt they could turn up the heat despite being 2–13 since the Palace at Auburn Hills had opened. Yes, the Bulls seemed self-assured.

The visitors' locker area in the Palace, unlike most in the NBA, is divided into two rooms. Jordan occupied the stall next to the inside door in the back room. He was relaxed preparing for Game 3; he hadn't been at his best, yet the Bulls had won the first two games rather easily. As a result, he seemed to have the confidence against the Pistons he'd never had before, even if he doubted his personal feelings toward the guys he played with would change.

"The thing is, this is a business, and in business you don't have to like everyone, but you've got to work with them," Jordan said. "What we've been able to do this season is separate. Basketballwise, our focus has been the same from game to game. It's been proven the best teams don't always have to get along together, and if everyone likes one another, it doesn't mean you're going to win. The difference is in the play.

"But I can't say that I saw it coming," Jordan admitted. "I can see it with Pippen and Grant now. I think they feel the pressure now, the pressure that I've felt. The blame is going to be on them now if we lose and they know it. And they're playing like it. I think that's the difference. If they don't continue to step up, we're not going to win, and they're under the microscope to perform. I don't think they've ever felt like that before. They didn't seem to care. But they're different this year."

And so was Jordan, at least from the Pistons' perspective. They'd studied him hard and made it to the Finals twice by taking advantage of his temper, his stubbornness, and his lack of faith in his teammates. It didn't seem as if it was going to work this time.

"Last year," said John Salley, "if we made a rally, Michael would start yelling at everybody and they'd get pissed off. This year they seem to have more confidence and aren't always looking for Michael."

And Michael, the Pistons realized, wasn't always looking to score as in the past.

"I think he finally realized," said Pistons assistant coach Brendan Suhr, "that one player can't win at this level, that the farther you get in the playoffs, teams can always stop one man. He finally sees that."

•

JACKSON HAD FINALLY come up with a quote he liked for this series. It came from Jung.

"Perfection is only possible with God," he wrote on the players' scouting reports. "We expect excellence."

The Bulls had that to open Game 3. First they knocked down a psychological barrier, then a mental barrier, and then a physical one.

They took on the "bad basket" in front of the Pistons' bench and scorched it. The lead was 24–8 before the Pistons' closed the quarter with 8 straight points. Detroit would rally for a 38–36 lead in the second quarter, but the Bulls didn't wilt. They were all over the place, forcing the Pistons into 3 straight turnovers (2 consecutive Grant steals) and getting 2 baskets from Pippen and 3 from Cartwright to go into the break ahead 51–43. They had shot nearly 55 percent in the half and turned back the Detroit surge. More than that, they had taken the Pistons out of their slow, bruising style and were getting into their own faster transition game. The Pistons had gone to a smaller, scoring lineup in an effort to counteract the Bulls' speed and quickness. The change reduced the Pistons' brute strength, their biggest advantage. It now seemed just a matter of time before the Pistons crumbled.

The Pistons remained helpless and the Bulls unflappable as the third quarter of Game 3 unfolded.

"They stole our playbook," Salley would complain later. "Talking junk, talking garbage, their intensity on defense, making sure there is only one shot, keeping people out of the middle, making us beat them with the jump shot. That's what we usually do." And one more thing: remaining cool.

Edwards knocked Grant down hard in the third quarter and Grant started to pick himself up slowly when Jordan came running at Grant, demanding, "Don't let him see you're hurt. Don't touch anything. Don't look hurt. Just get back in there."

The Bulls would lurch ahead by 16, but the Pistons zoomed within 5 on a run lashed together by Thomas with a tip-in, a three-point play, and a rebound of his own miss. The Pistons were heading into the fourth quarter down 8 and their championship clearly was on the line, for no team has ever recovered from a 3–0 deficit to win an NBA playoff series.

The Pistons fought desperately, but the Bulls would not fold. They hit 6 of their first 8 shots on the friendlier rim and took a 94–83 lead with about seven minutes left in the game. The Pistons were battling; they would come away with 9 offensive rebounds in the quarter in the kind of game they'd always won. Vinnie Johnson put in his own miss and Thomas did, too. Laimbeer hit a jumper and Aguirre a three-pointer. And when Laimbeer tipped in an Aguirre miss, the Bulls lead was just 5 with 2:31 left.

Pippen brought the ball up, and Aguirre got a hand on it, swatting it ahead to Johnson, who was breaking alone for the basket. It would be Bulls by just 3. But in came Jordan, zeroing in on Johnson. Jordan started to extend his pace and Johnson took a look over his shoulder. Seeing Jordan ready to swat away his lay-up attempt, Johnson slowed to try to let Jordan go past so he could drop the ball for Joe Dumars. But Jordan anticipated the move.

"I basically was trying to maneuver defensively to confuse him," Jordan would explain later.

With Jordan in position, Dumars could only throw up an off-balance shot, which Jordan would rebound.

"One of the great stops of all time," Jackson would say later.

And a stop, finally, for the Pistons, as Pippen stepped up to hit a jumper to give the Bulls a 105–98 lead with two minutes left and little for the Pistons to do but offer some petty assault, Rodman fouling John Paxson hard and then shoving the ball into Jordan's stomach during a break in play. The Bulls would just laugh. The final score was 113–107 Bulls. The Bulls shot 57.5 percent and grabbed as many rebounds as Detroit in the game Detroit had to win. Jordan led with 33 points, but Pippen had 26, Grant 17, and Cartwright 13. The Pistons' starting front line combined for 12 points. There was no more emphatic way the Bulls could win.

•

IT WAS 3–0 Bulls on a bright, sunny Sunday before Memorial Day. The Bulls were having a picnic at the daily media session. For the conference finals and NBA Finals, the league arranges a half-hour media session for each team. One team practices, then stays an extra half hour, and the other team comes a half hour earlier and then practices. Jackson had warned the players about saying anything incendiary before the first session in Detroit. He didn't want to provide any fuel for the Detroit fires, but the players hadn't been sure what he'd meant with a story he told that day to reinforce the point.

"My wife often tells me I'm talking way up here," said Jackson, motioning with his hand above his head. "But I've always felt that even if you catch a little, something's got to stick."

But some chose not to listen.

Jordan took the stage and got a few things off his chest. "People are happy the game is going to get back to a clean game and away from the bad-boy image," he said. "People don't want this kind of basketball, the dirty play, the flagrant foul, the unsportsmanlike conduct. It's bad for basketball." He continued for almost the entire half hour, saying how the Celtics were more worthy champions than the Pistons because they played a classy game, how everyone he knew wanted the Pistons to lose because they were dirty, how evil could triumph on occasion but never conquer. It's doubtful it was all meant to chasten the Pistons; he was just pointing it out, really. It would be a headline story in all the Detroit newspapers the next day, before Game 4.

"So what about your message to the team about not supplying ammunition for the opponent?" Jackson was asked before Game 4.

He offered a sly grin.

"Some guys," Jackson said with a wink in his voice, "have their own media agenda."

•

THE PISTONS HAD one last stand left in them, although the Bulls were not too worried. "We'll be watching our backs," said Jordan, and for much of Game 4 he refused to leave his feet. Even Jordan knew just how far he could carry his bravado.

Before the game, Pippen sat and thought about Rodman, who had been his insulting best throughout the first three games, taunting, pointing, jabbering, challenging, and then patting everyone on the butt in an ersatz gesture of good sportsmanship.

"They really need to get him some help," Pippen was saying to Grant. "Really. This guy is crazy. It's the one thing I'd never realized before and I was always too stupid to not let his stuff bother me. But now I can see it. I think he does have mental problems and needs help. Really. I don't like him, but I think he is sick and it's just not right that people like that are allowed to walk around free on the streets. They ought to get him some help. The boy is flat-out crazy."

And Pippen was sure about something else, not just the impending victory. The Pistons had named the street leading into their new arena One Championship Drive, and when they won a second time they changed it to Two Championship Drive. Pippen was wondering aloud if it would now become Four Sweep Drive.

"You can tell M.J. has more confidence in everyone," he added. "And I'd have to say it's come just in these playoffs. He's playing team ball and for the first time I can say he's not going out there looking to score. He seems to have the feeling, and we all seem to, really, that if we play together everyone can help. It's like even with Will [Perdue]; when I throw him the ball now, I feel like he's gonna score. Nobody felt that way two months ago. But I just have confidence in him and I think M.J. does, too. It's just a feeling, but it seems to be working."

The Pistons were working hard at the outset of Game 4, trying to run with the Bulls, a sure way to run to a quick defeat. The Bulls coaches loved the strategy, but Pistons coach Chuck Daly felt he had no alternative; he was adjusting as best he could. And it didn't take long for the Pistons to start taking their best shots.

Laimbeer was first, shoving Paxson hard out of bounds as Paxson drove for a basket.

"I'm not backing down from you," Paxson yelled at Laimbeer.

"I won't back down from you," Laimbeer shot back.

As he walked to the free-throw line to shoot, Paxson thought the confrontation stupid. But Paxson admitted, "It got me going a little bit."

Paxson made his two free throws, then hit three straight jumpers with two more free throws in between for 10 consecutive Bulls points, 12 in all in the quarter, and a 32–26 Bulls lead after one. "The question was not whether his shot was going in," said Cartwright. "It was whether he was getting the ball."

The Pistons would never get closer than 5 the rest of the way before the game turned into a rout for the Bulls in the third quarter. But before then, the Pistons would give their critics plenty of ammunition.

Midway through the second quarter, Rodman shoved Pippen hard out of bounds and into the stands; Pippen slammed into the floor behind the basket and suffered a gash in his chin that would take six stitches to close. The Bulls' bench exploded and moved toward midcourt as a flagrant foul was called. Assistant coach Jim Cleamons engaged in a colorful screaming match with a fan who began making obscene gestures. Pippen moved hazily into a sitting position.

Watching at home, owner Reinsdorf was both incensed and worried.

"That's good, Scottie, relax, relax," he said to the TV screen. "Don't retaliate. You're behaving like a man."

Pippen would later tell Reinsdorf that he didn't retaliate because he couldn't remember where he was.

"You play, you play, we don't get involved in that stuff," Grant instructed Pippen as Pippen rose unsteadily to his feet.

But Rodman wasn't done. He had let himself loose into that hysterical world that Pippen had wondered about, even if Pippen was in no condition to hear.

"You think that's something, I'll do it again," he screamed at the referees. "Makes no difference to me. We don't want no fags out here and he's a fag. I'll get him again. He's going down. He's going down harder this time and see if I care. We don't put up with none of that fag-ass shit out here."

Detroit was a beaten team. These guys were done. Jordan, with 29, and Pippen with 23 points and 10 rebounds, took over from Paxson after the first quarter, and the Bulls led by 17 after three. The final would be 115–94.

The only surprises would come at the end. The fans began to chant for the Lakers in the Finals; this series had become so bitter and Jordan's comments were so stinging that the fans of the tough guys came to favor tofu. And with a few seconds left, several Pistons players marched off the court over Daly's objections, directly in front of the Bulls bench and out to the locker room, without offering any congratulations to their conquerors. This gesture would set off a storm of protest within days as columnists called for Daly to be removed as 1992 Olympic coach and writers around the country castigated the Pistons for their boorish exit.

For the Bulls, there was almost a stunned kind of relief in the locker room immediately after the game.

"We didn't come this far just to get here," Jackson told the team. "No one remembers who finishes second in the Finals."

A somber note modulated the players' joy. Dennis Hopson began crying as soon as he sat down in front of his locker. He'd played three minutes at the end of the game, when the Bulls led by 25, his first playing time against Detroit. He'd played the least of anyone on the team, getting token appearances at the end of blowouts in four of the twelve playoff games. It wouldn't change in the Finals.

"I'd never cried before at a game or after or any time, and never in front of guys," Hopson would say afterward. "But I couldn't help myself. I wasn't a part of this team and I knew it. My own team didn't need me and it hurt."

So Hopson, a likable, quiet man, sat and couldn't control himself. Paxson patted him on the back and assured him he was a part of the team. Cartwright also tried to console him, as did his close friend Armstrong. But Hopson couldn't stop. Tears rolled down his cheeks and he could barely catch his breath. He was gasping for air. Several of the players looked on and all could understand. Hopson had been the king before, in college and as the leading scorer with the lowly Nets. Now all he could be was a cheerleader while those around him shared in the glory they would never forget.

He called his mother and told her. She was quiet for a long while. There was nothing to say.

The plane ride home took on a more lively tone. Jordan sipped from a bottle of champagne. "All I ever asked for is one shot," he said. "One shot. This ain't the time to come in second."

Krause, the portly and unpopular general manager, began dancing in the aisle.

"Who said I can't shake my booty?" he started to chant. "Watch this, watch me shake my booty."

The players became hysterical.

"I know the pilot's up there calling the tower going, 'Problem up here. Someone seems to be shaking the plane,' " Perdue said to Cartwright.

"Shake it, Jerry, shake it," yelled Pippen as he got up to do a mock dance with Krause.

"You guys made me look good," Krause gushed in trying to put his arms around Cartwright and Perdue, who were sitting together.

"Nobody could do that," said Perdue.

It was a happy team that stepped off the charter at O'Hare. Rookie Scott Williams would prove to be the only casualty; his troublesome left shoulder would pop out again on the way home when he saluted his teammates with his arm thrust out his car window as they drove by. He had to pull over and flag down Horace Grant to help him pop his shoulder back in.

June Jackson came to the airport to pick up Phil. She rarely did it, but this was a special night. And Phil wasn't that great a driver, anyway. His family always questioned whether he could drive a car safely because when driving he tended to lose concentration. June could remember him making dozens of snap decisions in a basketball game and then leaving and driving around a parking lot for thirty minutes until he decided what parking spot he wanted. Phil talked about the pleasure of sweeping the Pistons, about the emotion of the game, about Hopson and about the coming Finals. As June wheeled the car into the family's north suburban Chicago home, Jackson smiled.

His children had encircled his car with dozens of brooms.

12

GLORY TIME

6/2 v. Los Angeles; 6/5 v. Los Angeles; 6/7 at Los Angeles; 6/9 at Los Angeles; 6/12 at Los Angeles*; 6/14 v. Los Angeles*; 6/16 v. Los Angeles*.

*If necessary.

MICHAEL VERSUS MAGIC. That's the way they saw it in Chicago. Magic versus Michael. That's the way they saw it in Los Angeles. Dollar signs. That's the way NBC and the NBA saw it, for this NBA Finals between the Bulls and Lakers was going to be big. No last names, please; Elvis against John, Paul, George, and Ringo couldn't have been much bigger. This was more than just hero worship, it was idol gossip. Michael Jordan, the greatest individual player in sports history, was meeting Magic Johnson, perhaps the greatest team player. It was Jordan going for his elusive first title and Johnson probably going for his last. Scorer against playmaker. Coke against Pepsi. Nike against Converse. McDonald's against Kentucky Fried Chicken. If Jordan was the most popular and well-known player in the NBA, Johnson was 1a. It was a dream matchup, but the rela-

301

tionship between the two had long been a nightmare for both and still had its bad days.

Jordan and Johnson had pretty much reconciled their differences at the 1988 All-Star game in Chicago, but they still cast eyes warily at one another from across the NBA landscape.

When Johnson won his NBA MVP award in 1990, Jordan congratulated him, even though he had campaigned hard during the season for Charles Barkley. But privately, his thoughts were much harsher. "It's not so bad that I didn't get it," Jordan would remark afterward. "But I just hate that *he* got it."

Bulls owner and managing partner Jerry Reinsdorf would tell friends that he rooted for Johnson to remain an active player in the NBA because Jordan had said he intended to play for one year after Magic retired to get one time around the league without Magic's shadow.

"Magic always has been the guy Michael's measured himself against," explained Jackson. "Magic has the rings and the MVP awards."

And for a long time, he had Jordan's ire. It developed mostly from that alleged "freeze-out" of Jordan at the 1985 All-Star game. It really was unclear that such a freeze-out ever occurred; Jordan was 2 for 9 for 7 points, but many stars had not done well in their first All-Star games. Jordan's retinue said something had to be wrong for Jordan to do so poorly, and an associate of Johnson's and Isiah Thomas's told reporters that several players had conspired to make Jordan look bad because they felt he had tried to show them up by appearing at the slam-dunk contest in his Nike outfit when everyone was told to avoid commercial apparel for the All-Star weekend.

Jordan also saw Johnson's heavy hand involved in an effort to get Jordan's former teammate, James Worthy, traded to Dallas a few years back for Johnson's friend Mark Aguirre. Jordan saw Johnson as a man without the proper respect for people. Johnson saw Jordan as a brash hot dog promoting himself at the expense of others. Each resented the other's stardom. Egos at twenty paces.

"I guess it was jealousy," Jordan said on the eve of the Finals about his once-rocky relationship with Johnson. "All of the things happening to me, like my [multimillion-dollar] shoe contract, were things that should have been happening to him, but they weren't. And I got a lot of notoriety when I came into the league and I guess he didn't feel—I guess a lot of players didn't feel—that I deserved it. But I didn't have control over that."

So for years they both burned, Johnson over Jordan's commercial success and Jordan over Johnson's athletic success and acclaim as the game's most valuable player. But the game has increasingly become a business for both of them, and businessmen can forget their personal differences when money is involved. After all, nations usually resume trade even after wars. They needed each other for their All-Star games and charity fund-raisers. So a truce was worked out at the 1988 All-Star game and they agreed to attend each other's games and summer basketball camps. And they smiled and shook hands. No kissing, though.

Jordan even began to enjoy some of the time he spent with Johnson. And he especially enjoyed becoming a wedge between Johnson and Isiah Thomas.

Jordan agreed to play in Johnson's All-Star game in the summer of 1990, but he didn't want to miss a day of golf if he could help it. He went to Los Angeles, but played thirty-six holes the day of the game and was running late. Johnson decided to hold up the start to accommodate Jordan. Thomas fumed and finally went to Johnson and angrily demanded they not wait for Jordan. Johnson ignored his pleas. Jordan loved hearing the story.

But now Jordan had the chance he long craved. Everyone was looking at the Finals as his battle with Magic and that was fine with him. Jordan was certain he'd triumph this time.

•

PHIL JACKSON DIDN'T realize how crazy the NBA Finals were going to get until a Bulls time-out late in the first half of Game 1. He'd been to the Finals (back before they were trademarked and capitalized) a few times as a player with the Knicks in the early 1970s, but the media attention had grown exponentially since then. Jackson told the players before the Finals that they'd have to practice in Chicago at the Stadium to accommodate the national media instead of at the Multiplex near their homes in the north suburbs. That would mean an extra two hours' drive each day. The team hired a bus, but the players preferred to drive themselves.

"That makes it only twenty minutes for Jordan," some of the

Bulls joked. Jordan had become famous for driving on the shoulder
of the Kennedy Expressway into Chicago on his way to games. And
he always kept a few basketballs and game tickets in the car for
overaggressive police officers.

Jackson had also warned the team about family distractions, which
were already mounting. Several of Scottie Pippen's eleven brothers
and sisters were staying at his North Shore home. Reinsdorf said
he would hire a plane and get rooms in Los Angeles for the families
of all the players and staff, but he couldn't provide enough extra
tickets. When asked on the eve of Game 1 what his biggest concern
about the series was, Jackson said, "Getting tickets in L.A."

The distractions would be enormous and the demands incredible.
An old friend of Bach's had called. Could he get tickets for Bach
and then get a picture of his son with Michael Jordan? Jackson's
friends were calling for tickets every day. The coaches told the
players how Buck Williams had to make three trips to the airport
on the day of one of the games in Portland in the 1990 Finals to
pick up friends and relatives. It was getting big. And the city was
going Bulls crazy.

So was the Bulls marketing department. Not content with the
usual assortment of light displays, dribbling races, and ear-
shattering music, the marketing department came up with something
special that left the coaching staff dumbfounded.

"Tell me," Jackson said to the players forming a semicircle around
him while he had his back to the court during that time-out, "that
I didn't just see what I thought I saw."

Dwarfs. Trying to shoot baskets. Unable to get the ball closer
than a few feet from the basket.

The stunt threw John Bach into a rage. "They're making a mockery of the game," he began to shout. The coaches tried to calm him
for nearly the entire time-out. Tex Winter actually found it pretty
funny. He hadn't seen Bach this way since the guy had whistled the
national anthem. "It's a really big shew, a really big shew," trainer
Chip Schaefer joked in an Ed Sullivan voice.

Finally, Jackson gathered the team and quickly went through the
next play call. But he continued to shake his head and mutter, "I
don't believe this."

The game, too, was becoming a problem, and one Jackson had
worried about. How would Jordan react in his first Finals? They

had talked about it again a few days earlier and Jordan agreed it was best for him to take a backseat at the start, that for the team to succeed either Cartwright or Grant had to get going early.

But Jordan wouldn't have too much patience. Grant threw a bad pass to Pippen for a turnover and then missed a lay-up as the Lakers moved ahead 10–5. Cartwright missed a turnaround jumper.

"Uh-oh, here we go again," Jordan thought to himself. "These guys are uptight, they're nervous. They're not going to be able to do it at this level. I'm gonna have to take over."

Jordan drove and slammed, and on the next Bulls possession, drove and was fouled. Then he twisted around two defenders and slammed again. Then he drove and missed, but put in his own miss. Then he got caught in the middle and passed to Pippen for a slam dunk. Then after Paxson slipped in a pair of jumpers, Jordan drove and slammed again and finished the quarter with a jumper and a bank shot for 15 points. The Bulls had pulled ahead 30–29 after one quarter. The Stadium crowd was delirious. Everyone among the Bulls knew there was trouble.

"When M.J. goes off like that," Pippen would say afterward, "it messes up the other guys. I'm gonna get my points, but the others can't."

Pippen would score 19 in that game, the only other Bull besides Jordan in double figures. Jordan would score 36 and the signs on the floor were troublesome. Once, when Perdue had the smaller Terry Teagle guarding him, Jordan waved Perdue out of the post so he could go against Byron Scott, screaming, "I've got the advantage, I've got the advantage."

But the Bulls couldn't control Sam Perkins. He hit a pair of three-point field goals in the first quarter, and by halftime both he and James Worthy had 14. Jackson switched Cartwright onto Perkins because the Bulls didn't feel Grant could deny the stronger Perkins his position in the post-up game. But Worthy was moving well despite an ankle injury, and the Lakers were having their way inside. It had become their game.

The days of the Showtime express were gone. The Lakers had become a walk-it-up team with Magic Johnson drawing the double-team and then finding an open man. Worthy was a particularly good passer out of the post, so the Lakers were able to slice up teams in the halfcourt game now. New coach Mike Dunleavy, having seen how the aging Lakers were run out of the playoffs by Phoenix in 1990, had changed the team's style, and despite a rocky start in November the Lakers came to the Finals with a good chance to win.

But a fatal flaw would be revealed early. The Lakers moved out to a 41–34 lead against the Bulls' bench to open the second quarter, but when Johnson left the game five minutes into the second quarter the Bulls went on a 10–0 run. It would happen again early in the fourth quarter with Johnson on the bench. Jackson saw that the Lakers lost too much when Johnson left the floor. And Johnson clearly was tired after a rough series against Portland. It was at this point, despite the outcome of Game 1, that Jackson realized the Bulls would win.

"I think we have more answers for them when Michael is out than they have for us when Magic is out," he would say somewhat diplomatically later.

The Bulls still held on to a narrow 53–51 lead at halftime. Jordan and Pippen had combined for 29 points, the other three starters, 10. And when Jordan and Pippen began pulling up for jumper after jumper in the third quarter, the Lakers inched ahead 61–59. Jackson called for a time-out.

"What the hell is this one-on-one shit?" Jackson demanded. He'd often raise his voice in the team huddles, but rarely singled out either Jordan or Pippen. He didn't this time either, but the targets were unmistakable. "Let's run the offense," he continued. "We're not doing anything. What the hell is going on out there?"

Late in the third quarter, a quarter in which the Bulls scored 15 points while falling behind 75–68, Jordan would ask out of the game. He was tired. The coaches could not remember Jordan asking out of a game so early or for so long. There were clearly a lot of jangled nerves among the Bulls, including Jordan, who had worn himself out expending so much nervous energy early.

And he was hardly alone. Grant, for one, hadn't slept much the previous night and was at the Stadium three hours before game time, out on the floor shooting. Normally, players arrived ninety minutes to two hours before a game. Levingston said he felt fine when he got up. Then he threw up three times. Cartwright had told a friend staying with him, "It's just another game." The friend knew that meant Cartwright was nervous. "He only says that when he's uptight," the friend said. Jordan, too, would admit some nervousness before the game, but claimed he'd rid himself of it after the first few minutes. He was clearly exhausted midway through the third quarter, however, something nobody could remember seeing before.

With Johnson out of the game to open the fourth quarter, Jordan returned and moved on top of the floor to play point guard. The move triggered another 10–0 run that gave Chicago a 78–75 lead. Pippen, though, picked up his fourth foul early in that sequence, spoiling one strategy Jackson had wanted to try: He wanted to put the long-armed Pippen on Johnson to negate Johnson's height advantage over most guards, but he couldn't afford to with Pippen in foul trouble.

The game swung back and forth throughout the fourth quarter, although the Bulls seemed in control, leading 91–89 with forty-five seconds left and the ball after Vlade Divac missed a wide-open jumper. Divac had played well, getting 16 points and 14 rebounds, and he would play well throughout the series, though he was the player the Bulls chose to leave open on the double-team rotations. But Jordan missed a runner with twenty-four seconds to go, and then after a time-out Perkins, Jordan's North Carolina teammate, took a pass from Johnson, stepped back, and hit a three-point field goal for a 92–91 Lakers lead.

The odd thing about it is that no one had talked about taking a three in the Lakers' huddle, even though the strategy in the NBA is generally to go for the win on the road. But Perkins thought he was supposed to take the three-pointer anyway.

"I thought there was too much Magic–Michael hype," he would say later, echoing a thought popular on both teams. "Obviously, someone else was going to be involved."

Jordan then drove the ball toward the middle, but the Lakers, playing an umbrellalike zone against Jordan as they would throughout the series, forced him to drop off the ball. It went out of bounds off the Lakers. With nine seconds to go, Jordan again found himself going against Perkins, as a high-pitched buzz flowed from the stands. Jordan shook him and put up a jumper from about eighteen feet. It hit the back of the rim, then the front, then the back again and out. The Lakers rebounded and added a free throw for the 93–91 final.

"It wasn't meant to be," Jordan said softly as he slumped into his chair in the locker room.

For the Lakers, it was what they had come for. They'd wrestled away the home-court advantage and seemed to establish that their experience was going to defeat the Bulls' youth and athleticism. But Jackson felt the Bulls had much going for them, despite the loss. They'd gotten a poor refereeing crew with Jack Madden, who'd blown a crucial call in Game 6 in the Boston–Detroit series that denied the Celtics a chance to win the game. He'd make a highly questionable traveling call on Jordan early in the game and was censured at halftime by chief referee Darell Garretson, who was at the game but not working it. The Lakers had shot 34 free throws to 18 for the Bulls, and Jackson knew that would change. And the Bulls had come close, with Jordan's shot rattling in and out, even though Grant, Cartwright, and Paxson had played almost no role offensively. That would change, Jackson knew.

So Jackson wasn't all that dismayed as he joined his wife, June, who was deeply depressed over the loss.

"Wasn't it a great game?" Jackson said when he saw June. "Close, coming down to one shot, could have gone either way. That's the way it should be."

"Oh, for God's sake, Phil," she pleaded. "We lost!"

•

AS THE BULLS prepared for the collective game of their lives on Wednesday—perhaps the first "must-win" game for the team all season—several among the Bulls had plans.

First was Pippen. He would finally sign his contract extension. It had to be done before the team left for Los Angeles because the Bulls wanted to use the salary-cap money they had been holding for Toni Kukoc, and the NBA rule is that any salary-cap money remaining in a season has to be used before midnight of the last day of the Finals. No one among the Bulls thought the series would end in Los Angeles, but they couldn't take the chance. And by using that cap money now for Pippen, the Bulls could pay Pippen less in the later years of his $18 million five-year extension, so they'd have cap room to take another run at Kukoc if he eventually decided to come to the NBA. Krause insisted the signing be done in secrecy so Pippen wouldn't be questioned by reporters for the remainder of the Finals about his new deal.

Krause told Pippen's agent, Jimmy Sexton, that he didn't want Pippen coming downtown and that they should meet at some remote location to be determined by Krause. It was typical Krause in his best cloak-and-dagger mode. Billy McKinney, when he was an aide to Krause, used to call him on his car phone and say jokingly when he was bringing a college prospect in, "Agent X2 reporting in. I have the package." But Sexton would have none of that; the signing would take place in the Bulls offices.

To celebrate his newfound security, Pippen went to Bennigan's for a cheeseburger.

Grant, meanwhile, was bitterly disappointed and embarrassed about his play in Game 1, in which he had 6 points on 3-of-8 shooting. Already, it was being said in the media the Bulls really were a one-man team after all, and many of the Bulls were annoyed, for they knew Jordan had missed open players throughout the game.

"Hey, if Sam Perkins was on our team, he'd be Stacey King," Grant said after Game 1—less a condemnation of Perkins, whom Grant respected, than a comparison of the style of play of the two teams: Magic Johnson was looking to get the ball to Perkins to try for the game winner, or at least a tie, while Jordan once again looked primarily to himself.

Cartwright was not any happier, though he tried to be diplomatic about the way Jordan tried to rule. "Everyone likes to shoot twenty times, but in reality that doesn't happen," he told a reporter. "Ideally, we want a better dispersal of shots than we had Sunday, at least I know I do, but you guys ought to remember, we were one shot away from winning that game."

Later, a few of the players grumbled about Jordan's insistence on still calling them his supporting cast. Perdue noted that Jordan had scored 36 points, his third-highest-scoring game of the playoffs. The Bulls had lost two of those three games—their only losses of the playoffs so far. "He needs us," Perdue said. "We're not as good as he is, but he's got to start to realize he needs us to win."

"They're angry," Jackson said about his team. "They let one slip away they know they should have won."

Chip Schaefer, meanwhile, decided to take still another run at Grant about the glasses. He'd gotten a pair from Orth that were similar to the ones that John Salley wore, clear plastic and designed to fit more snugly. Grant agreed to try them for Game 2. He would shoot 10 of 13, saying afterward he intended never to take the goggles off. From Game 2 through Game 5, Grant would shoot 29 for 43.

Bach also had some persuading to do. After Game 1, he took home the tape of the game to analyze and continued to pore over tapes of the Portland–Lakers series. The Lakers had cut up the Bulls in Game 1 with their post-ups and quick passing out of the post to open spot-up shooters. Bach, though, had seen that toward the end of their series with the Lakers, the Trail Blazers had started to send their double-teams along the baseline, in effect *behind* the Lakers' post-up players, and it seemed to upset them. It would be too late for the Trail Blazers, but Bach felt this was an essential move for the Bulls. He lobbied Jackson hard at practice Monday. Jackson said he'd think about it. But he seemed in a good mood. When asked by a reporter the difference between the playoffs for him now and when he had played, Jackson said, "I went to bed about eleven-thirty Sunday and got up around six. When I was a player, it would have been the other way around."

Bach was even more convinced after watching tapes again Monday night. The Bulls had been sending their double from the top of the floor or across the court, in full view of the Lakers' post players, and they had time to read it and pass. Bach had Winter on his side; Winter had come up with the same idea but wasn't usually as forward with his suggestions as Bach. Initially, Jackson had reservations. "We only lost by a basket," he said. "Let's not scrap the defense that has taken us so far." But by Tuesday, Jackson had agreed. The team practiced the defense for almost two hours.

•

LIKE HIS PLAYERS, Jackson had been disturbed by Jordan's shot selection, but he decided to be oblique for now. There was no time to waste, but he felt sure the Bulls would win Game 2. Before the game, he instructed the team, "Okay, we've got guys open on the perimeters. We've got to find these guys."

Everything worked for the Bulls in Game 2.

They got both Cartwright and Grant going early as the duo combined for 18 of the Bulls' 28 first-quarter points; Grant spun left and right by defenders and Cartwright was active on the boards for putbacks and easy jumpers. Even a quick second foul by Jordan proved beneficial to the Bulls; Jackson had toyed with moving Pippen onto Johnson in Game 1, but this forced his hand. And Pippen would surprise even the coaches with his aggressiveness, his long arms distracting Johnson and his bodying tactics bothering the Lakers' star. Pippen had been desperately angry at himself for getting into foul trouble in Game 1 and hadn't slept well afterward. He was determined to make amends.

The Bulls remained in control in the second quarter, and held a 48–43 halftime lead. Jackson liked their togetherness thus far. Before Game 2, he'd spliced together some clips from a movie about Indians, *The Mystic Warrior,* which was a film version of the book *Hanta Yo.* The tapes showed scenes of the tribe working together matched with clips from Game 1 in which open shooters went unnoticed and ball handlers banged fruitlessly into the Lakers' zone defense.

And the Bulls came out smoking after halftime. Several players had complained after Game 1 about the rim at the east end of the Stadium being a little tight; this surprised the coaches, because they'd never heard the team complain about the Stadium rims, as they did about the Detroit baskets. But this night the Bulls would set an NBA record by hitting 17 of 20 shots in the quarter on that basket, with Jordan and Paxson hitting all 10 they attempted, and the Bulls would have a 19-point lead after three. They would go on to hit 61.7 percent of their shots, a record shooting percentage for a playoff game.

The fans in the Stadium were dancing, and so was Jordan, so much so that at one point Lakers assistant coach Randy Pfund had to restrain Dunleavy from going after Jordan. Jordan had started mocking his opponents during the Detroit series, and the practice would carry over to the Los Angeles series as he began to taunt the Lakers' bench after baskets. One time Pippen restrained Jordan as he shook his hands in front of the Lakers' bench as if he were rolling dice, and several times Jordan pumped his arm vigorously after baskets. Jordan's tactics weren't lost on the Lakers, who complained afterward about them; guard Byron Scott warned that such behavior was risky so early in the series.

But Jordan did have reason to celebrate, for he would perform the highlight-film move of the series early in the fourth quarter. It was a move that could only have been performed by the greatest individual performer ever to play basketball. Jordan had gotten the ball on the run after an A. C. Green miss and started to rise toward the basket for a right-handed slam. But he saw "long-armed Sam Perkins there," as he would later explain it. So, as only Jordan can, he hung in the air while he switched the ball into his left hand, lowered his left shoulder, and scooped the ball in left-handed. The crowd first gasped, for this was art, poetry without words, an instant for eternity. Then the crowd exploded. Jackson marveled later that it was something even he'd never seen Jordan do before. Dunleavy called a meaningless time-out with almost eight minutes left in the game, the Bulls lead at 26, and the 107–86 rout virtually complete.

The Bulls had accomplished much besides evening the series, as all five starters, led by Jordan's 33, scored in double figures. Jordan again had gone up to the top of the floor, even before Jackson had ordered it, and opened up the offense in a manner that spread the Lakers' packed-in defense. This, perhaps more than anything else, demonstrated Jordan's determination to win the game and do every-thing he could. He was a brilliant competitor; it was the attribute Jackson most admired in him. "It seems he always needs a chal-lenge," Jackson had once remarked. "I think that's why he's always hurling these insults all around the locker room, looking for someone to challenge him so he can back them down." He took the challenge when Jackson moved Hodges into the game for Paxson; Jordan would move to point guard and stay there, even when Paxson came back, telling Paxson to get out on the wing. It worked this time because Jordan virtually willed it to.

The Bulls also quieted Perkins, who scored 11 points, and the Lakers shot 12 fewer free throws than in the previous game. Jordan was phenomenal, hitting 15 of 18 shots and handing off for 13 assists. Paxson got just 8 shots, but hit them all. He'd had 7 in Game 1, hitting just 3.

Oddly, Jordan had singled Paxson out after Game 1, noting the 4 open shots he missed. Paxson thought it curious that Jordan was now counting his misses. But Jordan offered a beautiful anecdote for the media at the press conference after Game 2. He said he had told Paxson that he had to keep Johnson honest on defense, that he had to go down with no bullets, that he had to take his shots. Advised of this, Jackson carefully backed his star. "Michael is a challenging type of guy," said Jackson after hearing what Jordan had said. "He's not the type of guy who's going to commiserate or put his arm around someone's shoulder. He's going to say, 'Step up, chump, and make some shots.' "

It was a beautiful story: the big star, the leader, pushing, cajoling his team to greater heights.

Of course, all the Bulls knew it was a fantasy. Jordan had never said a word to Paxson between Games 1 and 2. He rarely spoke to any of the players about their play. But he'd heard Jackson tell Paxson that he was being run off his shot, that he had to step up and take his shots. It was something Jordan did often: He'd hear someone say something he liked and then say that he'd said it. It was much the same with his "supporting cast" comments; the phrase was something he'd picked up and repeated. It hadn't worked out as well as his supposed motivation of Paxson, but he sort of liked the taste of it anyway.

Jackson was restrained as usual after the game.

"All right," he said, "now we prepare to get two wins in L.A."

"Three, P.J.," Jordan yelled back.

Suddenly, the Bulls felt good enough to dream again.

·

THE BULLS COACHES had one other advantage as the team moved on to Los Angeles June 6 for Game 3 the next night.

They now had the Lakers' plays.

Of course, they already knew what plays the Lakers liked to run. That was no secret around the NBA. All teams had sophisticated advance scouting teams and films of opponents' games, which they'd spend hours analyzing. So the Bulls could tell in an instant what it meant when a team yelled "Savior"; that was a Dallas play that called for a double screen for a shooter. When Gene Littles cocked his finger as if shooting a gun, that was an isolation play. There's "Snake," for an action in which a player moves like a snake toward the basket, and there are times when coaches employ colors or hand and arm signals as in baseball or simply words like "Chop," or "Power," or "Dive," all denoting various actions toward the basket.

Red Holzman, Jackson's coach in New York, used to run "What the Fuck," a last-second shot. It was the arcane world of NBA strategy.

Over the years, Bach had kept a list of all the plays around the league, and the Bulls had become expert at intercepting the calls. Jackson happened to be an excellent lip-reader, and the Bulls coaches usually began time-outs by peering downcourt into the other huddle to try to see what the other coach was calling. They were well prepared for what the Lakers would try.

But now they also had twenty pages of Lakers' plays drawn out in Dunleavy's handwriting with all the options, which are sometimes hard to figure. The Lakers had left them under their bench when the walked off the court in disarray after Game 2. The Bulls had picked them up and begun to study them. They revealed nothing new, but they did confirm for the Bulls just what the Lakers were trying to do and what their options might be off those plays. Leaving the plays behind couldn't have made the Lakers very happy going home. The Bulls weren't sure if that was the reason, but the Lakers' scheduled practice for Thursday was canceled at the last minute.

There was some Hollywood business to sort out first as the Bulls readied for Game 3. Pippen had agreed to appear with Craig Hodges on the late-night Rick Dees program. No way, said Arsenio Hall. Pippen had also agreed to be with Arsenio, so it had to be no to Rick. Hodges was stuck and asked B. J. Armstrong to go with him. Hodges found himself answering lots of questions from Dees's lawyers.

·

THE BULLS WERE staying at the Ritz-Carlton Hotel in Marina del Rey. With an unprecedented media crush owing to the matchup of Michael Jordan and Magic Johnson, the game's two greatest marquee attractions, you didn't have to be Jerry Krause to be concerned about security. To ward off distractions, the Bulls had all the players and coaches register under pseudonyms; only callers asking for them by the proper pseudonyms would be put through. Horace Grant chose Clemson Tiger, his college's mascot, and was known as Mr. Tiger to the switchboard. John Paxson, out of Notre Dame, selected the name John Irish. And Jordan used the name Leroy Smith, as he often does on the road. Leroy Smith was the player who had beaten Jordan out for the last spot on his high school varsity basketball team. Smith now lived in Los Angeles; he and Jordan had remained friends, and he became one of the regulars in Jordan's late-night card games all through Finals week.

Phil Jackson also took a name, but it was one he'd actually been given long ago. The name was Swift Eagle. It was the name given him by the Native Americans he'd befriended in South Dakota during the summers of his playing career; he would ride the almost thousand miles from his Montana home to the reservation on his motorcycle, inspiring the name. (At the Bulls' victory party, Jackson would see his wife, June, dancing with several of his players and offer her her own new name. "We'll call you Dances with Bulls," he said.)

While the names cut down on the phone calls and demands, there was no way to eliminate completely the distraction Jackson had alluded to before Game 1: the demand for tickets. This was one more area where Jordan's fame and the resources that come with it served to drive a wedge between him and his teammates.

Jordan could do wonderfully unselfish things like bringing all his teammates to center court for the presentation of the MVP award in the Stadium, or sharing his slam-dunk contest winnings with his team, as he had done several years back. Another gracious gesture would follow the Finals: The Disney people had contacted both Jordan and Johnson, wanting the winner to declare his intention of "going to Disney World" after the final game. Both agreed, but Jordan said he would only do it if the commercial featured the whole starting five. Each would get $20,000 instead of $100,000 for him.

But he loused it all up in the locker room before Game 3. The ticket squeeze was severe, even for the players. Many had numerous friends and family members in for the Finals and couldn't even buy tickets. Paxson couldn't get one for his father; Cartwright couldn't buy one for his oldest friend. Jordan had obtained more than two dozen from the Bulls and other sources. They'd asked him to be discreet, but instead he spread the tickets out in front of himself in the locker room in a rather grand display, sorting them out for different friends and family while stuffing them into envelopes to be taken to the gate by the ball boys. The procedure went on for about a half hour as player after player glared right through Jordan.

It was an angry Bulls team that would take the floor that night.

·

THE LAKER SURGE at home that the Bulls anticipated would come, but not until much later. The Bulls were hitting their shots early and started to look more for Paxson. The Bulls had identified two further ways to thwart the Lakers. One was against Byron Scott. He'd shot well in the playoffs, so Jackson instructed Paxson to play him close. This generally wouldn't scare anyone, since Paxson can be beaten off the dribble, but Scott doesn't finish plays to the basket well; he's best at taking the pass off a double-team for his jumper. Paxson's defense, which was tougher than even the Bulls coaches expected, seemed to throw Scott off balance. He would shoot 0 for 8 in forty-three minutes in Game 3.

Then there was Johnson. He likes to play a zone defense, dropping off his man, in this case Paxson, and clogging the lane to stop the drives of players such as Jordan and Pippen. He'd been allowed to do it effectively in Game 1, and the Bulls' hot shooting in Game 2 made the Lakers' defense nearly irrelevant. But Jackson felt that making Johnson play Paxson was crucial, and it was time to stop sparing Jordan's feelings. He put together a tape after the first two games showing Johnson cheating over to the middle and leaving Paxson.

"M.J.," he said before Game 3, "you've got to see who's open. You've got to find Paxson. He's open. You've got to get him the ball. It's something we've got to do."

The message, delivered to Jordan in front of the whole team, was having another positive, bonding effect. The players were beginning to feel some sense of equal justice. "Phil did a great job of staying on everyone in the playoffs," Paxson would say later.

Jackson would update the tape after Games 3 and 4 and show it to Jordan again with the same message. He'd show Jordan setting up in the post, the defense collapsing, and open shots developing that Jordan passed up. He'd show Jordan at virtually every spot on the court missing Paxson. Jordan went along, and in the end Jackson would say, "Michael at some time became capable of giving up more of the spotlight and the ball. He understood this is what it took to get to the Finals and win."

The Bulls led 48–47 at halftime, but the game was about to turn.

Jackson had kept Jordan on Johnson, with Jordan still pushing Johnson and making him work hard for position. After halftime, though, Pippen said he wanted another try on Johnson and the two switched without consulting Jackson. The change would prove disastrous. The Lakers had been waiting for the move as Jackson had sensed, and Johnson quickly hit Divac, now defended by the much smaller Jordan on the switch, three times for baskets. Jackson called a time-out and was furious.

"What the hell are you guys doing out there?" he stammered, staring at the two. "Let's get back the way we were."

But the momentum had swung hard to the Lakers. Perkins drove and scored. Divac, emboldened by his success, scored on another pass from Johnson and then hit a jumper. The Lakers led by 67–54 with 4:46 left in the third quarter. Time-out again.

Jackson simply said the Bulls had to get a basket and designed a play for Paxson to go to the hoop. It worked. The Lakers, with the usually docile Forum crowd hooting and screaming, held on to their double-digit lead, but the Bulls strung together 6 straight points to close the quarter as the Lakers committed 3 straight turnovers. The lead was down to 6.

Dunleavy dared not take Johnson out. But Johnson was tiring, as was Worthy, whose ankle was starting to throb, limiting his movement to the boards for rebounds. He would score 12 points the rest of the series. "We felt," Jackson would say later, "that come the fourth quarter we would have the edge in conditioning, that they would be tired."

It was happening. After Perkins opened the fourth quarter with a driving hook, the Bulls scored 8 straight points to tie the game at 74 with 8:42 left. And suddenly Levingston would prove worth that season of investment.

First he blocked Perkins. Then he rebounded a Scott miss. Next he stole a Johnson pass. Finally he tipped in a Grant miss to make it 88–84 Bulls with 3:10 left.

"He was the glue that held us together," Jackson would acknowledge later.

It was the moment Levingston had long waited for. A few years back in the playoffs, he'd helped sink Atlanta in a memorable conference semifinals series against the Celtics by missing a wild shot. He hadn't played much all season, but that was becoming something of an advantage; his was a fresh body to match up with weary Lakers. "It's been like a fairy-tale year," said Levingston. "It was a good beginning to come to a team like the Bulls, but a bad middle. It's looking like a happy ending."

But the Lakers weren't done quite yet, even though the Bulls, on their way to a massive 46–29 rebounding advantage, got four chances on one possession before finally scoring to take a 90–87 lead with 1:07 left. Perkins scored, Jordan missed, and Divac, drawing Pippen's sixth foul, stumbled into the lane and put up a wild shot that went in for a three-point play and a 92–90 Lakers lead with 10.9 seconds left. Divac jumped into Johnson's arms, but there was much more to come.

Despite Jordan's failure in Game 1, he remained the greatest last-second player in the game. Jackson decided to take full advantage: Rather than take the ball at halfcourt after the time-out, Jackson told Jordan to take it full court so he could size up the floor and find his shot. Jordan wove his way downcourt against Scott without the Lakers showing much of a double-team; Divac would come too late. Jordan simply worked Scott into position about fourteen feet away from the basket, pulled up, and dropped in the tying score with 3.4 seconds left. The Lakers wouldn't get a shot, and the game moved into overtime, the Lakers' big third-quarter lead a bitter memory.

Overtime was the last thing the tired Lakers wanted. The game was tied at 96 after the first half of the five-minute session, but Jordan then put in his second daring reverse driving basket, Grant rebounded a Jordan miss for a basket, and Jordan was fouled for a pair of free throws while Perkins clanged a couple of jumpers off the front of the rim. The final score was 104–96.

The Lakers staggered off the court. The thirty-one-year-old Johnson had played a whopping fifty minutes, and Perkins, thirty, had hung around for fifty-one minutes. Scott, thirty, had gone scoreless in forty-three minutes and Worthy, thirty, was limping while Pippen and Grant, both a bouncy twenty-five years old, had grabbed as many rebounds as the entire Lakers' starting five.

"Those old legs can hurt you," Cartwright would agree with a laugh later when reporters raised the question of age.

All game long, Arsenio Hall had been taunting the Bulls from near their bench, waving a Lakers jacket at them. When the buzzer sounded, Levingston, who had 10 points off the bench, turned and stuck a finger at Hall.

"In your face, Arsenio," Levingston shouted. "In your face."

•

MISSED AMID THE shouting over Jordan's game-tying shot Friday was his reentry. Jordan landed hard on his right toe and felt a shooting pain. It was not unlike what he'd felt almost six years earlier when he'd broken his foot. He always carried a fear of such an injury with him, despite his acrobatic forays to the basket and often reckless play. He returned to the bench and said he might have broken the toe, but it would feel better as the overtime progressed and the scare seemed gone. Bulls' doctor John Hefferon examined it and said Jordan wouldn't even need X rays. Just swollen, he said, although the next day at practice, when Jordan took off, Hefferon would be bombarded with questions: "Will he lose the nail?" asked one TV reporter breathlessly. "Is it mostly black or blue?" asked another. These would be just a few of the dumb questions raised during the week, the two stupidest probably being when Jordan was asked if he had the most famous tongue in the world, and Cartwright was asked to comment on Phil Jackson getting a double off Satchel Paige when he was in high school and Paige had a barnstorming team that came through town. Hefferon answered the questions asked him as if they were serious. "Fifteen minutes of fame," he said later. "Got to take it seriously."

The Bulls knew the questions were more serious than Jordan's injury.

"Where's M.J.?" Pippen had roared Saturday morning when the Bulls boarded the team bus at the Ritz-Carlton for the media session and brief practice.

"He's not going," PR man Tim Hallam said. "He's injured."

"Oh, man, I'm hurt, too," moaned Pippen. "I got to get out of here. My arm, no, my hip is hurtin', no, my back, Tim. Tell Phil I can't make it."

Jordan had told Jackson that morning he didn't want to practice or talk to the media. "I'll cover for you," Jackson said, "but you've got to stay in your room. You can't let anyone see you go out."

Jackson never checked to find out where Jordan was that day, although the league was threatening to fine the Bulls for allowing Jordan to miss the media session. Jackson had told the players to try to rest, eat well, and lead a sedentary life in L.A. But after Game 4, Jordan played thirty-six holes of golf Monday and another eighteen before practice Tuesday morning. He was still relying on his youth and athleticism to carry him, and it still would, but the coaches wondered just how much longer Jordan could get away with his life-style off the court. They had begun to see subtle signs of slippage in his game, and he was developing a recurring tendinitis.

Suddenly, the Bulls were celebrities, even in Hollywood. Pippen had gone off with Jimmy Sexton to look for some clothes. They'd decided to go to Beverly Hills. "They see celebrities there all the time, so we won't be bothered," Sexton told Pippen. But Pippen ended up signing autographs for a half hour and never could get enough time to look for clothes. A Japanese company had approached Hodges; the firm would pay $100,000 to any Bull to come to Japan to give basketball clinics for a week, and it would be $550,000 if that Bull was Jordan. The players mostly spent their time lounging lazily by the pool amid the palm trees, taking turns doing interviews with the TV crews in from Chicago against the backdrop of the boats in the marina. It was a mild, breezy week, the temperatures cooler than when the team had left Chicago a few days earlier. The players were no longer thinking a team had to lose one of these things before it could win, as the rule seemed to be.

When the Bulls arrived at the arena Sunday afternoon for the 4:00 P.M. start of Game 4 (NBC was trying to get as many games of this glamorous matchup as it could into eastern prime time), Pippen dressed quickly and went out to shoot. It was his habit now to be the first on the court before games. But security guards had the court blocked. The Lakers were going through a full practice. It seemed an act of desperation to the coaching staff, and Bach recalled an NIT game in which Abe Lemons had his team scrimmage at halftime after a poor opening half. Jackson remembered Hubie Brown in New York putting his team through similar rigors.

Pippen scored first for the Bulls, then Paxson hit a jumper and a three-point field goal, and then Cartwright hit two jumpers on the way to a team-high 9 points in the first quarter. The Lakers would storm the boards for 7 offensive rebounds in the quarter, but the balanced Bulls attack kept them within 1, 28–27, after one quarter. The Lakers, it would turn out, had taken their best shot.

Johnson took a rest early in the second quarter and the Lakers never recovered. They shot just 25 percent in the period and scored 16 points. Worthy was now in severe pain and would play just one more quarter in the series. Hodges came in and knocked in a pair of jumpers and Scott Williams hit a bank shot as the bench erupted in high fives. But Williams was mostly there to help bother Perkins, who would finish with an ignominious 1 for 15 as the Bulls played to his left hand and he missed shot after shot. It would be a moment of personal glory for Williams in the shadow of his own personal horror; the house where his father had shot his mother and then killed himself was just a few miles from the Forum. (Williams would occasionally go out onto his balcony at the Ritz and look toward the house, but he didn't want to go back there, and he refused to speak about his old neighborhood.)

Jordan scored 11 points while Levingston added 5 rebounds as the Bulls went to halftime leading 52–44. The Lakers had to win or face going down 3–1, a hole from which no NBA team had ever climbed—a ditch, Dunleavy would call it later—to win a Finals. And they were starting to lose sight of the light at the top.

Jordan sensed the third quarter was the time for the Bulls to jump on the Lakers. He saw that Johnson was particularly animated as he led the Lakers out of their locker room. When the Bulls' starters gathered in a circle for the start of the second half, Jordan said, "Magic's disgusted with them. Let's go!"

Jordan was right. Johnson cajoled and pleaded throughout the third quarter for his team to get something going. But the Bulls hit their first 5 shots to take a 14-point lead. "C'mon," Johnson yelled, "doesn't anybody want to play?"

"We've got 'em," Jordan thought.

The Bulls' defense was now suffocating the Lakers. They scored just 14 points in the third quarter and left the court to boos, trailing by 16, their one-time express train stuck in the yards, their players wearing the expressions of bored commuters.

The Lakers opened the fourth quarter with 7 straight points, but

Perkins then missed a pair of jumpers, one a three-pointer after a Bulls turnover, and the Lakers would never recover. Hodges drove and put in a wild leaner and Jordan hit a jumper to get the Bulls back up by 13. And then Paxson thwarted every other Lakers hope: He hit a twenty-one-footer on a pass from Pippen after the Lakers scored 5 straight points to energize the crowd, and then a twenty-footer after Divac drove and put in his own miss. With the Bulls ahead 91–79 with two minutes left, Jordan blocked a Perkins shot and then leaped into the second row to try to save the ball. An unnecessary move, though one with a message: We'll even outhustle you, baby. The Bulls won going away, 97–82.

The team of the eighties, the kings of the fast break and the Magic show, had been buried. The Forum was deathly quiet. There was something great happening, but there would be no applause. The Lakers' 82 points were a Finals low for them since the NBA adopted the twenty-four-second clock in 1954. They were the fewest points a team had scored in any Finals game in a decade. They were the fewest points the Lakers had scored in a playoff game in three years. The Bulls were now holding their playoff opponents to 91.6 points per game, an all-time low. Every Bulls starter had taken at least 10 shots, led by Jordan's 20. And Jordan had 13 assists, so not only was he leading everyone in scoring but he had as many assists as Magic Johnson. Jordan was especially enjoying that, even if Johnson would eventually nose him out in assists after Game 5.

It was over and everyone knew it, and Craig Hodges braced himself for the coming charge. It had almost become a ritual now, and, in fact, the players had started to feel sorry for Hodges: Early in the playoffs, Krause had been going around the locker room yelling, "Fifteen, fifteen," for that was the number of games a team had to win to be champions. No one paid much attention, but the likable Hodges played along, and when Krause would come into the locker room after wins, Hodges would yell "Thirteen" or "Twelve" or "Ten," as the countdown kept going. Krause liked that and was now running into the locker room and charging Hodges like a wild rhino.

"Hooooooodddddgggggyyy," he would wail. "Twooooooooo."

"He's comin', Hodg, he's comin'," Armstrong began yelling.

"Look out, Hodg," Grant was squealing. "Here he comes."

The door burst open and Krause was there, yelling:

"Hooooodddddggggg." And now he was charging the naked Hodges.

King was making squealing sounds like a pig.

"Oonnnnnneee, Hooooodddggg, oooonnnnneeee," Krause yelled on the run.

The antics continued on the bus back to the hotel.

"Hey, P.J.," Jordan yelled mockingly from the back. "I ain't goin' to no White House. I didn't vote for that guy. I know you didn't vote for him."

Jackson said he hadn't voted for George Bush either, for Jackson said he wasn't really a member of any organized political party— he was a Democrat.

"Well, you won't go either, right, P.J.?" Jordan yelled. "You'll join me. We ain't going to no White House."

"Tex, this is gonna be trouble," Perdue was adding to the chorus. "You're gonna have to write another book. Everyone's gonna want the triangle."

That night, Mike Dunleavy went to a favorite restaurant with his wife. Just moments before he walked in, Jackson and his wife walked in and were being seated. As Jackson moved to his seat, a big round of applause grew. Jackson looked around and began to nod when he noticed Dunleavy. The applause was for the Lakers coach. The Bulls weren't the heroes quite yet.

The scene reminded Jackson of a story he'd heard about football coach Don Shula of the Miami Dolphins. Shula vacationed at a remote retreat in Maine where he was sure he was unknown. One night, though, he walked into a movie and the nine people spaced out around the theater began applauding loudly. Shula was shocked and a little embarrassed. Could his fame have extended this far? He sat down and leaned over to a man sitting a few seats away and said, "I didn't think they knew me here."

"Hell," the man shot back, "I don't know who you are. But the guy said he wouldn't start the movie until he had ten people in the theater."

Jackson stopped by and chatted with Dunleavy briefly and then the two couples ate dinner across the restaurant from each other.

The next game would be on Wednesday, so the players had some time on their hands. Pippen went to do that appearance with Arsenio Hall and several players went to a James Brown concert. Jordan played golf when Jackson gave the team Monday off after a brief stop to meet the media in the morning.

On Tuesday morning, a weary Jordan, wearing sunglasses, was last to step onto the bus for the trip to practice. He climbed to the top step. "Good morning, world champions," he said.

Jackson tried to curtail the celebration. He showed tapes of Games 3 and 4, and pointed out that in Game 3 the Bulls were a Jordan shot away from losing and in Game 4 the Lakers had so many open shots that they just missed. The Bulls could easily be down 3–1, he said. No one was buying it, but practice was as hard as it had been in months, with players banging one another harder than any had been hit in the Detroit series.

"Last practice for the season," Jordan said. "Let's make it a good one."

•

ON THE THRESHOLD of his own personal redemption—he would gain the Finals' Most Valuable Player award in a unanimous vote a few hours later—Jordan was as nervous as a kid facing his first day of school.

"I don't know what to do," he confided as he sat in his locker stall just before the start of Game 5. "I'm nervous. Should I pass? Should I shoot? I really don't know what to do. We're right here and there's no guarantee we'll ever be back. Who knows what this organization will do? I know what they said, but they wanted to make a trade as bad as I did. They just couldn't do it. But we're here. And now what do I do?"

What Jordan did to start the game was throw the ball to Paxson, who hit a jumper. So did Pippen, and Paxson hit another jumper. But both Bulls stars were nervous. Pippen hit just 2 of 9 shots in the first half, but Grant and Cartwright got 5 rebounds each and the Bulls were hanging in.

The consensus in the press room was that it would be over within minutes, that this would be a dolorous day in L.A. Worthy and Scott were both out. The Lakers started Terry Teagle for Scott and A. C. Green for Worthy. But the damage was being done by rookies Elden Campbell and Tony Smith. The Bulls had worried about Smith; he had beaten them in that February game after Johnson was hurt by penetrating and beating Paxson to the basket. And with Johnson on the floor, Jordan couldn't help out. The Bulls were grateful the Lakers hadn't gone to him sooner and had wondered why not throughout the series. He would hit 5 of 6 shots in Game 5. And Campbell was taking quick passes from Johnson, who would finish with a gallant triple double, and slamming around the late-rotating Bulls.

The Bulls were in a fight, trailing 49–48 at halftime. Jackson instructed his team at halftime to play their defense and the shots would come. Pippen finally started to shake loose, both rebounding and getting to the basket on the way to a game-high 32 points, the first time in the playoffs that a Bull other than Jordan would lead the team in scoring. But the score was still 80–80 after three periods.

With Green and Campbell doing most of the scoring, the Lakers took a 91–90 lead with 6:47 left. Time-out Bulls. The Forum crowd, much maligned by the Bulls in comparison to their home Stadium crowd, was playfully impassioned. Not only weren't they leaving early, as was their reputation, but they were cheering through the time-out. They were all standing. Was this smug, cool L.A.?

Jordan had taken 5 of the Bulls' 8 shots of the quarter so far. He had 26 points, apparently on the way to 40—and a trip back to Chicago for Game 6.

Jackson huddled with the coaches near the free-throw line while the starters took seats, as was the custom in time-outs. Jordan usually liked to peer out into the crowd during time-outs, but for the most part in these playoffs Jordan had been attentive. Jackson liked the eye contact he was getting from Jordan, and on several occasions just nodded to him in an unspoken "Okay, take over." But Jackson didn't like what he was seeing now. He decided to be sharp with Jordan.

He kneeled in the huddle and stared into Jordan's blazing eyes.

"M.J.," he demanded, "who's open?"

Jordan looked at him and didn't answer.

"Who's open?" Jackson asked again.

"Paxson," Jordan said.

"Okay, let's find him," Jackson said.

He clapped his hands and the team went back onto the floor.

Campbell, on his way to 21 points, slammed off a pass from Johnson for a 93–90 Lakers lead. Pandemonium. The Lakers had decided they would not let another team celebrate in their living room. It was just a matter of pride, Johnson had said earlier.

But Jordan found Pippen circling on the outside and Pippen dropped in a three-pointer to tie the game at 93.

Jordan stole the ball from Johnson, but Paxson missed. Jordan then stole the ball from Smith, and Pippen missed. "What the hell's going on?" Jordan thought. Smith missed, and Divac then blocked Cartwright, but Cartwright recovered and passed to Pippen nineteen feet away. Good!

Perkins lined one off the front rim—he was becoming adept at this—and Jordan took the ball up and found Paxson in the left corner eighteen feet away. Good!

It was 97–93 Bulls with 3:24 left.

Perkins tried a three-pointer coming out of a time-out and missed. Pippen recovered for his game-high 13th rebound, and found Paxson dashing to the basket. Paxson laid the ball in for a 99–93 Bulls lead with 3:03 left. He would score half his 20 points in the final four minutes of the game.

By this time, Jerry Reinsdorf and Jerry Krause had been brought to a room opposite the Bulls' dressing room to await the final moments. Sitting there was NBA commissioner David Stern. The three would go right into the Bulls' locker room for the trophy presentation if the Bulls won. Krause was up, pacing. His face was turning deep red and his jowls were shaking. He was having trouble breathing. "Jerry, Jerry, are you okay?" said Reinsdorf.

Krause didn't answer.

"Hey, it's only a game," Stern said.

"No it's not," Krause spit out.

Perkins came back with a driving bank shot, but Jordan weaved through the Lakers for a lay-up and a 101–95 Bulls lead with 2:27 left. Perkins was fouled and converted one of two free throws, and then Jordan passed in to Cartwright, who found Paxson lurking at the top of the key. Good!

Perkins came back with a drive, Jordan traveled, and Perkins hit a runner and was fouled for a three-point play. The Lakers had drawn within 2, 103–101, with just over a minute left. There was a chance.

This was it, Jackson thought on the bench as he watched Jordan dribble toward the basket. Jordan went left and then turned back to his right, but he was going across court instead of to the basket. He was not looking to shoot, Jackson noticed. *He was looking for Paxson.* He wasn't looking to score.

Jackson leaned back. He knew the game was over, the Bulls would be champions, and the whole season's effort had been worth it.

Jordan lured the defense to him and whizzed the ball to Paxson, standing eighteen feet away in the left corner. The shot barely rippled the net going down.

The Lakers would not score again. The final score was 108–101 Bulls. The Chicago Bulls were world champions.

.

WHEN THE FINAL buzzer sounded, a year's worth of effort and emotion burst forth like a river breaking a dam.

"Sweet," shouted Cartwright. "This is sweet."

"Seven long years," Jordan yelled as the players rushed from the pandemonium of the court to their locker room. "Seven long years. I can't believe it."

Emotion and exhilaration washed over the players. It was purifying, purging the jealousies, resentments, and feuds of the season. What remained was pure, unrestrained joy. And madness.

The Disney people had wanted to have the five starters pose for their "goin' to Disney World" clip on the court, but it was impossible; they would later adjourn to the rest room in the locker room for the brief commercial message. Pippen, dribbling the ball out to end the game, darted from the court as hundreds of Chicago fans stormed their heroes; the fans were representatives of the folks back home, who were pouring into the streets around the Chicago Stadium, around Wrigley Field, and in the downtown area to celebrate the victory.

"Twelve long years," Cartwright yelled to Jordan. "Twelve long years."

Jordan smiled.

"Everyone was just being crazy," Grant would recall later. "It seemed like all we were doing was screaming, acting like kids, yelling and screaming."

"Nineteen eighty-seven, nineteen eighty-seven," Grant and Pippin chanted as they fell into each other's arms. It was an old joke;

the two would always say that was when the Bulls started to turn around, in 1987, after they drafted Pippen and Grant. "Nineteen eighty-seven, nineteen eighty-seven," they yelled at one another and danced around in circles.

Hopson was yelling now too, dousing himself in champagne and receiving warm congratulations from every teammate. They all remembered Detroit.

June Jackson looked desperately for Phil on the court, unable to find him amidst the throng, and later edged her way into the bulging locker room, where the players' wives had also gathered. She thought Phil joyous, but later he would say his biggest thrill came in the last minute of the game when he knew it was over. "It's in the game," he said. "That's where the excitement is for me."

People, people everywhere in that locker room. TV cameramen wrestled for position and thrust microphones into everyone's faces. Commissioner David Stern began the trophy presentation and no one could hear. "Hey, I got to be a part of this," Paxson shouted and dashed to the end of the room. Everyone wore champagne like a shiny new suit, and Krause hugged every waist he walked into. But this wasn't the players' time. This was for TV and the reporters and fans who had crashed the party. Finally, Jordan got up to leave for the team bus back to the hotel and the locker room began to clear.

The players boarded the bus and moved to the back, as was their custom, the coaches in front and staff and broadcasters in the middle. It was there they had their moment. All were still in uniform. There would be no showering, at least with water, this night. In fact, the next morning when he boarded the bus for the ride to the airport and home, Jordan was still in his uniform, clutching a champagne bottle and chewing on a big, fat cigar he had used to puff rings of smoke in the face of almost everyone he saw the night before. Jordan still clutched the championship trophy that he had cradled for the TV cameras in the locker room. It was their Holy Grail, so elusive and so desired.

They passed it from player to player. Paxson stroked it as if it were a newborn son. Pippen kissed it. Everyone handled it so gently, almost afraid it would break, as they themselves had threatened to as a team so many times during the season. But Jackson's gentle handling and Jordan's secure hold and everyone's confident support kept the dream from splitting apart. Scott Williams shrieked when the trophy came his way. "Look at me now," he said exuberantly.

"Easy, easy, be careful," Jordan counseled. He watched it the way a mother does her baby. The trophy moved across the aisle to Armstrong and back to Hodges and up to Perdue and back to Jordan, finally, everyone putting a mark on it as the others watched.

"We did it," whispered Paxson to himself as he leaned back in his seat as the lights blinked by outside the speeding bus. "What do you know? We did it."

ACKNOWLEDGEMENTS

A FEW WEEKS following the end of the Bulls' 1990–91 championship season, I called Horace Grant to confirm a piece of information for this book. I had taken all of the players and coaches aside early in the season to tell them I'd be working on a book this season, and Grant had only vaguely remembered.

"That's right," he agreed. "I guess it should be interesting after everything that happened." Grant seemed to be thinking for a while, and then he finally said, "I don't know if you're going to write any things that make me look bad, but as long as they're the truth, that's okay with me."

I relate this conversation only because it's indicative of the way Horace Grant deals with people, but he was hardly the exception among the Bulls. It's easy to come away from this season wondering how such a disparate bunch could win a title.

The Bulls won for reasons discussed throughout the book. But I would take exception with the notion that their behavior—often angry with one another and management—suggests that they were an unusual team. I suspect many teams in pro sports exhibit the jealousies, anger, and resentments that often occur in this story. And why shouldn't they? Frankly, it's unnatural to take twelve young men united only by their athletic ability, put them together for about eight months, pay them varying fortunes of money, give them one ball to play with, and then expect them to maintain some sort of storybook, harmonious relationship.

Athletes too often are depicted as something less than complete human characters. They're supposed to be heroes and role models; they're not supposed to have to stay up all night with sick children, face cranky mothers-in-law in for long visits or have angry or ailing wives. But they do. And they have the same problems everyone else has. It's just that no one pays to see such problems or hear about them. Athletes are paid to perform. The Bulls did that as well in 1990–91 as perhaps any team in NBA history. But they also fought and feuded and were angry some days, giddy others. They ran the range of human emotions, although when the interviewers were around they mostly gave them what they expected to hear.

This book has been an attempt to look past that, to open the door to the locker room, take you on the team bus and plane, and let you sit with the players while they talk about their teammates, their coaches, management, and friends. Imagine your family with a reporter coming into your house to record everything that occurred during a year. Would some of the things that reporter heard surprise your friends and change the impressions they had of you?

That's essentially what I did. Although I didn't have access to the team plane or private meetings, I was able to piece together events that occurred there and elsewhere through relationships built up with this team. This is really a three-year project, that being the time I've covered the Bulls for the *Chicago Tribune*. I traveled with the team, saw virtually all their games, sat for hours in the locker room before and after games talking with players and coaches, met them at their hotels on the road and regularly after their daily practices. This book is the product of those sessions and literally scores of hours of interviews with most of the principals over that period.

A word about them: I cannot point to a player or coach among the Bulls whom I dislike. Some I found more interesting than others, like Bill Cartwright, Michael Jordan, B. J. Armstrong, Scottie Pippen, John Paxson, Craig Hodges, Will Perdue, and Grant. Some I didn't spend as much time with, like Scott Williams, Cliff Levingston, Stacey King, and Dennis Hopson. But I never found any uncooperative or unattractive in any way.

I was routinely amazed by the ease with which Jordan handled

himself in all public situations, his inordinate patience with an adoring public, and his fascinating magnetism and charisma. I respected
Cartwright's grace, intelligence, and dignity, and Paxson's ability to
charm people and mean it. I enjoyed watching Pippen mature and
remain playful, while Armstrong always was a kid you wanted to
hug. Perdue always showed a remarkably perceptive side and quick,
engaging wit. King rarely let his personal troubles, which extended
beyond basketball, interfere with his commitment to a smile. And
Hodges remained an encouraging beacon of faith for anyone who
cared. Hopson was always a gentleman, like his old friend Brad
Sellers, and Grant was a welcome port in stormy seas.

And a few words about some of the men who pulled the strings.
I discovered managing partner Jerry Reinsdorf to be one of the most
misunderstood men I've ever known, a guy whose heart and head
were constantly at odds, with his heart winning more often than
anyone would like to admit. The assistant coaches were a glorious
bunch, especially the sagacious John Bach, a true renaissance man
of the era. Which brings me to the head coach, Phil Jackson. When
my agent read some preliminary parts of the manuscript, she remarked that Jackson was the hero of the story. I think he would be
the hero in whatever story he was a part of. Every time I talked to
him, I came away knowing something new or thinking about something I'd rarely considered before. I spent four years in Washington,
D.C., covering Congress and the White House and never met anyone as interesting. He was calm and smart and funny, and often
with a distinctly left-handed view of things. And he was as engaging
to be with at the end of the season as he was at the beginning.

I'd also like to get in a few thank-yous, principally to literary
agent Shari Lesser Wenk, who was a source of strength and encouragement throughout the year. I'd like to thank Simon & Schuster editor Jeff Neuman for willingly taking a chance and sticking
with a first-time author and impressively living up to his title. I'd
especially like to thank my *Tribune* editors, Jack Fuller, Dick Cic-
cone, Dick Leslie, and Bob Condor, for their support throughout
the long season. There are several others who helped along the way
I'd like to thank, like Gary Graham, George Andrews, Mike Imrem,
Mike Conklin, Don Sterling, Mike Kahn, Jimmy Sexton, Bob Ford,
Kent McDill, Dale Ratermann, Rick Pauley, Pete Vecsey, David
Benner, Jeff Denberg, June Jackson, Dean Howe, the Bulls PR

and executive staff, and especially my wife, Kathleen, for accepting the abnormal life of an NBA beat writer/first-time author and for keeping our son, Connor, from hitting the kill button on the computer.

And as for Horace Grant, well, after being around him for three years, I still can't even think of anything that would make him look bad.